The Money Book

THE
MONEY BOOK

Your Money and Your Life

MARGARET ALLEN

SIDGWICK & JACKSON
LONDON

First published in 1977 by
Sidgwick and Jackson Limited

Copyright © 1977 by Margaret Allen

ISBN 0 283 98387 6

Printed in Great Britain by
The Garden City Press Limited
Letchworth, Hertfordshire

for Sidgwick and Jackson Limited
1 Tavistock Chambers, Bloomsbury Way
London WC1A 2SG

Phototypesetting by
Print Origination, Merseyside L20 6NS

For my daughters,
'FREDDI' *and* JACKI,
and my friends,
SILVANO *and* ROSS.

Acknowledgements

I would not have been able to write this book without the co-operation of many of my friends and my family. The contribution of my researcher Gillian Seeley was vital. She happily took on all the chores of the usual work, checking and rechecking without complaint and I am very indebted to her. My secretary, Jacqueline Neighbour proved of invaluable comfort when the task seemed impossible and without her assistance and that of Juliet Walker and Susan Whippey, the manuscript would never have been completed in a form acceptable to the printer. They not only typed out the manuscript but read it carefully and came up with many queries and suggestions which were most helpful.

In a book like this there are many sources and a great number of organizations and people have given their help unstintingly. Here, alphabetically are some of the organizations without whose assistance I could not have finished the book:

Automobile Association; Australian High Commission; Avis; Barclays Bank; British Insurance Association; British United Provident Association; Building Societies Association; Central Office of Information; Commercial Union; Customs and Excise Department; *Daily Mirror*; *Daily Telegraph*; *The Director*; Department of Education; Department of the Environment; Department of Health and Social Security; Department of Inland Revenue; Department for National Savings; Electrical Association for Women; Electricity Council; Equal Opportunities Commission; Extel; Finance Houses Association; *Financial Times*; *The Grocer*; Hatton Garden Gem and Precious Metal Company; H.M.S.O.; Ladbrokes; Law Society; Life Offices Association; Littlewoods Pools; Lloyds Bank; Lloyds Insurance Brokers Association; London Assay Office; London Graduate School of Business Studies; Manchester Business School; Martins Bank; *Mother* magazine; National Association of Funeral Directors; National Home Improvement Council; National Westminster Bank; Nationwide Building Society; Office of Fair Trading; The Post Office; Office of Population Census and Surveys; Quotel; Royal Institute of Chartered Surveyors; St Christopher's Motorists Security Association; Stock Exchange, *The Sun*; *Sunday Telegraph*; The Trustee Savings Bank; *Which* magazine; Wine Development Board.

I am particularly grateful to Danny O'Shea of M. and G. Unit Trusts for his invaluable help in the section on the Stock Exchange, and to Dryden Gilling-Smith, an expert on pensions, for his assistance in that area. William Halden of the Automobile Association was equally generous in his help in the motoring field, as was John Gaselee in insurance, James Dubois in all aspects of tax, Ronald Irving on the law, and Bevis Hillier on the antiques world. Without their help I could not have finished the book. Among newspapers who were generous in allowing me to quote them, I must especially thank my own newspaper, *The Times* and also *The Financial Times,* who have permitted me to reprint many of their regular tables. 'Brom', in The Times Business News library found anything I wanted in the financial area in seconds, and Jack Lonsdale, head of the Intelligence department, helped me considerably in the more general areas. Michael Cudlipp very kindly read the manuscript for me, pointing out areas which might not have been absolutely clear to anyone not familiar with the financial world. My daughters, Margaret and Jacqueline, have also read the manuscript and Margaret has checked many of the calculations.

Finally, I am most grateful to my Editor, William Rees-Mogg, for giving me permission to write the book.

To all of them, many thanks.

Margaret Allen
June 1977

Contents

SECTION TWO

YOUR MONEY AND YOUR JOB

SECTION THREE

FAMILY FINANCE

SECTION FOUR

TAXATION

SECTION FIVE

INVESTING

SECTION SIX

YOUR MONEY AND THE LAW

Author's Note

I have written this book to help ordinary people with a wide variety of their financial problems. I have not designed it as a technical manual for those in the financial world, but for individuals and families who may have little experience of how our lives can be affected by various financial rules and regulations, and how we can best use them to our advantage. But this is a book, not an encyclopaedia. There may be areas which it does not cover for everyone, but I hope that the general information given will point readers in the right direction in the solving of any of their financial problems.

One warning: money, and the rules surrounding it, are everchanging. Interest rates change from week to week, sometimes even from day to day. Banks change their rules regarding their account holders. New financial services may be launched, others abandoned; certain tax levels may change without requiring a Budget; building societies, finance houses and insurance companies alter the rates and conditions of both borrowing and lending; credit controls may be varied by the Government and its payments under the social security system can change. Bear this in mind when you read this book; you must be careful to check exact current conditions before you take any action.

The book takes in all the facts and figures which applied to the best of my knowledge at the end of June 1977.

This book went to press before the 1977 Finance Act was passed, and before the Government had reached agreement on Phase 3 of the pay policy. For this reason, the standard rate of tax is given as 35 per cent throughout the book.

Introduction

This book is all about money and how you can make the most of it. Whether you are rich or poor the chances are that you do not manage your money efficiently. Perhaps you are afraid of the whole subject of money. Throughout history it has been praised and castigated; it has been alleged to be the root of all evil; it has been said to make the world go round; it has been described as like muck, not good unless it is spread.

Money is probably all these things, but if you are to benefit from this book, remember Dr Johnson's maxim, 'There are few ways in which a man can be more innocently employed than in getting money.' You may then actually begin to enjoy taking proper care of your money.

It is all very well to say that, but in a time of inflation, like the one we have suffered for the past decade, money can be a source of constant worry. Most of us have been asking ourselves at least some of the following sorts of questions: Will my salary go round? Will I be able to cope with the next increase in the mortgage rate? Will I be able to live on my pension? Will the telephone have to go? Have I seen the last of steak? Where will the money for my next, even more expensive, season ticket come from? Will I still be able to use my central heating now that gas and electricity prices have gone up again? Can I still afford to educate my children privately? Are my annual holidays a thing of the past? How much will the wedding cost?

Problems like these used to be solved fairly quickly – by getting a rise in salary in one's existing job, by getting promotion and thus a higher salary, or by getting a new job that offers more money. Most of us used to be able to count on at least one of these things happening, so that we were able to maintain our standard of living. This is no longer true. Britain's poor economic performance in comparison with that of other industrialized countries since the end of the 1939-45 war has put paid to all that. Wages and salary increases are strictly controlled by government policy; unemployment is high; industry has not been able to develop new opportunities. But most important of all is the real monster, inflation, which is rapidly eating into the money we already have.

Inflation is a financial word for something we all know a great deal about today; it is the term used to describe the rate of the fall in the value of money. It is happening all over the world, but here in Britain we have been suffering it to a far greater extent than many other countries.

This is what happens. If the rate of inflation is 20 per cent a year, every £1 sterling at the end of the year will only buy four-fifths of the goods it would have bought at the beginning of the year. If your wages do not keep up with the rate of inflation, your standard of living falls by the amount of the difference. That is what is happening to many of us, so we must use our available money more efficiently to maintain our standards.

There is nothing new about inflation. It is part of the history of mankind. Ever since commercial activity began – and that goes way back beyond the Greeks and Romans – prices have been rising. But they have risen at different rates from time to time and from country to country. Today we are in a period of relatively high inflation. This chart shows you what has happened to the value of the pound since the end of the First World War.

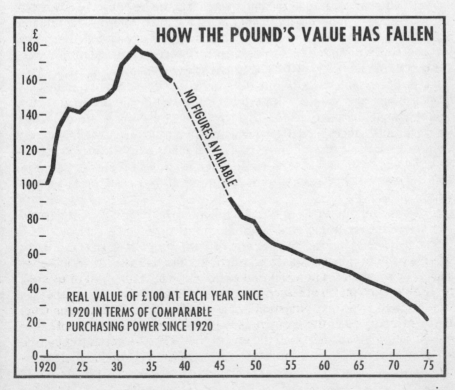

HOW THE POUND'S VALUE HAS FALLEN

NO FIGURES AVAILABLE

REAL VALUE OF £100 AT EACH YEAR SINCE 1920 IN TERMS OF COMPARABLE PURCHASING POWER SINCE 1920

As you can see, the pound today is worth less than 20p compared with 1920. This means that you need over £5 today to buy what £1 would have bought then.

One thing we must all realize is that there is no way of escaping inflation. No amount of adjusting and adapting of your life style will provide you with enough cuts and savings to match completely the extra money you will have to pay for the goods and services you use. But by thinking about your spending and your saving, you can minimize the effects of rising prices and husband your resources in such a way that you can cope without too much strain – and when times get better you will reap the benefits.

Sensible money management can bring savings to everyone, regardless of his income. Money may seem boring when you do not have enough of it, but if you use it like you use any other product, to give you the best possible value, you will be able to go through life with money in its right place, and not a dominant worrying thing which can ruin your enjoyment of life.

The first thing to do is work out precisely where your money goes. This in itself can be highly revealing. Maybe your car is too big (and expensive) for your needs; perhaps the children have grown up and you could move to a smaller house to cut costs; perhaps you leave too much in your current account at the bank when it could be put somewhere else to earn interest; or perhaps you are paying too much overdraft interest in order to keep some money on deposit at the bank or post office; perhaps you are over-(or under-)insured. These are just a few of the hundreds of instances of financial mismanagement which can come to light if you just sit down and set out your outgoings.

You must also look at what you really earn. If you are in full-time employment the chances are that you will be paying some tax. Once your tax allowances have been set against your income the government will take away at least a third of the remainder. With sound money management you can at least make sure they don't take more than they are entitled to, and that you are claiming all the allowances you are eligible for.

Always think in terms of your *net* income, not your *gross*. It's no use thinking you are doing well because you earn £5,000 a year or £100 a week gross; that figure is before any deductions. As well as tax, you will have to pay national insurance contributions, and your firm may well take 5 or 7½ per cent in pension contributions – which provide income, it is true, but not until you retire.

This book, then, is a practical guide on how to manage your money; it is not an economic treatise. I do not have any complete solutions to offer to the problems of inflation. This book is designed to help you make the best of your economic and financial situation as it is.

Basic Money Management

Chapter 1

YOUR PERSONAL BUDGET

Why, you may well ask yourself, should you bother to budget? You may feel that you simply don't have enough money, that you scrape by from day to day, and that there is nothing that can be done about it. You may feel that you can leave all that sort of thing to your husband, wife or parents. Or you may, of course, be so rich that you do not need to budget at all. In that case this section is not for you, and you can pass on to section V, on personal investment, to make sure you stay rich.

A personal budget is important for everyone, and no matter how little money you have it is highly likely that you could use it more efficiently. This is most important for the average family with young children. It doesn't take much experience of life to know that quarrels about money are one of the most upsetting things in married life, and not infrequently a cause of divorce.

THE 'AVERAGE MAN'

The first step in budgeting is to see how near you are to the national average. Even if your income level is exactly on the average, your own pattern of spending will be quite unique and will depend on your and your family's individual aims and priorities. Only you can answer certain questions about your spending. Do you want to own your home? Do you want a colour television set, a car, or wine with your meals, rather than savings in the bank? If you have spare money, would you

1

prefer it to go on your child's education, on 'educating' them through foreign travel, or on extra-curricular activities like music or sport? These may be substantial items requiring once-and-for-all decisions, but hardly a day goes by when the average family does not have to choose some financial alternative rather than another.

Your budget will change with the composition of your family. Housing costs may rise as a couple has children, then decrease again as the children grow up and leave home, and the mortgage, if there is one, is paid off. Holiday and entertainment costs usually seem to take a very large proportion of the family budget where there are no children, or they have grown up, in comparison with the family with small children, where food and clothes tend to predominate.

In short, there is no one 'budget'. The first rule is to make your budget fit your own requirements. Keeping up with the Joneses is a money-wasting activity; it may not even make you happy.

Even so, a look at the 'average' can be illuminating as regards your own spending.

If you notice that in any one area your spending is way out of line with the average, you would be wise to consider what adjustments you can make. If, for example, you spend a third of your net income on a mortgage or rent, you are probably spending too much. As the table below shows, the 'average' spending on housing is not more than 14 per cent, whatever the income level – though a young couple may prefer to pay rather more on a mortgage at the beginning of their life together. Later on, as their income rises, this proportion goes down, and of course, if they are buying a house on a mortgage, eventually disappears from the budget altogether.

HOW PEOPLE SPEND THEIR MONEY

	weekly income		
	£20-£40 %	£50-£60 %	£100+ %
housing	14.0	13.9	12.5
fuel, light and power	6.3	5.4	3.7
food	30.9	27.3	20.4
alcohol	4.5	4.3	3.7
tobacco	5.6	3.7	1.7
clothing and footwear	8.4	9.5	9.4
consumer durables	5.7	7.6	8.1
transport	10.7	12.5	12.9
services and entertainment	5.4	7.0	15.8
miscellaneous	0.4	0.8	0.8

These figures are adapted from the cash spending figures given in the government's annual *Family Expenditure Survey* for a married couple with two children at various income levels. They show what percentage of available money goes on various items of spending. Though they are averages, and few people will fit the average exactly, they show quite clearly that the poorer the family the more of its income goes on the basics of food and housing; the better-off it is the more there is available for non-essentials like consumer durables, entertainment and other services.

What you should aim for is a budget which suits your purposes and income level, and at the same time is flexible enough to meet any changes in your requirements.

INCOME AND OUTGOINGS

If you can make your income cover your basic outgoings and have something left over to give you a choice in the rest of your spending and, better still, something to put aside for savings, you are naturally a good manager of money. But most of us are not, and we need to plan carefully to make our money go round. Only young people who have not yet committed their money in definite directions can operate satisfactorily on a simple cash basis.

Many people find it rather horrifying to think of running their own budget like a company or a country in miniature. You should get over such reservations. It may be a bore, but you will certainly find it worthwhile when you see all the trouble it prevents.

Ask yourself these questions:

1 Do you know where your money will be coming from in the next few months, or possibly years?
2 Can you calculate exactly your fixed outgoings?
3 Do you know what you have left over for everyday spending?
4 Do you know what is left after that for luxuries?
5 Have you a realistic idea of what will be left at the end of all this for savings?
6 Can you fit today's spending into the long-term pattern of your spending so that you can achieve financial peace of mind and avoid staggering from one month to the next?

If you can answer yes to all these questions you are very unusual. Most people are hazy in some areas at least. The best way to start to achieve a financial balance is to start on the assumption that you will never have enough money to cater for all your needs and wants. If you get more money, you are likely to raise the level of your expectations – a bigger car or house, for example. Accept that you will have to sort out your priorities and forego some things to get others.

3

As you go along, always follow three rules, whatever other ones you may make for yourself:

1 If you are married, work on a joint budget. You are doomed from the start if you can't agree as a couple on your priorities.
2 Be flexible and always give yourself a personal allowance. You will run into deep trouble, particularly if there are two of you, if you have to account for every minor item you spend.
3 You must keep records. These need not be complicated – in fact, they should not be complicated. You are the master not your records. They are there simply to show you how your spending is going and to warn you if spending in any area is getting out of hand. They are to help you, not to put you in a straightjacket.

There are three steps you must now take to ensure that you can answer yes to all the questions I put above. You must:
First: work out exactly how much money you have coming in.
Second: provide for your fixed expenses.
Third: decide your priorities in everyday spending.

First: Assess your income

Before you can start managing your money properly, you must first find out how much you have. Draw up a simple chart to show just what you can expect to have coming in during the year. Include everything you can call family income: your basic salary; your husband or wife's; your children's as far as it contributes to the family income; any interest from savings or dividends from investments; any rent from property you own; any cash presents you may expect; any bonuses at work; any profit from selling your house, car or any other possessions; any rebate you may be expecting from the taxman; and anything you may get from freelance activities.

When you fill in your chart

1 Estimate *exactly* where you can, and if you are not sure put down a *minimum*.
2 Put down *net* amounts after tax and all other payments like national insurance and pension contributions. If you put gross amounts you are only fooling yourself.
3 If you work for yourself and your income is irregular, divide it evenly between months.
4 Don't *revise* your monthly totals *up* because you expect a rise, wait till you get it. Similarly revise everything downwards if your income suddenly falls.
5 Only put down items that you are sure of.

4

This should leave you knowing precisely what spending money you will have. Gear your spending to this and not to any estimates which you cannot itemize exactly.

Second: Provide for fixed expenses

Your second chart will show those items of expenditure which have to be paid for, and when you can expect to have to pay them. Although they are not fixed in the sense that you can always change your life style to make ends meet – you can sell your house, for example – they are not always avoidable at any particular point in time.

Plan as far as possible to stagger big single payments throughout the year, so that you have more or less the same outgoings each month. Your fixed outgoings will include your rent or mortgage; your general and water rates, unless they are included in your rent; ground rent if you own a leasehold property; your regular bills like gas, electricity, telephone, T.V. rental, and so on; any regular payments on hire purchase or insurance policies, holiday or Christmas clubs; once a year payments like house and contents insurance, car insurance and road tax; extra tax payments where you can predict them; subscriptions; any transport expenses which you can estimate like the cost of a season ticket or petrol; any extras like personal allowances for husband and wife and children; education expenses or extra lessons for a member of the family; any medical insurance like BUPA; any debts you may have. This list is endless, and every family will have its own particular pattern. As you can see, though these expenses are fixed at any one time, many of them can be flexible to suit changes in circumstances. They will swallow up a large proportion of your income.

Unlike your income, which you estimate at a minimum, put your expenses at a *maximum*.

Ask yourself whether you can include savings as a fixed expense. This may seem odd, but if you can regard any money you put away for the future as a fixed outgoing, you are very sensibly leaving a margin for any unexpected expense, as well as building up a nest-egg. I will look at the various forms of savings which may suit you in chapter 3 of this section, but it's worth emphasizing at this stage that regular payments into a savings account are relatively painless, if you regard them as a normal part of your outgoings.

Third: Decide priorities in everyday spending

Balance up your income and your outgoings. What is left is for day-to-day expenses and any extra saving when you have some money to spare. Now you will know whether you can actually make ends meet. If you can't, you will have to look at the current level of your fixed expenses to see which, if any, can be reduced. If none of them can – and this would be very unusual – look to ways of increasing your income. But on the whole most people have a float, however limited, to live on after dealing with their basic expenses, even though they may have problems in some months. These can often be ironed out by having a 'budget account' at a bank, of which more in chapter 6 of this section. Nevertheless, most of us usually find we have to do some juggling to get the money to go round all the things we feel are vital to our life style. Look at some of the items you may have to cover in your day-to-day expenses, and fill in yet another chart.

1 *Food and related items:* these usually take between 20 and 30 per cent of your total income, particularly if you include alcohol and tobacco. They may take more than half your floating money.
2 *Household expenses:* repairs, cleaning services, domestic help. Can you afford these? Are they a priority?
3 *Furnishings and consumer durables:* you may already be buying furniture or other items on hire purchase. Have you any money left over for this sort of thing?
4 *Clothes:* a very flexible item, but don't forget to include shoes, accessories, repairs and cleaning, whatever you decide your clothing budget can be.
5 *Transport:* try to estimate your costs over and above anything you have included in your fixed expenses. Don't forget car maintenance.
6 *The hairdresser or barber:* include here anything you need for personal use and care.
7 *Entertainment:* include your holiday spending here; all your sports spending; your reading material; eating out or your round at the pub; gifts to friends and relatives.
8 *Anything else:* we all have something.

This is the end of the beginning of personal budgeting. If you have followed the steps outlined above you will have a basis for the sensible management of your money. Before I go on to look in detail at the many aspects, here are a few tips:

*   **DO** set yourself sensible spending limits. This can't be done immediately, but after a few months' or a year's experience you will find it easier.
*   **DON'T** think you can solve all your problems by cutting down on one item too severely. Your food budget may look high, but don't imagine you can cut it by half.
*   **DO** allow yourself some luxuries. If having a holiday abroad is a

real need, it would be better to cut down on other forms of entertainment rather than go without it.
* **DON'T** forget the unexpected expense. Everyone has these. You may have to buy a new car before you really want to. Your children may suddenly decide to get married. Try to budget for something unforeseen every year. You can always carry anything saved this way forward to the next year.

Bearing these points in mind work out your planned spending for the year. If you look like spending more than you earn, make the cuts immediately. Don't hope for the best and carry on regardless. Keep records. Once you get used to it, you may actually enjoy it, particularly when you see the result in a nicely balanced budget – and you feel the relief when financial worries are cut down or even eliminated.

Above all when budgeting – *always minimize your income and maximize your expenses.*

Chapter 2

BRITISH BANKING

Before we go on to look at savings bank accounts, it will help you to know broadly how the British banking system works. Then you will be able to understand just why your bank manager's professional attitude to you may change, even though your own circumstances do not deteriorate, or even improve. Remember that the local bank manager is not his own master. He is subject to the policy decisions of his own head office and also to government instructions which come to the major banks by the government's own banker, the Bank of England. (All the facilities and services offered by the banks are discussed in greater detail in chapter 6 of this section.)

THE BANK OF ENGLAND

When the Bank of England was first formed in 1694 it was not the then government's intention to make it the core of all banking in Britain. It was just set up to raise money to finance Britain and her friends in the Grand Alliance to wage war against France. Like so many institutions, however, it did not disappear with the end of the war, but went on to develop until in 1844 the government decreed that only the Bank of England could issue bank notes in England and Wales. The Banks of Scotland and Northern Ireland are empowered to print their own notes, but though these circulate freely in Scotland and Northern Ireland, they are not in fact legal tender. Before 1844 many banks issued notes and the situation was very confused, with no one knowing just what was 'legal tender'.

Legal tender

What, you may ask, is legal tender? Bank notes and coins currently in use are legal tender; 'legal tender' is the term used to describe the things which can be used for the legal payment of a debt. But payment even in accepted notes and coins does not always amount to legal tender, and if it doesn't the person to whom you owe the money is entitled not to accept it. Legal tender is the only thing which a creditor is required to accept in settlement of a debt. He or she need not accept a cheque, or goods in exchange, or any unusual form of payment.

As far as coins are concerned, they are only legal tender up to certain amounts: 2p, 1p or ½p coins up to a value of 20p; and 10p and 5p coins up to £5. This means, for instance, that you cannot make anyone accept £1 in 1p pieces, or £100 in 10p pieces. Old coins, like the half-crown (12½p), are no longer legal tender, and no shopkeeper would accept them.

When it comes to bank notes, only Bank of England notes of current issues are legal tender in England, Wales, Scotland and Northern Ireland. These are Series 'C' green £1 notes, Series 'D' blue £5 notes, Series 'C' brown £10 notes and Series 'D' beige £20 notes. The notes issued by Scottish and Northern Ireland banks, which circulate freely in those areas, are *not* legal tender at all, so if you are visiting and have any left when you leave try to get them exchanged for Bank of England notes before you leave. The states of Jersey and Guernsey and the Isle of Man also issue notes, and these *are* legal tender, as well as Bank of England notes, on those islands, but not outside them.

Old notes

If you come across old bank notes which are no longer legal tender do not despair. You can always get your money back on a Bank of England note, because the Bank undertakes to honour its 'promise to pay the bearer on demand' in perpetuity.

You must apply to the head office of the Bank of England in Threadneedle Street in the City of London. If you cannot go there personally, your bank will do it for you and you will receive whatever is the face value of your notes. It is highly unlikely that you will have to pay a collection fee, unless your Bank has to pay an enormous amount in postage and insurance for a large number of notes.

If you do not have a bank account, any local branch of a bank will apply to the Bank of England for you. It may ask for proof of identity to make sure you are reliable and may well charge for any expenses it incurs.

If you have very old notes, they may be worth money as collectors' pieces. I have dealt with this in section V, chapter 8.

The bankers' bank

The Bank of England, then, is solely responsible for the issue of money, and it is accountable to the government. This means that it must constantly examine and assess the financial climate, and take action when necessary, say in the foreign exchange markets, to support sterling. It also controls the supply of credit to the other banks, and fixes rates of interest.

In co-operation with the Treasury, the Bank decides what will be the M.L.R, the Minimum Lending Rate. This tells the banking world the lowest possible rate of interest they can charge borrowers, and it also helps the government when it wants to borrow money from the public by the issue of its own stock (which I have discussed in section V, chapter 5). It also takes care of exchange control regulations; these are the laws which control the movement of sterling in and out of the United Kingdom.

It is also the bankers' bank, that is, the bank for the other banks, and it can, for example, insist that they leave money with it – what are called special deposits. In this way the money the banks have to play with when they are going about their day-to-day business is controlled by the Bank of England, and through the Bank by the Treasury and, of course, in the end by the government.

THE CLEARING BANKS

As far as most people are concerned the Bank of England has little direct influence in their daily lives, as it operates from behind the scenes. It is the clearing banks which look after most of the fifty-five in every hundred of us who have bank accounts. There are eight commercial clearing banks in England and Wales. In order of size they are National Westminster, with 3,600 branches, Barclays (3,200), Midland (2,700) and Lloyds (2,300). These are known as the 'big four'. Williams and Glyn's, with 300 branches, and Coutts (which is a subsidiary of National Westminster) are the other two long-established clearing banks. These six were joined by the Central Trustee Savings Bank in 1975. Previously, in February 1974, the existing members of the Clearing Houses

Association had agreed that the Co-operative Bank should have direct access to its clearing services, and in April of that year they offered these clearing agency facilities to other non-clearing institutions. This means that many more prople have access to clearing than ever before.

Scotland has its own system. The Bank of Scotland, the Clydesdale and the Royal Bank of Scotland with their subsidiaries are the clearing banks. There are some differences in day-to-day practice, but on the whole their services are similar to those offered by English banks, and Scottish banks, just like the English banks, are subject to the Bank of England.

Just as the Bank of England fixes the M.L.R, which serves as a guide to interest rates for all the other banks, so the clearing banks fix what are known as 'base rates'. Each bank then decides on the basis of the base rate what rate of interest it will charge on any money it loans to customers and the interest it will pay out to depositors. Every bank branch has a notice telling customers what the day's base rate is – it is fixed every Friday – and also what it is paying out on deposits. It will not always give a loan rate, because that is much more varied. Industrial borrowers pay one rate, there is another one for personal loans, and overdraft interest rates depend on how the bank manager personally assesses your status as a borrower.

What does the bank do with the money it holds?:

1 It keeps some cash to meet any demands customers withdrawing money may make.
2 It invests some of its assets, mainly in government stocks.
3 It holds some in reserve, usually in Treasury Bills.
4 The rest – usually about two-thirds – is available to its customers in the form of loans, overdraft facilities and so on.

DISCOUNT HOUSES

The Bank of England and the clearing banks are nothing like the full picture of banking in Britain, but outside the government banking area (see below) they are the parts which most affect our day-to-day lives. There are other institutions in the City of London which exist to aid business. They are just as subject to rules and regulations as the clearing banks. The discount houses for example, are concerned with the borrowing and investing of short-term money. Eleven of them make up the London Discount Market Association. All are public companies with shareholders. They do their business mainly by phone and work mainly with Treasury bills, short-dated government stocks, and local authority loans. By buying and selling these, they can have a considerable influence on the level of interest rates over the short term.

THE MERCHANT BANKS

The business of merchant banks is quite different from that of the clearing banks. They are mainly concerned in financing international trade. They accept bills of exchange to finance the trade of others, and as a result are also called 'accepting houses'. The seventeen members of the Accepting Houses Committee are the only true merchant banks, though in recent years other financial companies have chosen to give themselves the name. All seventeen members are in the City of London, but some have opened regional branches. Some of them have a few current account customers. Today they have expanded into many fields and you are likely to come across one eventually, if you set up a business. They will arrange loans for your company's development (corporate finance), manage your investments, deal with your foreign exchange transactions and gold dealing and give general financial advice. They are now also involved in hire purchase, equipment leasing, factoring (see section II, chapter 8), insurance, insurance broking, property development and shipping. They play a vital part in Britain's business life and international trade.

FOREIGN BANKS

Hundreds of foreign banks now have branches in the United Kingdom, mainly in London but also outside. Some banks operate through subsidiaries, which means that the bank is registered as a British company, but that it is owned by foreigners. Others simply set up a branch. Some operate as ordinary banks, but others are basically there for business contacts. The Bank of England issues a list of foreign banks from time to time, and they can be useful to you if you are thinking of exporting to their home country, or looking for a foreign partner in your business.

FINANCE HOUSES

These were originally set up so that people could buy railway wagons on hire purchase. But that was many years ago, and now they will finance the purchase of a great variety of goods and services. I have described the services they offer in detail in chapter 4 of this section. They are subject to government controls similar to those for the clearing banks. Most of the money they have available to borrow comes from the banks and other financial institutions. They do take deposits from the public, but this is only a small part of the total money they have available to lend.

FRINGE BANKS

There is no exact definition of a bank in the United Kingdom. Because of this all sorts of companies have been able to call themselves banks or banking corporations when they haven't really been banks at all. Many of these companies have been honest, but there have been a few sharks, and although strict rules are applied before these companies are allowed to set up, a few slip through the net nevertheless. The actual use of the name 'Bank' is strictly controlled today, and it is unlikely that any company would be permitted to call itself anything as wide as the European Bank or the British Bank, for instance, but names can and have been found which do not infringe the rules, but impress the potential customer.

If you have anything to do with a bank, check its credentials with one of the 'big four' before you leave money with it. Many of the 'fringe banks', as they are called, offer very tempting interest rates to depositors, but remember – *the higher the rate of interest to depositors the greater the risk of loss*, because the company may be lending at very high rates to unreliable borrowers. Many people have had their fingers burned this way, and some have even lost all their savings. The rules have been tightened up now, but you should still deposit your money with extreme caution. No interest rate is attractive if you lose all your money.

THE GOVERNMENT SECTOR

The private sector of banking is supplemented by the National Savings Bank and the National Giro. The National Savings Bank was established in 1861 when a lot of private banks were going bankrupt and its absolute safety was most attractive to depositors. Today it has 21 million active accounts and 21,000 outlets in post offices throughout the country. It is strictly a deposit bank, offering no other services. The National Giro, which was designed to transmit money through the postal system and to provide a cash back-up through the post offices, was formed in 1968. In 1975 its structure was reorganized by legislation and in future it may well become a real competitor to the clearing banks, offering overdraft facilities, credit cards and cheque guarantee cards.

THE TRUSTEE SAVINGS BANKS

There are eighteen regional Trustee Savings Banks who have branches all over the country. The Central Trustees Savings Bank, which is owned by the T.S.B. Central Board, operates in the money markets on behalf of all the regional banks. Until 1976 the Treasury exercised control over these banks through the National Debt Office. Now control is exercised by the Registrar of Friendly Societies jointly with the new

T.S.B. Central Board. At present T.S.B.s are not controlled by the Bank of England in the same way as other banks, but after a transitional period which ends in 1986 they will be subjected to similar (though not identical) rules to the commercial banks.

Chapter 3

A PERSONAL SAVINGS PROGRAMME

Setting out on a programme of sensible saving can be a bewildering business. There are an enormous variety of schemes, which go under different names. They may be called either *saving* or *investment*. Both have the same objective, that is, to increase your personal wealth, but there are important differences between them. With savings there should be no risk of losing your capital and an income should be assured. With investment, on the other hand, you take a chance as to the level of profit you will make – if any. For this reason the profit is generally greater, but there is a risk that the investment will not pay off to the extent you expected, and sometimes you may even lose part or all of your original stake. This chapter is concerned only with savings. If you have already worked out your savings plans and have money left over, turn to section 5, which sets out the various possibilities for personal investment.

CHOOSING YOUR ACCOUNT

Many people simply save when they have some money left over from their fixed outgoings. As was suggested in chapter 1 of this section, it is far better to regard your savings as part of your outgoings. In that way you can build up your capital on a regular basis. Of course, savings cannot come before some other expenditure, but when you are working out your budget try to fit in something for saving, however little.

If you are at the beginning of your financial life and do not have any capital, you probably do not want to take any risk with your money. This means that you must stick to assured savings with interest. You can choose from:

1   *National savings*. These are offered in various forms. The safety of your capital and interest is guaranteed by the government. Trustee

Savings Banks are also guaranteed, though they are midway between the National Savings Bank and the commercial banks.

2 *Local authority loans.* Members of the public lend money to various local authorities throughout the country. Every loan raised has to have government approval and is then guaranteed by the Public Works Loans Board.

3 *Savings at the commercial banks and finance houses.* These are private concerns, so the government does not guarantee the safety of your capital and interest. Failings in these are rare, however, and unknown among the leading clearing banks, where you will probably have a current account if you have one at all.

4 *Savings in building societies.* These, again, are not guaranteed by the government. There have been some failings in the past, but not among members of the Building Societies Association.

Interest rates are now very high indeed in comparison with, say, ten years ago. You will notice this if you go to the bank to borrow money or take out a mortgage. But high interest rates apply both ways. If you are saving money you will benefit from the high interest rates. In times of inflation the interest rate is very important. It is difficult to make your savings keep up with the rate of inflation, and any gap between the two is in effect a loss to you. So think carefully before you decide what to do with your money.

If for any reason you are prepared to take a risk with your money, even if you do not have any basic savings, turn to section V. Most people, however, will want to have some money put aside for a rainy day, and they will not want to take a risk with any of this money.

Short-term or long-term saving

Next you must ask yourself how long you can afford to have your money tied up in a savings account. This is important because:

1 If you may need money suddenly and urgently you should not put it into a scheme which does not allow you to draw out at short notice. If you do there may be a severe financial penalty to pay.

2 If you know you can leave your money where it is for some time, you will be able to find a scheme which offers higher rates of interest than many schemes which allow you to draw out immediately or on a week or month's notice.

Probably you would like to balance your savings between the two kinds of saving. As I go through, I will indicate with each scheme whether it is suitable for short-or long-term saving.

The question of tax

First of all look at section IV, chapter 1, for the rules on unearned income. That means any money which you do not earn directly from your employment, and includes interest on bank accounts, dividends from shareholdings, and rents from any property you may own. Income from savings is taxed as ordinary income until you reach a level of £1,501. After that you have to pay an investment surcharge of 10 or 15 per cent depending on the level. If you already have more than the £1,501 unearned income you will probably benefit from expert advice from your bank or from a stockbroker.

Some savings which I will discuss in this chapter carry certain tax concessions, or are tax-free. These are particularly useful for anyone who pays tax.

NATIONAL SAVINGS

Let's look first at the government sector. By and large the interest rates paid by the various forms of national savings change much less quickly than other interest rates. It is important to remember this, because it can affect their relative attractiveness in comparison with savings in building societies, banks or finance houses. The movement includes:

1 The National Savings Bank
2 British Savings Bonds
3 Saving Certificates
4 Retirement Saving Certificates
5 Save As You Earn
6 Premium Bonds
7 The Trustee Savings Bank

Remember, the safety of your capital and the interest promised is guaranteed by the government.

The National Savings Bank

This used to be called the Post Office Savings Bank and is probably still so called by many people. The government guarantee it carries was very important when the bank was first set up in the nineteenth century, when many private banks went out of business, but today it is less so. If you take care when choosing your savings account, there is no reason why your capital or interest should be at risk wherever it is.

Nevertheless, there is still a guarantee for those who are at all nervous about their savings. And to encourage people to go into national savings the government offers some concessions on certain national savings which are not available to savers outside this area. The National Savings Bank offers two kinds of account.

1 *The ordinary account.* This account, with a minimum initial deposit of 25p, is offering 5 per cent at the moment and the first £70 worth of interest you earn per year is tax-free. This is equivalent to £8.75 per cent if you are paying tax at the standard rate of 35 per cent and means that you can have up to £1,000 in your bank account before paying any tax on the interest. You should, however (if you are a tax payer), show the amount of interest on your tax return.

This kind of account is simply for saving in, and you are allowed a maximum of £10,000 in one or more accounts. You cannot have a cheque book or an overdraft, though you can get a crossed warrant for a minimum of £1 for some purposes, which can be used like a cheque, and you can get one regular monthly payment made through the account, for which there is a small charge.

You can withdraw up to £30 on demand from your account on any one day. But if you withdraw more than £10 twice in any one week your bank book will have to be sent to the head office to be checked. If you want more than £30 at any one time, you will have to allow a few days before you get your money, as you must either apply in writing, or pay for a telegram to the head office. You can give yourself greater flexibility by having more than one account.

2 *The investment account.* This can be opened with £1 and carries a higher rate of interest than an ordinary account. The upper limit to your deposit is £50,000. At present the interest rate is 10 per cent, but unlike the ordinary account the interest you receive is taxable. If you want to withdraw money from this account there is no limit, but you must give one month's notice and apply in writing. The investment account's other facilities are the same as the ordinary account. You can open both types of accounts at once and this is a good idea.

Any child over the age of seven can use the account himself. You can deposit or withdraw money at any one of the 21,000 post offices in the United Kingdom which transact National Savings Bank business, as long as you have your bank book with you. This will be supplied when you make your first deposit and all transactions are shown in it, so that you know exactly how much you have in the bank at any time. You cannot operate without your book so make sure you have it with you.

You will be earning interest from the first day of the month after you put the money into your account and go on earning it until the first day of the month in which you take the money out. It makes sense therefore to be organized about your payments. Get your money into the bank before the end of the month if you can and it will earn interest almost immediately. If you delay until the first few days of the month it will be anything up to four weeks before your money starts earning interest.

Both these accounts are for short-term savers, though the ordinary account is rather more short-term than the investment account, at least for small amounts which can be withdrawn without any notice.

Advantages

1 Accessibility. Very few of us live far from a post office and the hours are longer than in the commercial banks.
2 Money on demand. You do not have to wait to withdraw your money, so it is useful for day-to-day requirements.
3 Cheapness. There are no bank charges and you earn interest on the money you have deposited in the bank.
4 If you are paying tax above the basic rate, the tax-free element in the ordinary account is attractive.
5 It is a good way to save for short periods.

Disadvantages

1 There are much better ways of building up your capital than in the ordinary account or even the investment account, though the rate in the investment account is more attractive to non-tax payers than building society interest, which is effectively lower.
2 The other services are limited compared with some other accounts.

British Savings Bonds

National Savings Bank accounts are the best short-term method of saving offered by the government, but there are also a number of long-term schemes on offer. British Savings Bonds are especially good for anyone who wishes to put money aside for five years, as there is a tax-free bonus for anyone who holds them that long. At present the bonds, which are called the Jubilee Issue, offer 8½ per cent a year running interest with a 4 per cent tax-free bonus at the end of the five-year period. This is worth more than an extra 1 per cent a year, allowing for the tax which would normally be paid. The minimum you can put into the bonds is £5 and the maximum £10,000, and you can withdraw them at one month's notice, with the proviso that you lose the 4 per cent bonus, if you have not held them for a full five years. These bonds are sold in series and at different rates of interest. Only the most recent, the Jubilee Issue, is on sale at present, but some of the others still exist and interest (though not extra bonuses) is still being paid on them. You may well inherit some. If you do it is usually best to sell them and transfer to the current issue.

On page 18 is a summary of all the British Savings Bonds which have been issued.

You can buy the bonds at any post office which transacts bank business, in Trustee Savings Banks, or in branches of the commercial banks.

The interest you are paid every six months is liable for tax, but will be paid gross (before tax) to you, so make sure you include details on your tax return.

Summary of British Savings Bonds

issue		commenced	interest dates		years to maturity		limit
6%	1st	1 April 1968	15 March	15 September	5	102%	£10,000
1st	conversion	1 April 1968	15 April	15 October	5	"	no limit
2nd	conversion	15 June 1968	15 June	15 December	5	”	”
7%	1st	28 April 1969	1 April	1 October	5	”	£10,000
1st	conversion	15 May 1969	15 April	15 October	5	”	no limit
2nd	conversion	15 June 1969	1 January	1 July	5	”	”
3rd	conversion	15 Aug 1970	1 February	1 August	5	”	”
4th	conversion	15 Oct 1970	15 May	15 November	5	”	”
7%	2nd	3 May 1971	1 May	1 November	5	103%	£10,000
5th	conversion	1 July 1971	15 May	15 November	5	”	no limit
6th	conversion	15 July 1971	15 February	15 August	5	”	”
8½%	1st	7 May 1973	1 March	1 September	5	”	£10,000
1st	conversion	15 June 1973	15 June	15 December	5	”	no limit
2nd	conversion	15 Sept 1973	15 March	15 September	5	”	”
9½%	1st	3 June 1974	15 January	15 July	5	”	£10,000
1st	conversion	15 June 1974	1 January	1 July	5	”	no limit
2nd	conversion	15 Sept 1974	1 April	1 October	5	”	”
8½%	Jubilee	2 Aug 1976	15 June	15 December	5	104%	£10,000
3rd	conversion	15 Aug 1976	1 February	1 August	5	”	no limit
4th	conversion	15 Nov 1976	1 May	1 November	5	”	”

Note 1: Unlike previous issues of British Savings Bonds the current issue of 8½ per cent British Savings Bonds (Jubilee Issue) will not be brought on to the Trustee Savings Bank part of the National Savings Stock Register.
  Enquiries about or applications to deal with bonds already administered by the Trustee Savings Bank should be made to the Trustee Savings Bank.
Note 2: All the above mentioned bonds are encashable before maturity on one month's written notice by the bondholder.
Note 3: Bonds inherited from a deceased bondholder do not count for limit purposes.
Source: The Post Office.

Advantages

1 Accessibility.
2 The maximum amount allowed is better than in, say, savings certificates.
3 They come in small units of £5 each, so can be built up regularly.
4 Although you lose the bonus if you cash in before the five-year term is up, they are quite suitable for short-term savers as the basic interest rate is good. But they are also good for long-term savers. When the bonds mature you can always cash them and go into the most recent issue.
5 They can be bought for children and the interest credited to the child's National Savings Bank account.

Disadvantages

They are not always as good an investment as a building society, depending on the current rate of interest. Seek advice from your accountant or bank before buying.

Ulster Development Bonds

There is a special issue of bonds for Ulster, which are similar to the British Savings Bonds. They are called Ulster Development Bonds and the terms under which they are issued are exactly the same as savings bonds, except that they cannot be bought by anyone under the age of eighteen. If they are bought in the name of someone under eighteen the purchaser gets the interest not the child, and the amount is included on the purchaser's tax return.

These bonds are available from Northern Ireland post offices, from the Belfast Stock Exchange, the Ulster Savings Committee, 58 Royal Avenue, Belfast BT1 1DU, and finally from the Ulster Savings Branch, Crown Buildings, Artillery Road, Coleraine, Co. Londonderry, which will also send you further information.

Defence and national development bonds

Some Defence or National Development Bonds may come into your possession. They have now matured and are no longer earning interest. If you have any write to the Director, Bonds and Stock Office, Lytham St Annes, Lancashire, FY0 1YN, and he will redeem them.

Savings Certificates

These are a very popular method of saving for the long term, and all the interest on the certificates is tax-free. So far there have been sixteen different issues, and only one is available for sale at any one time. The terms of the newest issue are usually slightly better than the previous one, as would be expected at a time when interest rates are rising. The minimum investment is £5 and the maximum £1,000. The interest rate is highly attractive 7.59 per cent on the latest issue.

You can withdraw money at any time with eight days' notice, but interest paid to you is considerably reduced if you do this. There are some points to note about saving certificates:

1 You do not get interest on them in the usual way. The government simply announces the unit, usually £5, and tells us what that £5 will be worth on maturity. If you bought £100 of the latest issue it would be worth £134.00 in four years' time.
2 The value and interest builds up slowly like this:

Fourteenth Issue

Years after purchase	Value at end of year	Yield per cent for year
	£	£
1	1.06	6.00%
2	1.13½	7.08%
3	1.22½	7.93%
4	1.34	9.39%

Basic Money Management

Like other forms of national savings, savings certificates can be bought at post offices, commercial bank branches and Trustee Savings Banks. You will get a holder's card and a registration number which is printed on all the certificates you can hold. Take care of your card as this will have your registration number on it and details of all the certificates you hold. As a safeguard note the registration number down in another place, so that you can always find it. It is necessary for buying more certificates or cashing them in.

Advantages

Savings certificates are a very attractive form of long-term saving to anyone who pays tax, as all interest is tax-free.

Disadvantages

Those who do not pay any tax can get better gross rates of interest elsewhere.

Retirement Savings Certificates

The full name for these is Index-Linked National Savings Certificates Retirement Issue. They were first brought out in June 1975 and represented a new idea in government savings plans. Their value is worked out, not on the basis of added interest or an increase in value based on a certain rate of interest, but on the cost of living. So far they are limited to retired people, that is, men over sixty-five and women over sixty.

They are an excellent form of saving, protecting the holder to a great extent from any falls in the value of money and offering in addition – if they are held for five full years – a 4 per cent bonus. This is how they work. First of all, you buy the certificates in units of £10. The money that you eventually get back on them will be increased in proportion to whatever rise in prices there has been. The government uses the U.K. General Index of Retail Prices as its measure of the rise in prices.

This index is worked out every month. The government compares the average prices of many goods in day-to-day use like food, clothing, drink, tobacco, transport and fuel with the prices paid in the previous month. If prices have risen the index will rise; if they have fallen, the index will fall. The money you receive when you cash the certificates is calculated by seeing how much the index has changed between your purchase and sale. The national newspapers usually give the values of the certificates since they were first brought out. You can easily do the sum to find out what yours are worth:

$$\frac{\text{payment} \times \text{repayment month index}}{\text{payment month index}}$$

You get no extra at all unless you hold the certificates for a year, but after that their value is calculated from the level at the date of purchase. If prices rise by 20 per cent in a year, for example, you will get £12 for every £10 unit you have bought. And if you hold the certificates until they mature you will get an extra 4 per cent of the face value, or 40p on a £10 unit.

It is clear that these certificates are very attractive when inflation is running at a higher rate than the interest offered on most saving schemes. All the repayments, too, are free of income tax and capital gains tax, so there is no complication there either. In the first year of operation the potential profit was 24.4 per cent. After that there was a slowing down in the inflation rate, but it has now increased again (1977).

Not surprisingly with such an attractive scheme the government limits quite severely the amount it will let you buy in comparison with savings bonds or saving certificates. At present it is £500 per person. You need not be actually retired or getting a pension to buy them; you must simply meet the age requirement.

Advantages

Retirement certificates are eminently suitable for men over sixty-five and women over sixty:
1   who wish to protect the purchasing power of their savings.
2   who wish to buy in small units of £10.
3   who need a tax-free return.
4   who need the accessibility of the post offices and Trustee Savings Banks for their purchases.

Disadvantages

The only possible disadvantage of retirement certificates stems from the advantage. If prices generally stopped rising, the adjusted price of the certificates would also stop rising, or even begin to fall. This is something we have not seen for many years, but if the rate of inflation does slow down reconsider your position, in case there is something more attractive to be purchased.

Save As You Earn

The Save As You Earn scheme enables you to make regular payments directly from your wages or salary each month and build up your capital over a five-year period. It is the only form of government saving available to those of us who are still earning and not yet retired which offers any protection from inflation. Each contribution is separately revalued in line with the Retail Prices Index at the end of the five-year period. It is especially attractive because any gains are free of income tax and capital gains tax.

21

These are the rules:

1 You must make a minimum of sixty monthly payments (i.e. over five years) of a fixed amount.
2 The monthly payments can be any amount in whole pounds from a £4 minimum to a £20 maximum.
3 You can hold more than one contract as long as a month elapses between taking them out, provided that the total paid each month does not come to more than £20.
4 You must be over sixteen to hold a contract and you are not allowed to have a joint contract with anyone else.
5 You are allowed to miss six payments in total. When you miss one this has the effect of postponing the whole of the contract by one month, and so on up to six. If you miss a seventh, the contract is cancelled and you will be allowed interest at the rate of 6 per cent tax-free on what you have already paid in.
6 Partial withdrawals are not allowed.

What to do

Get an S.A.Y.E. proposal from a post office or write to The Director, Savings Certificate and S.A.Y.E. Office, Durham DH99 1NS. Check to see if your employer has a group scheme.

The contract will start from the first day of the month following the month in which the first contribution is paid. You can pay by cash through most post offices, or by standing order through a Giro or bank account.

Initially the contract runs for five years, after which time the contributions are individually revalued on the following formula – the same as with retirement certificates:

$$\frac{\text{payment} \times \text{repayment month index}}{\text{payment month index}}$$

Assume that you are paying the maximum £20 a month and the Retail Price Index was 150 when you made the first payment and 190 when the five years were up. The sum would be £20 × 190/150 = £25.33, which means a profit of £5.33. Each monthly payment is valued separately and the total sent to you, though you can if you wish leave the money where it is for another two years. You make no further payments, and when the two years is up the whole amount is revalued again. You will also get a bonus which is equal to twice your monthly payment. But if you withdraw the money at any time between the fifth and seventh years you will only receive the value as at the end of five years.

Like other forms of government saving, S.A.Y.E. comes in various issues. There is nothing to stop you taking up a new issue if you already have contracts on existing ones. Each issue has its own limits.

Advantages
1   S.A.Y.E. is an excellent form of regular saving and gives a guarantee that your savings will at least keep up with inflation, as far as the Retail Price Index reflects this.
2   It is particularly good for high tax payers, as all profits are tax-free.

Disadvantages
S.A.Y.E. is not for you, however, if:
1   You cannot spare even a small amount for regular saving.
2   You cannot be sure of leaving the money where it is for the full period. It is therefore only suitable for long-term savers.

Premium Bonds

Most forms of saving offered by the government are secure and unexciting. They are meant to help us build our nest-egg for the future. Premium Savings Bonds are the one way of gambling with the government. You do not get any interest on the bond, but instead have a regular once a month chance to win a tax-free cash prize.

An unusual feature in the gamble, however, is that you never lose your original stake. You can sell your bonds at any time for the same price as you paid for them – though you have, of course, been losing any interest you could have got on any other form of saving and, because of inflation, your original stake is almost certainly worth less in *real* terms than it was when you bought the bonds. Of course, you may win a prize, which alters the situation completely.

Do not make premium bonds your first expedition into savings, if you are to stand any chance of keeping up with inflation, but once you have your nest-egg secured they are a good way of having a flutter without losing your initial stake.

When the bonds were first introduced in 1956, the maximum holding allowed was 500 of the £1 units. This has risen steadily over the years and you can now hold 2,000 of them. If you hold the maximum holding it is reckoned that you will get at least one prize each year, but that is likely to be only the minimum prize of £25, which is equal to only 1½ per cent tax-free a year – or just over 2 per cent taxable – not much compared with the other savings I have looked at.

The way prize winners are selected is basically the same as in a raffle. But it is rather a sophisticated raffle. The main draw is held at the beginning of each month and there is a further smaller draw each

23

Saturday. The winning numbers are selected by ERNIE, who is not a man but a computer which selects at random (Electronic Random Number Indicator Equipment).

The monthly prize money is set by calculating one month's interest at the rate of 5⅝ per cent a year on all the bonds which are eligible for the draw in that particular month. You have to hold the bonds for three clear months following the month in which you bought them before you qualify for the draw. This is how the money is divided at present:

Each week

1 prize of £50,000   25 prizes of £1,000 each

Each month

1 prize of £100,000   1 prize of £25,000

Each remaining complete £100,000 is divided into:

1 prize of £5,000   10 prizes of £1,000
10 prizes of £500   25 prizes of £100
1,000 prizes of £50   1,000 prizes of £25

Of the remainder, each complete £10,000 is divided into:

1 prize of £1,000   1 prize of £500
10 prizes of £100   100 prizes of £50
100 prizes of £25

Any residue less than £10,000 is divided into £25 prizes with any sum less than £25 being added to the prize fund for the following month.

The odds on you winning one of these prizes has been calculated at about 10,800 to one bond. The odds vary a little depending on whether there are four or five weekly draws in a particular month. If you have won one prize in a month, you are not eligible for another one. If the bond number is actually drawn twice, you will receive the higher prize. If you win you will be notified by post, and if the prize is over £100 you will be sent a claim form. All prize-winning numbers, apart from the £25 ones, are also given in many newspapers. A complete list is given every month in the *London Gazette*.

You can claim a prize later if you have failed to do so at the time of the draw. All the numbers of prize-winning bonds won eighteen months or more ago and still unclaimed are listed at the end of the *London Gazette* in January, April, July and October. Copies of this are usually on display at the larger post offices.

As with all government schemes, the bonds can be bought from all post offices. You must be sixteen to purchase them, though a parent or guardian can buy bonds on behalf of their children.

Since ERNIE started twenty years ago, it has often been claimed that it is biased towards certain numbers, or places in which bonds have been bought. This is not so: every time a check is made over a reasonable length of time it shows that ERNIE is completely impartial.

Advantages and disadvantages

Obviously premium bonds are no use in any plan to build up your capital. You may be lucky and win but that is not the same as having a guaranteed plan. But they are attractive to someone with just a few pounds to spare who likes the idea of a gamble without too much risk.

Trustee Savings Banks

Trustee Savings Banks run parallel with the National Savings Bank and are a kind of halfway house between it and the commercial clearing banks. They are non-profit-making and supervised by the government; they are also part of the total National Savings Movement. They are organized on a local basis and are all independent from one another, though the rules are the same throughout.

In general, accounts operate in the same way as those in the National Savings Bank. There are available:

1 *The savings account.* Like the National Savings Bank this is offering 5 per cent at the moment (1977) and the first £70 of interest is tax-free. The only difference compared with the ordinary account at the National Savings Bank is that you can draw out more money at any one time – £100 can be drawn on demand.

2 *The investment account.* This pays more than the savings account, the rate at any time being displayed in your local branch of the T.S.B. As a rule you need to give one month's notice before drawing from this account. The interest paid is all taxable. T.S.B.s also issue cheques, which I have dealt with in chapter 6 of this section, on banking, and they offer other services as well.

Advantages

The T.S.B. is a good place to keep money you may need at short notice, particularly if you do not pay tax.

Disadvantages

Though T.S.B. accounts are very useful, if you are trying to build up your capital there are better ways of doing it.

LOCAL AUTHORITY LOANS

Anyone who pays rates knows that it costs money to run a borough.

25

Basic Money Management

Local authorities raise the money not only through the rates but also by borrowing money from members of the public and paying them interest (which comes from the rates) on the money. The loans they require are generally advertised on most days in the paper; the Sunday papers are a particularly good vehicle for this kind of advertising.

Though local government is part of the official life of the country each authority is free to decide what terms it wishes to offer for money lent to it. They all vary, and careful study is worthwhile if you want to get the maximum interest on your money. Do not simply go to your own local authority. In general, big powerful authorities can get away with offering lower terms than small authorities, though there is no difference in the security of your investment. Every loan raised is guaranteed by the Public Works Authority after getting government approval.

Here are the mid-1977 rates and minimum amounts accepted by some of the larger authorities:

Authority (telephone number in parentheses)	Annual gross interest	Interest payable	Minimum sum	Life of bond
	%		£	Year
Alyn & Deeside (0244 531212)	11	½-year	100	2-3
Barking (01-592 4500)	12⅜	½-year	5,000	4-6
Erewash (0602 303361)	12	½-year	5,000	4
Liverpool (051 227 3911)	11¾	½-year	500	3-4
Liverpool (051 227 3911)	12¼	½-year	500	5-7
Merthyr Tydfil (0685 3201)	11½	½-year	500	3-4
Merthyr Tydfil (0685 3201)	11¾	½-year	5,000	3-4
Merthyr Tydfil (0685 3201)	12	½-year	500	5-7
Merthyr Tydfil (0685 3201)	12¼	½-year	5,000	5-7
Poole (02013 5151)	11½	½-year	- 500	3-5
Poole (02013 5151)	12	½-year	500	6-7
Redbridge (01-478 3020)	12	½-year	200	4-7
Sefton (051 922 4040)	11½	½-year	2,000	3-5
Slough (0753 23881)	12½	½-year	1,000	5-7
Thurrock (0375 5122)	11¾	½-year	300	4
Thurrock (0375 5122)	12¼	½-year	300	5-7
Wandsworth (01-874 6464)	12½	½-year	5,000	5-7
Wandsworth (01-874 6464)	12¼	½-year	1,000	5-7
Worcester (0905 23471)	12	½-year	1,000	4-10
Wrekin (0952 505051)	12¾	maturity	1,000	3
Wrekin (0952 505051)	12¼	annually	1,000	4

Reprinted with the kind permission of the *Financial Times*.

The first thing to remember about these loans is that they are not designed for short-term saving. As a general rule you will be asked to leave your money for a period from two to five years – though sometimes you can lend for a year or even less. The length of time will depend to some extent on what the local authorities think is going to happen to interest rates. Say they offer you 10 per cent, but expect that by the end of a year most savings will be offering only 8 per cent, they will encourage you to lend to them for only a year. If, on the other hand, they expect rates to go on rising, they will try to get you to leave your money with them at the 10 per cent rate for as long as possible. This is how you should go about selecting the loan to suit you.

Watch the newspapers carefully. Cut out advertisements which interest you and write for more details. The advertisement will give you the name of the borough, the rate of interest being offered, the minimum period for which you can invest and the minimum amount you can invest. You then apply to the treasurer of the local authority. You will not be likely to be able to invest less than £100, and the minimum may be as high as £1,000. At present you may get 12 per cent or more before tax, depending on the amount you put in and the length of time you leave it with the authority.

It is worth considering, however, whether your own local authority would not be more convenient than one a long way off, particularly as that way you can do business personally.

Advantages
Excellent for those who pay little or no tax who can leave their money tied up for a long time.

Disadvantages
1 The interest quoted is always gross, but it will come to you with tax deducted. If you are not a tax payer, you will then have to reclaim the tax. If you would find this a burden, perhaps another form of saving would suit you better.
2 It is hard to get your money back before the loan period is over. Do not leave any money with a local authority which you are likely to need unexpectedly. Remember that it means you will have a relatively large amount of money locked up for a set period. Local authority loans are strictly for long-term saving.
3 Local authority loans are obviously not for small savers.

FINANCE FOR INDUSTRY DEPOSITS

It is possible to put money on deposit with Finance for Industry, a government-sponsored institution which is the parent holding company of the Industrial and Commercial Finance Corporation (I.C.F.C.) and

27

Finance Corporation for Industry (F.C.I.), both of which lend money to companies to finance expansion. The deposits are similar to local authority loans and are available at differing rates of interest for periods of from three to ten years. Current rates are published by the *Financial Times* for amounts from £1,000, which is the minimum investment permitted, to £25,000. Rates on larger amounts are given on request. Currently, interest rates vary from 12½ per cent to 14¼ per cent, the rate being higher the longer the period the money is committed.

Send your deposits to, or get further information from: The Chief Cashier, Finance for Industry Limited, 91 Waterloo Road, London SE1 SXP (telephone 01-928 7822). If local authority loans appeal to you, F.F.I. deposits make an interesting secure alternative. The advantages and disadvantages are the same.

SAVINGS AT THE COMMERCIAL BANKS AND FINANCE HOUSES

The clearing banks

For most people it is their *current account* which is important to them in their dealings with the commercial clearing banks. These accounts do not earn interest and are designed to cope with day-to-day financial transactions. I have described them in chapter 6 of this section. Banks also offer *deposit accounts*. These are useful places to put money which you may want to transfer quickly to your current account, as it will earn interest until you have to. They are also useful for building up your savings, as regular transfers can easily be made from your current into your deposit account. You can open a deposit account at any bank branch. It need not be the one at which you have your current account, though that would probably be most convenient. And of course you do not need to have a current account at all.

The most important difference between saving with the government and with the commercial banks is that the rate of interest changes far more quickly with the latter. It is based on the official Minimum Lending Rate, which is decided by the Treasury through the Bank of England each Friday. The deposit rate is usually between 4½ and 3 per cent points below the M.L.R., and the current rate is usually posted in bank branches. If the M.L.R. is 14½ per cent, for example, the deposit rate will be 11-11½ per cent; if it is 13 per cent the deposit rate will be 9½-10 per cent; and if it is 8½ per cent, the deposit rate may be as low as 4 per cent.

There are other minor points of difference:

1 You will not usually get a bank book with your deposit account in a clearing bank. You will get a bank statement from time to time as

with your current account. It will show deposits and withdrawals and the interest earned on the account.

2 Interest is paid on a daily, rather than a monthly, basis. The rate is often much higher than in the Post Office, but the fact that the interest is taxable brings the net rate down if you are a tax payer.

3 There is no minimum or maximum amount which you can have on deposit.

4 You can only withdraw money at the branch at which you have an account. With the National Savings Bank account, you can withdraw money at any post office which does bank business.

5 You can draw out as much as you like on demand, though you will usually lose seven days' interest when you do.

A bank deposit account has all sorts of uses, but once you have built up enough money to cover emergencies it is a good idea to look around at the various forms of long-term saving. Even the usually attractive rate of interest is not generally enough to compensate for the fall in the value of money through inflation.

Finance houses

Finance houses work rather like building societies: they borrow money from the public at one rate of interest and lend it out to people who take out hire purchase contracts at a higher rate. Unlike building societies, however, they are ordinary public companies which exist to make a profit for their shareholders. This generally means that the interest rate they charge and the rate they offer is higher than in many other financial institutions, but the rate on deposits varies enormously depending on how much you leave with them and the terms on which you leave it.

More than in any other area of banking and finance, take care and investigate, through your bank or accountant, the company thoroughly before putting your money with it. Most of the companies which advertise for deposits today are absolutely reliable, but, in spite of the law, what are called 'fringe banks' have crept into the business from time to time. Some of these have succeeded, but others have gone bankrupt and depositors have lost all or most of their money. You can spot higher risk companies by the higher-than-average rates of interest they offer. Such schemes may look very attractive, but a promised high return is no use if you lose all your money. Let's look at the reasons why there is some risk with certain of these companies.

Finance houses are primarily a twentieth-century development. They were set up to provide finance as hire purchase and credit sales developed. It was beyond the reach of most retailers to finance these kinds of sales themselves, and they turned to companies specializing in this work. Defaults on H.P. are far more more common than defaults on

29

mortgages. These sometimes small periodic payments are often the first thing to be stopped in times of financial stress. Consumer protection for people buying on H.P. has meant that, more and more, finance companies have had to make proper provision for bad debts. They have either had to go to court to repossess their goods in cases of payment default, or to agree to extended terms for those people in difficulties who have paid more than one third of the total purchase price (see section VI, chapter 4, on the law relating to credit sales).

The bigger and older established companies have countered these problems by developing their business away from hire purchase, and today many of them operate in a similar way to banks. More and more they have turned to personal loans rather than H.P. contracts, because with a loan a defaulter can be taken to court. Many finance houses now have the status of banks. You need have no fears about leaving your money with one of the big established companies, especially if it has bank status, or is associated in one way or another with a clearing bank.

I repeat, this is the most risky area of banking. Do not be led astray by greed. If you want to save with a finance house:

1 Write to the company and ask for details of all its deposit schemes.
2 Or contact your bank manager, who may be prepared to accept money for any finance company which is connected with the bank.
3 Remember that the longer you leave your money and the more there is of it, the better terms you will get.
4 Remember that, unlike with building societies or some forms of government saving, you will have to pay tax on the interest you get. Allow for this when working out the real rate of interest. If you do not pay tax, of course, the interest rates will be highly attractive. Rates vary from company to company, but at the moment you can get between 9 and 10 per cent if you are prepared to put your money on three months' notice.

SAVINGS IN BUILDING SOCIETIES

A building society is an organization set up to finance house purchase. It does this by lending money to borrowers and charging them interest. It gets the money which it lends on mortgage by a variety of savings schemes, which can be very attractive in certain circumstances. It pays depositors rather less interest than it charges its mortgagees, and the difference – which varies according to the type of saving scheme – goes towards running the society's business and providing a reserve of money in case of default by borrowers. It is not a profit-making organization. There are several good reasons for investing in building societies:

1 There are tax advantages to tax payers.
2 The schemes on offer usually, though not always, compare well with other forms of saving.
3 People who have put money into a building society often get preferential treatment when it comes to getting a mortgage.

You have plenty of building societies to choose from. There are well over 500 scattered throughout the country, with more than 2,000 branches altogether. Some cover the whole of the United Kingdom and others – generally the smaller ones – are more localized with only a few branches. You may think that size has something to do with reliability but this is not the case. There have been failures among building societies in the past, but other larger societies have usually absorbed the failing company, and there have been none at all since the law concerning building societies was tightened up by the Building Societies Act of 1960.

If you want to be absolutely on the safe side, however, choose a society which has 'trustee status'. This means that it measures up to certain government criteria as being suitable for executors dealing with estates to invest in. You should also check that the society is a member of the Building Societies Association. This has firm rules for its members and not one of them has ever failed.

Building societies use all sorts of fancy names for their various accounts, but although there are some minor differences between societies they all basically offer the same kinds of scheme. The interest rate is higher the longer you leave your money, and a higher interest rate is generally also paid for regular savings, because the society knows that it can rely on your funds for some time.

Here, as an example, are the types of saving schemes offered by a London-based building society at the present time. You should be able to find something similar either among the country-wide societies, or at your own local one.

type of account	*interest rate* %	*taxable equivalent* %
Shares	6.70	10.31
Premium Shares (3 months' withdrawal notice)	6.95	10.69
Centenary Shares 'C' (6 months' withdrawal notice)	7.45	11.46
Subscription Shares (monthly savings)	7.95	12.33
Deposits	6.45	9.92
Centenary Shares 'B' (4-year term)	8.20	12.62 (issue discontinued)

You will notice that the last column of the table shows a higher interest rate than is actually paid. This shows the interest you would have to earn to get an equivalent amount if you had to pay tax on it at the current standard rate of 35 per cent. But interest in building societies is not, as this might suggest, tax-free: it is 'tax-paid' at the standard rate. The building societies have negotiated special tax concessions for their account holders, as a result of which interest is tax-free to account holders who are paying tax at the standard rate of 35 per cent. If you are paying tax at the higher rates you will have to pay tax on your account. However, although the interest is tax-paid rather than tax-free you cannot claim it back if you are not a tax payer. This means that *building*

	Deposit Rate	Share Accnts.	Sub'pn Shares		**Term Shares
	%	%	%	%	
Abbey National	6.75	7.00	8.25	8.00	3yrs., 7.50% 2 yrs. £1,000-£15,000
Alliance	6.75	7.00	8.25	8.00	3yrs, 7.50% 2yr, 7.25% 1yr min. £100
Anglia	6.75	7.00	8.25	8.00	3 years min. £500 7.50% 2 yrs.
Birmingham Incorporated	6.75	7.00	8.25	7.50	2 years min. £500 7.25% 1 yr.
Bradford and Bingley	6.75	7.00	8.25	8.00	3 yrs., 7.50% 2 yrs., min. £500
Bristol and West	6.75	7.00	8.25	—	
Bristol Economic	6.75	7.00	8.25	7.25	3 months' notice
Britannia	6.75	7.00	8.25	8.00	3 yrs., 7.50% 2 yrs., min. £1,000
Burnley	*6.75	7.00	8.25	7.50	Minimum £500 2 years' term
Cardiff	7.55	8.30	9.30	—	
Chelsea	6.75	7.00	8.25	7.75	Minimum £500 6 months' notice
Cheltenham and Gloucester	6.73	7.00	—	8.00	3 years
Citizens Regency	7.55	8.12	9.50	9.37	3 years £5,000 minimum
City of London	7.80	8.30	9.25	9.13	3-year increment £500 min.
Coventry Economic	6.75	7.00	8.25	8.00	7.50% 3 mths. notice aft. 9 mths.
Derbyshire	6.75	7.00	8.25	7.50	Minimum £5,000 3 months' notice
Gateway	6.75	7.00	8.25	8.00	3 yrs., 7.50% 2 yrs. Min. £500
Greenwich	6.00	8.00	9.00	9.00	2 yrs fixed 1% over Share Acts
Guardian	7.55	8.05	8.30	8.75	Minimum £1,000 3 months' notice
Halifax	6.75	7.00	8.25	8.00	3 yrs., 7.50% 2 yrs.

	Deposit Rate %	Share Accnts. %	Sub'pn Shares %	%	**Term Shares
Hastings and Thanet	6.75	7.00	8.25	8.00	3 yrs., 7.50% 1½ yrs. £250–£15,000
Heart of England	6.75	7.00	8.25	8.00	3 yr. 7.50% 2 yr. min. £500
Hearts of Oak & Enfield	7.55	8.00	9.60	9.75	4 yr. 9% 3 yr. 8.75% 2yr. min. £1,000
Hendon	7.00	7.50	—	8.00	Minimum £2,000 6 months' notice
Huddersfield & Bradford	6.75	7.00	††8.25	8.00	3 yrs., 7.50% 2 yrs. £100–£15,000
Leamington Spa	6.85	7.10	9.36	6.97	rising to 8.47 % in year 6
Leeds Permanent	6.75	7.00	8.25	—	
Leicester	6.75	7.00	8.25	8.00	3 yr. 7.50% 2 yr. £100–£10,000
Liverpool	6.75	7.00	8.45	8.30	Min. £1,000 over 2 yrs. 6mths. not.
Magnet & Planet	7.55	7.80	9.05	9.05	3 yrs. min. £100 8.80% 2 yrs.
Midshire	6.75	7.00	8.25	8.25	Min. £500 3 yrs. Top Yield
Mornington	†6.70	7.60	—	—	
National Counties	7.80	8.05	9.05	7.75	6 months
Nationwide	6.75	7.00	7.50	8.00	3–4 yrs. min. £500 2 yrs. 7.50%
Newcastle Permanent	7.55	7.80	8.30	—	
Northern Rock	6.75	7.00	8.25	8.00	3 yrs., 7.50% 2 yrs. min. £100
Norwich	6.75	7.00	8.25	8.00	Minimum £500 2 yrs.
Paisley	7.55	7.80	9.05	—	
Portman	*6.75	7.00	8.25	8.00	3 yrs., 7.50% 2 yrs min. £500
Property Owners	7.55	8.30	9.55	8.80	3 months notice
Provincial	6.75	7.00	8.25	8.00	4 yrs. 7.75% 3 yrs., 7.50% 2 yrs.
Skipton	6.75	7.00	8.25	7.50	2 yrs. 8.00% 3 yrs. min. £500
Sussex Mutual	7.00	§§7.15	—	8.00	3 months notice. Min. £500
Town and Country	6.50	7.00	10.00	8.00	3 yrs., 7.50% 2 yrs. £1,000–£15,000
Woolwich Equitable	6.75	7.00	8.25	8.00	3 yrs., 7.50 2 yrs. Min. £500

*From 1 June 1977. **Rates normally variable in line with changes in ordinary share rates. ††Moneymaker Shares. §§£5.00 and over 7.40%. †Rates from 16 May 1977.

Reproduced by kind permission of the *Financial Times*. An up-to-date table is published every Saturday.

society savings are best for those who are paying tax at the standard rate. Other people can find a better net (after tax) interest rate in other places. They are suitable for either short- or long-term saving.

Interest rates in building societies change more slowly than in some other parts of the private sector. This means that from time to time saving with a building society may not be as attractive as other forms of saving. Keep an eye on interest rates and switch backwards and forwards if this is financially advantageous to you. On pp. 32-3 are the current interest rates offered in 1977 by some of the larger societies.

CHOOSING YOUR SAVINGS PLAN

Everyone will have a different priority when it comes to saving, and we must each work out the scheme which suits us best. This scheme will depend on many things, including

* age
* marital status
* profession
* salary level

1 *Age.* The younger you are the less you will probably need for your nest-egg, but even so try to save £100 or £200 a year. It makes a useful deposit for a car, or can be used to finance a holiday.

2 *Marital status.* As soon as you marry, or indeed think about marrying, your savings should become a more important item in your budgeting. The more money you can get together before you marry the better. Try, if possible, to save a deposit for a house or flat before you become involved in family budgeting. Once bought, a house is an investment for life. If you are divorced or widowed, try if possible to keep up some saving, however small. More than most, you may find you need your nest-egg.

3 *Profession.* If you are in a steady job with prospects of an increasing salary, tailor your savings to increase as your salary rises. Don't try to save too much at the beginning, but gradually build up. If you are in an uncertain profession, where your earnings may be erratic, it is even more important to make sure you have some money put by for emergencies.

4 *Salary level.* This is most important. It should be a guide to the kind of savings plan you follow. Tax-free savings are of less use to those who do not pay tax than to those who do. If you pay tax at the standard rate, or more especially at the higher rates, get as much tax-free saving as you can.

To start with, as I said in chapter 1 of this section, try to think of saving as part of your normal outgoings. Then you must divide your money into:

1 Short-term savings.
2 Long-term savings.

Everyone will need some money for emergencies, and to begin with you may have to concentrate on building up a reserve which you think will cover any sudden payments you may have to make. For short-term saving you should choose from the following:

1 National Savings Bank Ordinary Account (especially if you are paying tax).
2 Trustee Savings Bank Ordinary Account (for the same reasons).
3 A deposit account with a clearing bank (this offers a better interest rate than the above, but the interest is taxable, so this is better if you are not paying tax).
4 A building society deposit or share account (good for those paying tax at the standard rate, less good for those who do not pay tax or who pay at the higher rates).

In all these you can get your money out quickly without much fuss or loss of interest.

When you have built up your reserve you can turn to longer-term plans. Choose saving schemes where there is a bonus for fulfilling the whole plan, and choose the best terms to suit your circumstances. Choose from:

1 National Savings Certificates (the interest is free of tax, which makes these very attractive to high tax payers).
2 British Savings Bonds (better for those not paying tax, as the interest is taxable).
3 Save As You Earn schemes (these are free of tax and allow you to build up your long-term capital on very favourable terms, but they are limited to a maximum saving of £240 a year).
4 Local authority loans (the high rates of interest are good for those who do not pay tax or pay only at the standard rate).
5 The longer-term schemes offered by the building societies (good for standard rate tax payers).
6 The longer-term finance company deposits (high rates of interest, but take care in choosing your company).
7 Retirement Savings Certificates (if you are retired).

Do not buy premium bonds as part of either your short- or long-term savings plans. These are quite separate and only for those who like to gamble without losing their original stake.

The following table will help you to choose sensibly:

Type of saving	State/private	interest rate *	interest rate changes	tax status
National Savings Bank: Ordinary Account Investment Account	State		Periodically Periodically	Tax-free to first £75 Taxable
National Savings Certificates	State		Fixed for term	Tax-free
Retirement Savings Certificates	State		Linked to Index Retail Prices	Tax-free
British Savings Bonds	State		Fixed for term	Taxable, but tax-free bonus at end
Premium Bonds	State		Erratic; now equal to 5⅝%	Tax-free
Save As You Earn	State		Linked to Retail Prices Index	Tax-free
Trustee Savings Banks: Ordinary Account Investment Account	State		Periodically Periodically	Tax-free to first £75 Taxable
Local Authority Loans	Guaranteed by government		Fixed for term	Taxable
F.F.I. Term Deposits	Guaranteed by government		Fixed for term linked	Taxable
Clearing Bank Deposit Accounts	Private		Linked directly to M.L.R.	Taxable
Building Societies	Private		Changes slowly but follows trend	Tax paid at standard rate
Finance Companies	Private		Linked to M.L.R. for fixed or term	Taxable

*Interest rates change all the time. Fill this column in as you make your savings plan.

When you have built up a good reserve of savings, you may feel you would like to 'diversify' and put some of your money into a wider range of investments. If you have reached the point where you can take some

36

interest paid	current min/max amount	best long/short term	withdrawal terms	best for
Monthly Monthly	26p/£10,000 £1/no upper limit	Short Either	£30 on demand; rest in few days; one month's notice	Beginners and tax payers Non-tax payers
At end of term	£5/£5,000	Medium	8 working days' notice, but on penal terms	All tax payers
When cashing in	£10/£500	Minimum one year	8 working days' notice, but returned only at purchase price if held less than one year.	Men over 65, women over 60, especially tax payers
15 June 15 December	£5/£10,000	Medium/ Long	One month's notice; bonus lost if term not completed	Non-tax payers and standard rate payers
As monthly or weekly prizes	£1/£2,000	A gamble	8 working days' notice	Gamblers, who do not like losing stake
At end of term	£48/£240 per year	Long	8 working days' notice, but bonus lost if term not completed	Wage earners, especially high tax payers
Monthly, but added annually on 20 November	25p/£10,000 £1/no upper limit	Short Either	£100 on demand; rest in a few days; one month's notice	Beginners and tax payers non-tax payers
Monthly, half-yearly, or yearly	By negotiation usually not less than £100/no upper limit	Long	Varies between one & 10 yrs; difficult to break term	Those with ample funds and non-tax payers.
Half-yearly	£1000/no upper limit	Long	Minimum 3 years; maximum 10 years	As with local authority loans
Daily	No limits	Short	7 days' notice	Non-tax payers
Monthly, but credited twice a year	£1/£10,000	Depends on scheme	Varies with scheme. Usually £100 on demand, rest in a few days	Those paying standard rate tax
Varies from company to company	By negotiation no upper limits	Depends on scheme	Varies; penal terms if contract not fulfilled	Those with ample funds and non-tax payers.

risk with a portion of your savings in the hope of a better return on your money, turn to section V, where all the possibilities open to you are discussed.

Chapter 4

WHEN YOU WANT TO BORROW MONEY

GETTING CREDIT

Let's clear away right at the start any idea that there is anything wrong with borrowing money to buy the things we need. Most people borrow at some time for a particular purpose. Some who quite happily take out a mortgage regard any other form of hire purchase or credit sale as best avoided. This is a mistaken view. It is, of course, wrong to over-extend yourself in your hire purchase commitments, as with any other regular payments, but many people's lives are made much more comfortable by the possibility of paying for purchases over a period of time. By borrowing in this way you can have the use of something you need now by committing part of your future income in the contract.

To get some idea of the extent of the credit business, look at the figures. Total borrowing by the British public at the end of 1976 had reached the massive figure of £2,662,000,000 in outstanding instalment credit. That is equal to £75 for every adult in the country. Personal loans from the banks now amount to £3,274,000,000 and the building societies are lending £6,000,000,000 a year.

You may think that if you want something it is worth saving for. An admirable idea, but just think of saving up to buy a house. That would take many more years than the period of the average mortgage, and you would be paying tax on interest over the years, rather than getting tax relief on your interest payments on a mortgage. Few people today would not buy a house simply because they disapproved of mortgages, and once you have taken the step of getting a mortgage there is no valid reason for not financing other major purchases – a car, furniture and household fittings, even a holiday or expensive items of clothing – in that way too – though there is no tax relief when you borrow for anything except a house, or improvements to a house.

The big development in hire purchase has come about because of a change of attitude towards borrowing not only on the part of the borrowers themselves but also on the part of the lenders. To begin with, only people with 'security' were offered loans and the conditions were strict. Borrowers had to have other assets with which to back their application for a loan. Lenders naturally want as much security as they

38

can get to ensure that their money is repaid, particularly following changes in the law, which are very advantageous to anyone buying goods on credit (see section VI, chapter 4, on protection for borrowers).

But lenders have come to realize that it is not only physical assets which represent security. Regular wages or salary can be just as good as actual capital or other assets. In other words, the man or woman (women need no longer provide a male guarantor if they have regular earnings or assets) who is in a steady job, but who does not have sufficient capital or savings to buy, say, a car, can be just as good a risk as the person who owns a house, or has some money in the bank, or a few shares.

As a result, most of us are either borrowers or lenders, and few follow the old adage 'Neither a borrower nor a lender be'. In today's society it is sensible to borrow. Do remember, however, that with credit facilities so widely available there can be a danger of over-reaching yourself if you are not careful. Make sure you know exactly what your total borrowings add up to: a bank overdraft or personal loan, or money outstanding on a credit card, is just as much a debt as the hire purchase you may arrange when buying a car or furniture.

It is important to remember that borrowing is rarely free, unless perhaps you are borrowing from a friend or a member of your family, or sometimes if you are borrowing for no more than six months, for example from some department stores. And interest rates charged on hire purchase are some of the highest that there are.

This fact may not be immediately apparent when you borrow. The stated interest rate may seem quite low, but there is sometimes a great deal of difference between the 'flat rate' and the 'true rate'. In general, you can work out the true rate by using the following formula.

Say you borrow £100 over two years, and you have to pay back a total of £120 in eight quarterly instalments of £15 each. You work out the 'flat' interest rate by taking the difference of £20, which is 20 per cent of £100, and dividing it by two, because the repayment is taking place over two years. This gives an annual 'flat' rate of 10 per cent. But this is not the 'true' rate, because you are reducing the debt in quarterly instalments, and the interest is fixed for the period of the full loan and does not decrease as your debt goes down. You must multiply the flat rate by 1.8 if you are paying quarterly, by 1.9 if you pay monthly, and by 2 if you pay weekly. This means that the 10 per cent flat rate becomes a true rate of 18, 19 or 20 per cent, and that interest rates are really much higher than they appear. The true rates work out like this at different 'flat' rates:

flat rate	quarterly	monthly	weekly
%	%	%	%
5	9.0	9.5	10
6	10.8	11.4	12
7	12.6	13.3	14
8	14.4	15.2	16
9	16.2	17.1	18
10	18.0	19.0	20
11	19.8	20.9	22
12	21.6	22.8	24
13	23.4	24.7	26
14	26.6	26.6	28
15	27.0	28.5	30
16	28.8	30.4	32

Rates are sometimes given on a monthly basis. In the next chapter, on credit cards, I have set out what they mean on an annual basis.

It is sensible to get a loan carrying the lowest possible interest rate. Let's look at the sort of rates available for car purchase, which is often the biggest item of hire purchase after a house. The following table shows the kind of rates being offered by different lenders earlier this year (1977); it also shows the difference in total payments over a two-year repayment period where the loan is reduced monthly. The sum borrowed is in all cases £1,000.

You can see two things from this table. Most important, there is a lower total repayment of £678.24, or more than 38 per cent, for the cheapest form of borrowing compared with the dearest on exactly the same loan over the same period. Second, the stated interest rate has no direct significance. Depending on how the company calculates them, the repayments can vary enormously with fairly similar flat rates of interest. The odd one out is a bank overdraft, where interest is charged daily, so that the true rate and the flat rate are the same.

type	flat rate p.a. %	true rate p.a. %	total payment over 2 years
special deal hire purchase	5	9.5	£1,190
bank overdraft	14.5	14.5	£1,290
personal bank loan	9	17.1	£1,342
A.A. finance house loan	11.0	20.9	£1,418
finance house loan	13.5	25.65	£1,513
hire purchase	15.5	29.45	£1,589

Of the examples above, the cheapest way to borrow is under the low-interest scheme offered by some motor dealers; the second cheapest is a personal bank loan; the dearest is an H.P. finance house loan. For this reason, the A.A. has put out guidance for those buying their cars on hire purchase. The rules they suggest are, with modification, generally sensible for any H.P. or credit sale for cars or anything else.

1 Make your initial deposit as low as possible. You can lose interest on your money if delivery is delayed for a month or more.
2 Check the true rate of interest before signing any agreement. Look at everything available before making your final choice.
3 Do not raise any money through a finance broker. You may be charged a brokerage fee as well as interest, which will make the loan very expensive.
4 Avoid finance houses which do not have a good reputation. Deal only with those which have a reliable record. These are usually associated with one of the clearing banks.

Above all, when you sign a hire purchase contract, or one for a credit sale, read all the small print, and know exactly what you are committing yourself to. Read section VI, chapter 4, to make sure you are aware of the legal implications of what you are doing.

Hire purchase rates vary from company to company. If you are very lucky you may manage to get money at a true rate of interest around 25 per cent. The more reputable firms charge interest at about this level. If you are unlucky you may pay up to 60 per cent a year. Avoid this if at all possible, and insist that the lender tells you the true rate of interest he is charging you. When the Consumer Credit Act is operating fully, you will be entitled to know the true rate of interest, but at the moment you may find the lender reluctant to tell you. When this happens the rate is almost certainly unduly high.

There are government rules covering hire purchase and credit sales. You may be required to put down some deposit, unless you are buying what is regarded as an *essential* item like a cooker, fridge or gas fire. If you agree to pay back the money very quickly in any credit sale – that is, within nine months – you may not have to leave a deposit. You may borrow for up to two and a half years for what are called 'controlled goods', but only up to two years on a car. If you are buying essential items there is no limit on the repayment period. Your retailer will tell you what sort of goods you are buying.

There is an important difference between goods bought on hire purchase and those bought on a credit sale. You do not own the former until you have made the final payment, but goods bought on credit sale are yours legally from the moment you buy them. Turn to section VI, chapter 4, where I have set out the legal implications of this difference. Hire purchase and credit sales are the most common ways of borrowing to finance your purchases, but there are many other ways. Let's review the most important of them.

Your bank. I have dealt with this in detail in chapter 6 of this section, on current bank accounts. All you need to know here is that an overdraft, rather than a personal loan, is generally – though not always – the cheaper way to borrow.

Your credit card. Again, this is covered in detail in the next chapter of this section. Do not assume that the money outstanding on your credit card is not a loan. It most certainly is.

Your insurance company. If you have an insurance policy which carries a cash-in (or surrender) value you may be able to borrow on it. The most common types of policy where this is available are usually a whole-life policy, or an endowment policy with a surrender value. The policy is used as security, and you may be allowed to borrow up to 90 per cent. These are attractive, because you do not need – though you can if you wish – to repay the loan until the policy matures. The interest rate you are charged will be relatively low, and is unlikely to be more than 15 per cent. The longer you have held the policy the better.

This is an excellent way to borrow, but remember that surrender values are low in the early years of a policy (see this section, chapter 13), so you will not be able to borrow for some time after you have taken the policy out. For this reason, it is not a good idea to take out a policy *simply* to provide yourself with a borrowing opportunity.

Personal loan from a finance company. You can use this for whatever purchases you choose. Finance companies prefer this kind of contract to a straight H.P. loan because it is easier for them to get their money back if the borrower defaults on his repayments, and the minimum loan may be £100 or even £200. As I said earlier, it is an expensive way to borrow.

Credit accounts with shops. Sometimes these are interest-free, if you are only asking for the credit until the end of the month when you receive the bill. A great deal depends on how the particular store runs its credit accounts. Those that insist on immediate payment monthly generally charge nothing, or very little; those who allow you to pay back over a period in the same way as Barclaycard or Access (see next chapter) may charge a high rate of interest. Some stores allow you the option of paying either way, and you can vary your paying policy as it suits you.

Budget accounts with shops. The holder pays a set amount each month, usually a minimum of £4, and is then allowed to buy goods up to eight times the amount of the monthly payment. As each payment is made the credit limit moves up by the same amount.

These accounts are dear, though the interest may be shown not as a straight payment but as a 'service charge'. This can be up to 5 per cent of the amount outstanding each month. Get an ordinary account if you can, but if you have no security or a low income, a budget account may be all that the store will allow you. After holding it for some time they may be prepared to let you move over to an ordinary account.

Check trading. This form of borrowing is only for those who want small amounts and cannot raise money in any other way. It is a very expensive form of borrowing, with the interest rate going up to 70 per cent overall. It is also expensive for the retailer who accepts the check in payment.

Check trading first developed in the north of England in the mutual clubs in the industrial centres. It works very simply. The check trading company sells checks of values from £1 to £20. These can be used in any shop which accepts them. The repayment is made in twenty weekly instalments, which are usually collected from the borrower by one of the agents of the company. If the borrower pays, say, 5 per cent back on the value of the check the flat rate of interest annually is around 25 per cent. The *true* rate is far more. When the retailer turns the check in, he has to accept a discount of 15 per cent, or 15p in the pound, so the check trading company makes money from both the borrower and the retailer. Retailers, particularly in poor areas, are prepared to accept the high discount because it brings them in business which they would not otherwise get.

Nevertheless, check trading is useful for those with little money. As the collector sells checks as well as calling for the repayments, he or she often gets to know a family well, and in cases of real hardship it is possible to get the repayments deferred.

Mail order. This is probably the most common form of borrowing in the United Kingdom. The companies offering mail order vary enormously in size. Some are one-man businesses serving only their local area, where the customer may also be able to visit the shop and buy over the counter, but usually there is no discount for cash. But the really big area of mail order is the giant companies. These produce very large catalogues which they send to agents, who organize sales for them and take a commission on the value of the goods they sell. The mail order business has a long history, and, as with check trading, the amounts involved are relatively small, as a rule. The business developed from the old shop clubs which grew up in the Victorian era. Mail order firms normally operate on a credit-only basis. Prices are usually 'credit prices', and very often no cash price is given, so you gain nothing by paying cash.

It is rather difficult to work out what interest you pay with mail order. Repayments are generally made in twenty weekly instalments, and if that is the case you are unlikely to be paying more than an annual interest of 20 per cent. Sometimes the period is longer, particularly if expensive items like domestic appliances are involved. But interest is not that important with mail order, because although you pay a high rate you may occasionally find that the 'credit price' is actually lower than the price in shops. This is because mail order companies do not have anything like the overheads which shops and stores have to include in

43

their prices. Mail order companies have few retail outlets, and generally agents are cheaper to run than large department stores.

The real bargains are usually to be found in branded goods. This is a selling ploy, for the customer can then compare prices in the mail order catalogue with those in the shops. Non-brand names will usually be a little dearer, though not much, than non-branded goods in the shops.

Small loan societies. There are not many of these, and if you find one you are fortunate, because the rates of interest are comparatively good. They tend to lend small sums of money to their members for fairly short periods. This type of loan is gradually dying out, but you may still find a small loan company, a friendly society, or a non-profit-making credit union, which will lend small amounts.

Second mortgage lenders. This type of lending is growing fast. Basically, it works on the principle that if someone has had a first mortgage for some time the value of the mortgaged house has probably risen sharply. This means that the house can be used as security for more borrowing, and that comes from second mortgage companies. They act as go-betweens. After checking the borrower's credentials, they introduce the prospective borrower to the prospective lender, which may be an insurance company, a finance house or some other kind of financial institution.

There are pitfalls, some of which I mention in chapter 8 of this section, on mortgages, and borrowers should be absolutely certain that they know what they are letting themselves in for. Interest rates are higher than on first mortgages, sometimes much higher, and the borrower may be persuaded to take more money than is actually needed, so that the repayment burden is heavy. If you are seeking a loan for house improvements, try to get one from whoever is lending you the money on your first mortgage. That way you will avoid paying a higher rate of interest. Only get a second mortgage if you can find no other way of getting the money you need.

WHERE NOT TO BORROW

There are some forms of borrowing that you should avoid unless you are desperate, and even then it's wiser to keep on trying rather than resort to them. These are money lenders and pawnbrokers. It is difficult to decide which is the worst bet, but I opt for money lenders: all you lose in pawnbroking is the stuff you have pawned, whereas money lending rates are punitive.

Money lenders. This is an expanding business, despite the pitfalls for borrowers. There are nearly 3,000 licensed money lenders in Britain, and many more who have tried to avoid being licensed. Obviously, if you must use them, go to a licensed one. As a rule, they lend no more than a few hundred pounds – £100 or £200 are the most popular amounts – and the interest rates are prohibitive. If you have some security for your loan – and if you have, it is unlikely that you would go to a money lender in the first place – you may pay anything between a 20 and 40 per cent flat rate of interest.

If you cannot secure the loan – and this is true of most people who go to money lenders – the flat rate will rise to 50 or even 60 or 70 per cent. As you can see, you should, if you are sensible, wait until you have been turned down by all other possible lenders before resorting to the money lender. He is just for those to whom no one else will lend – for the money lender will consider any loan at all.

Pawnbrokers. These traders make their money from defaulters. The business is dying out now in Britain, but further severe economic difficulties could bring a revival. You must pay the money back within six months and one day. If you are lent less than £2, the pawnbroker has an automatic right to the goods you have left with him as security if you default. If you borrow more than £2 and default, the goods have to be sold by public auction. The maximum profit the pawnbroker is allowed is ½p for every 25p he has lent, after allowing for all his costs, which can mount up. The real cost of a loan can be high, and when you consider that most loans given by pawnbrokers are between £1 and £4 it seems much better to try to tide yourself over in some other way, say by taking a temporary evening job, or a part-time job if you are a woman at home.

The pawnbroker will lend you money on anything which is saleable at a higher price if you default. In the past, jewellery has often been 'pledged' – the term used to describe the security you leave with the pawnbroker – but items like cameras, radios, cassette players, musical instruments or even small antiques might also be acceptable. Remember that if your financial problems are more than very temporary you are quite likely to lose a treasured object.

WHAT KIND OF BORROWER ARE YOU?

When anyone lends you money, whether for a house or to pay for a holiday, they will want to be as certain as possible that you will be able to pay it back. The lender is likely to want to know whether you are in a steady job, and how long you have held it. If you want a very large loan he will want to know whether you are also buying a house on a mortgage, and what other security you might be able to offer.

So the first thing any prospective lender determines when a loan is being sought is the personal credit-worthiness of the borrower. Do not despair if you cannot prove that you are a good risk because you have only just started working, or for any other reason. Just try to get someone to guarantee your loan. Be clear what this means, however, for if you default the guarantor will have to pay off any remaining debt. Minors, that is anyone under eighteen when they take out a loan, must always have a guarantor, because they cannot be sued for debt. Parents will be held responsible for any minor's debt, if there is no guarantor.

Many people take on loans on such terms that they are unable to maintain the payments. The lender does not wish to take court action any more than you will wish it to be taken, so if you run into difficulties inform the lender immediately and he will usually adjust the repayment period.

From time to time, *the rules* about credit sales and hire purchase are changed by the government. Check what the current rules are before you actually start negotiations. Once you have taken on a loan on certain terms these cannot be varied (except in the case of bank overdrafts), even if the rules change. New rules only apply to future contracts.

Finance companies have to obey the same 'credit guidelines' as those set out for the banks. This means that from time to time the money they have available to lend will vary, so even if you have been turned down in the past do not hesitate to go back again, either because your own circumstances are better or because the general economic atmosphere has improved.

Keeping your record clean

If you are in a reasonable financial position you will usually find that you can get a loan, unless you have a record of bad debts, that is, failures to repay previous loans. It is now extremely difficult to keep these secret. There are private companies who track down the debtor's record for the lender, and if you get a 'thumbs down' from them you are unlikely to get your loan.

Credit reference bureaux like the United Association for the Protection of Trade Ltd and British Debt Services Ltd keep records of all court actions for debt recovery and also seek out any other information which might be useful for a lender to know.

There is also an official organization, the Register of County Court Judgements, which files all the records of judgements which are unpaid for twenty years, and these are available for public scrutiny for those twenty years. The Register has been losing money at the rate of £30,000 a year, and because of this the government may decide to abolish it, as part of the overall cuts in public spending. By the time you are reading this the Register may well no longer exist. Good news, you may think, for bad debtors, but this is not so. If companies find that their bad debts increase without the Register, interest rates will almost certainly rise for all borrowers.

How likely are you to get into too much debt?

Over the years a picture has gradually grown up of the sort of family which is likely to get into more debt than it should. With some adaptation, you can see if you come into this category. If you can see yourself in the following, take extra care before increasing your borrowing.

* You are likely to be young with more than the average number of children.
* Your total family income is likely to be above average.
* Neither husband nor wife takes financial responsibility for the family's debts (go back to chapter 1 of this section on personal budgeting and forward to section III, chapter 2, on setting up a home). Matters can soon get out of control if husband and wife buy what they want without reference to the overall family budget.
* Either husband or wife, or both, is rather happy-go-lucky, preferring to buy anything they need, or think they need, whenever they want to, rather than work out whether they can meet the financial commitment involved.
* As a family, the unit is inclined to blame its financial problems on outside factors which are not really to blame, instead of admitting that it has over-stretched itself.
* You are unlikely to do much reading, so it is certainly a remote chance that you will be reading this, unless you are already desperate. You are far more likely to rely on your T.V. set when making your financial decisions, rather than reading and looking around at the options open before you buy.
* Your family probably moves around a lot from house to house.
* You may recently be separated or divorced, and find the same money has to keep two homes.
* Finally, but not to be ignored, as it can be at the root of all overspending, a husband may well be happy in his job but his wife unhappy about the level of his income. This can lead to overspending on both sides, the wife through sheer frustration and the husband to prove that he can keep up with his neighbours.

From this list, it is easy to guess which age group tends to be in financial trouble; it is among those aged between eighteen and thirty that the total amount of money owed is way above the level it should be. You can work out more or less the amount of monthly outgoings you can afford; the precise figure will vary in every case. Factors which will influence it are your marital status, the size of your family, your other dependents, your travelling costs, and, of course, your salary and prospects of advancement at work.

In general, try to limit your total borrowing to no more than 15 per cent of the disposable income you have after you have paid your rent or mortgage. Even if you have few other commitments, never go above 20 per cent. Make sure that in any one year you do not owe more than 30 per cent of your annual income after tax and your basic needs. Above all, consider how stable your job is before you get into any debt at all.

Signs of over-borrowing

* You have too many small debts in different places. Your credit card limit may be near. Your overdraft is at its limit. In any revolving credit account your spending is always close to the maximum.
* You find yourself asking for longer and longer term credit and paying as little as possible on deposit.
* You have to stretch the payment of your bills to the point where some of the next instalments fall due before you have paid the current lot.
* You start thinking about putting all your debts into one place in an attempt to keep them under control. You may feel that it is better to have just one debtor, say your bank. This is sometimes a good idea, but there can be a temptation to start building up new debts all over again, unless you are very strong-willed.

The solution to too much debt

1 Sit down and work out the level of your debts and the periods over which you owe the money. If the total is way above the level it should be, look at those debts where the repayment period could be lengthened to ease the burden of your repayments, then contact the debtor and ask whether you can spread the repayment over a longer period.
2 If the excess debt is small, and two or three months of severe budgeting will solve the problem have these two or three stringent months. It will be well worthwhile in the long run. Look at your future commitments and see which can be avoided altogether or cut down. A smaller car, perhaps? A less expensive holiday? It is likely you will find *something* you can do without.
3 If there really is no way in which you can economize, inform your debtors, and ask for an extension of the loan period, even if you were at the limits when you started. Many of them would prefer to get their money back a little more slowly than not at all.
4 If you decide that you must consolidate your debt, then try to make sure that this overall loan is at the lowest possible interest rate. Check back to earlier in this chapter for what is best for you. In general, it will be your bank if you have an account with one of the clearing banks, or a loan through the National Giro or Trustee Savings Bank if you do not.
5 Above all, *do not panic*. Few of us go bankrupt, but many learn a

sharp lesson in avoiding it. If you do reach this stage, turn to section VI, chapter 5, to see what going bankrupt means. Even that is not the end of the world.

Chapter 5

USING A CREDIT CARD

Credit cards are possibly the most important development in borrowing since the end of the war – though the wrong use of them has almost bankrupted many people. Used properly they can be extremely valuable in planning your spending because, to some extent, you can choose the method and timing of repayments.

What a credit card does is to take away the need for a cheque, cash, or a formal hire purchase agreement when you are buying. You can either repay the whole amount at the end of the month, or stagger it over several months.

BANK CARDS

The two main bank credit cards in Britain are *Barclaycard*, which, as its name suggests, is issued by Barclays Bank, and *Access*, operated by National Westminster, Lloyds and Midland and their subsidiaries. Barclaycard is the oldest in this country – it was formed in 1963.

They are very easy to use. You simply sign a bill when you buy something and keep a copy. The bill is sent each month. Naturally, you have to pay something for this service. At the moment it is 2 per cent a month. Not much perhaps, but remember that 2 per cent a month works out at 26.8 per cent a year.

Between them Barclaycard and Access cover most big department stores and many smaller ones, most big garages and hotels and the smarter restaurants. You can also use them abroad. Access is interchangeable with Mastercharge and European Eurocard, Barclaycard with Bank Americard and Ibanco, Carte Bleu and Visa. The frequent traveller may find that they are not sufficient abroad, and not all countries make much use of them.

Snags

* The cost of borrowing. The bank cards are geared to the bank, and therefore to bank profits. For this reason, the interest rate will vary with the bank's prosperity.
* The credit limit. The bank will decide just how much credit it will give you. Students – if they get a card at all – may be limited to £50; £100 is average, and very few people get over £500.

INDEPENDENT CARDS

Because of these limitations you may decide to use one of the independent cards. The main two are *American Express* (Amex) and *Diners Club*. These can be widely used throughout the world, and there is no limit on credit. *Clients get generous free credit* – forty-five days from Diners and sixty from Amex. After that they charge 1½ per cent a month, or 19.6 per cent a year, on your outstanding balance. *But,* and it is a big but, they do not like lending money: you are expected to settle the whole of the bill when you receive it. If you make a habit of delaying payments, they will pursue you vigorously and will eventually take away your card. They make their main profit by charging the outlets.

Snags

* Not as useful in the U.K. as the bank cards, because there are fewer outlets. Do not make either of them your only card.
* They charge you for your card, which the banks do not. At present, the cost is £7.50 a year.

DEPARTMENT STORE ACCOUNTS AND OTHERS

In many department stores the old monthly accounts are giving way to a system similar to the bank credit cards. If you settle a bill immediately you get it, there is no interest to pay. If you delay or stagger your payments, there will be an interest charge of between 1 and 2 per cent a month (12.7 per cent to 26.8 per cent a year).

Most stores issue a card like the ordinary credit card, either for one store alone (Harrods, for example) or for a group of stores (like Debenhams). Very few charge as much interest as Barclaycard or Access.

You can also have a *Budget account*, which has a credit limit. You put in a regular amount each month, and can spend to the limit of your credit. This is called 'revolving credit', because as you put more money in each month so you automatically extend your credit limit by that amount.

There are many other small credit cards, which tend to be for a particular purpose – airlines, hotels and car hire firms sometimes issue them, for instance. Some offer discounts to card holders. Naturally, they are hard to come by and go only to privileged customers.

DISCOUNT CARDS

A recent development is discount cards. They have been in evidence for a long time, but limited to one particular store or service. Now 'blanket' cards are beginning to be issued. *Countdown,* for instance, allows its customers a discount for paying cash at about 8,000 outlets. You pay a fee of £7.50 a year and are entitled to a discount of 10 per cent.

Even if you do not have this card, you can always ask for a discount if you pay cash, particularly in any establishment which takes cards.

PROTECTING YOUR CREDIT CARD

It is possible to insure yourself against the loss of your credit card and the possibility of it being used fraudulently. Insurance companies will insure you to the credit limit you are allowed on Barclaycard or Access, and to an agreed limit on other cards. Many credit card companies offer insurance. Check if their rate is better than the insurance company's.

Remember, you are responsible for any bills, even if you have lost your card, *until you inform the company of the loss.* So phone or telegram them immediately you find your card is missing. Confirm this by letter. The company will then inform its outlets and the card will not be able to be used by anyone (even you) if it happens to turn up. You will be supplied with a new card.

Chapter 6

YOUR CURRENT ACCOUNT

DO YOU NEED A CURRENT ACCOUNT?

Bank advertising always implies that everyone should have a current account at a bank. So far they have managed to convince 55 per cent of us that they were right. Are we correct in assuming then that the other 45 per cent are wrong? Quite simply, no. Not everyone needs a current account.

A current account differs from the deposit account, which I have already discussed, in that you pay in one way or another for the services which you are offered and the degree to which you use them, rather than the bank paying you interest on the money you have in your account.

A current account operates very simply. You can open one with a clearing bank with any sum from a few pounds upwards. In return you will be provided with a cheque book, which you can use either for cash withdrawals from the bank, or to make payments without having to use cash. Life today would be impossible for many of us without the cheque facility. Just imagine carrying around £1,500 £1 notes if you were going to buy a car, or always having to send cash through the post. Transmitting money by means of a piece of paper, which is protected by your signature and the details you must fill in on it, is obviously much safer than sending actual cash.

Another vital difference between current and other accounts is that you can have access to more money than you actually have – with your bank manager's permission. He may be prepared to allow you an overdraft, which will be fixed at a certain limit depending on your needs and circumstances.

Before agreeing to open an account for you, the bank will probably ask you for two references. Quite reasonably, the manager will want to know if you are who you claim to be, whether you can be relied upon to be honest and responsible, and whether your employers are prepared to recommend you.

There are several questions you should ask yourself before deciding whether the services of a bank would be useful to you and make the management of your money easier, or whether, when the glamour of having a cheque book wears off, you would really be throwing money away by having a current account.

1 Are you paid monthly or weekly, and does your money come in cash or by cheque or credit transfer? You can usually choose, but your employers may be reluctant to use one method for you and another for everyone else.

2 Do you have enough transactions to justify the use of a current account? This isn't just a matter of the cheque facility. Banks will deal with all sorts of payments for you: rent, mortgage, annual orders to clubs, electricity and gas bills and a host of others.

3 Is earning interest on your money less important to you than the very obvious advantages of having a cheque book? This makes it much easier for you to move money around, but at a cost. Remember, other institutions apart from banks will give you interest on money deposited with them. This may be better for you than a deposit account at a bank.

4 If you need to borrow money, is the bank the best place? You can

get money from building societies and finance houses. To borrow from a bank you will almost certainly have to have an account with a particular branch and a steady source of income coming in to pay off your debt eventually.

You may feel after answering these questions that a current account is not for you. You can take it that you do not need a current account if:

1 You are paid weekly in cash.
2 Your rent is collected from you at the door.
3 You always use cash when shopping.
4 You pay for your gas and electricity by putting coins in a meter.
5 You do not have a regular enough income to make an account worthwhile.

If you fit into this pattern, look at chapter 3 of this section on savings accounts.

YOUR BANK MANAGER

Remember that banks are more than a convenient place to put your salary and savings. They offer many services to their customers – travel facilities when you are going abroad, insurance, financial advice on investments, executor and trustee services, advice on setting up a company. I have dealt with these where they arise in other parts of the book, but mention them now to illustrate just how important a person your bank manager will be in your life.

So choose him with care. The best and most troublefree banking comes from a long-standing relationship with one bank. People who move about will be treated with caution. By all means, argue with your bank manager if you do not think you are getting the best possible service, but only change your bank as a last resort. It is better, too, if possible, to stay at the same branch. Over the years succeeding bank managers will get to know you well, and if you have conducted your affairs properly and within your means your bank manager will always be prepared to help you if you are in temporary difficulties, or, say, you want to expand your business.

Make sure your bank manager knows everything about you. Don't try to fool him; he is trained to notice subtle changes in your payment policy. So, if you get married or divorced, come into some money, start a new business, get a rise, make sure he is one of the first people to know about it. *Your bank manager is the best financial friend you can have.*

BANK CHARGES

The basic difference between a deposit account and a current account is that your money will earn interest in the former whereas you will pay for having the facilities the latter offers.

If you manage your current account properly, however, you can reduce – and even eliminate – the charges you will have to pay. Every bank has its own rules, but there are some broad principles to follow if you want to keep your bank charges to a minimum. Remember, though, even if you pay no actual charges, you are in effect paying something because you could be earning interest somewhere else with the money you have in your current account.

This is why the banks are able to offer some of their customers charge-free accounts. They assume that the client's money carries a nominal rate of interest, so until that amount is used up in the carrying out of the services the account offers, account holders do not pay charges. The banks say that about three-quarters of their customers have charge-free banking, because they meet certain conditions. These conditions, as I write, are generally that you must keep at least £100 in credit, or have an average credit balance of £200 in your account during the half-yearly charges period. If you do this all your cheques, statements and standing orders or direct debits will be free. If your balance falls below these levels, charges gradually increase. The bank will charge you 10p for each withdrawal, less an allowance of 5 per cent a year on the average amount of money you have in your account. If you are overdrawn, you will of course pay not only for withdrawals, but also interest on any money you owe the bank.

This is how Barclays Bank describes its charges system to its customers:

Example (1)

The average of the money kept on your account	£150	£100	£50
20 withdrawals from your account during the half-year at 10p each	2.00	2.00	2.00
Notional interest allowed on your account equivalent to 5% p.a.	3.75	2.50	1.25
Bank charges for half-year	FREE	FREE	.75

Example (2)

The average of the money kept on your account	£150	£100	£50
30 withdrawals from your account during the half-year at 10p each	3.00	3.00	3.00
Notional interest allowed on your account equivalent to 5% p.a.	3.75	2.50	1.25
Bank charges for half-year	FREE	.50	1.75

Example (3)

The average of the money kept on your account	£150	£100	£50
40 withdrawals from your account during the half-year at 10p each	4.00	4.00	4.00
Notional interest allowed on your account equivalent to 5% p.a.	3.75	2.50	1.25
Bank charges for half-year	.25	1.50	2.75

Most banks offer charge-free banking to students, even if they do not have the required level of credit, as long as they do not overdraw their accounts. This is because the banks see students as their future account holders. Most banks usually allow the charge-free arrangement to continue for a year after the student starts work.

CLEARING CHEQUES

Clearing is simply the process used by all the banks in co-operation with one another to get money from one place to another as fast as possible. That is what banking is all about – *the transmission of money*. In the past the system was a mechanical one, with cheques and money whizzing about the country. Today the computer has arrived and a company, Bankers' Automated Clearing Services, provides facilities for the transfer of magnetic tapes containing details of customer transactions from bank to bank. As well as this, of course, the banks themselves deal with transactions between their own branches. The system is fast and accurate, but mistakes can occur. So if you decide to have a bank account keep your own record of the payments you make out and the money you pay in and check it against the statement of your account which the bank will send you from time to time.

This is how it works:

1 A cheque is a written instruction to your bank to pay a certain amount of money on your behalf, debiting your account.
2 When the payee receives the cheque, either from you directly, or through the post, he deposits it in his own bank, or gets cash for it.
3 The cheque is then sent to London to be 'cleared'. To make the system fast and efficient cheques are not cleared individually, but centralized. All the cheques are added up and each bank gives just one payment to, or gets one from, its competitors. Putting the system on the computer has made this process even faster in the past decade.
4 The cleared cheque is then sent back to the branch on which it is drawn – that is, your bank. Your account is then adjusted for the amount of the cheque, assuming you have enough in the account to pay. If not, the bank may refuse to pay. This is known as 'bouncing' your cheque. So make sure you either stay in credit or have arranged an overdraft with your bank manager.

As you can see, this is quite a complicated procedure. Clearing usually takes only two days, as the banks are highly efficient.

CHEQUE CARDS

Being able to make payments by cheque is certainly the most important benefit offered by the bank to the account holder. But the system would not work if the people to whom cheques were made out were not virtually 100 per cent certain that they would be honoured by the bank. A shopkeeper must be sure that a cheque is as good as cash, and there are still a few – a very few – who refuse to take cheques at all.

In recent years the banks have taken steps to put the bank's backing behind the individual customer's cheque. They have introduced the cheque card, which guarantees that they will honour cheques up to a certain amount, regardless of the state of the customer's bank account. At present the level is £50. The customer produces his cheque card when paying, and if the number is noted on the back of the cheque by the *payee,* the bank guarantees payment. If the account becomes overdrawn the bank takes the matter up with the account holder. If the holder persistently runs into overdraft, or over his overdraft limit, the bank may take away the card.

All the clearing banks now offer a cheque card. For customers of Barclays their Barclaycard counts as a cheque card as well as a credit card. You should try to get a cheque card; the banks now automatically offer them to all their creditworthy customers. You may not get one if you are a student or have no regular income going into your account, but try to persuade your bank manager to give you one. Some parents are willing to guarantee their student children's cheque cards, and banks are usually happy to accept this guarantee. Remember, an honest face, or a driving licence, is no substitute for the guarantee of a cheque card.

There are some snags, however. A cheque drawn on a cheque card cannot be stopped in any circumstances, even if you instruct your bank before it arrives. So if you are buying something you may wish to take back don't use your cheque card.

HOW TO USE YOUR ACCOUNT

Paying in

Banks are not fussy about the form in which you pay money in to your account. They will accept cash, cheques, money orders, foreign currency and postal orders. Nor are they fussy about where you pay it in. You need not go to your own branch, or even your own bank. At your branch you simply fill in a credit form; anywhere else you use what is known as a 'bank giro form'. Fill it in and the money will be credited to your account in a few days. You can also pay money into anyone else's account as long as you know their branch and account number.

Writing a cheque

It may never have occurred to you that there are right and wrong ways of writing a cheque, but they are in fact one of the easiest things to add to or forge. Here are some sensible rules for cheque writing:

* *Never* give a signed blank cheque to anyone you cannot trust completely. I would even say never sign one at all, because it can be lost and then it's as good as cash.
* *Never* change your signature after you have given the bank a specimen signature for their records.
* *Never* leave any space either at the beginning or the end when you are writing in the amount, or putting in the figure. The pound figures should be as close to the sign as possible with a dash which does not allow a number to be slipped in and which finishes right up against the amount of pence.
* *Never* use Mr, Miss, Mrs or Ms, and, if you are a married woman, don't use your husband's name rather than your own christian name (it can confuse the bank).
* *Never* write cash cheques for anyone you can't completely trust.
* *Never* lend anyone one of your cheques, or borrow from anyone else. Technically you can write a cheque on anything, but banks do not like this and will scrutinize very carefully any cheque which looks unusual.
* *Do* write in ink; pencil is legal but can easily be tampered with.
* *Do* date the cheque properly. Try not to date cheques ahead. This may worry the bank, or the payee, who may wonder whether you will have enough to pay when the time comes.
* *Do* write the name of the payee very clearly.
* *Do* write the figures in the box as well as writing out the amount fully. Since decimilization the banks have advised customers to use a hyphen and not a decimal point between the pounds and pence – £5-73, not £5.73. Always put two figures after the hyphen – £5-03, not £5-3. Write the figures carefully: a 3 can become an 8 or 9, a 1 a 4 or 7 written sloppily.
* *Do* cross a cheque which has to go through the post. Write 'A/C Payee' or 'not negotiable' on it. It is as well to cross *all* cheques; this means cash cannot be drawn on it, it has to go through the banking system.
* *Do*, if you have to endorse a cheque – sign it on the back – write in exactly the same way as you have written your name on the front. If that is not your usual signature, add it as well. Wait until you are depositing the cheque before you endorse it. If you lose an endorsed cheque, anyone can cash it.
* *Do* fill in the counterfoil. It's simple common sense and will help you to check statements, which are not as detailed today as they used to be. If you have no record yourself, it may be difficult for the bank to trace a lost cheque.

Protecting yourself against forged cheques:

1 Follow the rules for writing cheques set out above.
2 Guard your cheque book as well as you guard your money. A cheque can be better than cash, because it can be written out for any amount.
3 Tell your bank immediately, by phone, if you lose even one cheque.
4 Check your bank statement for any discrepancies.
5 If you change your name, address or bank number, destroy all your old cheques.
6 Avoid a sloppy signature; it is much easier to forge.

If you are a shopkeeper accepting a lot of cheques, there are tell-tale signs to enable you to spot the possible cheque-bouncer. You should be suspicious of:

1 Anyone who does not have a cheque card.
2 Anyone who is impatient and tries to hurry you.
3 Anyone who makes a fuss about providing identification.
4 Anyone who tries to persuade you to take a cheque larger than the amount of the purchase and asks for change.
5 Anyone who drops names. It may be an attempt to make you believe he or she is well-connected.
6 Anyone who is a minor, that is, under eighteen years old. Minors are not responsible for their debts.

Stopping a cheque

When you sign a cheque you are in effect making a contract to pay the amount of money stipulated on the cheque to the person designated on it. It is therefore a serious matter to cancel a cheque before the payee has had a chance to pay it in. Such an action can lead to legal proceedings.

Nevertheless, sometimes in your banking life you may feel that you have to stop a cheque. You may feel that the payee has acted fraudulently towards you. Whatever the reason, think very carefully before taking this step.

For your action to be successful, you should get in touch with your bank as quickly as possible, and also the payee, unless you anticipate trouble. This means telephoning. Follow up the telephone call with a letter immediately. Give the cheque number, its date, the payee's name and the amount. If the bank has paid out before your instructions arrive, it's too late.

Cheques written under a guaranteed cheque card cannot be stopped. If you are in dispute with the payee, you will have to pursue your quarrel in some other way. Remember this when you are buying clothes, particularly shoes, if you are in any doubt about the purchase.

BORROWING FROM YOUR BANK

Most of us at some time or another will need more money than we have in the bank. You may decide that none of the methods of hire purchase suit you, that you need a bridging loan between buying one house and selling the one you live in, that you want to renovate your house and do not have the ready cash, that you need some money to expand your business, or that you are temporarily short of cash. In circumstances like these the bank will consider your request for money, and if it feels you will be able to pay it back from your regular income will grant you an overdraft or a personal loan. An overdraft simply means that your current account is allowed to go from being in credit into debit without the bank bouncing your cheques. The bank will usually set a limit on the amount you can go into the 'red' and it is usually only prepared to lend money in this way for a short period. If it grants you a personal loan instead this means you are getting money rather than goods on hire purchase. You get a lump sum and pay it off in fixed instalments. You will have to pay interest on both kinds of facility.

Overdrafts

There is no doubt that an overdraft is the cheapest way to borrow. You pay interest on a daily basis. This is usually charged at a few per cent above the bank's Minimum Base Rate, depending on your credit rating by the bank. This means that the amount you are charged fluctuates from time to time. It will go down as your wages or salary go in and then rise as the payments go out. *You are only charged on the amount you owe each day.*

The rate of interest you pay on your overdraft will depend on two things: the current base rate which the bank has set, and how your bank manager assesses you as a borrower. The rate can vary from as little as 1 or 1½ per cent above base rate to as high as 5 per cent. If your general financial position is not sound you are likely to have to pay at the higher end. It is generally the big industrial corporations which manage to borrow at the lower rates.

Banks are tough when it comes to overdrafts. Private customers provide most of the deposits which come into the banks, but get only one-sixth of the loans, so getting an overdraft is not always easy. But money is always available to the right customers, even when getting any credit at all is difficult.

Remember, however, that no bank will let you treat an overdraft as a long-term loan. It is rarely any use going to a bank to buy a house. The most the bank will be prepared to do is to finance the 'bridging', that is the time between your buying your new house and getting the money for the sale of your old one. And if the loan is likely to be for more than six months, you may find the bank very reluctant to help you at all. If your roof falls in, the bank will very likely lend you the money for repairs while you negotiate with the insurance company. It may finance a short-term car purchase, or allow you to overdraw if you suddenly have a number of once-and-for-all bills to pay.

If you have difficulties in paying off the overdraft you may find you are an unpopular customer for life. The bank will want a good reason about every six months if you wish your overdraft limit to continue, for overdrafts are not designed to let you live permanently beyond your means.

Never go in to your bank manager with a request he can easily turn down. It is highly unlikely he will finance your holiday, or the purchase of a fur coat or a hang-glider. If that is your secret intention, be careful.

It will help if you have someone or something which will guarantee your overdraft. The bank manager may look more favourably on rather a frivolous request if you are prepared to lodge share certificates, or house deeds, with him, in case you can't or don't pay up. He will also accept another person as guarantor, if they can prove that they have assets to cover your overdraft. But remember that if you do not pay, your guarantor will have to. It is a lot to ask of someone.

Personal loans

These are an alternative to overdrafts, but they cost more because the interest is generally fixed for the term of the loan. The bank manager may prefer to lend in this way, not because the bank will make more profit – though it will – but because he may feel you should have the discipline of paying back a fixed amount each month. If you have a persistent overdraft, he may ask you to turn it into a personal loan and run your account in credit. Try to persuade him not to do this. A personal loan has some advantages, however.

First, you may have to pay regularly, but you can spread the payment over two, three or even five years in some banks. Midland Bank are particularly sympathetic to five-year borrowers. Second, you can do what you like with the money. If your bank manager lets you have a loan, it is because he thinks you can pay it back, as with any hire purchase contract – though he will probably, but not invariably, ask you what the money is for.

Lloyds Bank have some tips for customers when they go to their bank manager for a loan or overdraft. First of all, they say, you must have the answers to these questions:

1 How much do you want?
2 What do you want it for?
3 When will it be repaid?
4 Where will the repayment money come from?

They also suggest:

* ★ Be honest about your commitments.
* ★ If you run into trouble, don't be afraid to shout early.
* ★ Don't ask for too little, as it is as bad as asking for too much.
* ★ Don't anticipate future income which may not mature, or legacies from relatives.

Tax relief on bank interest

There is a widespread – but inaccurate – belief that you can no longer get any tax relief on interest you pay to the bank. It is true that over the years tax relief has been reduced, but it still remains for certain items:

1 *Home loans.* Few people can buy their houses through a bank today, because the term of the loan is not long enough for most of us. But if you do this, you get full marginal tax relief on the interest on the loan just as you do with a mortgage. As with mortgages, you are allowed a limit of £25,000 advanced and can only have relief on a mortgage on your principal residence.

These rules came in with the 1974 Finance Act. Where people were already getting relief on bank loans over £25,000, or for their second homes, the relief is still permitted on any amount without limit, but this will stop in 1980 when they will have to come into line with the rest of us.

You can also get tax relief on any loan which is for improving your home, as long as you keep inside the £25,000 limit. This does not mean you can get tax relief on your current maintenance and repair bills; it must be a real improvement like a second bathroom or central heating.

2 *Bridging loans.* It frequently happens when you are buying one house and selling another that the two deals don't coincide. When this happens you can get a bridging loan to tide you over, and can get tax relief on the interest on such a loan. Without this tax relief many people would not go through with the deal, but usually the relief only lasts for twelve months, by which time you are expected to have your deal settled.

3 *Personal loans.* Applicable only if you are borrowing for strictly business purposes. It doesn't matter whether you are employed by someone else or self-employed: if you can prove that the purchase is strictly for business – say a typewriter, car or van – you will get tax relief.

4 *Overdrafts.* Once again only if the loan is strictly for business purposes.

OTHER SERVICES OFFERED ON A CURRENT ACCOUNT

Standing orders and direct debits

Cheques are not the only means of using your bank account for making payments without using cash. There are two other ways: standing orders and direct debits. Standing orders have been in operation longer and cost more, and direct debiting is now taking over a great deal of this business.

If you have regular bills of a fixed amount – say, annual subscriptions, rent, or insurance policy premiums – you can pay them by means of standing orders. These can be very useful, because the bank takes over the 'remembering' for you and transfers the money on the particular date stated by you each year, month or even week. You will, of course, have to remember it yourself when checking your account. To arrange a standing order, simply fill in a form. It can be cancelled at any time.

Direct debiting is particularly useful when payments are likely to vary. The person or company to whom the payments are due is given the right to approach your bank directly and ask it to debit the appropriate amount from your account whenever a payment falls due, and credit its own account. This is cheaper than payment by standing order because the banks deal directly with one another. The customer is always asked for his permission before any new regular payment is debited.

But be careful: if you already have a standing order, it may be transformed into a direct debit without your being told. Some customers do not like this, and if you are one of them get the company and the bank to return to the standing order procedure.

Cash facilities

One of the problems for working people with bank accounts is getting to them – banks are open only between 9.30 a.m and 3.30 p.m. from Monday to Friday. The banks have given up Saturday morning opening, and late evening opening which replaced that has also stopped. This is actually no more than a mild nuisance, unless your bank is not prepared to give you a cheque card, because the banks have expanded their cash dispensing services to tide their customers over the times when they are closed, or when they cannot get to their own branches. As usual each bank has its own system, but the services they offer amount to broadly the same thing.

1   *The cheque card.* This can be used at any branch of any clearing bank to obtain up to £50 cash, just as it can be used for purchases. Some shops, too, will cash cheques outside banking hours for people they know.

2　*The cash card.*　This is usually a small plastic card which can be inserted into a cash dispenser at some branches. You tap out on a keyboard your own personal code, and a certain amount, usually £10, is delivered to you. The machine keeps the card, and you then have to wait until it is returned to you before you can get a further £10. Your account will be debited by £10 when your card eventually makes its way back to your branch. The whole process can take up to a week. As such a facility is of very limited use, some banks have devised a new dispenser which gives you the £10 and also returns your card.

3　*The cash service card.* This is even more sophisticated and works in the same way as the £10 cash card, but the maximum amount you can draw is arranged between you and your bank. In this case, you tap out your number and the amount you want. Some bank branches provide this service outside the bank twenty-four hours a day, but others only inside the bank. All the latter does is help you avoid queueing; it does not effectively extend your banking hours. These new dispensers can sometimes do other things, apart from giving you the cash you need – provide you, during the week, with a written record of the balance in your current account; take an order for a statement of your current account; take an order for a new cheque book.

The snag about all these services is that they are not yet available at all bank branches. The machines are costly to install and it will be many years, if ever, before there are as many machines as bank branches. Make sure, if you have a cash card, that you always carry a list of where the machines are.

Deposit boxes

These are used by people who wish to keep valuable jewellery, important papers, etc., outside their homes. There is no doubt that they are far more secure from burglary in the bank than in the average home. The bank takes as much care of its customers' personal items as it does of their money and charges a fee for so doing. There is a safe custody fee, which may be under £10, and a further charge for the security box itself, which goes up to around £25. You need not have an account at the bank.

Many people put things in security boxes because they wish to keep them secret. They don't ask what is in the box and they don't want to know. It is not unknown for people to store items illegally, and the banks don't want to be involved.

But banks do get robbed. Banks make it quite clear that they do not accept responsibility for loss or damage caused by criminals. To protect yourself you must take out insurance. Shop around. As with all insurance, the rates vary enormously. Any company which does household contents insurance will probably quote a special 'all risks' premium for the contents of your box.

JOINT ACCOUNTS

A current account need not be for one individual only. Many married couples have a joint account, and some banks require parents to hold one jointly with their child until the child reaches eighteen. You can, if you persist, make sure that only the child has drawing facilities and – though even more persuasion is needed – that only he gets the bank statement. In this case, the parent is acting as guarantor, and the bank will not be slow to inform him or her if the child gets into overdraft.

Joint accounts can be convenient for married couples, but they have serious drawbacks, which married couples should consider before pooling all their money:

1 Many banks still regard the wife as only the agent and not the principal in a joint account. This means that they will send the statement to the husband only and in the event of his death will not allow the widow access to any money until probate is proved. Make sure that joint really means joint when you open the account.

2 Husband or wife may not always know what the other has drawn out. Unexpected moves into the red can cause family rows.

One possibility is to have a joint account to which you both contribute, if you are working, which is designed to pay household bills and nothing else, and separate personal accounts. An account just for bills is in any case useful, even if you are single, but it also means that married couples can keep their private spending quite separate – no one can complain if you are treating yourself on your own money, after making your contribution to the joint fund.

BANK BUDGET ACCOUNTS

If you are new to banking, uncertain about your money management, or have to make fixed regular payments every week or month, you may find that a budget account in addition to your ordinary current account will make your financial life easier. The banks have recently brought in this kind of account to help people who find that their bills come in batches, whereas their credits tend to be spread evenly throughout the year.

What you do is add up all the bills you expect to have to pay during the year, excluding those like rent or mortgages which you pay every month anyway:

rates	£150(payable twice a year)
gas	£120(payable quarterly)
electricity	£130(payable quarterly)
life insurance	£90(payable annually)

house insurance	£20(payable annually)
car insurance	£60(payable annually)
T.V. licence	£18(payable annually)
season ticket	£200(payable annually)

This sample gives a total expenditure of £788. Now divide this sum by twelve (or thirteen if you prefer) and transfer the money (£66 or £60.61) from your ordinary current account each month by means of a standing order or direct debit. If you can, add a margin to allow for increases in your bills. The bank will then supply you with a special cheque book to pay the specified bills. It does not matter if you run into an overdraft in one particular month. This will almost certainly happen, but you will end the year in balance.

A budget account is not free, but it can save you money because:

1 Annual season tickets are much cheaper – and save you still more money when fares rise – than weekly, monthly or quarterly seasons.
2 Car tax is cheaper if you pay by the year, rather than every four months.
3 Overdraft charges are higher than budget account charges.

The banks calculate the cost of budget accounts in different ways. Some charge a higher basic fee based on the total amount passing through the account during the year, with no charge when you are overdrawn. This way the cost for every £1,000 is about £28 a year, as I write. Others charge a lower basic fee, but charge you 4 per cent above their base rate at the times you are overdrawn. Work out which one suits you best. If you pay out heavily at the beginning of the year, the first kind will probably pay off for you. If, on the other hand, you can build up a credit in the earlier part of the year, the second method will be best.

Before choosing your bank, consider all these aspects of the bank's services before you make your final decision.

THE NATIONAL GIRO

The National Giro was set up by the government to provide some of the services provided by current accounts for people with no bank account. To begin with it offered just a simple and cheap money transmission service, but since it was set up in 1968 it has developed into something much wider.

When it started a Giro account was much cheaper to run than a current account at a bank. Since then the clearing banks have reduced their charges a great deal, so that the difference is small. Nevertheless, there are some advantages in having a Giro account:

1 Deposits can be made at any one of the 21,000 post offices that do bank business. As with clearing banks you can have your salary paid directly into your Giro account.

2 Most post offices are open for six days a week, including Saturday, and, as you can withdraw up to £30 in cash every other business day, you have access to your account more days of the week and for a longer business day.

3 You can transfer your money by means of a Giro cheque free to other Giro account holders. All envelopes for postal transactions are postage paid and supplied by the post office.

4 Standing orders are free.

5 Statements are free.

You get all these services because you do not earn any interest on the money in your account.

Unlike current account holders, holders of Giro accounts cannot get an overdraft. A personal loan scheme for account holders has been introduced, however. It has been arranged through Mercantile Credit Limited, one of the leading finance houses in Britain. You must be over eighteen and not live in the Isle of Man to qualify. Details are available at any branch of Mercantile Credit, and preferential interest rates are available to Giro account holders who have their pay credited directly to their accounts.

The main problem with Giro is its acceptability. Not everyone yet accepts Giro cheques, and there is little point in having an account which cannot be used freely. The number of shops which accept Giro transfers is growing all the time, but it is still not large. But you can pay a Giro cheque to someone who does not have a Giro account. All they have to do is to pay it into their own bank account, or cash it at any post office.

TRUSTEE SAVINGS BANKS

The Trustee Savings Banks are gradually becoming more and more like the clearing banks and in the next few years the transformation will be complete. They offer cheque accounts as well as deposit accounts, and using one tends to be rather cheaper than using a clearing bank current account. Cheques and standing orders are free as long as you keep a minimum of £50 in your account during the six month's charging period, and if your balance falls below that you are charged only 2½p for each cheque you use, or for each standing order paid by the bank. The Trustee Savings Bank also provides a cheque guarantee card for amounts up to £30, and, if you have a T.S.B. card with the Eurocheque card symbol on it, you can cash cheques up to £30 in the major banks in Europe, just as you can with the ordinary bank cheque card. The main difference betwéen the T.S.Bs. and the clearing banks is that overdrafts are not available. This is expected to change in a few year's time, but until then you may be able to get a personal loan, which is arranged by the bank with the finance house on lines similar to the National Giro/Mercantile Credit scheme.

T.S.B. cheque accounts are very useful for those who wish to keep their bank charges down, but the lack of overdraft facilities would be a disadvantage to many people. T.S.B. cheques, if backed by a cheque card, should be just as acceptable as any other cheques, but they are not as familiar, and retailers may occasionally - and quite wrongly - be reluctant to take them.

The T.S.B.s also offer many other services. They sell certain government stocks at a low rate of commission, run a Save As You Earn scheme, provide travellers' cheques, and have their own unit trust.

Chapter 7

GETTING A ROOF OVER YOUR HEAD

DECIDING TO BUY A HOUSE

There few of us who do not think about buying a house at some time in our lives. Normally it is a sensible thing to do. It gives you and your family a guaranteed roof over your heads, and eventually it can yield a substantial profit, which can either go to your heirs or, if your family has grown up and left home and you decide to move to a smaller house, provide a nest-egg for yourselves.

Since the end of the last war, house prices have risen just about twice as fast as the cost of living. This means that house buyers have beaten inflation handsomely. Of course the rise in house prices has not been uniform over the years. There have been 'bubbles' in the upward trend when prices have barely moved, and sometimes they have even fallen. So it is not enough to say that buying a house is a sound investment. You need to think about buying at the right time. If prices were at their highest ever, and all the signs in the economy indicated a general slump, you would be wise to defer your purchase in case you have a chance to buy at a lower price later. Of course most of us cannot choose the time we buy. You may marry, change jobs, see the house of your dreams, at a time which is economically inconvenient. Then you will have to make the best of the opportunities which come along.

During the 1950s house prices were fairly stable: the price of new houses rose by 1½ per cent a year, that of old houses by about 2½ per cent. During the 1960s house prices increased by around 7 per cent a year. Then in the early 1970s the house market went quite mad; in the first three years house prices doubled.

A shake-out from these high levels was inevitable, and there were some very sharp falls in prices – though in some areas they remained fairly stable. In the past two years the increases have been in the order of 9 and 10 per cent respectively. This is a trend which seems likely to continue; the very sharp increases of the early 1970s seem unlikely to recur, at any rate for some time.

This is what has happened to new house prices since 1965:

1965	£3,830		
1966	£4,060	+	6 per cent
1967	£4,290	+ 10.6	per cent
1968	£4,569	+ 10.6	per cent
1969	£4,788	+ 10.5	per cent
1970	£5,093	+ 10.6	per cent
1971	£6,167	+ 12.1	per cent
1972	£8,725	+ 14.1	per cent
1973	£9,784	+ 11.2	per cent
1974	£10,876	+ 11.1	per cent
1975	£12,732	+ 13.2	per cent
1976	£13,307	+ 10.5	per cent

Source: Nationwide Building Society

You can see from this table that, if nothing else, your investment will be safe, while at the same time providing you and your family with a home. Since 1965 house prices have risen on average by nearly 350 per cent, that is, three and a half times.

Figures like these will seem enormous in relation to your wages and the various other demands on your financial resources. For most of us buying a house is the single most important financial transaction of our lives. We should therefore go about it with care; mistakes are expensive. First, let's look in a bit more detail at the advantages of house buying.

Unless you are fortunate enough to have been left a property you will have to pay money wherever you live – whether you buy a house or rent one.

A *cash payment* means that you will own your house outright. This may give you peace of mind, but it is not always the best way to buy a house. You pay what the pound is worth at the time you buy, whereas if you stagger your payments over a number of years, you will in effect be paying less because the value of the pound will decline.

Most of us buy a house on a *mortgage* (see next chapter); few people have the money available for an immediate outright purchase. If you have a mortgage you can take advantage of inflation, and – in Britain at least – get tax relief on any interest you pay. This means that the cost of a mortgage is relatively low no matter what the interest rate.

Rent is money down the drain. You can easily pay as much in rent as you do with a mortgage, and rents are more affected by inflation. So you lose in three ways: you have no asset at the end of the day; your payments may not go down, relatively speaking, over the years; you get no tax relief.

After weighing up all these factors most of us would decide to buy a house if possible. There are other plus factors in owning a property:

1   You can resell it at a profit.
2   You eventually stop paying for your house at all when you finish paying off your mortgage. Until then a mortgage is like a subsidized rent.
3   You can sometimes let off part of your house, either as a flat, or as rooms, and so provide yourself with an income. Be careful though: if you are still paying a mortgate the building society will want to know and you will need its permission. Some ban sub-letting outright.

CHOOSING A HOUSE

Once you have found a house you like you should ask:

*   Is the price right?
*   Is the size right?
*   Is it a good long-term investment?
*   Is it in the right area?

Let's look at these aspects in turn.

The right price
This depends not only on the value of the house compared with others similar to it, but also on your ability to pay the deposit and to cope with the mortgage repayments and the running and maintenance costs. Here the building society manager may give advice. Remember the legal and survey fees involved in the purchase. You must also make some estimate for initial repairs or redecoration. You must decide what new household equipment you will need. Your old curtains may well not fit your new house; your old cooker and fridge may be too small, or too big. You must decide if you need central heating, if your proposed purchase does not already have it. Finally estimate your travelling costs to work, and you

will have some idea – though only an idea – of the minimum cost of your proposed purchase.

The right size
Again this depends on what you can afford and what you want. A seven-bedroomed flat is no use to a couple whose children have left home, while a four-bedroomed house is sensible for the couple with a number of children who will be around for some time. Some families can manage with very little private space; others find a small place claustrophobic and unsatisfactory. Work out your family needs in a realistic way with regard to money. Try if possible to anticipate your future needs. Buy a larger house than you need at present if you intend to have more children – if you can afford it. The costs of buying and selling to meet the needs of a growing family can be prohibitive.

A good long-term investment?
You can *never* be certain, but you should try to assess whether your house will be a good long-term investment. First, go carefully over the points mentioned earlier and check the house itself fully before buying. It is a good idea to have the house surveyed for yourself instead of just relying on the survey done on behalf of the building society. Always try to have two houses in view in case one turns out to be full of dry rot or damp, for example. This way you can avoid being too disappointed.

Second, you need to know whether the value of the house you choose is likely to move up more than the general average for the country, or – much less likely – whether you could possibly lose money. Ask yourself some questions:

1 *Is the area in which you propose to buy changing in character?* It could become more or less fashionable. Islington in the London area, for example, from being an area where living standards – and therefore house prices – were low, has partly changed into a middle class area. This district shows the possible pitfalls clearly. Some streets have not changed at all; others are unrecognizable compared with twenty years ago. There have been vast profits in the latter sections, but only small ones elsewhere. Hastings, on the other hand, has declined as a resort in recent years and the rate of increase in house prices has been less there than in many other areas. This is typical of many seaside resorts.

2 *Is your proposed house near a projected motorway?* This can have a marked effect on house prices in an area, if commuting to work then becomes a practical proposition. The same applies where the property is close to a good rail service. The closure of railway lines has had a dampening effect on areas which were previously well served by them.

70

But new developments are not always an advantage. You can be too close to a motorway, or, usually worse, an airport.

Do not underestimate the importance of these points. They can make all the difference to whether or not your house is a good long-term investment – and a nice place to live in at the moment.

The right area?

There are a few more questions you should ask yourself about the area in which you propose to buy:

1   Are other municipal costs likely to mean that you are stretched financially? In London, for example, it costs ratepayers far more to live in the Camden area than in Wandsworth. If you are a house owner, you must pay rates.
2   Is the house so far from your work that commuting costs are likely to more than outweigh any benefit you get from a lower purchase price and lower mortgage repayments?
3   Are there suitable schools for your children? Will they have a long way to travel to school?
4   Is the area so remote that you will have to have a car to live comfortably?

Regional variations in price

House prices are not uniform throughout the country, and there is some variation between flats and houses, and between different types and ages of house. There are always individual variations within an area, but on the whole prices are higher the closer you are to the centre of a city, and highest of all in London and the South-east. Here are the latest valuations put out by the Nationwide Building Society:

		Existing	
	New	Modern	Older
All house prices	£13,307	£12,873	£10,665
London and S.E.	£16,317	£15,560	£13,768
Southern	£16,464	£14,994	£12,694
Scotland	£14,181	£14,096	£11,812
South-western	£11,918	£13,010	£11,322
Eastern	£13,253	£13,007	£11,136
Northern Ireland	£13,413	£12,065	£10,738
Midlands	£12,209	£11,387	£9,357
North-western	£11,702	£10,930	£8,652
Wales	£11,508	£11,706	£8,876
North-eastern	£10,847	£11,123	£7,856

You can see that houses in London and the South-east tend to be more than 50 per cent dearer than houses in North-eastern England, and even within the London area it costs more to buy in Chelsea or Hampstead than in Willesden or Whitechapel. In some areas new houses are dearer than existing ones, whereas in others the reverse is true. New town houses will probably cost more than existing ones, because they tend to be in very modern developments in already expensive areas. But existing houses can cost more than new ones, especially if they are detached or semi-detached.

These figures are only averages, but they may give you some indication of whether your house is correctly priced for your area.

FREEHOLD OR LEASEHOLD?

When you are buying you must enquire whether the property is freehold or leasehold. The former means that the owner has sole and permanent control over his house and the land on which it stands. This is the way most of us buy today. But, particularly with a flat, you may find that you are only buying a lease and that somebody else owns the freehold. This means that someone else has the permanent right to the house and land, and that you have it only until the lease ends. Many years ago leaseholds were considered a bad thing, but successive government action has protected many leaseholders. When a lease runs out many holders now have the right to take on a new lease – at a negotiated price – if they wish.

Some leases are so long – ninety-nine years is quite common for a lease on a newly built house – that having a lease is virtually the same as owning the freehold. In such cases the annual payment for the lease – the ground rent – will usually be quite small, just a few pounds, and the freeholder's rights are merely technical.

If you live in Scotland and Northern Ireland remember that customs and laws are rather different than in England and Wales. There it is the rule rather than the exception to live in leasehold rather than freehold property.

THE BUYING PROCESS

You will probably buy your house through an estate agent, though people do sometimes advertise their houses privately. In any case it costs the buyer nothing to use an estate agent: it is the seller who pays his fee, which is based on the size of the house. Estate agents also advertise. They keep details of some of the houses on their books in their windows, and some of the bigger ones also send out lists of houses and flats.

The first thing to remember is that the price asked is what the seller hopes to get for his house. It is by no means fixed, and it is up to you to make an offer if you do not think the house is worth the asking price. Some sellers state straightaway if the price is not open to negotiation, but even then it may be worth a try, especially if the house is in need of expensive repairs. Many owners, however, deliberately fix on a higher price than they expect to get, so that the prospective buyer is more likely to think he is getting a bargain if he offers less than the asking price. But, even if you do have an offer accepted, things can go wrong and you may find yourself gazumped.

Gazumping

A gazumper is someone whose word in house-selling cannot be taken at face value, someone who will accept an offer for his house but still leave it on the market in case a better offer comes along. There is not much you can do if this happens to you, as unfortunately there is nothing in the law to prevent it. Neverthless, gazumping is a thoroughly reprehensible practice, and most unfair on the *bone fide* buyer. It usually only happens when house prices are rising sharply and there is a scramble among buyers. It is best, however, to bear this possibility in mind, especially if a house is particularly attractive, and it is yet another reason for having more than one house in mind when you are buying.

Chapter 8

FINANCING YOUR HOUSE PURCHASE

THE ADVANTAGES OF A MORTGAGE

Few of us today have sufficient cash to pay for the entire purchase of a house in one go. Even if you do have the money, it is not always a sound idea for several reasons:

1 You are entitled to tax relief on any interest you pay on money borrowed for house purchase.
2 You can borrow in an insurance-linked way, so that if you die the insurance company pays up the full value of any remaining borrowing.
3 In a period of inflation the value of money is falling, so that over the years you gradually pay less and less in real terms, even if your

repayments rise now and again because of rises in interest rates. Anyway, as the interest rises so does the tax relief.

4 If you have ample cash available, it would probably be better invested in some other way, for the reasons given above. You can then build up your capital from two or more directions at the same time.

5 If you are not a tax payer, or pay so little tax that relief on mortgage interest would bring you below the tax threshold, you can opt to pay lower interest on your mortgage.

For all these reasons most people buy their houses on what is called a 'mortgage'. Basically a mortgage is just like any other hire purchase contract. You put down a deposit and pay off the remainder at a certain rate of interest. But it differs from most hire purchase in that the contract will probably run for much longer, and you are entitled to tax relief on the interest you pay. The interest charged, too, will probably vary over the length of the mortgage.

Mortgage rates are at their highest level ever at the present time. Nevertheless, a mortgage is still a cheap way of buying a house, because of the tax relief. Deposit rates are similarly high, but even so not enough money is coming in to the building societies to meet the demand for mortgages, so you may have to shop around before you get one. The situation can change rapidly, however, so check before despairing of getting a loan.

TAX RELIEF ON MORTGAGE INTEREST

Tax relief effectively reduces your monthly payments by about a third if you pay tax at the standard rate, and by even more if you pay at the higher rates. The actual monthly payment remains the same, but the tax relief is reflected in higher take-home pay.

Relief on mortgage interest is one of the most generous forms of tax relief. But in recent years it has been limited to some extent. Tax relief ceases at a mortgage level of £25,000, and each person is only allowed tax relief on a mortgage on one house. Married people living together are counted as one for this purpose, and can only get tax relief on one mortgage. The average mortgage today is well below this ceiling at £8,024, so the limit affects only the relatively well off. Again, few people buy more than one house at any time, so that limit is largely academic as well.

At present the mortgage rate is 12¼ per cent. This table, supplied by the Building Societies Association, shows how every £1,000 borrowed over twenty-five years at 12¼ per cent will be repaid, the net payment after tax relief has been deducted at the standard rate, and how the balance shrinks. You will see that in the early years, you pay off very

74

little capital. The interest charges are so large that they swallow up almost all your monthly repayments. Gradually more and more capital is paid off, but the interest element remains large almost until the end of the payment period. It is not until the nineteenth year that you will be paying off more capital than interest. At the end of twenty-five years you will have paid £2,457.68, after tax relief, for every £1,000 borrowed.

TAX RELIEF

Year	Annual Repayment £	Net repayment after tax relief at 35% £	Balance outstanding at year-end £
1	129.72	86.85	992.78
2	129.72	87.16	984.68
3	129.72	87.50	975.58
4	129.72	87.89	965.37
5	129.72	88.33	953.91
	648.60	437.73	
6	129.72	88.82	941.04
7	129.72	89.37	926.60
8	129.72	89.99	910.39
9	129.72	90.69	892.19
10	129.72	91.47	871.76
	1,297.20	888.07	
11	129.72	92.34	848.83
12	129.72	93.33	823.09
13	129.72	94.43	794.20
14	129.72	95.67	761.77
15	129.72	97.06	725.37
	1,945.80	1,360.90	
16	129.72	98.62	684.51
17	129.72	100.37	638.64
18	129.72	102.34	587.15
19	129.72	104.54	529.36
20	129.72	107.02	464.49
	2,594.40	1,873.79	
21	129.72	109.81	391.67
22	129.72	112.93	309.93
23	129.72	116.43	218.18
24	129.72	120.36	115.19
25	129.30	124.36	—
	3,242.58	2,457.68	

Option mortgages

What happens, you may well ask, if you do not pay tax or pay so little that you will not get the full benefit of the relief available? This problem has been tackled by bringing in a new type of loan called an 'option mortgage'. Right at the start, when the mortgage is taken out, the borrower can opt to pay interest at a lower rate, if they give up their

TAX RELIEF

Annual Repayment	Option After tax relief Subsidy (4.2%) to Building Society	Balance outstanding at year-end
£	£	£
94.08	42.00	986.42
94.08	41.43	971.75
94.08	40.81	955.90
94.08	40.15	938.77
94.08	39.43	920.26
470.40	203.82	
94.08	38.65	900.26
94.08	37.81	878.65
94.08	36.90	855.30
94.08	35.92	830.07
94.08	34.86	802.81
940.80	387.96	
94.08	33.72	773.36
94.08	32.48	741.54
94.08	31.14	707.15
94.08	29.70	670.00
94.08	28.14	629.85
1,411.20	543.14	
94.08	26.45	586.47
94.08	24.63	539.60
94.08	22.66	488.96
94.08	20.54	434.24
94.08	18.24	375.12
1,881.60	655.66	
94.08	15.76	311.24
94.08	13.07	242.21
94.08	10.17	167.63
94.08	7.04	87.04
94.05	3.66	—
2,351.97	705.36	

rights to tax relief. At present the subsidy is 4.2 per cent of the normal rate of interest and it is paid to the building society by the government. Once you have opted for the mortgage it cannot be changed, so these mortgages are only for those who pay little or no tax, or those who are likely to move into this bracket before long. Even if you are not paying tax at the moment, think carefully whether you are likely to do so in the future. The early loss by not taking out an option mortgage is likely to be more than regained in later years. But it does make a difference to the monthly payments. Over twenty-five years with an ordinary mortgage, you will make a total payment before tax relief of £3,242.58 for every £1,000 you borrow and £2,457 after tax relief. With an option mortgage this shrinks to £2,351.97, as the table on page 76, also from the Building Societies Association, shows.

To qualify for an option subsidy the borrower must fulfil the usual conditions: the dwelling mortgaged must be occupied by the mortgagee, or a dependent relative, as the only or main residence and the amount of the loan must not exceed £25,000.

HOW MUCH CAN YOU BORROW?

The amount of money you can borrow depends, generally, on three things:

1 The type of house or flat for which the loan is asked and the value that the lender sets on it.
2 The status and salary of the borrower.
3 Who you borrow from.

The type of house or flat

Lenders have all sorts of preferences. Some may not lend on flats at all; others do not like leasehold property, unless the lease is so long that it is equivalent to a freehold; some do not like older houses; others may not lend on properties in the centre of a city. If one source fails, shop around until you find someone who will at least lend you some money in principle.

Anyone lending money is bound to be cautious. Having accepted the house or flat as suitable for a mortgage, they will then have it valued independently before deciding the amount of the loan. They will want to be sure that the sale value of the property is enough to cover the amount of the loan they give you. This is why they are unlikely to offer you 100 per cent of the price – though this can occasionally happen with new property developments where the developer building the estate negotiates an overall deal in principle. The valuer will then come up with a price. It may be the same as you are paying, or it may even be more, but usually it is less – if only a little less.

If the value of the house is set at less than you are paying for it, you will have to pay the difference. The mortgager (the person giving you the mortgage) will only lend up to the limits of his own valuation, and will set particular limits depending on the age of the house – and, of course, on the borrower's ability to pay, which we will come to later.

Say you are buying a house for £15,500 and the mortgager values it at £14,500, you will have to put down at least that £1,000 difference, and to be on the safe side the lender will probably not give you 100 per cent of his own valuation. If it is an old house you may only get a maximum mortgage of two-thirds of the valuation, and almost certainly not more than 80 per cent. On new houses the percentage may be 90 or 95 per cent, or, occasionally, 100 per cent. Let's take the above example for an old house:

purchase price	15,500
valuation	14,500
66 per cent of valuation	9,603
balance of valuation	4,897
difference between valuation and purchase price	1,000
total balance	£5,897

Here the borrower will have to find a total of £5,897.

But the picture is different with a brand new house at the same price. To begin with the gap between the purchase price and valuation will probably be narrower.

	£
purchase price	15,500
valuation	15,250
90 per cent of valuation	13,725
balance of valuation	1,525
difference between valuation and purchase price	250
total balance	£1,775

In this case the borrower will have only to find a total of £1,775.

When the lender says he will offer you a 66 per cent or a 90 per cent mortgage, he does not usually mean 66 or 90 per cent of the purchase price. In the first example he is actually offering 62 per cent of the purchase price and in the second 88½ per cent. The difference between what you would regard as a certain percentage mortgage and what the lender does can be quite wide.

The *ideal* house is a new three-bedroomed semi-detached house on a housing estate which is covered by the National House Builders' Registration Council's guarantee, and which is close to shops and a mainline station.

The status of the borrower

To get a mortgage you must basically be in work; if you are self-employed you must be able to produce figures to show you are capable of paying off the loan. It no longer matters whether you are a man or a woman. What matters is your earning level and the reliability of your earnings.

It is extremely difficult to set down fixed rules. What one lender finds acceptable another may refuse outright. Some lenders, for example, would not consider actors or writers – both notoriously erratic professions – but others accept them if their average earnings figure over a number of years is adequate. On the whole, however, to borrow easily you must have steady and regular earnings and your requirements must relate to your ability to pay.

As a general rule you will find that you cannot get a loan

1   more than two and a half or at the most three times your current yearly wage or salary, or
2   which would involve you in repayments of more than one quarter of your monthly earnings. The average borrower spends 18 per cent of his or her gross pay on a mortgage

These limits are set so that the lenders can be as certain as possible that you will be able to repay the loan.

But salary levels on their own are not enough. The lender will want to know a great deal about you: your age, which may limit the length of time for which you can get a mortgate; your health, which may affect your ability to pay; your work record, which may suggest that you are an erratic employee; sometimes even details of your family and nationality.

A good mortgage prospect is a family man (or couple) in a good steady job with a record of past saving, preferably in the building society which will be lending the money. The worst mortgage prospects are those who work for themselves, on commission or in uncertain professions, who at the same time have a history of bad debts. So if your earnings pattern is at all uneven, do at least avoid bad debts.

Today women are entitled to be treated in the same way as men, if their incomes justify it. It is still possible, however, for a lender to refuse to take into account the whole of a working wife's income in deciding how much to lend, particularly if she is young and likely to stop working to have children before long. Single women should find no more difficulty than men in getting a mortgage. If you think you have been unfairly treated contact the Equal Opportunities Commission in Manchester for advice. Its address is Overseas House, Quay Street, Manchester M3 3HN.

The *ideal* borrower, then, is a happily married man with a steady job, earning about £4,000 a year. That is ample to support the current average mortgage of £8,024, or even a little more.

If you don't meet these conditions, don't give up your search for a mortgage. Few of us are ideal, and even if we are, we do not always choose an ideal house.

Who you borrow from

You may get better or worse treatment depending on whom you approach for a mortgage. Local councils usually limit their loans to people who already live and work in their area, or who are planning to move into it. Occasionally, too, they may give priority to a particular class of borrower. For example, they may be trying to help the lower income groups, or to help people to buy the houses and flats they live in as council tenants. Councils tend to be rather more generous with loans than building societies; insurance companies tend to lend more on higher priced houses than either councils or building societies, and are often more flexible about the state the house is in. Building societies may insist that you first save with them before granting you a mortgage.

You can often increase the amount of the loan you are offered by providing additional security in the form of savings or an insurance policy, and sometimes you can borrow more money from an employer or even your bank. But take care not to overstretch yourself financially by borrowing more than you can comfortably repay.

You may also be a borrower who is treated as a special case. This happens sometimes to tenants on a lease who have the opportunity to buy the freehold because the owner wishes to release some capital on his property. Certain leaseholders have the right under the Leasehold Reform Act to buy the freehold at a price which is generally well below the market price for the property. In such cases the lender may be persuaded to give a bigger mortgage than usual because the real value of the house or flat is way above the current asking price.

WHERE TO GET A MORTGAGE

Mortgages come from three main sources: local councils; building societies; insurance companies.

You can also borrow in a variety of other ways – all of which are eligible for tax relief if the loan is to help you buy a house. Friends and relatives may lend you money. Some employers have mortgage schemes for employees, which depend on length of service, status, etc. You may have a family trust fund which can help. Your bank manager may be prepared to forward you part of the money, though usually not for more than five years. Finance companies will sometimes 'top up' your mortgage with what is called a second mortgage, if you do not have quite enough to meet the purchase price. Occasionally – though this is rare – the person selling the house, may be prepared to let you pay him off gradually in the form of a mortgage rather than demanding the purchase price outright, at the time of sale. On the whole, however, except in exceptional circumstances, it is best to raise your mortgage through the usual channels.

Councils

If you can get a council mortgage, you may be going to the best possible source. Councils cover only 5 per cent of the total mortgage market, but they operate on rather different principles from building societies and insurance companies. They lend through a sense of social duty. They are trying to ensure that the people who live in their borough are decently housed, whether in council houses and flats or in owner-occupied homes. Many consider that it is cheaper in the long run to help you buy your own home than to build new council-owned property. Not all councils operate mortgage schemes, however. Check to see if yours does. Because they view loans as part of social policy, councils tend to see their priority as helping the borrower, rather than balancing the value of the house with the ability of the borrower to pay. It is therefore sometimes easier to get a big – even a 100 per cent – mortgage from a council than from the other sources available, who are basically in the mortgage business either to balance their ingoings and outgoing (building societies) or to make a profit (insurance companies). The one disadvantage is that their interest rates may often be higher than those in building societies. And in times of financial stringency they may suspend their schemes altogether. In the circumstances anyone who gets a council mortgage can count himself lucky.

Building societies

If you have read the chapter on savings (chapter 3 of this section) you will know that the building societies were set up solely to finance house purchase. They provide more loans than all the other organizations that lend for house purchase put together. They use the money they get in deposits (paying interest at one rate) to lend to suitable borrowers (who pay interest at a higher rate). They do not make a profit, but the difference in rates covers the day-to-day running costs and provides a reserve in case of a sudden withdrawal of savings, or an unusually large failure rate in mortgage payments. So far they have never needed to call on this reserve.

They tend to have stricter requirements for their loans than local councils, but there is no doubt that the building society provides the best opportunity for the average borrower to get a mortgage.

Building society rates of interest change only slowly, but they do follow the general pattern of interest rates. If they rise, mortgage interest rates will rise, and it is wise to remember this when taking out a mortgage. Try not to borrow so much that even a small increase in monthly payments will overstrain the family budget.

The amount available for lending by building societies varies from time to time, depending on how much money is going into them. This varies because building society rates of interest to depositors change slowly in comparison with interest rates in some other areas, so the societies are not always the most attractive way of saving in a period when interest rates are rising. When this happens depositors shift their money to areas offering higher rates of interest, and, correspondingly, there is less money available to borrowers. If mortgage money is tight, it is a good idea to save up in a building society if you are thinking of applying for a mortgage at a later date. It is no guarantee of a mortgage, but it does mean that your application will be more favourably looked at in a difficult period.

What else can you do to ensure you get a building society mortgage? First, choose the sort of house which building societies regard as a good risk. This means a house built after 1921 – though this rule is breaking down somewhat today. They like the sort of houses that 'normal' families live in – not too close to the centre of a city, but not too far away to make commuting difficult. The semi-detached post-war house is typical of what they favour. They do not like flats, unless they are purpose-built with a ground landlord who is responsible for certain services, which will maintain standards.

If after a few years you decide that you wish to extend your present house rather than buy another one, building societies will usually listen sympathetically to any request for a topping up mortgage, as they see this as increasing the value of the house eventually.

Insurance companies

Some insurance companies will finance the whole purchase of your house through a special insurance policy, but most link themselves with a building society, so that the borrower pays not only normal repayments on the outstanding loan but also a (sometimes hefty) insurance premium to cover the purchase in the event of death. This provides protection for the building society, which is then guaranteed to get its money back, and also gives security to the borrower's dependents in the event of his or her death.

It is useful to get the extra cover that an insurance policy gives to a mortgage, because building societies can then be pursuaded to make bigger loans. The borrower also gets tax relief on the insurance payments as well as on the mortgage interest, and some policies may have a surrender value after as short a time as one year. Mortgages are also good business for the insurance company, for most mortgages go their full term, which brings a profit to the company.

In general most people will go first to a building society, but people who are seeking a higher than usual loan, or who are buying a house which may need a lot of money spent on it for it to become habitable, may find an insurance company more willing to listen to their request than a building society or a local authority.

Finance houses

Not a major source of mortgages, but they will often lend on second mortgages (which are eligible for tax relief if they don't break the £25,000 barrier). They are useful if you are a little short of what you need, but they usually carry a higher interest rate than normal loans, and you must make sure that the loan is not so loaded with awkward conditions as to be barely worth having. They are also useful for those who want to raise more money when they have been living in their house for some years, and can be used for home improvements. They are a useful standby, but no more than that, in the total mortgage business.

The rest

There are all kinds of other sources for mortgages, but remember, if you go in for any kind of private borrowing you will have to meet any terms the lender sets. So take great care and only borrow when the terms are fair and reasonable.

WHAT KIND OF MORTGAGE?

There are four basic kinds of mortgage:

1   Repayment mortgages: gradual repayment over the whole loan period.
2   Endowment mortgages: repaid totally at the end of the loan, or on the death of the mortgagee if that is earlier.

3 A combination of one and two.
4 Option mortgages.

There are also other, less common kinds, including:

1 Standing mortgages.
2 Joint income mortgages.
3 Low start mortgages.
4 Escalator mortgages.

Repayment mortgages

These are the most common. They are repaid in monthly instalments, which represent the repayment of a combination of capital and income. They are either eligible for tax relief or for the government subsidy if the option mortgage is chosen. Those who choose the former get most tax relief in the early years when the interest payment is highest.

Interest only mortgages (standing mortgages)

The borrower pays interest charges only. The interest is calculated at a maximum rate fixed over the whole period of the loan. The capital borrowed remains outstanding until redeemed. Payments are therefore fairly low and are wholly eligible for tax relief. When property prices are rising repayment of capital normally presents no problems when the house or flat is sold. This is a relatively expensive way to borrow, but to those paying a lot of tax the high tax relief can be attractive.

Endowment mortgages

Standing mortgages can be linked to life assurance through endowment mortgages. The borrower takes out an insurance policy for the same amount as he wishes to borrow. Its timing is the same as the loan period for the mortgage and it provides extra loan security. These mortgages are rather costly, particularly in comparison with an ordinary repayment mortgage, because not only must continuing high interest be paid on the loan, but there are insurance premiums as well. What the policy does is insure the mortgage for the full loan period and then redeem the loan at the end. Unlike ordinary insurance premiums, which carry tax relief of only 17½ per cent, endowment mortgage policies qualify for relief at the rate of 40 per cent, but like ordinary insurance these policies can have a 'with profits' element (see under Endowment in chapter 13 of this section). These cost more but can provide a healthy extra profit at the end of the mortgage period. Like insurance policies, too, endowment mortgages carry a surrender value after a period.

84

Combined mortgages

These are the best for many people, carrying an insurance guarantee combined with monthly repayments to the building society. The option is available on the repayment part of the mortgage, but only normal tax relief can be claimed on the insurance element.

Option mortgages

There is no need to elaborate further on these. They have a government subsidy and work in principle in the same way as repayment mortgages. They are useful only for low or non-tax payers.

Joint income mortgages

These are simply a variation of the ordinary repayment mortgage. The incomes of both husband and wife are taken into account in deciding the amount of the loan, and the payments are phased in such a way that they are larger while both are earning and then tail off. This is usually done on a fixed formula, with the first, say, three years' payments at the rate of a fifteen-year mortgage and the rest on a twenty-five year basis. You may find that you have to pay a slightly higher rate of interest on this type of mortgage, but it is very useful for a young couple who want to pay off as much of their mortgage as possible before starting a family.

Escalator mortgages

These are the absolute opposite of joint income mortgages. The payments start off low and increase steadily. They are useful if you know your income will rise, but the lender may well want proof that this is likely to happen. They are useful because they mean mortgages are paid off faster and interest charges are lower, but they can be dangerous if your expected rise fails to materialize.

Low start mortgages

The borrower pays a reduced rate of interest for the first five years and then increases the payments. Once again these are attractive for people who know that their income will increase and so can take on rather larger commitments than their present income would justify. Mortgages like these are generally limited to professional employees or civil servants.

WHEN INTEREST RATES CHANGE

As I have already said, mortgage interest rates change slowly, but they do eventually change if interest rates generally move up or down. Building societies tend to raise their rates after other financial institutions have done so, but they also lag behind when it comes to lowering them. When there is a change the amount of your monthly payments will change – though if you have a straight repayment mortgage you can extend or reduce the period of your mortgage rather than changing your monthly payment. The following table shows what you will pay each month on every £1,000 borrowed over twenty-five years at different rates of interest. These payments do not allow for tax relief, which will usually effectively cut the payment by about a third.

Mortgage rate	*monthly repayment*
10½ per cent	£9.54
11 per cent	£9.50
11½ per cent	£10.26
12 per cent	£10.63
12¼ per cent	£10.81

Remember, it is not possible on all mortgages to keep your payments steady, and even where you can there may come a point when you are in effect extending the repayment period for ever. It is possible to extend repayment mortgages. The societies recommend, however, that you do not let your payments extend beyond twenty-five years. The same applies to option mortgages. But extension is not possible with endowment and interest only mortgages. Your monthly payment must increase or decrease in accordance with the revised amount that will be sent to you by the society. If you make payments through your bank you will be required to authorize them to change the payments.

If you have taken out a mortgage in recent years, you will be forgiven for thinking that mortgages rates do nothing but rise. Although they have risen sharply in recent years, there have been two cuts recently and if you look at the total picture over more than fifty years you will see that there have been long periods of falling mortgage interest rates. See table opposite.

WHEN YOU CANNOT KEEP UP REPAYMENTS

If for any reason you cannot keep up your mortgage repayments, tell the lender immediately. Whether an institution or a private person, the lender has the right to foreclose on the loan and sell the house to pay the debt, but few will take such action immediately if you explain the circumstances to them. Building societies, for instance, may permit you to make interest only payments for a time until your circumstances improve, and your local social security office may help towards these. If

MORTGAGE INTEREST RATES FROM 1925

(Owner Occupiers)

Date	Remarks	Rate %
1 January 1925 to 30 September 1932	Approx. dates	
1 October 1932 to 31 May 1933	Approx. dates	5½
1 June 1933 to 30 April 1935	Approx. dates	5
1 May 1935 to 31 December 1939	Approx. dates	4½
1 January 1940 to 30 April 1940	Approx. dates	5
1 May 1940 to 31 December 1941	Approx. dates	5½
1 January 1942 to 12 August 1943	Approx. dates	5
13 August 1943 to 31 December 1943	(£1,000,000 only)	4
1 January 1944 to 31 August 1945		4½
1 September 1945 to 20 January 1952		4 *
1 November 1946 to 31 October 1948	(Properties of new construction)	3½
21 January 1952 to 14 August 1955	Terms up to 20 years	4½ variable (5 fixed)
21 January 1952 to 13 May 1952	Terms 21-30 years	4¾ variable (5¼ fixed)
14 May 1952 to 14 August 1955	(Properties of new construction) Terms up to 35 years	4½ variable (5 fixed)
14 May 1952 to 19 May 1954	Terms 26-30 years	4¾ variable (5¼ fixed)
1 January 1954 to 14 August 1955	Class 1 Properties Terms up to 25 years	4½ variable (5 fixed)
12 March 1954 to 14 August 1955	Class 2 Properties Terms up to 25 years	4½ variable (5 fixed)
20 May 1954 to 14 August 1955	Class 1 Properties Terms up to 30 years	4½ variable (5 fixed)
1 February 1955 to 14 August 1955	Class 1 Properties Terms up to 35 years	4½ variable (5 fixed)
15 August 1955 to 21 May 1956	Terms up to 35 years	5½ variable (6 fixed)
22 May 1956 to 22 July 1956	Up to 15 years	5¾ variable
	16 to 25 years	6 variable
	26 to 35 years	6¼ variable (fixed + ½)
23 July 1956 to 30 September 1957	Up to 25 years	6 variable
	26 to 35 years	6¼ variable (fixed + ½)
1 October 1957 to 31 December 1958	Up to 25 years	6¼ variable
	26 to 35 years	6½ variable (fixed + ½)
1 January 1959 to 21 May 1959	Up to 20 years	6 variable
	21 to 35 years	6¼ variable (fixed + ½)
22 May 1959 to 22 May 1960	Up to 20 years	5½ variable
	21 to 35 years	5¾ variable (fixed + ½)
23 May 1960 to 7 June 1961	Up to 20 years	6 variable
	21 to 35 years	6¼ variable
8 June 1961 to 31 January 1963	Up to 20 years	6½ variable
	21 to 35 years	6¾ variable
1 February 1963 to 31 January 1965	Up to 35 years	6 variable
1 February 1965 to 19 May 1966	Up to 35 years	6¾ variable

(Owner Occupiers)

Date	Remarks	Rate %
20 May 1966 to 30 April 1968	Up to 35 years	7⅛ variable
1 May 1968 to 31 March 1969	Up to 35 years	7⅝ variable
11 March 1969 to 31 March 1969	Up to 35 years	7¾ endowment
1 April 1969 to 31 October 1971	Up to 35 years	8½ variable
		8⅝ endowment
1 November 1971 to 30 September 1972	Up to 35 years	8 variable
		8.2 endowment
1 October 1972 to 5 April 1973	Up to 35 years	8.5 variable
		8.7 endowment
6 April 1973 to 14 August 1973	Up to 35 years	9.5 variable
		9.7 endowment
15 August 1973 to 14 September 1973	Up to 35 years	10 variable
		10.2 endowment
15 September 1973 to 30 April 1976	Up to £11,000	11 variable
		11.2 endowment
1 May 1976 to 24 November 1976	Up to £11,000	10.5 variable
		10.7 endowment
25 November 1976 to 30 April 1976	Up to £11,000	12¼ variable
		13¼ endowment
1 May 1976 to 30 June 1977	Up to £11,000	11¼ variable
		11½ endowment
1 July 1977 –	Up to £11,000	10½ variable
		11 endowment

Source: Nationwide Building Society

the situation persists, however, and the lender does foreclose, you are entitled to have any capital returned to you which you have paid off, less any expenses the lender may have incurred in the sale. If the situation does arise that your house has to be sold because you cannot pay the mortgage, it is best to try to do this yourself and then pay off the outstanding loan.

MORTGAGE PROTECTION

You can buy mortgage protection or guarantees for your house to protect your heirs in the event of your death, even if you do not have an endowment-linked mortgage.

The guarantee is secured through a special insurance policy and should only cost a few pounds. It ensures that the mortgage will be fully paid off if you die. The payments can be added to your mortgage loan if you wish.

Protection costs more, but is useful not only if you die but also if you are unable to keep up your payments because of ill-health or unemployment. Premiums vary, but are rarely very high

WHEN YOU WILL NOT GET A MORTGAGE

Some properties are extremely difficult, if not impossible to mortgage.

They include buildings which are not normally used as homes, like windmills, oast houses, old barns and the like. You may get a small loan on such a building, but nothing like the loan you can get on an ordinary house or flat. Many building societies are also reluctant to lend on thatched or timber houses. They require massive insurance, which again is more expensive than on an ordinary house or flat, before considering giving a loan.

Chapter 9

KEEPING DOWN THE RUNNING COSTS OF YOUR HOUSE

Wherever you live certain costs are unavoidable: mortgage or rent, rates, water rates, and compulsory service charges if you live in a block of flats or an estate.

After that it is up to you to make the best or worst of the running costs of your house – though you may not always have a choice about every item of your spending. Your business may be such that you have no option but to have a telephone. Your house may already have electric central heating or storage heaters when you buy it, and you may not be able to afford to change them, or the area may not be served with gas, which might well be more economical. Think about these things before you actually buy your house. Later on may be too late.

Remember that government policy may change. Some years ago many people bought electric storage heaters because of the favourable tariff available if they were used at night. That tariff has now been scrapped and owners are left with an expensive, and not necessarily efficient, form of heating.

Remember, too, that the price of any service is likely to increase steadily. There was a rush to gas central heating when natural gas was discovered in the North Sea. It was thought it would make gas cheaper. Well, allowing for inflation the price of gas has not risen as much as other fuels, but nevertheless prices have risen steadily as more and more gas has been piped ashore.

The rule when you are setting up home and estimating running costs is *always assume the worst.*

If you are actually buying an appliance, buy soon rather than later –

the price is sure to increase. When estimating your gas and electricity costs, assume a minimum rise in prices of 10 per cent a year and ask yourself whether your funds are likely to increase enough to cover the higher costs. It is no use installing central heating if you are going to find it too expensive to use properly: far better to heat individual rooms separately, so that you have more control over the cost.

YOUR FUEL BILLS

Electricity: Study the amounts of electricity you could use in any one week (of course some of the items have a seasonal bias). The following are the average number of units of electricity the average family uses in a week, as estimated by the electricity board. One unit is equal to 1,000 watts, or one kilowatt.

Approximate amount of electricity used by domestic appliances

appliance	units per week
refrigerator	7
freezer (12 cu. ft)	20
cooker (family of four)	21-28
lighting (3-bedroomed house)	7
T.V. – black and white (9 hours' viewing for 1 unit)	3½
colour (6 hours' viewing for 1 unit)	5
dishwasher (1 unit per washload)	7
electric blanket – under	1
over – on all night	2
portable room heater (2 units per hour)	112 (8 hours' daily use)
washing machine – automatic cold fill (2 units per washload)	8-9
twin-tub (3 units per washload if water used once only)	11-12
tumble dryer (2 units per hour)	6
toaster (70 slices per unit)	1
shaver (1,800 shaves per unit)	-
clock	12 units *per year*
hair dryer (3 hours per unit)	1
immersion heater (only form of water heating in winter)	75

You will probably not have all these appliances, but it is easy to work out the weekly cost of any one item at the current average rate of 2.61p per unit of electricity, and from that your total bill.

Gas: There are, of course, fewer gas appliances, but those where a comparison can be made cost about 10 per cent less to run.

You will notice I am looking at the running costs of domestic appliances before going on to the purchasing of them. This may seem like putting the cart before the horse, but it is the right way to go about it. Estimate what the costs will be *before buying,* even if you have the cash to buy or will have no problem getting a hire purchase agreement. No appliance is any use if you find it too expensive to run.

Let's assume that you are moving into a new house, or renovating a very old one, and have complete freedom of choice about what kind of appliances you install. Here are just a few examples of the differences in running costs. You can easily work out any others by consulting your local gas and electricity boards.

Heating

In winter, and perhaps during part of the spring and autumn, heating is likely to be one of the biggest items in your bills. As I write, these are some of the points you must consider when deciding how to heat your house:

* All central heating is expensive. You can ignore what advertisements say about 'cheap' and 'efficient'. It may be efficient, but it is never cheap.
* Electricity is the most expensive heating.
* Electricity has some advantages over the rest. It is very clean and easy to use. Gas requires rather more servicing, while solid fuel needs more work by the householder, but less professional servicing than either oil or gas. Electricity, too, is the only type of heating which does not need a flue or chimney. If by any chance you do not or cannot have one installed, you will have to have electricity, despite its cost disadvantages.
* Electricity is available everywhere. Gas is not, and if you choose oil or solid fuel you will have to be sure that you can arrange for regular delivery. Just as important, you should have enough storage space to allow you a reserve should your delivery be late.

Think about all these points and then ask yourself whether:

1 Your family is out all day (though you can get a time clock which automatically switches off your heating while you are out or sleeping).
2 You generally use only a few rooms and the others just occasionally.
3 You would find your total budget under pressure while you are paying for the installation and running costs at the same time.

(This, of course, will not apply if you buy a house which already has central heating.)

If you decide against central heating, you will have to think about some kind of individual room heater for each room, or a heater which you can carry around from room to room. Among these the dearest to run is the portable electric heater which blows out hot air. The cheapest are gas convector fires, though these must be linked in some way to outside air, and solid fuel closed stoves.

Paraffin heaters and gas radiant/convector heaters, for some considerable time after purchase at least, are, taking into account purchase price and running costs, the most economical. Remember, if you use gas for heating in any way you will qualify for special tariff rates, which has the advantage of making your cooking cheaper if you cook by gas.

Here are the current comparative running costs for central heating a three-bedroomed semi-detached house to 70 degrees for one week, in order of expense:

gas	£4.32	(including £22 annual standing charge)
coal	£4.60	
anthracite	£5.30	
oil	£5.90	
coalite	£6.00	
electricity (mainly night heating)	£8.57	(including £14.16 annual standing charge)
electricity (day heating)	£15.77	(including £14.16 annual standing charge)

If you consider the cost per room over a year, it can be as little as £50, if you use closed boilers or fires, or as high as £180 if you pay the standard full price for electricity.

How to keep your heating costs down

First, insulate your house as much as possible. You can insulate the loft with the thick wadding which is available cheaply; you can have (more expensive, but only a once-and-for-all payment) cavity wall insulation; and you can install double glazing on the windows (the price varies according to whether you do it yourself or have it done professionally). *Efficient insulation can save you up to 50 per cent of your fuel bills, and up to 75 per cent of your heat loss.*

Here are the approximate costs of the different kinds of insulation:

professional double glazing	£350
installing double glazing yourself	£175

cavity wall insulation	£175
loft insulation (done by householder)	£50
draught proofing	£18
lagging hot tank	£5

The total cost of all this will be £598 if you have the double glazing done professionally and £423 if you do it yourself. At today's prices, you are likely to have recovered your money in five or six years.

Second, if you have central heating, find out the minimum temperature in which you feel comfortable. For every degree centigrade lower that you fix your thermostat you can save up to £15 a year. Put individual thermostats in each room. A thermostatic radiator valve in each room is the most economical. Check your radiators regularly to make sure they are all working properly.

Heating your water

If you have central heating, the price of heating your water will be included in the central heating costs. To make sure you are using it as economically as possible:

1 Make sure the tank is lagged. This can save you up to £40 a year.
2 Do not put the thermostat too high. This costs more, and is of no benefit if you always have to add cold water when you run any hot.
3 Use your hot water economically. Don't heat up a whole thirty gallon tank when you only need a little. Use a pan or kettle instead for small amounts. Have showers rather than baths; they use far less water.

If you use round 250 gallons per week – again the average consumption of hot water by the average family of two adults and two (not quite two) children in a three-bedroomed semi – this is how your costs work out. You may not believe that you use that much, but the average bath alone takes 10 gallons. If your family are all daily bathers, you are likely to be well over the average.

The following table shows the number of gallons of hot water you can expect per pence from the different forms of heating at 1977 prices. They will probably rise by at least 10 per cent a year.

Electricity:	instant heater	1.2 gallons
	immersion heater	1.0 gallon
Gas:	instant sink heater	10.0 gallons
	instant bath heater	6.9 gallons
	boiler	4.0 gallons

Oil:	central heating boiler		3.0 gallons
Solid fuel:	central heating boiler		
		- coke	3.0 gallons
		- coal	4.0 gallons

These amounts are only approximations. They will simply give you an idea of the different costs of the various types of water heaters.

Lighting

Lighting uses very little power in comparison with heating. In a three-bedroomed house you will be unlucky if your lighting costs you much more than £1 a week.

The dearest light bulb you can buy, combining initial and running costs, for a given amount of light is the longlife single coil, which has an estimated life of 2,000 hours. The cheapest is the pearl coiled coil. Pearl bulbs give more light than opal ones, and clear give the most light of all. But you may not like the glare which comes from a clear bulb.

As well as the three different finishes, there are also three different internal structures. These are the single coil, the coiled coil and longlife. The coiled coil gives out more light for the same amount of electricity than the others, but the longlife (which gives out less light for the same electricity and wattage) lasts twice as long as the other two.

Here is how you can save:

1 Hundred watt bulbs work out cheaper combining purchase price and running costs, so use them if your lighting design permits it, rather than the lower wattages. This applies whether you are considering levels of light or the cost of electricity.

2 Longlife bulbs are dearer to buy and give out less light, but if you do not mind this they work out cheaper to run if you are using a lot of light.

3 Fluorescent tubes can be cheaper than bulbs in the long run. You will need to buy special fittings and the tube itself is expensive, but they last up to seven times longer than an ordinary bulb and give out far more light for the amount of electricity used. Thirty watts from a tube will give as much light as a 100 watt bulb. But don't keep switching the light on and off. It will blow far more quickly if you do. You also have to ask yourself whether you can actually stand living in a room lit by fluorescent lighting.

4 A light dimmer can reduce the amount of electricity you use, but it is only worthwhile if you use it often. If you use one three hours a night on average (and this is a lot if you take the summer months into account) the dimmer, if you buy one of the cheaper ones, might pay for itself in about a year. A dearer one would take four

or five years to pay for itself. It is best, therefore, only to buy and use a dimmer if you like it for decorative purposes in your lighting.

Cooking

The cost of your cooker

There are three basic kinds of cooker. The two most popular are gas and electricity. The third is the solid fuel, sometimes called the Aga-type, which can also be run off gas or electricity and can be used to heat water. It is by far the most expensive to run, takes up more space, and costs more to buy. Gas and electric cookers both cost a little less than £100 for a standard model, though you can pay up to £250 for a model with extras, and even more if you buy a continental or American model. The Aga-type costs around £450.

Gas is the cheapest to use, particularly if you are on a preferential tariff, often called the gold star tariff. Gold star cuts the cost by more than half and a gas cooker may well then only cost a little over £10 a year to run.

Electricity will probably cost at least three times more, and an Aga anything from nine times more, if run on gas to fifteen times more if run on oil. Solid fuel Agas will cost about £160 a year. Agas clearly are only for devotees of that kind of cooking.

How to cut the costs of cooking

No matter what you do, you will only save a few pounds, but with prices at their present levels and with further rises in the offing, we should consider all possibilities. Here are some suggestions:

1 Buy gadgets like pressure cookers, toasters, slow roasters, electric kettles and the like for use when appropriate. They are generally cheaper than using a cooker.
2 With an electric cooker, make the pans fit the ring as exactly as possible. On gas, do not use pans so small that the flames go up the side of the pan and waste heat.
3 Use very little water when cooking vegetables. This is not only economical; it is better cooking too.
4 Keep the lids on saucepans, unless you are cooking something which requires them to be off. You will cook more cheaply and quickly this way.
5 Use matches rather than a gas pilot light. It's surprising what a pilot light can add to your bill – it can be £5 a year.
6 Don't over-cook food. It tastes better, is more nutritious and costs less!

I haven't mentioned microwave ovens yet. These are expensive –

around £200 – and have limited uses. You cannot, for example, cook beef which is crispy on the outside and rare inside, as the microwave cooks evenly throughout, but it will reheat frozen food very quickly and cook a joint in less than half an hour. It has its uses for those who are at work all day, or who use a freezer a lot. Microwave ovens are very cheap to run, but they are an extra rather than a first choice for the average family, because of the expense of buying.

Gas and electricity bills

If you do not pay your bills, the supply will be disconnected and will not be restored until you pay up. If you are elderly, or on social security, you are likely to receive help with paying your bills, and in many areas of the country, especially if you are elderly, the supply is no longer disconnected simply because in the winter months, when your bill is heavier, you are unable to pay.

For the vast majority of us, however, fuel bills have to be paid, however difficult we may find it. They come in four times a year and consist of a standing charge (for the use of the service) and a charge for the amount of fuel used.

In addition to the normal electricity charges there has been since August 1974 a 'fuel cost adjustment', which is in effect an extra charge. It is worked out by multiplying 0.00047p by the number of pence by which the fuel price is more than £20 per tonne. At present this is 0.369p per unit, and is worked out like this:

cost of fuel in power stations	2785p per tonne
basic cost	2000p
difference	785p

adjustment = 785 × 0.00047p = 0.369p per unit

There are a variety of gas tariffs. They suit different people according to the amount of gas they use. Before you start paying, ask the local office for advice on which one will suit you. If you use only a little, the General Credit tariff will be best, but if you have gas central heating or a lot of other gas appliances choose the Gold Star tariff. With the former you pay a lower standing charge, but a high price for the first 100 therms of gas you use. With Gold Star, the standing charge is almost four and a half times as much, but the cost per therm is one third less.

How to pay
1 You can simply pay your gas or electricity bill as it comes in by cash or cheque.
2 You can open a budget account at your bank, so that it does not

matter whether you have the actual cash when the bill comes in (see chapter 6 in this section).

3　You can make regular monthly payments which are one twelfth of your *estimated* bills for the year. If you do it this way, an adjustment is made either way at the end of the year. You can pay these either through a standing order at your bank or through a National Giro account.

4　You can buy special savings stamps issued by the gas and electricity boards whenever you have some spare cash and these can then be used towards paying your bills. If you bought one 50p stamp each week, for example, you would have £6.50 towards the bill at the end of the quarter.

If you do have a problem in paying, *tell the local gas or electricity office immediately*. If your difficulties are going to be only temporary, they may arrange a special easy method of paying off your debt over a period.

Your washing

This is the last really major item for most families. Prices of washing machines vary enormously, depending on what you want your machine to do. Automatic machines which do the whole process in one go including spin drying are usually the most expensive to buy; twin tubs are cheaper. There is quite a substantial difference in price between different makes. You can also wash by hand or use the launderette, or simply buy a spin or tumble drier after doing the washing by hand.

Taking our average family again, they are likely to be washing about a ton of clothes a year, so it is very important to work out the costs of washing correctly. The price of detergents must not be ignored, nor the cost of the electricity involved in an average wash.

The amount of electricity used in a washing machine will vary depending on the type of wash you are doing. The most expensive is the hot white wash; the cheapest, the cool wash with no spin drying. It is obviously cheapest to dry your clothes outside on a line, but this is not always convenient if you live, say, in a flat.

Let's assume you are washing clothes which need hot water, that the main drying is done in a machine, and that you are buying your washing machine on hire purchase. Here then is the approximate cost of your weekly wash.

hand washing – dried on line	£0.40
dried in a spin drier	£1.09
dried in a tumble drier	£1.20
twin tub – dried on line	£1.15

dried in a spin drier	£1.20
dried in a tumble drier	£1.28
automatic machine – dried on line	£1.18
dried in a tumble drier	£1.26
launderette – two loads a week tumble dried	£1.05

There seems little advantage in using the launderette when you consider the inconvenience of having to go to it. If you have a service wash – that is, you leave your washing there for one of the attendants to do – you will have to pay at least 10p extra. This may be well worthwhile if you have no space for a washing machine, or if you are out at work all day, and have little time to spare.

Twin tubs will, unless you are unlucky, cost less in repair bills than automatics. They also spin dry better and are quicker than automatics, but automatics are less bother to use, they rinse better, and usually have a bigger capacity than twin tubs.

Dishwashers

So far the dishwasher has not caught on very well in Britain. It is expensive – usually between £120 and £200 – and is obviously well down on any priority purchase list. It costs more than £1 a week to run, as against about 30p for washing up by hand. It may also not be very good at washing up very dirty pans, and you may find that you have to do these yourself. To be run economically, it should always be fully loaded, and this means you will need a reserve of plates and cutlery, etc., unless you have a large family always sitting down at one go. It is very hygienic, but whether it saves time or not is a moot point. It takes time to load, sometimes as long as to wash by hand, and if you leave washing up on the sink to dry and drain there is little to commend a dishwasher in its drying properties.

Freezers

In normal times it is unlikely that a freezer will save you a lot of money. What you save in bulk buying may be swallowed up by running costs. Freezers are basically for making your life easier, not cheaper. In times of inflation, however, when food prices are rising almost weekly, useful savings can be made. To save money on perishable foods, you will definitely need a freezer. Savings accrue in three basic ways:

1 You can buy food in bulk and pay less per pound.
2 You can save as prices rise by having bought earlier.
3 You can store your own produce, or buy when prices are seasonally low.

Against these advantages you must set the running costs:

1 Electricity. The cost of running a freezer is relatively low, but it will certainly rise as time goes on. The actual amount will depend on the size and type you choose; the length of time you leave the lid open and the number of times a day you open it; the average temperature of the room around the freezer and the temperature of the food you put in it.
2 Depreciation. Your freezer will usually last about fifteen years. Work out an average cost each year for depreciation, including in this any interest charges if you have bought on H.P.
3 Insuring yourself against breakdown and food loss.

When you have worked out these costs, you will probably find that even with bulk buying you will not save a great deal by using a freezer, unless you have plenty of your own home produce.

You should also consider what using a freezer costs in non-monetary terms. You must plan your menus more carefully. You must find space for the freezer in your home. You must remember that it takes times to unfreeze food. Such irritations may outweigh any advantages of a freezer for some people.

However, despite the drawbacks, more and more people are deciding that the advantages of having a freezer far outweigh the disadvantages.

Choosing your freezer

Before you start looking at particular models, decide whether you want an upright or chest freezer, or a combined freezer/fridge.

Chest freezers take up more space than the other two types, and loading and unloading is more difficult. Make sure that you can reach the bottom when you bend over. On the other hand, chest freezers accumulate far less frost, use less electricity, and maintain a more even temperature than upright ones. They also offer a good extra working space in your kitchen. *Upright freezers* are becoming increasingly popular because they generally take up no more space than a fridge. They are easier to defrost than chest freezers, but cost more to run.

Only consider a combined *fridge/freezer* if you have no room for both separately. Usually the freezer space is relatively small, and there is almost always more room in the fridge than in the freezer section. Many people might consider this the wrong way round.

When you have decided which type you want:

* Buy as big a freezer as your space and income will permit. Reckon anyway on about four cubic feet for each member of the family and you will not go wrong. If you have a lot of your own produce you will need more space than this.

* Extras cost money. Decide whether you really need them. You can get automatic defrosting, interior lights, extra-fast freezing compartments, door locks, warning lights when temperatures change and special racks or baskets for storage.
* Shop around. Fix yourself a price and stick to it. Wait for special offers. Freezer prices can vary enormously on the same model.
* Always buy from a good dealer. Freezers are reliable and tend not to cost much in repairs, but things can go wrong and you will then need faults put right within twenty-four hours if you are not to lose all your food.
* Even if the guarantees all appear sound, insure the contents of your freezer against spoilage.

If you follow these tips you are unlikely to go wrong, but before buying insist on:

1 A test run before delivery.
2 Proper installation. Do not let the delivery man leave the house until the freezer is in place – *and running*.
3 A lesson from the delivery man on the best use of your freezer.

Two final tips: have a special electric point which you use for your freezer and nothing else. Cover the on/off switch with sellotape, so that you cannot switch it off accidentally. I once lost a lot of food by accidentally switching off the freezer switch, which happened to be one on a panel of four. And remember, a full freezer is heavy. A big one can weigh as much as half a ton. Can your floors stand such a weight?

You've bought your freezer, had it installed, it runs properly – then *use it*. To get the maximum savings, fill it up as much as you can afford. Keep it full. Rotate its contents. Never switch it off, except for an annual clean-out.

Freezer insurance

I have already mentioned getting insurance to cover lost food. You should also remember that – though it is unlikely – your freezer can break down, and once it is out of guarantee repair bills can be high. There are many freezer and breakdown policies available which automatically cover you for food loss and freezer breakdowns.

A typical policy should, if your freezer is less than ten years old, cost a maximum about £10 a year. This will cover food loss of up to about £100, labour and parts to about £150. As few freezers for the average family go much above this price the cover is good enough.

Small appliances

Small appliances cost relatively little to run. Whether you buy them or not depends upon your priorities. Probably only a vacuum cleaner is a must. Using, say, a mixer or a liquidizer is always more expensive than doing the job by hand. Whether these sorts of appliances save time is also doubtful. What they save in preparation they very often lose in the more complicated cleaning and washing after use.

Buying your appliances

There are certain rules to be observed when buying your domestic appliances:

1 First and foremost, *buy the appliance which best suits your needs*. It is no use buying an enormous freezer if a small one would suit you better, or a small cooker if you have to supplement it by a number of gadgets.

2 *Look at* Which *magazine,* the journal of the Consumers' Association. It comes out monthly and is extremely useful if you want to be certain you are getting the 'best buy' out of a range of models. One that costs more to purchase may be safer and more economical to run. Take time before making your final choice. Even after consulting *Which,* insist that you are shown how an appliance works in the showroom. You might find, for instance, that *Which's* 'best buy' is at the wrong height for you to use.

3 *Shop around.* This is all important. Prices vary enormously. You may have to pay far more in a store which will deliver goods than in one of the discount stores which encourage you to take whatever you buy away with you – and even if you don't they have relatively low delivery charges.

Discount warehouses are cheapest of all. They do an enormous amount of advertising in the national press, setting out their prices against what they describe as 'normal prices'. Sometimes the difference seems very large, but it is generally possible to buy below the higher prices stated in other stores. Nevertheless savings can easily be of the order of 20 per cent. Specialist electrical and domestic appliance shops come next cheapest, with general department stores dearer, except at sale time. Some highly specialized shops may carry only the expensive ranges, and they usually charge top prices when they do so, particularly among radios, television and stereo equipment, which is very much a matter of individual taste and which I will look at in chapter 11 of this section. But the same considerations about shopping around still apply.

4 *Use the sales.* There is absolutely nothing wrong with sale goods so far as domestic appliances are concerned. They are just as safe and efficient as any bought at full price. Shops and stores, and electricity and gas showrooms, are simply clearing their stocks for new designs to come in. You can get real bargains.

Chapter 10

BUYING FOOD

If you have read chapter 1 of this section, you will know that, after the rent or mortgage, food is easily the biggest item on the average budget. The days of cheap food which the British enjoyed so long are gone, and the increases in prices are by no means over. Food is going to loom even larger in our total budgets, until finally we approach the European pattern where in some countries it takes more than half of a family's available money.

It makes sense then to look carefully at the way we spend money on food and, if necessary, to change old habits for new and more economical ones.

YOUR BASIC GROCERIES

The Grocer magazine has worked out a basic shopping basket. You probably do not buy exactly these items, but something very similar.

Basic shopping basket

food	
Anchor butter	8 oz
Birds Eye fish fingers	10
Birds Eye frozen peas	1 lb
Cheddar cheese (UK)	1 lb
Cookeen fat	8 oz
Del Monte tinned peaches	15½ oz
Eggs (standard white)	6
Golden Delicious apples	1 lb
Heinz baked beans	15¾ oz
Heinz tomato soup	15¼ oz
John West sardines	4¼ oz
Kellogg's corn flakes	500 g
McDougalls self-raising flour	3 lb
McVitie's chocolate home wheat biscuits	200 g
Mothers Pride sliced white bread	large

Nescafé instant coffee	4 oz
PG Tips tea	4 oz
Robertson's strawberry jam	1 lb
Stork SB margarine	1 lb
Tate & Lyle granulated sugar	1 lb
Wall's pork sausages	1 lb

non-food

Ajax scouring powder	1 lb 2 oz
Daz washing powder	E3 size
Fairy Liquid washing-up liquid	19 fl oz

Fresh fruit and vegetable basket

apples	1 lb
carrots	1 lb
new potatoes	1 lb
tomatoes	1 lb

As you can see, the list consists of branded goods. If you use supermarkets regularly you will know that very often a particular store will offer what are called 'own brands' which can bring down the price of your 'basket' considerably. The prices you pay depend to some extent on the shop you use and to some extent on exactly where you live. You cannot do much about that, of course. It would be crazy to move house simply to get to cheaper groceries. But it is quite useful to know where you stand nationally as far as expense goes.

On pages 104-5 there is a selection from *The Grocer* price list for a branded basket in various chain stores. The table shows the name of the chain and of the chain's own brands, the area serviced by the chain, the number of branches in the country, whether trading stamps are available, and the price of the total basket in four regions.

The Grocer estimated that the savings in own brands could be as high as follows:

washing-up liquid	at least 30 per cent
scouring powders	at least 20 per cent
self-raising flour	at least 15 per cent
sardines	at least 15 per cent
baked beans	at least 10 per cent
chocolate biscuits	at least 10 per cent
coffee	at least 10 per cent
corn flakes	at least 10 per cent

continued on p. 106

The Grocer's PRICE LIST FOR CHAIN STORE

grocery chain	main own brand name	area covered	Number of branches			stamps	Price of branded basket			
			total	superstores	discount stores (name)		Greater London £	South-east £	S. Wales S. West £	Mid-lands £
Asda	Asda	N. England, Midlands, Scotland, Wales	56	36	-	-	-	-	-	4.34
Bishop's	Bishop's	London, Midlands, Home Counties	73	-	9 (Bishop's Discount)	-	4.83	4.87	-	4.79
Budgen	Budgen	S.E. England, Midlands	154	-	-	G.S. or own (most)	4.95	4.92	-	-
Co-op	Co-op	UK	7,500	18	-	dividend (most)	4.81	4.80	4.72	4.75
Fine Fare	Fine Fare	U.K.	800	7	22 (Shoppers' Paradise)	-	4.82	4.79	4.80	4.77
Gateway	Gateway	S. England, S. Wales, Midlands	91	-	5 (So-Lo Discount)	G.S. or P.S. (most)	-	4.86	4.81	-
David Greig	Key	London, Midlands, Home Counties	75	-	-	-	4.84	4.85	-	4.85
International Stores	International	England, Wales	742	3	40 (Pricerite) 6 (Payantake)	G.S. or P.S. (most)	4.90	4.91	4.78	4.86

Key Markets	Key	Midlands, S. England	104	2	14 (K.D. Discount)	-	4.64	4.56	4.54	4.57
Liptons	Sunshine	England, Wales	1,000	-	80 (Presto)	-	4.77	4.72	4.68	4.73
Mace	Mace	U.K.	4,500	-	-	G.S. (few)	4.95	4.97	4.89	4.95
Mac Markets	Mac	England	71	-	-	-	4.79	4.62	-	4.56
Safeway	Safeway	England, Scotland	82	-	-	-	4.75	4.78	-	4.64
Sainsbury's	Sainsbury's	Midlands, S. England	217	3	-	-	4.77	4.78	4.75	4.76
Spar	Spar	U.K.	3,900	-	-	G.S. (few)	4.98	4.88	4.90	4.92
Tesco	Tesco	U.K.	740	16	-	-	4.84	4.79	4.80	4.77
V.G.	V.G.	U.K.	3,300	-	-	G.S. (few)	5.07	5.04	5.01	5.00
Waitrose	Waitrose	Midlands, S. England	57	-	-	-	4.87	4.86	4.82	4.82
Woolworths	Winfield	U.K.	610	53	-	-	4.78	4.69	4.71	4.70

cooking fat	at least 10 per cent
fish fingers	at least 10 per cent
tea	at least 10 per cent
tomato soup	at least 10 per cent
washing powders	at least 10 per cent
butter	at least 5 per cent
strawberry jam	at least 5 per cent
soft margarine	at least 5 per cent
tinned peaches	at least 5 per cent
frozen peas	at least 5 per cent
pork sausages	at least 5 per cent

Savings were only unlikely with sliced white bread and sugar.

You can see from this table that wherever you live you can make a considerable saving by buying a grocery chain's own brands. Do not think you are buying an inferior product when you buy an own brand. It has probably been manufactured in the same place as the branded goods and the composition of the product is likely to be the same. Often only the packing is different – generally less elaborate in the own brand range. But why pay for packaging?

The saving in buying own brands applies wherever you live and is quite consistent throughout. You can save 10 per cent of your outlay, sometimes more, by careful selection of own brands.

The Grocer's chain store table also shows you how considerably overall prices differ from one grocery chain to another. Wherever you live Key Markets are the cheapest for the full basket and V.G. the dearest. Safeway and Sainsbury's are fairly close in price to each other, the Co-op a little dearer and Tesco a little dearer still. The differences are very small, however. It would hardly be worth making a long journey by car or bus to save the few pence involved. Obviously, the prices in the table will be out of date as you are reading this; if current trends continue you will probably find you are paying more everywhere.

The Grocer also does regular assessments of the cheapest places to shop in the various regions it studies. Consider changing from one chain to another, if one is cheaper and equally convenient to shop in. Here are its conclusions:

The Midlands. Asda was cheapest for brands and as cheap as any chain for own brands. Key Markets and Mac Markets came next, with Mac being a little cheaper in own brands. Key was cheapest for fruit and vegetables.

North. Asda and William Jackson came out best, with Asda being a little cheaper except for fruit and vegetables. Mac was about the same for own brands, but dearer for branded goods. Liptons was about the same as Mac, as were Safeway, Woolworths and Tesco.

Scotland. The Co-op was the best bargain here, if you collect stamps. Otherwise Safeway and Woolworths were cheapest for brands and own brands.

Greater London. Key Markets was cheapest for brands, and only Mac Markets was cheaper for own brands. Next best came Sainsbury's, Safeway, Woolworths and Tesco and if you collect stamps the Co-op. There was little to choose here. Tesco was marginally cheaper than the others for fruit and vegetables.

South-east. Here again Key Markets and Mac Markets came out on top, with Key slightly cheaper for brands and Mac for own brands. Next came Tesco, and the Co-op for the stamp collectors. Liptons and Woolworths were cheap for brands and Sainsbury's as cheap for own brands.

South Wales and the South-west. Key Markets came out best, followed by Tesco, and the Co-op (with stamps), with the Co-op a bit cheaper for brands and Tesco for fruit and vegetables. Liptons, Woolworths, Gateway and International Stores were as cheap as any others for brands but not own brands. Liptons was cheapest of all for fruit and vegetables and Sainsbury's as good as the Co-op and Tesco for own brands.

You can see from this that by picking and choosing between brands and own brands, and between supermarkets, you can make quite considerable savings – though interestingly *The Grocer* found that very often people preferred the atmosphere of the dearer shops.

Rules for supermarket shopping

You can follow all the rules for sensible shopping, go to the cheapest stores, choose own brands, and still waste money. To avoid this:

1 Make a list of what you need and stick to it.
2 Don't be tempted by anything new or exotic. The chances are that it is overpriced.
3 Take advantage of special offers when they occur, like so much off toothpaste or detergent, rather than waiting until you actually need the item, when the offer may be over.
4 Don't buy too much or too little. If you live alone, or have a small family, it is a waste of money to buy a bumper size and then have to throw some of it away.
5 Know exactly the price of what you are buying. This means working out the unit cost of every item you buy. This is most important.

MEAT

When you are buying meat, remember that the cuts which you can grill or roast quickly will cost the most. This does not necessarily mean they are the most nutritious or even that they taste the best.

Even if you are out at work all day try to organize your cooking routine so that you can take advantage of the cheaper cuts. If you have a freezer this is easy. You can cook several meals at the weekend and use them during the week. If your family has no experience of anything but grilled steak and chops, try to educate them on to something new.

Here are the bargains among the different meats:

Beef

Fillet steak is by far the most expensive, followed by sirloin and the best topside roast. Rib roast is rather cheaper. Chuck steaks and flank steaks can be grilled if the quality is good and they come cheaper than the prime grills.

Cheaper still are braising and stewing cuts which will take a long time to cook. These are beef shank, brisket and shin beef. Lastly there is minced beef, which can be cooked slowly or quickly as hamburgers, meat balls and meat sauces.

Lamb

The most expensive cuts are the chops cut from the rib or loin and leg of lamb for roasting. Shoulder is far cheaper. It roasts well, and although more fatty it is often more succulent than leg.

Chump chops and best end of neck are cheaper, and cheapest of all are neck chops. These are not popular in Britain, but they do not need such long cooking as the cheaper cuts of beef and are excellent in casseroles.

Pork

Loin and leg for roasting are the dearer cuts. Shoulder is cheaper and also roasts well, but it is difficult to cut unless the butcher bones and rolls it for you. Chops, too, are expensive, as is pork fillet.

Only belly is cheap. This can generally be cooked quite quickly and makes a good roast if stuffed, boned and rolled – though it may be too fatty for some tastes. It also makes a beautiful hot pot-style dish, with potatoes and onions, which is cheap, tasty and filling.

Offal

This is often the poor relation in cooking in Britain – though in many countries it is regarded as a great delicacy. Except for calves' liver and, a little less dear, lambs' kidneys, it tends to be cheap.

Veal kidneys, hard to get but worth searching for, are remarkable value, and a little patience can make a good meal out of almost any kind of liver, kidney, tongue, heart, brains, sweetbreads or tripe. This last, much misunderstood food can be made into delicious casseroles for a fraction of the price of a beef or lamb stew. It is also very nutritious.

Veal

Veal is young beef and what goes for beef also goes for veal, though on the whole the stewing cuts of veal are leaner than beef and more tender, so take less time to cook. Though the expensive cuts of veal are as dear as any meat, stewing veal is often a great bargain and can be used in as many dishes as stewing lamb or beef. It is a sadly neglected meat in Britain, so look out for it.

Poultry

Most poultry in this country is sold as a total bird. It is worth experimenting with larger ones and roasting, say, only a part and using the rest for stews and finally as stock for soups.

This applies particularly to turkey. When you buy a turkey, however, do not buy one so large that you have to go on eating it indefinitely. Probably more turkey is thrown away uneaten because a family becomes more bored with it than any other meat. It is no wonder turkey is generally only popular at Christmas; we spoil our appetite for it for the rest of the year. Try buying it in pieces and making escalopes of the breast, or roasting only one leg of an enormous bird.

How many portions per pound?

As a rough guide here is the number of portions you can get from one pound:

beef	
fillet steak	3
sirloin steak	3
other steaks	3
top rump roast	3
rib roast (with bone)	2
casserole beef	3
lamb	
leg	4
shoulder	4
lamb chops	4
stewing lamb	3
pork	
leg	4
shoulder	4

| loin chops | 2-3 |
| loin roast | 3 |

poultry
| chicken | 2-3 |
| turkey | 2-3 |

Ham goes a little further than pork, because eating the fat is more acceptable to most people.

Weight loss in cooking

When you buy meat you must also consider how much it will shrink when you cook it. This is why you do not get the same servings pound for pound from every kind of meat. Some lose more when cooking than others, and the more slowly you cook the less the loss will be. Frozen meat loses rather more than fresh meat.

The amount of meat loss is a measure of how much extra you are paying for one pound of meat. Chicken is generally the cheapest meat to buy, but it does not always work out cheapest when you consider the net weight after cooking. On the whole New Zealand lamb shoulder, which originally costs nearly 50 per cent more than chicken, works out the cheapest meat of all, taking into account both price and weight loss in cooking. Here are some examples:

joint	weight loss
beef topside	37%
port neck end roast	38%
sirloin steak	38%
pork loin	43%
English leg of lamb	47%
N.Z. leg of lamb	48%
English shoulder of lamb	48%
N.Z. shoulder of lamb	48%
pork leg	51%
beef rib roast	54%
frozen chicken	69%

When you are buying you must allow for this loss of weight when calculating the real price of the meat. If you are making a casserole, the weight loss will go into the gravy, so do not use more water than you need if you want your casserole to have a rich taste.

FISH

Though we live on islands surrounded by waters rich in fish, the British have never been really big fish eaters. This is a pity, because ounce for ounce, fish is as rich in protein as meat and it is not nearly as fattening.

You can often eat almost twice the amount of fish as meat for the same number of calories. This does not apply to all fish. The more expensive sorts like salmon and lobster are heavy in calories. It is with the white fish like cod, haddock, hake, halibut, sole, plaice and turbot that the gains really come.

There used to be an enormous price advantage in buying fish rather than meat, but this has largely disappeared, except with fish like mackerel, herrings, sprats and coley. All these are rich in nutrition, but some people find them fiddly to eat. The small effort of filleting these fish can be well worthwhile.

The main thing when buying fish is to buy it fresh, preferably from a fishmonger. There will be nothing wrong with the frozen fish you buy in a supermarket, but its texture will have changed, and there is no doubt that fresh fish tastes nicer.

Prices vary enormously every day, so you should buy the bargain of the day. And try the cheaper fish like coley and rock fish, which are excellent when cooked and have not climbed in price to the same extent as cod and other popular fish.

If you are thinking of freezing fish yourself, buy it as fresh as possible and get it home and into the freezer as quickly as you can. Never freeze shellfish yourself. You can buy it frozen and get it into your freezer, but there is a real danger of shellfish going bad if you buy it fresh and freeze, however quickly you freeze it. Never exceed the recommended maximum freezer periods, as given later on in this chapter.

Some fish, like lobster, salmon, prawns, turbot and halibut are now definitely in the luxury class. They will be at least as expensive as the most expensive cuts of meat.

The only consolation is that there is very little waste at all, and far less is lost in cooking fish than meat.

VEGETABLES AND FRUIT

Unless you have a freezer, or grow your own vegetables and fruit, you will be at the mercy of seasonal prices, for most fruit and vegetables last only a few days, and not only do they go mouldy, but with each day left uneaten they lose some of their nutritional content.

So buy only as much as you need at any one time, or as much as you can accommodate in your freezer. Always beware of out of season items. They may be tempting, but the prices are almost certain to be ludicrously high. If you have a freezer, soft fruits are generally a good buy in season and freeze very well.

THE STORE CUPBOARD

It makes good sense in these days of inflation to buy food now instead of later if it can be stored for a time, to keep ahead of price rises. The obvious way to do this is to buy tins, jars, bottles and packets. Food will go off, eventually, however. The length of time it lasts depends on the product itself and the way it is preserved. In the end seals will break and even tins deteriorate, letting in air and bacteria.

Rotate your purchases. Don't use the tins you have just bought. Bring older ones forward and you should have no problems. Do not keep food until it has lost its colour and flavour, even if it will do you no harm.

RUNNING YOUR FREEZER

Nor does food last forever in a freezer. Even if it has not actually gone 'off', some food changes texture, colour and even taste if left too long. To avoid disappointment in these ways, make sure you rotate the food in your freezer. It takes time, but you must move the food round, so that you do not take out first the things which you have only just put in. Here are a few maximum storage times:

beef	12 months
lamb	10 months
veal	10 months
pork	9 months
mince	2-3 months
offal (liver, kidneys, etc.)	2-3 months
sausages	6-8 weeks

Cured meat lasts less well than fresh meat in terms of taste. It also needs wrapping well, so that it doesn't dry out and to prevent all the contents of the freezer tasting smoked. Smoked bacon will usually last from four to ten weeks and unsmoked for three to six weeks.

chicken	12 months
turkey and ducks	9 months
game birds	6-8 months
white fish	12 months
Salmon, trout and herring	9 months
shellfish	1 month
vegetables	6-12 months (depending on variety)
fruit	12 months
cream	3-6 months
butter, unsalted	4-6 months

butter, salted	2-4 months
margarine	12 months
cheese	4-9 months
	(depending on variety)
beaten whole eggs or yolks	6 months
egg whites	12 months
milk	3-6 months
bread	6-12 months
cakes	4-6 months

If you are freezing composite dishes like stews and casseroles, or soups, try not to leave them in the freezer for more than three or four months.

Remember that if you go beyond the recommended storage times, the food may not necessarily be bad – though you are taking a chance on it – but it will probably not be worth eating.

Not everything will freeze. Most salad vegetables go limp and watery. Frozen tomatoes can only be used for cooking. Bananas turn black. Mayonnaise curdles and single cream separates. Hard-boiled eggs get leathery yolks. So don't waste money freezing anything which is not suitable.

Don't freeze things either which can be stored better in another way. Pasta will freeze, but it keeps just as well and cooks as quickly if you start straight from the packet. Its texture is better, too.

These are just some of the traps to avoid. Buy a good book on freezing – there is a large choice. They go into enormous detail and can help you use your freezer in the most economical way.

Bulk buying for your freezer

If you shop haphazardly or just buy normally at, say, your local butcher, you will certainly not save any money by having a freezer. It is essential to plan your spending. Many butchers will give you a discount for bulk sales, but there are also companies who do nothing but sell in bulk. Be careful, though. If it is beef you want make sure you are not being sold poor quality.

If your family will not look at liver and kidneys, or can't stand stews, it's no use buying big packs which include these. And, again, watch the quality before you buy. Is the meat properly trimmed? Is there too much fat? Would you be better off as far as your family's tastes are concerned if you bulk bought half a dozen legs or shoulders of lamb rather than half a sheep? These are all important considerations. Before you start on your buying, consult your family and try to tailor your purchases to their requirements.

Look carefully at any freezer food purchase plans. These can appear

113

very tempting. You may get a rent-free freezer and a certain amount of food free to start you off. But there will be snags. You may have to sign up for a long-term contract, which you may not be able to afford. You may have to contract to buy a certain amount of food every month. The minimum purchase may be too much for your needs. Again, the packs may not suit your family needs, so they turn out more expensive than they look at first sight.

In all these schemes, use extreme caution before committing yourself.

FOOD CO-OPS

A new way of saving on food bills has been growing in popularity recently – the food co-operative. When a number of people get together to buy in bulk they can save 15 to 20 per cent. To start a co-operative you need at least a dozen people and not more than about fifty, otherwise the co-op gets unmanageable. Around twenty-five is a good number.

Get together with your friends or even advertise for co-op members. Make sure you run your co-op in an orderly way. Have meetings about once a month, and keep proper books of your incomings and outgoings. Work out a cycle of ordering, buying and distribution. Charge a small membership fee to cover your distribution costs. Decide whether you will distribute from one point, or whether you can manage door-to-door deliveries.

Work out your expenses properly and be very careful that you do not underestimate them. These are the kind of savings you can then expect:

1 Meat: between 15 and 20 per cent. But be careful: co-op members will need freezers to take real advantage of bulk buying.
2 Fruit and vegetables: about 30 per cent. Once weekly buying is all you can manage here. Don't buy highly perishable vegetables, or fruit that is too ripe.
3 Cereals, pulses: about 50 per cent.
4 Eggs and dairy produce: about 15 per cent. You will need refrigeration for this.

You will not save much on frozen foods and groceries – particularly frozen food – after you allow for running costs.

Some rules to follow:

* Search around for the best discount stores. Try buying from farmers directly. Local butchers will give you a discount, but not as much as meat wholesalers.
* Find out the smallest bulk order you can get.
* Find out if you can get delivery: this is important if no member of the co-op has a large car.

* Find out if you must pay in advance.
* Find out if substandard orders can be returned.

Friends of the Earth, 9 Poland Street, London W1V 3DG (telephone 01-434 1684), have produced a useful little booklet on food co-ops. It tells you the best buys, what to look for, and how to run your co-op.

TIPS FOR SAVING WHEN BUYING FOOD

1   Plan well ahead. Work out your menus. Do not buy more than you need of perishables.
2   Avoid buying ready-made meals if possible. These can be very useful if you have to leave a hungry family to take care of itself now and again, but for ordinary family catering they are total disaster pricewise.
3   Do not be taken in by fancy packaging, or, even more so, by fancy descriptions of food. It will rarely come up to the promise on the package.
4   If you know you will have leftovers, buy things you can easily use up.
5   Do not send anyone to do your shopping for you. Do it yourself, or you will end up spending more than you have to.
6   Avoid health foods unless you are buying them for the taste. They are expensive and there is no evidence – yet – that they are better for you than ordinary food.
7   Be flexible. If beef costs too much, rework your menu, so that you can take advantage of what is cheaper. This applies to vegetables, too. It is best to buy what is in season. All of us should be able to buy a few strawberries or even asparagus when they are in season. Out of season prices may be three or four times higher, or even more. Try to avoid the beginning of the season, when prices may be at the absolute top, because the produce is so tempting.
8   Use your freezer sensibly and shop when items are in season for use later on.
9   Always check the unit cost of what you are buying, however rough your calculation is.
10 Try to work out the cost of every portion when you buy meat, fish or vegetables. If the cost per portion is too high, choose something else.
11 Try to make quality and quantity go together.
12 If you can buy by the ounce, gram or pound, you may well be able to save money. Unfortunately, because of pre-packaging, this is getting more difficult.
13 Do not buy in such quantity that your stocks will have finished

their reasonable shelf life before you get round to using them. This applies particularly to dried goods like peas, beans, lentils and barley. The fact that they do not actually go off does not mean that the flavour is not impaired by keeping them too long.

14 Buy the size which is most useful to you. Do not be too mean or too generous. One way you will be forced to open another (relatively expensive) small package, the other you will be throwing things away.

15 Look at what you are buying and compare the price with other forms of the same food. Do fresh, frozen, tinned or freeze-dried peas work out cheapest for you? As a rule frozen food is a bargain only when used in small quantities.

Know the cost of what you are buying

Packaging can be deceptive: elaborate labels, boxes, shapes and coverings can mask the real size of what you are buying – and so hide its true worth. Make sure that you are not one of the ones who are deceived in this way.

Very few people check the *unit* cost of what they are buying – this is the cost per ounce or pound, gram or kilo. By buying in quantity you can usually lower the unit cost, but not always. Rarely – but it does happen – the price per ounce or gram is higher for larger amounts, so it is wise to check before buying. This may reflect increased packaging costs.

It is a bore always having to make calculations as you go round a store, so try to memorize a few prices per pound and per kilo, so that you can do a quick check between brands and get the best bargains. You must always look for the *net* weight – the gross weight includes the packaging.

Learn to recognize the unit cost automatically. Carry a copy of the list below around with you for a time until you get used to it, or even take a small calculator with you to calculate unusual amounts. Many people – including me – do this today. Then you will know exactly what you are getting for your money.

Try at least to remember a few key amounts:

> 1 kilo is just over 2 lb.
> ½ kilo (500 grams) is just under 18 oz.
> ¼ kilo (250 grams) is just under 9 oz.
> 100 grams is rather less than ¼ lb.

Chapter 11

PERSONAL AND FAMILY PURCHASES

CLOTHES

The customer may always be right in theory, but certainly not in practice. More money is probably wasted on clothes than any other area of personal spending. That dress or suit which looked so good in the shop may be all wrong when it gets home. Nothing is lost – take it back immediately. You are entitled in law to your money back and you don't have to settle for a credit note (see section VI, chapter 2).

More often, clothes, and particularly shoes, develop faults after very little wear. If this happens, take them back. More and more shops automatically take things back today, but some still try to refer the buyer back to the manufacturer. Do not accept this. Demand your money back; it's the shop's job, not the customer's, to deal with the manufacturer who supplied the faulty item.

When you've decided what you want to buy, don't hand over your money until you have done your own quality check. Make sure, as far as you can, that you are getting value for money. Generally the more you pay the better the quality, but beware of fancy trade names where prices may be higher than the quality of tailoring justifies. Quality is in any case not always what people are looking for. Fashion garments, in particular, may be best bought cheaply and thrown away after a season. Examine shoes very carefully: there are more after sales complaints about them than anything else.

The good clothes buying guide

Decide why you want to buy. Don't pay a fortune for something you intend to keep only for a season, or, conversely, pay too little for something you will want to wear for a few years.

Make sure you buy the right size. This isn't so daft as it sounds. Even the same size can vary; one size 10 may not be the same as another. Try on whenever you can. British, Continental and American sizes are all different. Here's how they vary:

WOMEN'S CLOTHING

Dresses, Knitwear, Blouses and Lingerie

British	American	Continental (bust/hip)
32 ins (10)	8	81/86
34 ins (12)	10	86/91
36 ins (14)	12	91/96
38 ins (16)	14	96/102
40 ins (18)	16	102/107
42 ins (20)	18	107/112

Skirts

British (waist/hip in ins)	American	Continental
24/36	10	42
26/38	12	44
28/40	14	46
30/42	16	48

Stockings

British	American	Continental
8	8	0
8½	8½	1
9	9	2
9½	9½	3
10	10	4
10½	10½	5
11	11	6

MEN'S CLOTHING

Socks

British and American	Continental
9½	39
10	40
10½	41
11	42
11½	43
12	44
12½	45

Shirts

British	American	Continental
14½	2	37
15	3	38
15½	4	39
16	5	41
16½	6	42

Suits and Overcoats

British and American	Continental
36	46
38	48
40	50
42	52
44	54
46	56

Shoes (men and women)

British	American	Continental
3½	5	36
4	5½	37
4½	6	37/38
5	6½	38
5½	7	39
6	7½	39/40
6½	8	40
7	8½	40/41
7½	9	41
8	9½	42
8½	10	42/43
9	10½	43
9½	11	44
10	11½	44/45
10½	12	45
11	12½	46
11½	13	46/47
12	13½	47
12½	14	47/48
13	14½	48

Examine every garment for possible faults. Does the hem droop? Will it fall down? This is evidence of bad cutting and hasty sewing.

Are the seams skimpy? Is the sewing even? Will they split on wearing? Is there enough margin to allow alterations?

Will the buttonholes fray, the buttons fall off, or the zip break? Zips which are too light for the weight of the material, for example, will not last long.

Will the lining split because it has been too skimpily cut? This is a common fault in cheap clothes.

Will any decorations fall off in wearing, washing or dry cleaning?

Check whether a garment will wash. Dry cleaning is expensive. Many garments carry a dry cleaning label when it is perfectly possible to wash them. The manufacturer is protecting himself against deterioration in washing. If you take a chance and wash when the instructions say dry clean, you won't get anywhere if you complain.

These are all commonsense rules, but it's amazing how many people try something on, like it, and buy it without any check. It's a very English habit. In Europe people care almost as much about the inside and basic quality of the garment as about the style.

Avoiding pitfalls in shoes

As I have already said, shops get more complaints from buyers about shoes than any other article of clothing. Most shoe shops now obey the law and give you back your money, but some will try to persuade you to take a credit note instead. Do not accept this, unless there really is another pair of shoes in the shop that you like. Complaints mostly arise from 'fashion shoes', which may look substantial but quickly fall apart.

Whatever the price of shoes, you can help avoid problems if you bear in mind a few things when you are buying:

1 Make sure they fit. This is not as obvious as it sounds. Your feet change size during the day. They are smallest in the morning and largest at night. So buy about midday.

   Don't just sit down when you are trying them on. Walk about. The height of the heel or the shape of the toe can reduce comfort as you walk. Don't cram your feet into a particular size because you think it is your usual one. The same size does vary with make and style. Don't try on just one shoe. Your feet are likely to be marginally different in size.

2 Spend most money on your work or walking shoes. Save on sandals, or shoes which only match a particular outfit.

3 Choose a style that will last. This probably means not buying the height of fashion, but then your feet will still look good after the fashion has faded.

4 Remember, children's feet grow quickly. Buying at sales is a false economy if the child will then not get enough wear out of them. Up to the age of fifteen, a new size is needed every few months, and even after that, many people's feet are still growing. It is best and most economical to limit the number of shoes a child has. Otherwise he or she may end up wearing shoes that are too small because they are not worn out.

5 Only wear shoes for the purpose for which they were intended. Fashion shoes will deteriorate very quickly if worn too often in the rain. If your shoes do get wet, bring them back into shape by stuffing them with paper and letting them dry slowly away from heat.

6 Try to change your shoes once a day. Shoes get tired too and will

120

keep their shape better if you don't keep them on too long at any one time.

7　Remember, you get what you pay for. Leather is dearer than synthetic materials and it wears in a different way. Don't economize on uppers, but there is no harm in paying less because a shoe has some sort of synthetic sole and heel. Examine the shoe properly before you buy. Is it stuck or stitched together? What is the lining like?

8　Look at the name of the manufacturer and its source. If something goes wrong you are unlikely to be able to get an exact replacement for a foreign-made shoe, so you may be better off buying from a reputable British manufacturer.

9　*Always keep your receipt.*

Choosing your sewing machine

You can save an enormous amount of money by making your own clothes, and the key to success is your sewing machine. Choose the right one for your needs. There is no point in buying a complicated machine with every possible gadget that can do all sorts of embroidery if you are just going to make simple clothes.

The basic choice is between hand-operated and electric machines. Most people today choose the latter because they are less tiring to use, quicker, and easier in that you have both hands free to work the material. But if you are a beginner, hand machines run more slowly and are easier to control, and some people choose them because they don't want to be tied to an electric power point. The chances are that you will choose electric.

If you are going to do anything more than simply sew seams, it is worth paying for a few extras. If you buy a machine which only does *straight stitching* you will find it difficult to sew stretchy or knitted fabrics. A buttonholing attachment is particularly useful; a *zigzag* machine often incorporates a number of different attachments; a special presser foot means you can sew on buttons, or hem. All these are well worth buying, because the additional cost is small and an enormous amount of time can be saved. Unless you think you will do quilting, smocking, cording, gathering, etc. – and not many people do – don't buy those attachments.

All machines on the market will sew competently for you, but designs vary a lot. Look for the following:

*　The light: it is better to have one above the needleplate.
*　The case: some are easier to carry than others.
*　The weight: if you will want to carry your machine around, don't buy one which is too heavy. Heavier is not necessarily better.

121

* Be sure you have extra bobbins, spare needles and any other bits and pieces.
* Check the guarantee. You should get five years on the machine and two on the motor and foot control.

Finally, make sure you have a demonstration before you buy. The specialist sewing machine shops may be most helpful, but you may find that you can get a discount in an ordinary shop or department store.

Having bought your machine, have it serviced now and again. Sewing machines are tough, but they run more easily for a little oiling and care.

FURNITURE

The kind of furniture you buy for your home is largely a matter of personal taste. No one can decide for anyone else what is or is not a good buy. There are, however, a few guidelines you should take into account, whatever style you choose.

Make a proper buying plan. Few people can afford to buy a whole house full of furniture in one go. Work out how much you can afford on hire purchase and do not go over your limit. Decide what is essential and buy that first. With some items it is best to pay for as good a quality as you can possibly afford. This applies in particular to beds. You will spend a third of your life in bed, so you might as well do it in as much comfort as possible.

You will be surprised how few things you need to get your house looking like a home. A bed, chest of drawers, settee, table and chairs and you are off. Put everything in the same room if necessary at the beginning to make it look lived in. Make it look individually yours with a few lamps, cushions, pictures and mirrors. Above all, do not be tricked into over-extending yourself to impress your family or neighbours.

If you really do not have much money to spend, buy as cheaply as possible and rely entirely on these accessories to give the rooms their own, and your, character.

And if you have very small children, do not buy expensive furniture anyway, unless you have a special room for the children to do their destruction in, or actually do not mind your furniture being ruined. You cannot expect a small child to appreciate the value of your treasured object.

Do not buy anything until you have inspected it thoroughly. Bounce on the bed, lean back hard in the chairs, wooden or soft, to see if they can take it, make sure a table you may have to work at is a comfortable height. Do not buy an 'easy' chair that is not easy and comfortable to sit in just because it looks attractive.

Be especially careful when buying carpets. These are often offered as 'bargains', which they may well not be. Cheap carpets are often not hardwearing. Check the fibre content before you buy. Wool is the most expensive and hardwearing but it must be mothproofed. Nylon and acrylic are less resilient and easy to clean.

Try to imagine everything in its setting in your home. What looks nice in a showroom may be totally unsuitable for your room. Think about the size. Is it too small for your rooms, too big, or the wrong shape?

If you will be moving soon, buy as cheaply as possible in case some things do not fit into your new home.

Re-upholstery. Before you consider getting your furniture re-upholstered, find out what you will really save. If it is not much and the actual structure of your settee is showing signs of wear and tear, you might be better off in the long run buying a new one.

If you are going to re-upholster, get several estimates; they can vary tremendously. If you have a lot to do, consider doing it yourself. You can enquire with your local authority about classes, or, if you are naturally handy, there are many easy-to-follow books.

Delivery. Use your connections to get discounts. But if you use a discount store, check that its prices item for item are genuinely cheaper, because you may find you have to pay for delivery.

Delivery can be a problem, but do not let the store bully you. Ask when delivery is and make sure that they stick to the date. If there is any sign of doubt about delivery, shop around a little. Most items of furniture are similarly priced wherever you shop. Go to the firm which offers the best delivery terms.

MAIL ORDER

Buying on mail order may save you money (see chapter 4 of this section). Branded goods bought this way may be cheaper, quality for quality, than those bought in shops, though non-branded goods are usually dearer. The customer can also save on expensive shopping trips, particularly if he or she lives out of town. But there are snags:

* The customer cannot examine the product until he takes delivery, when it may well not come up to expectations.
* There is nothing to be gained from paying cash, as the quoted prices are always credit prices and there is no discount for cash.
* Delivery can take a long time, sometimes too long, and the product may be no use when it finally arrives.

Taking the following precautions will save you both disappointment and money.

1 Make sure you fill in the form correctly – a lot of people don't. Have you ordered the right size, quantity, colour, etc?

123

2 Order well in advance and allow at least a month for delivery – more at Christmas, especially if you are buying gifts.

3 Look at the conditions attached to the sale. Is there a guarantee? What are the money-back terms?

4 Don't rely on any illustration in an advertisement or a brochure. Read the description – its weight, colour, size, contents. If anything is missing, don't buy.

5 Don't pay cash if you can avoid it. A cheque can always be stopped. But you cannot get a refund (unless the mail order firm is prepared to give you one) if you use a credit card when you are buying.

6 Examine the product as soon as it arrives to make sure the contents are as stated.

7 If you want to send the product back, do so immediately. Give your reasons in a letter attached to the parcel. Keep a copy of your letter.

8 Use only reliable mail order companies. If you buy through a national newspaper you have some protection at least on delivery. The papers have a fund which reimburses people who do not receive the goods they ordered or get their money back.

You must claim within three months of making your order, and the fund covers only undelivered goods. If you have a quarrel with the company over quality, you must take it up direct with them.

Remember, you have the same protection and rights in law if you shop by mail order as you do with personal shopping.

SEASONAL BUYS

If you do not have to buy at any particular time, you can often save a lot by buying at certain times of the year.

You may not wish to buy your clothes in the sales if you are very fashion-conscious, but in this 'anything goes' era for clothing being up-to-the-minute is less important than it was previously. In any case, you can buy underwear, tights, socks and children's clothing in the sales.

Sometimes buying in bulk – three pairs of socks in one pack, for instance – will save money. If this is not possible, wait for the cheap 'season' to buy whatever you want. Shops and stores like to keep trade moving in months when people would not normally buy, and they also need to clear their stocks to make way for new designs.

Garden furniture comes cheaper at the *end* of the summer, not the beginning. Fridges may be cheaper in the winter. Central heating can often be installed at bargain prices in the summer. When you are buying, think whether you could buy more cheaply if you waited a few months. I cannot give a totally exhaustive list, but here are a few items and the cheapest months to buy them:

product	time to buy
bedding	winter and summer sales
bikinis	summer sales from July onwards
blankets	late winter
camping equipment	late summer
clothing	
spring	summer sales
summer	summer sales
autumn	winter sales
winter	winter sales
crockery	winter and summer sales
seconds	any time
Christmas presents	any month except December
domestic appliances	
fridges	winter sales
cookers	winter and summer sales
washing machines	winter and summer sales
dishwashers	winter and summer sales
furniture	winter sales particularly
furs	June to September
gardening equipment	August and September
home furnishing	winter and summer sales
ski wear and equipment	March
toys	January and February

This short list shows that the best time to buy is generally the time when most people are not buying. It makes sense to think about whether what you are buying has a 'low' season and take advantage of it.

CUTTING THE COST OF YOUR ENTERTAINMENT

Entertainment at home

We all need some relaxation in our lives and most of us have it, even if it is only the *television*. One thing to be said for television is that it is cheap to run. If you watch it for four hours a night that will take up most of your leisure time and will cost about 1p an hour for colour or ½p for black and white – excluding the cost of buying or renting. Spread that among a family and it is highly unlikely that you will find any form of relaxation cheaper, apart from walking, and even that uses shoe leather.

When you include the cost of buying, say, a 22-inch colour television set, which lasts you for five years and costs little in repair, the cost of an

125

hour's viewing will rise to between 8p and 10p an hour, depending on where you buy your set. If you get it at a discount warehouse or store the price is likely to be more than 25 per cent less than in an ordinary store.

Or you may rent your set. If this is a black and white one, you may well pay less than 50p a week, particularly if you have had a long contract. This way you have no repair bills to think about, and if the set breaks down totally it will be replaced by the rental company.

But renting has been less attractive since the advent of colour television. Weekly rentals can be as high as £2-£3 per week, and if you are going to keep your set for more than two years, which is likely, you will be better off in the long run buying.

If *music* is your hobby, you will need rather more expert advice on record and cassette equipment than I am able to give. Try to get this for nothing. Go round several stores, describe your needs and accommodation, and decide what equipment you would like. Then buy at a discount.

A good stereo system costs about ½p an hour to run, without taking into account your buying costs, or the cost of records or cassettes, whichever you are using. Listening to music is therefore a much more expensive hobby than watching television.

It is a good idea to buy hi-fi units separately, but you must expect to pay about £50 for the deck arm and cartridge, really good speakers may cost up to £100 each, and amplifiers about £70.

Cost this out over a period of, say, five years, assume you are buying a dozen records a year and listening for about ten hours a week, and you will find that the overall cost comes close to 20p an hour. The more you use it, the lower the average cost per hour.

Entertainment outside the home

If you think the figures above are high, think what entertainment outside the home might cost an average family in a week.

parents:
one night a week at the cinema   £2

or the theatre   £4

one meal out each week   £10

mother:
two nights' bingo (say £2 a night)   £4

father:
one night at the pub   £2.50

children:

dancing lessons	£1 (each)
piano lessons	£1.50 (each)
going to football match	50p–£1 (each)

A family doing all this is likely to be paying out between £18 and £23 a week on family entertainment. Not many of us can afford that much.

Drinking at home

If you confine your drinking to your home you will certainly save money. Pub and bar prices have a service element built into them. If the brand you buy does not particularly bother you shop around various wine merchants. You may find the following discounts:

liqueurs and sherry	up to 40%
port and wine	up to 30%
beer	up to 25%
vermouth, vodka, and rum	up to 15%
gin and whisky	up to 10%

It is also worth looking in your supermarket: the brands they have on offer are more limited, but often cheaper. They occasionally have own brands too, which are sometimes, though not always, cheap. Do not buy these bulk, however, until you have tried one bottle to see if you like the taste.

This is particulary important with wine. Today anything only a little over £1 a bottle is usually rubbish. It is impossible to sell a decent bottle of wine at such a price and make a profit. This is how the price of a three-quarter litre bottle of claret builds up:

duty	57p
transport	7p
bottling labels	16p
overheads	18p
VAT	6p
	——
total	£1.04

You can see from this that, even if you pay only 6p for the wine and the grower's profit, you will have to pay £1.10 a bottle. At £1.30 you get 26p's worth of wine as the overheads will be the same, so the quality of wine can rise quite sharply after the basic costs are covered.

Costing your sporting activities

This book is not the place to go through every sport working out the possible costs you may face if you are to take it seriously. But before you embark on what could be an expensive pastime here are some questions you should ask yourself:

1   Have you got the time to take it seriously, or would it interfere with your other activities?
2   Just what, if anything, will it cost each time you play?
3   What are the transport costs involved in getting to and from the venue? Are they prohibitive?
4   What will equipment cost?
5   Will it involve you in a lot of expensive socializing after the match or game is over?
6   Is it dangerous? If so, have you got yourself properly insured?
7   Is it so expensive that it would virtually prevent any other member of your family taking up any sport or activity they would like?

These questions may seem trivial at first glance, but any hobby once taken up seriously can be difficult to give up. When times are hard, resentment can build up in a family which sees money going in one direction when other members feel it could be better used elsewhere. Always discuss your hobby and what it will mean in time and money with your family.

Chapter 12

INSURING YOUR HOME AND YOUR POSSESSIONS

INSURING YOUR HOME

Once you have bought your home, you should insure it even before you set foot inside the door. In fact you should do it as soon as contracts are exchanged. If you are buying on a mortgage, the insurance company or building society will insist that you insure it for at least as much as the original mortgage they allow you.

Previously you had no choice over the insurance company; the building society would simply include the annual premium in your mortgage repayments, so that there would be no question of the policy lapsing. Now you have some choice, but there is so little to choose between the bigger insurance companies that it is not worth making a fuss about it.

The lender may wish you to insure your home for rather more than the amount of your mortgage, or indeed for more than you have paid for the house. This is because he is basically insuring himself against the total destruction of the building. He will want to be sure that if this happens there is enough insurance money to replace the building. He may reckon that this will cost far more than the amount of the mortgage and set the insured value accordingly. This will be the value of the house, not the land on which it stands.

You need not insure your house for its market price; that includes the site. But take care, because the market value is often *less* than the cost of rebuilding.

If you are buying your house for cash, you should make the same calculations. If you own the freehold, you will have the land no matter what happens, but the cost of rebuilding your house will rise steadily with inflation. For this reason you should steadily adjust the amount for which the house is insured as time goes on.

Even if you have some insurance via your mortgage, it is worth considering taking out additional cover yourself on the building. If you are renting property, check to see if the landlord has arranged the house insurance. If not, do it yourself to safeguard your position.

How to go about it

1 Sit down with a reliable local insurance agent and talk the matter through. He will have a good idea of basic values in the area and will be able to advise you. He will take into account the exact location and condition of your house. A swimming pool or garage would obviously add to the value of a house, for instance. If you do not know an insurance agent, ask your bank or solicitor to help you. Or try the local Citizens' Advice Bureau.

2 If the house is new, get the builders to give you some sort of estimate of its replacement cost. It may well be more than their costs, even if the house has only just been completed.

3 If you have bought from someone else, try to find out if you can what they had the house insured for. If they had lived in the house for some time, however, it is highly likely that they were under-

insured – most people are – so use their estimate of value only as a starting point.

4   If all else fails, call in a surveyor and ask for his estimate of the value. While you are doing this you can also have the contents of your house professionally valued, which will be a help when it comes to insuring them.

Once you have decided on the value you are ready to go ahead with the insurance. Your policy will be basically a replacement policy for the whole house, but it will also cover you for minor damage from burst pipes, leaking roofs, etc. For small jobs, however, the lessor or owner of a property may be required to pay the first £15 of damage himself.

Check with your building society to see that the value for insurance purposes is adequate, then keep the insured value of your house up-to-date all the time. If the insurance company feel you have under-insured they may scale down any claims you make, even for minor damage. Some policies today are index-linked. Get one if you can, then you are safe. .

Do not make trivial claims. If the insurer gets several from you every year – particularly if, say, your roof always seems to be leaking, or your pipes bursting – he may well put up your premium.

What your policy can cover

Although most policies give the same kind of cover, there is actually no standard house insurance policy. Though they may make certain exceptions, or load the premiums in certain locations – if you live in an area known to be subject to flooding, for example, you will probably have to pay more than normal for that risk – most insurers will cover the following:

1   Fire, lightning, explosions or earthquakes. These can all happen in Britain. In 1976, for instance, there were many claims for earth tremors, if not for quakes.
2   The escape of water or oil from a water or heating installation. This includes such things as burst pipes.
3   Aircraft or car damage. This is becoming increasingly important, and many people, since the advent of supersonic aircraft, are trying to cover themselves against any damage sonic booms could do to their houses. This is particularly important if you are on a known flight path, though there have been some difficulties so far in proving that broken windows or cracks in the wall were caused by sonic booms.
4   Riots or malicious damage. Obviously this is more important in

some areas of the country than in others. The centres of big towns are the most prone to this kind of damage.

5 Storms or flood. We know all about these in Britain, but is this cover enough? Check your drought cover. The summers of 1975 and 1976 have shown that we can have droughts, and these can lead to serious damage. Drought can cause subsidence, leading to cracking walls. In the autumn and winter of 1976-77 many insurance companies had more claims for leaking roofs, because of the cracking and shifting of tiles due to the long drought, than ever before.

6 Theft. Burglars rarely steal a house (it has been known) but it is remotely possible that you may have an integral part of your house stolen.

You can see from what I have said that your house insurance policy can cover most contingencies. As far as burst pipes, floods, riots or malicious damage are concerned, the householder will usually be required to pay the first £15 of damage. If you want to avoid even this payment, your policy will probably cost you an extra £4 a year. You can also increase your cover to allow for further items, say, damage from falling trees. If you decide you want to be covered for 'all risks', most insurers will give you this for a slightly higher premium.

Normal house insurance is not dear. It is set at a maximum of 12½p for every £100 worth of house. This means that if your house is worth £10,000 you will only pay £12.50 a year to insure it, or £25 for £20,000.

Subsidence cover

Most risks are well-known, but from time to time new ones arise and the householder may then discover that he is not covered for them. One such instance is subsidence, which can cause minor or quite severe damage to a house. Areas of subsidence are well charted and include not only natural geological areas of subsidence, but also those created by old mine workings or other manmade underground activity.

In normal weather circumstances it has always been thought that at most one per cent of British homes would be liable to subsidence. The percentage was so small that it was not until 1970 that insurers provided cover for subsidence at all, and then it was included in the general policy. This meant that many householders were insured against a risk they did not face.

The dry summers of 1975 and 1976 changed all that. Many thousands of claims for damages have come into the insurance companies, from minor cracking and leaks to the severe sinking of a whole house. To cut down the costs to themselves of such claims insurers have been writing what are called 'excess clauses' into their policies to cover subsidence.

131

Most insurers now require householders to pay the first £150 of any subsidence claim, or 3 per cent (sometimes as much as 5 per cent) of the sum insured, whichever is greater. This means that if your house is insured for £10,000 you will have to pay the first £300 of the bill, £600 at £20,000.

This presents a dilemma for many householders: if they increase the value of their overall insurance to keep pace with inflation and make sure that their cover for, say, fire damage is adequate, they are at the same time putting themselves at the risk of having to contribute far more than they can afford if they are forced to put in a subsidence claim.

So far the insurance companies have not yet come up with a solution to this problem. All the householder can do is raise his insurance to keep up with inflation if he is pretty sure he is in an area which is not subject to subsidence. However, if he lives in one that is, he must balance the chances of finding himself inadequately insured should there be a fire against the more likely eventuality of having a smaller bill for subsidence damage. Not a pleasant choice to have to make.

Problems like this come up all the time in insurance, so you should pay constant attention to your house insurance. Not only do replacement costs rise, but the actual incidence of various forms of damage changes. Do not be caught out with a totally inadequate policy.

INSURING YOUR POSSESSIONS

Once you have got your home adequately insured, you must look to its contents. Remember that insuring your possessions is entirely your responsibility. They will not be covered by your house insurance. If, for example, you have a burst pipe which damages your carpets, your house insurance policy will cover you for the damage to the fabric of the building and the repair itself, but any replacement for the carpet or the cost of any cleaning will have to come from the policy on your possessions.

If you are arranging all the insurance yourself, however, contents can sometimes be included in an extras section. The rates for the two types of insurance are different, but there is the advantage of having only one premium to pay if you can have everything dealt with in the same policy.

The first steps

First of all, make an inventory of all your possessions. This means furniture, domestic appliances, pots and pans, curtains, carpets – everything. Work out what they all cost you and what you would have to pay to replace them. Break down the list into several sections:

1   Normal household furniture and equipment.

2 Pictures, antiques and anything else with no simple replacement value. If necessary take photographs of these. They may be useful to show to the police or your insurers in the case of burglary or fire damage. Get a professional valuation on anything particularly valuable.

3 Any very valuable items like paintings, furs, jewellery, or watches. These should be insured separately. It is highly unlikely that you would be able to persuade your insurer to give you the full value of a £500 diamond ring, if it was lost or stolen, unless it was separately insured in a list vetted by the insurer, and the premium for that part of the policy calculated accordingly.

When you have added up the value of everything you have, you will probably be surprised at what it amounts to. Get as much of it into the one insurance policy as possible, although, as I've mentioned above, very valuable items may need their own policy. If the premium is too high for you to pay in one lump, the insurance company may be prepared to let you pay half-yearly or quarterly.

When your list is complete, put one copy away safely then take another to the insurance agent or broker, or the insurance company if you are dealing with them direct.

The cover provided by different companies can vary considerably. It might be sensible, therefore, to use an insurance broker, who would be able to look at all the possibilities available and find the one that suits you best.

Remember, your insurance needs may change. As you add to your possessions, whether they are personal belongings or part of your family home, include them on your insurance.

How much cover do you need?

You may be able to get a single 'all risks' policy for everything you have, but this is likely to be extremely expensive. It is generally more economical to split your belongings into sections.

1 *Your normal belongings.* These can be insured at the standard rate of 25p per £100. You can include quite valuable items in this, like antique furniture, Persian carpets, etc., if the overall total makes full allowance for them. You should, however, mention them specifically when you take out your insurance, or you may find that you get only a proportion of the value when you make a claim.

The standard form of insurance policy will probably have certain restrictions on it, regardless of the total value. It may only cover the loss of money up to a certain amount, say £50, or 5 per cent of the total sum which you have insured. All your jewellery and other personal effects like furs may be regarded as not worth more than one-third of the total sum insured. 'Wear and tear' will be taken off before you get the amount of a claim. If you have been using an armchair for fifteen years and it gets burned beyond repair, it is highly unlikely that you will receive the full replacement cost.

If you want to cover yourself for full replacement costs, regardless of the age and condition of your effects, you may be able to take out a policy which allows this. If you do, you will have to insure for the full cost of replacing everything in the house. Consider very carefully whether this would be worthwhile: in not too many years the total of the premiums may well add up to more than any expected benefit from the replacement of one particular item.

2 *Belongings which have a particular value.* Could be a piece of furniture, or a picture, but more often single items of jewellery or watches, cameras and other equipment which you might carry around with you, including some items of clothing. These are commonly insured at a higher rate under 'all risks'. You may be able to get a worldwide 'all risks' policy, which means that wherever you go you can take these items with you secure in the knowledge that if they get damaged or stolen they will be replaced.

Try to get an 'agreed value' for all these items, because once something is lost it may be difficult to reach any agreement. You may need a receipt. If you have not got one, say, when you have been given a present of jewellery, get a jeweller to give you a professional valuation. When you have arrived at a total value for everything you want to insure, add on a little more to cover anything you may have forgotten, and anything else you may buy during the coming year.

You may be able to cover damage or loss of clothes under your 'all risks' policy, but you will generally have to pay the first £5 or more of any such loss on the wear and tear principle. It is, of course, always possible to get these insured separately. If you are a professional entertainer, for example, you will probably have to pay a fairly high premium, not only because your clothes are worth a lot, but also because you travel around a great deal and therefore expose them to greater risk of damage or theft.

What your policy will not cover

Now you may think you are completely protected, but even 'all risks' does not cover everything. Certain mishaps are excluded:

1 The breakage of anything brittle, unless it is done by thieves, or fire. If you are dusting your Ming vase and drop it, the insurers will not pay a replacement value for it. On the other hand, if you drop your non-waterproof watch in the bath and it stops, you

134

could then argue that the damage was caused by 'external means'. Whether your claim was met would depend upon the particular insurance company.

2 Damage caused by moths or vermin. Try to mothproof anything which may need it, and make sure that your possessions are as safe as it is possible to be from rats or mice.

3 Breakdown, gradual deterioration, or wear and tear. An insurance policy does not mean that you will never have to replace things; you will when they break down or wear out. The idea is to replace anything lost by accident, whether through theft, fire or sudden damage caused in any other way.

What it will cost

Normal cover for your household belongings is not very expensive; it costs about twice as much as cover for the building. You should be able to get most things covered for 25p for each £100 worth. This means that if you have £2,000 worth of furniture and equipment, you can insure them for £5 a year.

The 25p rate covers most of the country, but if you live in the centre of a big town and particularly the centre of London you are likely to find yourself paying more. This is because insurers believe – and the crime statistics confirm this belief – that theft is more common in city centres. Theft is the biggest area for claims, yet another reason why it is a good idea to have photographs of as many of your valuable items as possible.

You may also find yourself paying a slightly higher premium if you live in one of those fashionable and expensive areas outside towns which are such a natural magnet for thieves – for example, the so-called 'stockbroker belts'. If you live in such an area your insurance company may want to inspect your house to satisfy itself that it is adequately burglar-proofed.

If you keep making claims for thefts, the company may well refuse to continue to insure you unless you change to better locks, put gates across your windows, or install a burglar alarm. If you go to another company, they may well ask you how many times you have been robbed and stipulate the same conditions before they agree to insure you. If you have a great deal of jewellery, you may be asked to keep a safe in the house, or, if it is extremely valuable, to leave it in the bank for safe keeping.

It is impossible to set out any rate, or even an average rate, for the cost of an 'all risks' policy. It will depend on who you are, where you live, the sort of life you lead, your job, the particular type of item you are insuring and the total value of everything you have on 'all risks'. It is likely to be most expensive (yet again) if you live in London or any large city, or if the total insured is extremely large.

Making your claim

You are entitled to claim when anything is lost or destroyed, damaged, or stolen.

Inform your insurers right away. In the case of anything lost or stolen, inform the police immediately too, particularly if you discover the loss at night or in the evening when it is not possible to contact the insurers for some hours.

Do not touch anything until the extent of the damage has been seen by the insurers. You can only do essential repairs before informing the insurance company if by so doing you can prevent the damage from getting worse. For example, you could repair a burst pipe to prevent it from damaging your carpets still further.

If you have any doubts about getting an agreed value, you should employ an assessor. He will be able to haggle with the insurance company on your behalf. But you will have to pay his fee out of your own pocket.

You will have to fill in a claim form. Then the insurer may pay up, or he may wish to inspect the damage for himself before deciding what, or whether, to pay out on your claim. They do not always come themselves and may send an 'independent adjuster' to negotiate the claim with you.

Do not be surprised if, when the adjuster arrives, he tells you that you are under-insured. As I have said elsewhere, this is almost inevitable if you have kept your insurance at the same level for a number of years. Making a claim from your insurance company is one way – the hard way – of finding out you really are under-insured.

Chapter 13

ASSURANCE AT ALL TIMES

Most people's mistake when they come to insure themselves is that they do it too late. When they are sick, they suddenly discover that they could have covered themselves for periods away from work. When they get round to thinking about life insurance they all too often find that they have missed the best terms.

So sit down early – in your twenties – particularly if you are a man and married, and consider whether you have insured yourself properly against accident or sickness and whether you have adequately catered for your dependents in the unfortunate event of your unexpected death.

If nothing happens, and you have insured yourself properly, you will have acquired an easy way of saving with tax relief.

There is a difference between *assurance,* which covers something that will definitely happen some time, and *insurance,* protection against something which may or may not happen. This chapter deals mainly with assurance.

DIFFERENT KINDS OF LIFE POLICY

A straight life policy is called a *whole life* policy. You pay premiums every week, month or year for the rest of your life and the insurance company pays your heirs the sum assured after your death. The sum assured is agreed between the insurance company and the customer at the time the contract is taken out. There are two other kinds of policy which are now far more popular with the public than whole life:

1   *Term assurance.* You pay premiums for a fixed number of years – this is unlikely to be less than ten years, but may be a very long period. If you die during this period your heirs will be paid the sum assured. If you survive until after the term has ended, it pays out nothing.

2   *Endowment policies.* These give the best of both worlds. You pay premiums for a fixed number of years. If you live until the end of the period, you receive the sum assured. If you die while you are still making payments, the money will go to your heirs. These policies can be 'with profits' or without.

With profits policies cost more, but if you can afford the premiums you will get far more out than you put in if you survive the term, or your heirs will get the amount of profits credited until the point at which you die. 'With profits' simply means that each year the insurance company gives you some of the profit it makes from investing your premiums.

Most people do not think of *annuities* as insurance, but they are the same as whole life insurance policies in reverse. Instead of paying premiums until you die, you pay a cash sum to begin with and then you are paid a certain agreed sum of money at fixed intervals until you die. Then the annuity usually dies with you.

So that you understand what you are getting when you insure, let's look at some of the possible benefits:

1   First and foremost you can protect your family from financial hardship in the event of your death. You can do this by providing for some form of regular income, or a lump sum payment. If you are buying your house on a mortgage you probably already have an insurance policy which will repay your mortgage if you die when it is still outstanding.

2   You can save regularly for a nest-egg which matures when you retire, or provides a lump sum if you die first.

137

3　If your policy has been running some time, you can use it as security for a loan from your bank.

4　You can gear your endowment policies to mature at certain points in your life – when your children go to secondary school, when they leave school at sixteen, to pay for their further education, or even, if you want to splash out in a big way, for their wedding.

5　The maturing of an endowment policy can be an excellent wedding gift to your child (but beware capital transfer tax – see section V, chapter 1).

6　You can save tax. The government allows you to offset *part* of your insurance premiums against tax. At present this is 17½ per cent of the total premiums. From the financial year 1979-80 the system is to be changed in an attempt to make tax collection simpler. Then you will no longer have your premiums set as a tax allowance against your earnings; instead you will be able to pay premiums up to £1,500 to the insurance company after tax deductions, and they will have to get the money back in bulk from the Inland Revenue.

Whether you go for whole life, term or endowment policies, there are some differences within each type.

*　If the policy cover remains unchanged throughout its life, it is known as *level term.*

*　If the policy includes an option to change it later into a more valuable policy of the same kind, or even a different one, it is called *convertible.*

*　If the sum assured declines steadily to vanish at the end, it is known as *decreasing.*

*　If the sum assured is to be paid out in regular instalments in the event of the policy holder's death, rather than in a lump sum, it is called *family income.*

WHAT KIND OF ASSURANCE DO YOU NEED?

Whole life

Whole life insurance is suitable for anyone who wishes to leave his family or heirs with a lump sum when he dies. This will usually be a married man with children.

One problem is that the premiums must be paid until death, and after retirement it may become difficult to keep them up. You can get round this by taking out a *limited payment policy,* under which you pay full premiums until retirement, after which they stop.

With profit policies are dearer than straight policies, but you can take out something called a *decreasing whole life with profits policy.* The premiums are calculated as if the sum assured actually decreased over

138

the years. This does not happen, because the with profits bonus payments more than make up the gap. Eventually the sum assured reaches rock bottom and the decreasing period ends. You then stop paying premiums and the policy begins to appreciate in value rapidly.

The snag about whole life is that you can never touch the money yourself. If you have a policy for, say, fifty years, you may begin to think that you could have saved or invested the money more profitably somewhere else, particularly if inflation has eaten away at the true value of the sum assured. It is, however, not a particularly expensive form of assurance.

Term

This is the way of getting the biggest cover for the least outlay. You never get any money if you survive the term. People who do dangerous jobs or engage in dangerous sports often use term insurance as a means of getting high cover at comparatively low cost.

It is also popular with many people who have mortgages, especially the *decreasing term* type, more commonly known as a mortgage protection policy, when a decreasing sum is assured as you pay off your mortgage. A building society may even insist that you take out this kind of policy for the period of your mortgage. It is an additional security for them. There are varieties on the basic term policy: sometimes you may even get a paid-up whole life policy at the end of the term, or a cash payment.

Obviously this sort of insurance is suitable in some cases and some situations, but it's not in the end much use to anyone unless the policyholder dies before the term ends.

Endowment

Quite rightly, endowment with-profits policies are the most popular in the United Kingdom today. They are quite expensive, but they provide the policy-holder with a means of protecting his dependents in the event of his death and also with the prospect of being able to enjoy the money should he survive the full term.

The with-profits element can be most attractive, and may even mean that the policyholder gets double the sum assured. If you have read the chapter on mortgages, you will know that this kind of policy is most popular with building societies when they are arranging a mortgage. The policy is used as additional security for the loan.

Endowment with-profits policies are also the basis of most equity and any other linked contract investment schemes (see section V, chapter 5). What happens is that part of the money paid each month by the investor goes into an insurance policy which protects the saver.

Endowment policies come in all sorts of forms and for all sorts of purposes. Education policies have been growing in popularity in recent years. The parent pays premiums, usually but not always and not necessarily linked to the father's life, which guarantee that an agreed sum for a child's education will be paid for in the event of the parent's death, or that an agreed sum will be provided for an agreed number of years, when it is needed. As the policy is activated, the premiums rise. These policies vary enormously in what they offer. If you are thinking of taking one out, there are two rules you should always follow:

1 Take out the policy as soon after the child is born as possible.
2 Gear your premiums to much higher school fees than at the time you take out the policy. Fees have risen enormously in recent years, and what looks adequate today may be a mere flea-bite in a few years time (see section III, chapter 2).

Grandparents can also take out endowment policies to benefit their grandchildren. They insure themselves against dying before the child, and the policy ends when the child comes of age with either a cash payment or a fully paid-up life policy.

Endowments are very attractive to many people, but they can seem relatively expensive in the initial stages. If you are forced to surrender your policy before it matures (see later in this chapter) the cost can be high, so be sure that, unless something totally unforeseen happens, you can meet your commitments.

Annuities

When you buy an annuity you are taking a gamble on how long you will live. It is the reverse of the gamble you take when you take out a life assurance policy. You pay a capital sum to give you a regular income until you die: the older you are when you buy the annuity the higher the income in return for your capital payment the insurance company will be prepared to pay you.

As men have a shorter life expectancy than women, they usually get a slightly higher income at the same age than women. The longer you survive, the greater your chance of making a profit, though it always takes some years at least before you recover the capital sum that you have paid out. How long this takes will depend on your age when you take the annuity out.

There are various types of annuities:

* Guaranteed annuities, which give some form of capital repayment on death as well as lifetime income.
* Immediate annuities, where you pay a lump sum and start

receiving the income six months later, and afterwards in half-yearly instalments.

* Deferred annuities, which you buy before you wish the payments to begin. These are bought on an instalment basis, and may include a cash option as well as income.
* Joint survivorship annuities, which are for husband and wife together. When one partner dies the amount of the annual annuity usually falls by about a third.
* Minimum annuities, which guarantee a fixed income for a certain number of years, usually five. At the end of that period the person who holds the annuity has the option of a cash payment instead of continuing with the annual income. This is useful if you suspect that you may be able to get a better deal five years later, if annuity rates have risen.
* Reversionary annuities are another form of joint annuity. They can be taken out by someone who wishes to assure an income for a companion if he or she dies. If the purchaser dies first the companion gets the annuity, but if the companion dies first the annuity dies.

Annuities are useful because they provide attractive tax concessions which vary and would not be available if you simply invested your capital sum and lived on the income from it. With annuities you can usually get double the income you might get from investing in the stock market.

HOW MUCH ASSURANCE DO YOU NEED?

There is no fixed amount for you to aim at in the matter of assurance. If you are a young man or woman with no ties and responsibilities, you may well feel that the business of assuring your life can wait. And you may well be right. But once you are married with responsibilities you will need some kind of assurance to protect your dependents.

Many women feel that they need not concern themselves with assurance, but their death can bring considerable financial hardship to a family, particularly today when many wives work and the overall standard of living of many families is dependent to some extent on the wife's income. For this reason a married couple should plan their assurance together.

If you still need convincing, one of the major assurance companies has produced the following facts: 7,000 married women under the age of forty-five die each year in Britain. This means they are still likely to have children living at home. Yet only one in four wives is assured in any way at all. You could try, for example, to get joint life assurance on your mortgage. Discuss all these aspects with your broker when deciding what level of joint cover you need.

First of all, decide what income the surviving partner will need if the other dies. If it is the woman who is left, she is unlikely to be earning as much as her husband, or may not be earning at all, and will need to replace her husband's income as nearly as possible. A surviving man may not need so much, but it is wise to remember that if life is to be at all manageable some extra help in the home will probably be necessary – and it generally costs more than a wife.

Second, calculate your outstanding commitments should you die and try to make sure that any money coming from the insurance company will cover them. Additionally, you may want to insure your children's education and a variety of other projects.

All the time take care not to commit too high a proportion of your total income to assurance. We are nearly all worth more dead, but it is foolish to make life miserable just to ensure that this is the case.

Here is the sort of life assurance programme that the Life Offices' Association and the Associated Scottish Life Offices suggest that a man should follow through various stages of his life, from marriage to retirement:

First step: age 25 (newly married: intending to start a family)

Take out	Premiums	Cover provided
(a) Whole life policy, with profits, premiums to cease at age 65	£45 a year	£2,000
(b) Mortgage protection policy to cover £7,500 building society loan repayable over 30 years	£12 a year	£7,500 initially
(c) Family income benefit policy for £1,000 a year for remainder of 25 years	£18 a year	£25,000 initially (£1,000 a year for 25 years)
Total	£75	

Next step: age 35 (budget allows more savings)

Take out		New cover
An endowment assurance policy with profits payable at age 65	£100 a year	£2,000
Previous policies (above) cost	£75 a year	
Total	£175	

Third step: age 43 (eldest son leave school)

Take out	Premiums	Cover provided *New cover*
A second endowment policy payable at age 65	£120 a year	£2,000
Previous policies now costing	£175 a year	
Total	£295	

Retirement: age 65

Endowment assurances mature for payment ·	No further premiums payable	Benefits received (including bonuses)
		£5,000 first endowment assurance; £3,000 second endowment assurance;
		£8,000 cash payment
		Remaining cover £4,400 whole life policy (including bonuses)

Notes

1 The man for whom this programme was planned could look forward to a regular income on retirement from his employer's occupational pension scheme.
2 The actual cost to the policyholder is of course less than the figures given here, the precise amounts depending on the amount of tax relief to which he is entitled on his pay.
3 Premiums and bonus rates can vary a great deal from office to office. The above figures are only examples to show how a programme may be arranged.
4 Bonuses on the with profits policies have been estimated below current rates: the amounts actually payable will depend on future profits.

Copies of a booklet explaining this plan are available from LOA-/ASLO Information Centre, 60 Cheapside, London EC2V 6AX.

SURRENDERING A POLICY

I cannot repeat too often that you must take care not to overload yourself with assurance. If you have to give up a policy before it has run its course you will find that the penalties are severe, especially with a savings-linked or life endowment policy. Many people make the mistake of over-committing themselves, only to find that they cannot keep the payments up. *Nearly half the life assurance policies taken out are given up within ten years of starting,* long before the policies have matured.

When a policy actually acquires a surrender value varies from company to company, and you should check this before taking your policy out. Some policies acquire a surrender value after the very first payment, but most companies insist that you pay for a minimum of two or three years before the policy gets a surrender value, and some companies may make the policyholder wait as long as five years.

Let's consider a man of thirty taking out a with-profits policy for £10,000, maturing after fifteen years. The annual premium is £698, though the real outgoing is less because of tax relief.

Surrender after two years and a payment of £1,396 in premiums will bring him a repayment of only £912; after five years the figures are £3,490 and £2,280. It is only after about seven years that the repayment will equal the premiums paid. After that there is a profit, and when the policy matures after fifteen years and a payment of premiums totalling £10,470, he can expect a minimum payment of £18,905 – a very nice profit.

This final payment is likely to be more than you would have got from regular saving in the bank or a building society, but they would have been earning interest right from the start.

Why are assurance policies so different? When you surrender a policy you are paying a *penalty* for not giving the assurance company enough time to cover its costs in issuing the policy. It costs money to assure you, and expenses and commission have to be paid to whoever sold you the policy.

To avoid losing your money:

1   Stop and think before you commit part of your salary on a regular and long-term basis.
2   Don't just listen to the assurance salesman. He makes his living out of selling policies. Make sure he describes the contract for yours and explains the surrender terms. Get independent advice. You will have no comeback once you have signed the contract.
3   Do your own check on anything long-term. Set the spending against your other commitments. Make sure the policy is what you want.

HOW TO BUY LIFE ASSURANCE

You can get your life assurance through:

1   *The insurance company directly.* This can be a good idea if you know that the particular company offers good rates and returns, or has a deal

144

which will suit you particularly well. But if you are buying through one company, you do not have the benefit of being able to shop around, so it may not be the best you can do.

Remember the different kinds of companies. They are:

* Proprietary companies. There are like ordinary companies. Some of them may be very old and have been formed under Acts of Parliament or under Royal Charter. This makes no practical difference to the way they operate.
* Mutual companies. These have no shareholders; anyone who has a policy with them is a 'member' of the company, sharing in its profits and, of course, when they occur, its losses. Losses are rarely more than a few pounds, because some mutuals are limited by guarantee – and profits are more usual anyway.
* Mutual indemnity associations. You are unlikely to come in contact with these; they sell to the professions rather than the public in general.

2 *An insurance agent*. These used to be door-to-door salesmen, but this practice is dying out and may soon be forbidden by law. Agents include people like solicitors, accountants and bank managers, who deal with money every day and are often asked for advice by their clients. Car dealers are often insurance agents as well, though they, of course, limit their activities to car insurance. As a rule they work only for one company, so dealing with them has the same kind of disadvantages as dealing with the company direct. They make their money by commission on sales, so they won't charge you anything.

3 *An insurance broker*. All in all he may be your best bet when searching for life assurance, especially if your needs are a little complicated. He sells any sort of insurance, and although he, too, will tend to do regular business with certain companies, he will know where the best bargains are to suit your particular case. An insurance broker will:

* Look at your particular circumstances.
* Design total cover in all areas in the most efficient and economical way.
* Look for unusual cover for you.
* Review your policies from time to time to see that they still fit your needs.
* Deal with your claims for you promptly.

A warning: check up on any insurance broker before you consult him. Anyone can set themselves up in business and they may well know very little about insurance. Confine your dealings to brokers who are members of the Federation of Insurance Brokers, the Association of

Insurance Brokers, or the Corporation of Insurance Brokers. If the broker you choose is a member of one of these organizations, he will usually advertise the fact.

FRINGE INSURANCES

Today it is possible to insure yourself against an enormous variety of things, for either long or short periods. It is impossible for me to list here all the possibilities, but here are just a few you might consider worthwhile:

1   You could cause accidental injury to someone. We can all do this, but if you drive a car a great deal in your job it might be worth covering yourself against this eventuality.
2   You can insure yourself against having twins, a good idea if twins run in the family. If they do arrive, the extra money always comes in useful. You take out the policy as soon as you are pregnant. This costs about £5 for every £100 insured in each pregnancy, but will vary depending on how strong the family record on twins is.
3   In addition to your own life and that of members of your family you could also insure the life of a favourite pedigree pet, or a horse. You can also cover yourself for veterinary fees.
4   You can insure bits of yourself: your voice if you are a singer, your hands if a pianist, your legs if a dancer or footballer.
5   You can also insure yourself when you go on holiday, or against being unable to go as planned (more details in chapter 18 of this section on holidays).

Chapter 14.

COVERING YOURSELF AGAINST SICKNESS

If you are ill, you will have enough to think about without worrying about money. On the other hand, employers may well ask themselves why they should pay you when you are not at work. You can help solve this problem in many ways.

STATE SICKNESS BENEFIT

First of all, there is the state sickness benefit. We pay for this each week or month when we are working, through our National Insurance contributions. Like most benefits this has risen over the years, and is likely to continue to do so. As I write the rates are:

men, single women and widows	£12.90
married women	£9.20
additional payment for:	
wife, or other adult dependent	£8.00
first or only dependent child	£3.05
subsequent children	£2.55

This means that a married man with two children will get £26.50 to support his family with while he is away from work sick. This is not a great deal, particularly for a family buying a house and trying to run a car. This is generally partly overcome by the additional payment of an earnings-related supplement for twenty-six weeks.

No payment is made if you are away from work three days or less, and nowadays it is almost unheard of for an employer to make deductions for the first three days. It is just not worth anyone's time and money to go through the necessary administration. Of course, anyone who does piece-work or happens to be employed by the day will not get any money, but this is rare. The earnings-related supplement is not paid for the first twelve days.

These benefits apply whether you are employed or self-employed, but if you are unemployed you will continue to receive the usual

147

unemployment benefit. The self-employed do not get the earnings-related portion.

To get the benefit at all you must have a medical certificate, which now goes under the title of MED. This is a statement by your doctor that you are unfit for work. When you are ready to return he will produce a further certificate stating this and your benefit will cease from that date.

Most people assume that the state benefits will be enough to see them through. They do not expect to be ill very often and feel that it will be enough to tide them over difficult periods. Their medical treatment itself will, or course, cost them nothing if they use the National Health Service.

COMPANY SICKNESS FUNDS

In addition your company may have what is called a sickness fund. When you are sick you get a payment from the fund to help you out. There are almost as many varieties of these funds as there are firms. The fund may be provided entirely free by the company itself; more likely, employees will pay in a small contribution each week, and membership of the fund will be optional.

If it is a company scheme, your employer will very likely have taken out a permanent health policy to cover all his workers similar to that available to the individual (see later in this chapter). The insurance company will generally insist on its own doctor examining the person for whom the claim is made, to make sure that there is no malingering. The payment is usually made to the employer rather than directly to the employee. That way it is regarded as earned income and treated better from the point of view of tax. Were it paid to the employee direct it would be regarded as unearned income, which often bears a higher rate of tax.

Where the sickness fund is contributory the rate of benefit will depend to some extent on how much is in the fund and will be adjusted from time to time.

PRIVATE INSURANCE

You may feel, nevertheless, that your benefits are not enough, and wish to take out extra insurance for periods when you are ill. There are various forms of private insurance.

Hospital cash insurance

You can cover yourself for any period that you are in hospital. This is not the same as having *private* medical treatment in hospital, and the money can be used for any purpose you want: your family may have a long and

148

expensive way to come and visit you; maybe you would like a private room, or a semi-private one. A premium of between £15 and £30 a year will give you cover of £5 a day while you are in hospital. This is a rather high premium if you are not going to be ill very often, but only you can calculate that risk. It covers you only while you are in hospital (the average stay is ten days, and one in ten of the population spends some time in hospital every year), and not while you are at home convalescing. The insurance company will not normally pay out to patients in mental or geriatric hospitals. On the whole this insurance is not enough, and the premiums may rise if you make several claims. You would be wiser to look around for something more substantial to cover you for the total period that you are ill.

Permanent health insurance

It is far better to take out permanent health insurance. Once you have this the insurance company cannot cancel it, no matter what happens to your health, or how many claims you make.

If you want this kind of insurance, it is a good idea to take it out as young as possible. Premiums may rise sharply with age, as you become more likely to be taken ill. You may find, if you are a woman, that illness or absence from work through pregnancy and childbirth are excluded from all these policies.

What you get is a weekly payment all the time you cannot work because of sickness or accident, and the payments will go on as long as you are not working, or until you reach a particular age, which is set beforehand. As a rule the payments do not start as soon as you are ill; they usually begin after thirteen weeks.

This type of policy is not expensive. It will cost a man of thirty-five only about £25 a year for a £20 a week benefit. Women have to pay rather more.

All insurance premiums are based upon a calculation of what is likely to happen. The less chance there is, the less money you will have to pay to cover yourself. Permanent health insurance is rather new, and most of the policies so far have been taken out by men. Where women have taken them out, experience shows that they tend to have more long-term illnesses than men. As a result women find that they have to pay anything between 20 and 80 per cent more than men for the same cover. They win in other forms of insurance, though, as they tend to live longer than men: they pay less for life cover, for instance.

After six months your state sickness benefit stops and is replaced by an invalidity benefit, which is much less, so your income drops still further in comparison with what it was when you were working. This makes permanent health insurance particularly useful.

If you take out permanent health insurance the insurer will generally

149

let you insure yourself for up to three quarters of your earnings, less any state benefits you are allowed. You can choose when the payments will start – either one, three or six months after you become ill. The longer you defer payments the cheaper the insurance is. If you are prepared to wait six months, you will probably find that your annual premium will be half as much as if payments were to start after one month. A man just under forty with a hitherto good health record will pay about £45 or £21 for a benefit of £100 a month paid after one month and six months respectively. Premiums vary a little, however, from company to company.

Permanent health insurance may not be suitable for all of us, but it can be a great help to the self-employed and to those who have high incomes, whose standard of living would be most affected by long-term inability to work. Talk to your employer first and find out how long he will be willing to go on paying your salary in the event of your being ill, and fix your insurance policy accordingly.

Accident insurance

You can also insure yourself against accidents at work. This is fairly cheap and may be advisable if you are in the kind of job where accidents do occur. You will naturally have to pay more if you are, say, a manual worker on a building site than an office worker.

The building worker may pay out about £12 a year for a package of benefits worth £15 a week for two years' disablement or £4,000 for the loss of a limb or an eye. These policies are strictly for disablement caused by accidents at work and do not cover ordinary sickness.

PRIVATE MEDICAL TREATMENT

In addition to securing a reasonable income for yourself while you are ill, you can also insure yourself for private medical treatment, either in hospital or out of it.

It has to be said straightaway that you will not get better treatment because you pay for it privately. What you will get is a private room or a small ward, and you will be able to have the treatment immediately, or when you want it, even though your case may not be urgent. You can also choose your own consultant.

If you use the National Health, you may find that for a hernia, tonsils or varicose veins you have to wait up to three years for treatment, and that you then have to go for treatment whenever you are sent for, even if it is inconvenient, otherwise you may lose your place in the queue.

Many people, however, cannot afford the very high fees which must now be paid for private treatment, and to cover themselves they take out insurance to pay for it should the need arise. About 2½ million people are covered by medical treatment insurance in the U.K. They either take out this cover themselves or belong to the group schemes which are run by many companies.

Full cover, if you take out an individual policy, can cost a thirty-year-old married man with children £100 a year. This will include the maximum possible surgeon's fees and all accommodation in hospital. Group schemes are about a third cheaper. Sometimes the employer will make a contribution, sometimes not. Occasionally he may offer it free to some or all of his employees as a fringe benefit.

If you are attracted by the idea of private medical treatment, make enquiries with your employer first. If he has nothing to offer you, write to one of the non-profit making organizations that specialize in this type of work. They are, alphabetically:

British United Provident Association, Provident House, Essex Street, London WC2R 3AX.
Private Patients Plan, Eynsham House, Tunbridge Wells, Kent TN1 2PL.
Western Provident Association, Culverhouse, Culver Street, Bristol BS1 5JE.

All these companies offer basically the same sorts of schemes, but the specific benefits vary, as do premiums, from one company to another. Write to find out what they offer. All exclude some things, which may or may not be important to you. Treatment during pregnancy and childbirth is always excluded, although sometimes you may be covered if a caesarian section is necessary.

You will always have to pay for your own gold fillings, or trips to health farms, osteopaths or acupuncturists, and for a variety of other treatments. You will also have to declare any existing illnesses or medical condition and, unless you come to a special arrangement with the company, you will not be covered for treatment for these. There may also be a limit on the contribution which the insurer is prepared to make.

Do remember, if you want private treatment and have to pay for it yourself, accommodation and nursing can cost you up to £300 a week and a surgeon and anaesthetist up to £200 for a major operation. You can get cover for up to a year in hospital through private medical schemes. Nevertheless, think carefully before you take out this form of insurance. If you do not mind being in a ward or waiting for a minor condition to be treated, do not take it out. If you are suddenly struck down and need an operation immediately, there is no more delay with the National Health Service than with private medicine.

Chapter 15

BUYING AND RUNNING YOUR CAR

THE COST OF MOTORING

We take motoring so much for granted these days that it is sometimes difficult to appreciate that it is entirely a twentieth century development. Indeed, it is only in the last twenty five to thirty years that car ownership has become widespread.

To begin with it was the preserve of the wealthy; its growth has been linked with the growth in disposable income. It was still a status symbol in the 1950s and 1960s, but has now become an indispensable part of the way of life of millions.

Yet its cost is still formidable. This cost is not always realized at the time a car is purchased, and is all too often later ignored. As a result a family may have to sacrifice many other things in life simply to keep their car, which may or may not be providing a service which justifies the expense.

Today there are 55 million people in Britain and 14 million motor cars. The figure is not staggeringly large, but it has quadrupled in the last twenty years and doubled in the last ten. But most cars today have more than one driver – half the adult population possesses a driving licence.

Motoring has always been expensive, and never more so than now. Have no illusions about it. All calculations comparing the costs with the costs of public transport show that it is an expensive way to travel.

Just because you can get four people from Manchester to Sheffield in a car ostensibly more cheaply than by train, or fill your car up once a year with your family for a holiday, does not mean that it is cheaper overall to have a car than to use public transport. Your car, as we will see later, costs you money even when it is standing still in your garage.

For a few brief years at the beginning of the 1970s it looked as though the cost in real terms of buying and running a car would fall. Then in 1973 the oil war came and these hopes were dispelled. The following year motoring costs rose faster than in any other year since motoring began, and more and more motorists found their car was costing them as much as – and sometimes more than – their mortgage.

We are still feeling the effects of the events of 1973, directly and

152

indirectly. Though the rise in costs has slowed down a little, the price of petrol has now (1977) almost doubled to 80-90p a gallon, while servicing, repairs and insurance have all gone up by half as much again. All this means that the motorist's out-of-pocket expenses have risen sharply. Worst of all, the cost price of a new or second-hand car has doubled. If you already have a car, trading it in for another one may not present such problems as a first purchase, though the upsurge in prices upset many drivers who had felt that once they were over the hurdle of the first car, all problems were over.

If you had bought a brand new Mini in the summer of 1973, you would have had some change out of £700. If you had sold it a year later, you would probably have been pleasantly surprised at how little it had depreciated in price. But a year later you would have had to pay £80 more than the original showroom price to buy it back, and in the meantime a *new* Mini had more than doubled its price tag.

In spite of all this, you may feel that the car is still a source of pleasure for you and your family and still a comparatively inexpensive way of enjoying leisure activities.

More important, the reduction in public transport and the resulting relative isolation of many parts of the country mean that a car – no matter how expensive – is sometimes essential if you are to get around at all.

BUYING YOUR CAR

Before you buy

First, ask yourself whether you really need to own a car. If you live in a city and need your car only for occasional outings and summer holidays, hiring one whenever you feel you need it may make more economic sense than buying one. Using a taxi every day for your needs can be cheaper than running a car, and you then have no worries about parking. Even with the charges hidden away in most car hire company's contracts, a fortnight's hiring fees represent only one third of what a year's garaging could cost in a major city.

Second, if you have decided that you really do need a car, spend some time deciding what kind you want. It is useless to choose a two-seater sports car with a jump seat if you have a family who will expect to be taken out in it. An estate car is a good buy for a growing family, or for anyone who uses a car for holidays and touring. If you are a young and inexperienced driver, do not choose a sports car because you think it suits your personality. Insurance companies are aware of the temptations of such a car to the young, and the cost of insurance is correspondingly heavy. Do not buy an enormous car, which is costly to run, if you will generally be driving alone, or if you live in a city where parking can be difficult.

153

Third, make sure you can pay for your car – both for the actual purchase and for the running of it. Make sure you have enough cash or can get a loan, whether from your bank or from a finance house, or possibly through the car dealer. The cost of borrowing varies enormously, so look around rather than immediately accepting the first deal you are offered.

Fourth, if you are using a dealer:

1 Make sure he is reliable. Make enquiries with the professional dealers' organization before you start the process of buying.
2 Compare the different guarantees that dealers offer. What do they cover? How long are they for?
3 Do not automatically take the dealer's word that you are getting a bargain. It's highly unlikely that you are. Have the car checked independently. The A.A. or R.A.C. do this.

You may find that you get the best service from a local dealer, rather than one of the big more anonymous ones. He will depend for the successful continuation of his business on local recommendation.

Second-hand cars

It is likely, if you are buying your first car, that you will buy second-hand – unless you are a woman, as women often prefer new cars. As many as two-thirds of all Britain's motorists drive cars they bought second-hand, and many who could afford a new car prefer one about a year old, which has been run in properly and had all the snags ironed out.

As the price of new cars increases, so the demand for one- or two-year-old cars also increases; this applies even to company cars, which will generally have done around 17,000 miles in their first year, compared with the private motorist's average of 9,000. At least these cars have been regularly serviced and maintained, while the private owners may well have neglected their cars because of soaring garage costs.

One great attraction of buying second-hand is that you will not have to face such heavy depreciation as on a new car.

One snag, if the car you buy is three years old or more, is that it will need an MoT (Ministry of Transport) test every year. The test is now tougher than ever, and will cost you £4.10 whether the car passes the test or not. A re-test costs £2.05. Reasons for failure can range from such vital matters as steering and inadequate brakes and seat belts to minor faults like a defunct horn, worn windscreen wiper blades and blocked screen washers, or even a dud bulb in the stop lights.

Try to get a second-hand car which carries a guarantee from a reputable dealer. If it does not, have it checked by the A.A. or the R.A.C., the independent motoring organizations. They will charge about £10 for a full inspection – an amount well worth paying to know that the car is in good order. Some dealers offer cars complete with an independent A.A. report.

How much can you afford to pay?

Set yourself a maximum price that you are prepared to pay before you start – and stick to it.

New cars. With a new car the price is usually known beforehand, but there are still several ways of saving money. Extras can put the price up a good deal. Some of these are more or less compulsory, but others are genuine extras. Some manufacturers include delivery, and the price of number plates and seat belts (which arc now compulsory), in their prices, others do not. Most family cars are made with two kinds of interior, standard and 'de-luxe'. If you are set on one particular model, you may find that you have no option but to take the de luxe model, and the expensive trim can add between £100 and £200 to the basic cost of the car. This is not all bad, however, because the car will keep some of its de luxe aspects when traded in, so you may be able to recoup some of your money.

Second-hand cars. When you are buying a second-hand car, remember that you will never get a bargain unless you buy privately. All dealers, and many private sellers too, know exactly what the car or cars they arc selling are worth. If you get a few pounds knocked off the price, that will most likely be because the dealer had intended all the time to knock them off.

If the car you are buying genuinely costs less than most other similar models, take great care and have it thoroughly checked to see why it is being offered so cheaply. There is likely to be something wrong with it. Do not always believe the mileage reading. Mileometers can easily be tampered with. Learn the tell-tale signs which will give you an idea what mileage a car has really done:

* One that has driven 15,000 miles will still have a good tread on the tyres.
* One that has driven 25,000 miles will have a worn tread on the tyres and the battery may have been replaced.
* One that has driven 30,000 miles may have a brake pedal which is wearing out.

Test drives

It does not matter whether you are buying new or second-hand, always ask for a test drive. Surprisingly, less than half the buyers of new cars ask for a test drive. The fact that a car is new does not necessarily mean there is nothing wrong with it.

If you don't think you will spot any faults yourself, get someone with more experience and some technical knowledge to drive it for you. Do not simply drive along the road and back. Test the car for hill starts, try it on a poor road surface if possible, and in congested traffic conditions. Alternatively do not test drive the car at all, this may strengthen your position if you discover a fault later (see section VI, chapter 2).

Check the car carefully for scratches and dents before you drive it away. If you do not do this immediately, it may be difficult later to have things put right for nothing by the dealer.

Having test-driven it, check the boot to see that the spare tyre and any tools are all there. Do not leave the dealer until you are sure you have the logbook, warranty and handbook and, very important, the MoT roadworthiness certificate, if the car is more than three years old. Do not forget your insurance cover (see next chapter).

Negotiating the price

Once you have chosen your car, you should start negotiating on the price. Even when you buy a new car, you need not always accept the listed price, particularly if you are paying cash.

A main dealer gets a discount of about 18 per cent on a new car. Try to persuade him to give some of it to you. If you are lucky, you may get between 5 and 12 per cent off the list price. If the first dealer you try will not do it, try another.

Drive a hard bargain when you are trading in your car for another one. Take it to the dealer in tip-top condition, cleaned up and polished and with minor faults put right. The dealer will usually offer you between 20 and 25 per cent less than he expects to sell it for later on. You may find that it is better to sell your car privately first. That way you may get a higher price – but do not underestimate the problems of selling privately. Advertising can be expensive, and anyone buying from you will probably also try to drive a hard bargain. Remember that a dealer's second-hand price should include V.A.T. (see section IV, chapter 3).

Time your trade-in properly. Your repair bills may begin to get out of hand after you have driven 60,000 to 70,000 miles. Every car will vary, but do not trade in before you have had your car three years; and after six years you might as well drive it into the ground and then sell it for scrap.

RUNNING COSTS

Once you drive your car away from the showroom, you begin to spend money. It disappears in several ways, apart from petrol costs.

Depreciation. A 1,500 cc car worth over £2,000 depreciates in value by about £500 in the first year. That's almost £10 a week, more than £1 a day. Allow another £100 a year for every 500 cc increase in engine size. If you buy a new car, it will probably lose more than a third of its value in two years and half in three years, unless, of course, prices rise at an even higher rate than they have been doing since 1973.

Standing charges. Then there are the costs you incur without going anywhere. These are reckoned to amount to £650 a year if the car in your garage is between 1,000 and 1,500 cc – the most popular range owned by nearly half of Britain's motorists. As well as depreciation you must allow some interest – this is usually put at 7 per cent – for the amount your money would have earned if it had not been invested in your car. Garaging costs money, either in rent or extra rates, and street parking. Other expenses are road tax, your driving licence, insurance, and the MoT certificates where applicable.

If you are wise you will also join one of the motoring organizations. They are always useful, and not just when something goes wrong.

Repairs and servicing. Repairs can be a major item, even on the most carefully driven car. When you buy, look at the recommended servicing intervals – some models go 3,000 miles in between servicing, others as much as 6,000. Clutches on some cars take two and a half hours to replace, on others up to eleven hours. Now that labour charges have reached £6 an hour in London and £5 elsewhere the time a job takes can make a considerable difference to your final bill.

Do not run your car without proper servicing. It will only cost you more in the long run. If you wait until something goes wrong, your repair bills will be much higher. Regular servicing should bring to light any problems which might be developing before they become too serious, and replacement parts may not be necessary if a fault is found early on. Try to do some of your servicing yourself. It is not too difficult. Already over 4 million motorists have taught themselves how to do some, if not all, of the basic work. To help yourself in this try to buy a car where all the areas that need servicing are easily accessible.

Beware when you buy an imported car – spares may be 20 per cent or more dearer than those for British-made cars, and their servicing garages may be few and far between, with the result that servicing and repair jobs are not only more costly but also take longer. You may have your car off the road – costing money – for some time.

Petrol. This is the main cost involved in taking your car out on the road. As a rough guide, the A.A. says that small cars do 35-40 miles to the gallon, medium cars 30-35 and larger ones 20-30. If you have a G.T. version of your car, you will find you get five miles less to the gallon. Some very large cars manage only a few miles to the gallon, and if you drive mostly in town you will use up petrol more quickly than outside it. There is no point in choosing, buying and maintaining your car sensibly and then throwing all these savings away by paying too much for your petrol. Here are some ways of making sure you get value for money at the petrol pump:

* Do not buy high octane fuel if your car does not need it. Over half the cars in Britain do not.
* Get out of your car when you are buying petrol, so that you can keep an eye on where the petrol is going.
* Make sure that the pump reading is at zero before the attendant starts to fill up your tank, or before you do if it is a self-service station.
* Watch carefully to see that your bill matches the amount you receive.
* If the garage is making any kind of special offer, be sure you get it, because you will be paying for it in one way or another in the petrol price. Remember that a cut price may be better for you than any trading stamps offer, because it is money gained immediately.

Other running costs include replacement tyres, oil and batteries. And car parking fees, parking meters and (inadvertent) fines can add £20 a year to your motoring bills.

Total running costs for the family car now add up to more than 5 p per mile, which together with the fixed costs means that if you drive 10,000 miles a year it will cost you altogether 12p per mile, including depreciation, or £22 a week, a formidable sum of money for many average wage earners.

Good driving can cut your costs

If you want to cut your motoring expenses, good driving will help:

To save petrol. Accelerate smoothly and get into top gear as quickly as possible. Brake gently and take the correct line into a bend.

To reduce wear on your tyres. The tread wears almost twice as rapidly at 70 m.p.h. as at 45 m.p.h., especially in hot weather or when driving on curved or rough roads. Avoid striking sharp objects such as kerbs, rocks or holes in the road, and maintain the manufacturer's recommended tyre pressure. Do not do wheel spinning starts.

To avoid unnecessary repair bills. Do not over-rev your engine or slip your clutch unnecessarily. Above all, keep your car in peak condition by regular maintenance. Choose the service agent with care. Try to get to know the mechanics who do the job.

Motoring for most of us is still worth every penny it costs. But make sure you and your family get maximum pleasure for the minimum amount of money from your car.

Chapter 16

INSURING YOUR CAR

THE BEST INSURANCE FOR YOU

We generally have an option whether to take out insurance or not. There are two exceptions to this. One, which I have already discussed, is house insurance, when you are buying your house on a mortgage; the other is car insurance. It is against the law in this country – and most others to drive a car without insurance. However, you can choose what kind of insurance you have.

The minimum insurance required by law must cover your legal liability should you injure someone else on the road, including your passengers. Very few people have this minimum insurance by choice. If you have a very bad record it may be all you are likely to be offered, but if you are *that* bad you will probably already have been banned from driving.

You must get your car insured before you drive it away from the showroom or dealer. If you have not yet fixed up your permanent insurance, a temporary cover note will do. This can only be for a limited period, and can be issued to you by an insurance broker. The proper insurance certificate can come only from the insurance company with which you are dealing. Remember, if you let the temporary note run out – or indeed your proper insurance– you are breaking the law if you drive.

In recent years the cost of motor insurance has increased very sharply. Recent surveys have shown that today people tend to spend more insuring their cars than their lives – a natural development when there are so many demands on one's total budget.

We know that the price of most things has risen, but motor insurance seems to have outstripped many other items. The temptation, then, is to reduce the amount of cover to keep premiums within reason. Even so, the average motorist today spends £55 on his car insurance. There are three main types of car insurance:

1 *Act only (third party)*. This is the kind I have referred to above. It covers only your legal liability for the injury of others, whether you knock them down as you drive, or they are passengers injured in a crash in which you are involved. It applies only to people and does not cover damage to your own car or anyone else's.

159

This does not mean you will have to pay if you damage someone else's car and the accident is entirely your fault. It simply means you will have to find the money out of your own pocket, and this could spell financial ruin if the damage is extensive. Clearly you should if at all possible have more insurance than this.

2   *Third party, fire and theft.* Third party covers any damage to people and their property. Property here usually means someone's car, but it could extend to the windows of a house you have driven into, or a wall you have knocked down. Third party does not cover damage to yourself or your own car.

If your car either catches fire or gets stolen, it will be a write-off as far as you are concerned, so it is only sensible to be covered for this. Most claims in this area are for theft. You will not get the money immediately, however. The insurance company has to be satisfied that the car has disappeared for good before handing the money over to you.

If you have an old car, which is not worth too much money, third party, fire and theft is generally the best sort of insurance for you.

3   *Comprehensive.* Basically this means you are covered for damage to your own car as well as others, and it is not relevant how this damage is incurred. You, however, get all kinds of extras to your basic comprehensive policy, including:

* Cover for any other person or persons when driving your car with your permission. Driving without your permission can also be covered.
* Cover for third part liability when you yourself are driving someone else's car, again with their permission.
* Extra cover for your heirs should you be killed driving the car. This is unlikely to be allowed at much more than £1,000.

Whatever you do, you will probably not have covered every eventuality. If your car is a write-off, for example, you will not get the price you paid for it, but the depreciated price allowing for the age of the car. Repairs due to ordinary wear and tear are not covered.

It makes sense to have the widest possible cover, if you can afford it. If you cannot, you should ask yourself whether you can actually afford to run a car at all.

WORKING OUT THE PREMIUM

When you have decided which kind of policy you want that is not the end of the matter. The insurer may want to know the purposes for which you intend to use the car, and he may raise or – very rarely – lower the premium accordingly. On an ordinary car the highest premiums are paid by commercial travellers. If you use your car for business as well as private purposes, you may pay rather more than if you used it simply for private motoring.

The most common type of policy, which carries the standard premium, covers a car for social, domestic and pleasure purposes. It also covers the policy owner and nobody else if it is for business or professional purposes.

There is not, alas, one premium for one type of policy and one kind of car. The insurer will want to know a great deal about you when you apply for insurance, and if you do not tell the truth you will invalidate the policy. You will be asked the following questions:

1 How old are you, and what is the age of anyone else who will drive the car?
2 How long have you been driving and what is your record? Have you had any accidents? Have you ever been disqualified?
3 What is your profession? Is it likely to put your car at more than normal risk?
4 What make of car is it, and what model? Is it a sports car?
5 How much is the car worth?
6 Where is it when you are not driving – in a garage, or out in the open air?
7 Where do you live?
8 If you were not born and brought up in Britain, where do you come from?

Those questions all mean something to the insurer, and on the basis of past experience, called 'actuarial experience', he will assess your desirability as a policyholder. From the above questions you may have guessed that it is better: not to be too young or too old; to be British; and to have a clean record, a steady job and a not too speedy car.

The *worst risk* is a young man, under twenty-five living in central London, with only a couple of years' driving experience who has had a few major or minor accidents already. He will have been born in Latin America, and drives a sports car worth many thousands of pounds which he lets all his friends drive. He will be charged a very high premium, or the ordinary insurance company may refuse to insure him at all. He may have to go to the Lloyd's underwriters for a special policy. His premium will run into hundreds of pounds.

In contrast, actuarial experience shows that the *best risk* is the teetotal housewife in her thirties, who drives a solid family car worth less than £2,000, which she uses infrequently, perhaps to drive children to and from school and her husband to the station. She lives in the country, having been brought up there, and is the only driver of her car. Women, despite views to the contrary, have a better driving record than men.

Her premium for exactly the same cover will be far less than the young man's.

Age is an important factor. If you continue to drive blamelessly for fifty years, it is unlikely that your insurance company will put up the premium just because you have reached seventy. But should you try to change to a new insurer, you would probably find that the premium immediately shot up.

Apart from your own personal circumstances, two other considerations are all important: where you normally garage the car, and what model it is.

Where you live. Insurers divide the country into various sections. Generally if you live in town you will pay higher premiums. Greater London is the most expensive, then the other major conurbations. The country side is cheaper, and Devon and Cornwall cheapest of all.

Sometimes the premiums, in the lower rated areas may be only half as much as those in the towns, but rates vary greatly from company to company. Some companies, for instance, charge almost as little for cities as other companies do for Devon or Cornwall. You may get the worst of all worlds if you live in the suburbs: premiums may be as high as in towns, even though you never actually drive to town.

What model car you have. The various makes of cars (with the exception of some of the real sports cars, which are rated individually) are also divided into different categories. There will be many makes of car in a particular range in one category, so you can at least get a rough idea of the premiums before your own circumstances are taken into account.

Very few motorists pay the full premium, or a loaded one. That only happens when you first take out insurance cover for a car you have bought or where your circumstances are adverse from the insurer's point of view.

Let's assume first, however, that you are a man in your mid-thirties who has just bought a new car, having driven other cars for many years, and that you have the benefit of a nine-year no-claims bonus.

Premiums have risen sharply in recent years, and you will probably be asked to pay as follows, assuming that the only other person who drives is your wife. This situation is quite common.

Mini Clubman	Rover 2000	Morris Marina	Ford Capri
£40.68	£71.20	£74.00	£75.40

Ask yourself if the differences in the premium are such that you would prefer the smaller car.

If you are younger you may find yourself paying a higher premium, and if you have a poor record and have not earned any no-claims bonus you will be similarly penalized. It may happen that you will not be penalized in your premium for being young. Instead the insurer might insist that you pay the first £25 to £50 of any bill for damage.

How to earn a no-claims discount

Obviously we should all aim at getting a no-claims discount. If you can build this up over a number of years, you can reduce the cost of your car insurance considerably.

To begin with, you must have been driving your own car for some time. You do not normally get a no-claims bonus when you first take out insurance for your own car, even if you have had years of trouble-free driving, using other people's cars or hiring cars.

Some insurers may allow you a discount of about 20 per cent if you come into this category, but not all. Otherwise, the first cut in your premium comes after the first year of claim-free driving. The discount builds up over the years to a maximum of 60 or 65 per cent after about four or five years. You may not always lose your entire bonus if you have made only one claim during the year, but you will slip back a bit in the discount scale.

If you have a minor mishap, especially if you are near the maximum no-claims discount, it is often worth paying for the damage yourself rather than risking your bonus.

IF YOU HAVE AN ACCIDENT

Knock-for-knock agreements

When you and another car bump into one another, both cars and persons may sustain damage. To deal with this most insurers operate what they call knock-for-knock agreements, whereby each pays the damage to the car which it has insured. No regard is paid to which driver is responsible for the damage. A condition of knock-for-knock agreements is that the policy on the car must cover the damage risk in full.

This is all very well for the insurer, who is able to pay out any claim more quickly, thus saving on the administrative costs of dealing with another insurer and also avoiding litigation.

These agreements are not so good for the driver, however. He may find that he will not be paid for the amount of any excess damage under his policy, and he may lose his no-claims bonus when coming to renew his policy. It is up to the motorist himself to put a claim in for the excess, if he regards himself as in no way to blame for the accident. This can lead to litigation, though usually it does not. If the driver succeeds in his claim, it is evidence for his own insurers that he was not responsible for the accident and the no-claims bonus should remain intact. If you are sure that you were not responsible for an accident, persist in your claim – otherwise you will lose your bonus.

How to make a claim

Rule number one is to tell your insurance company as soon as possible. Delay on your part could result in some loss to you. Your insurers will then send you a claim form, which you should try to fill in and send back by return of post.

If your car is a write-off, either through fire or a crash, the insurance 'assessors' (the company's experts who specialize in working out the value) will decide the market value of your car immediately before the damage was done. Try to get an 'agreed' value at the beginning of each year of insurance. That way, you will have no problems if the car is a write-off. The same applies if your car is stolen, except that you will probably have to wait at least six weeks before your claim is settled.

You will be lucky to get the whole value of any necessary repairs paid out to you. Your policy may well limit this, but in any case the insurance company may argue that the car is in a better state than it was before the repair and that the motorist must pay for part of this 'betterment'.

Even if you do not make a claim, however, your insurers have a right to know every time your car is damaged. They should be informed in writing, and are on record as saying that this information will not affect your no-claims bonus.

If you read the small print in your policy, you will see that under its terms you are required to do this. This rule is really to safeguard the motorist. You can never know when claims may come from the driver of another car. If you have not told your insurance company, they will have some awkward questions for you.

IF YOUR INSURANCE IS NOT VALID

If you are responsible for an accident, someone may claim against you. There should be no problems here, apart from the loss of your bonus, unless for some reason your policy is invalidated. This could happen if you had been driving your car in a totally unroadworthy condition – perhaps with faulty brakes – or if the person driving the car was under the permissible driving age of seventeen years (eighteen if they were driving abroad).

If this happens you could find yourself saddled with a very large bill, particularly if in the most unfortunate chance someone is killed as a result of the accident. What happens then is that the injured party's damages are paid by his insurance company, or the Motor Insurers' Bureau. Then, however, either the insurers or the M.I.B. can take steps to recover the money from you. As your own insurance was invalid at the time of the accident, you will find no one to help you.

When your insurance runs out

As the car owner you are responsible for keeping your insurance up to date. As a general rule your insurance company will warn you that it is running out and send you a temporary certificate with a reminder. But they are under no legal obligation to do so.

If you have genuinely forgotten to pay, and can prove it to your insurers, they will generally accept the premium as soon as you send it, dating the new policy from the date the old one expired.

In some cases, they may even be willing to handle a claim for you during a time when you have been legally uninsured. If you suddenly remember that you have not renewed your policy, get on to your insurers immediately by telephone. *Never forget that a delayed renewal payment can leave you in serious trouble.*

The renewal notice will give you fifteen days' extra cover from the date your policy expires. Do not be under any illusion that you are getting fifteen days free – the new policy will date from the expiry of the old one. The fifteen days' grace only gives you the minimum cover required by law, and it only applies anyway if you are intending to renew with the same insurers.

Some motorists run into trouble because when they see the renewal premium they decide to look for something cheaper and to take advantage of the fifteen-day temporary cover while they look. This can be a serious mistake. If he has an accident after he has sent a proposal form and cheque to another insurer but before it has been accepted, the driver will find that he is covered by no one. By sending off another proposal form and cheque, the motorist is clearly indicating that he has no intention of renewing his old policy, and any claim under that policy will be rejected if the accident occurs after the original expiry date.

Filling in the proposal form

Similar problems can also arise if you do not complete the proposal form properly. This may mean that you cannot claim, even if your insurance has not run out. It is dangerous simply to sign the form and then leave the rest to the salesman.

Supposing a proposal form did not indicate previous convictions for dangerous driving; the car owner might not have mentioned them to the salesman simply because he hadn't been asked. Should the car be a write-off later, the owner would have to reveal these convictions on his claim form. The chances of the claim being rejected out of hand are very high.

165

WHERE TO GO FOR YOUR POLICY

There are many insurance companies which do motor insurance, and you will have seen a lot of them advertising in the national and local press. You can also go to the underwriters at Lloyd's. A few insurance companies do not handle motor insurance. There is nothing to stop you from walking into a local branch of an insurance company and doing your business directly with them, or you can fill up a form from the paper and do your deal by post. Otherwise you can use:

1 *An insurance broker.* He may filter through the various companies to find the one which suits you best, and therefore save you time. If you want to deal with Lloyd's anyway, you cannot go there directly and you must use a broker. He will normally not make any charge to you for this service: the money he makes will come from the insurer.

It is worth finding out if the company you work for has a particular insurance broker, through which it does its business. If this is the case, the broker will often make a special effort on behalf of employees, though the particular policy may not amount to much in terms of total business from the firm.

2 *An insurance agent.* Many of the larger insurance companies have full-time or, more often, part-time agents. They may use a firm of solicitors, for example, or a large garage or motor car dealer.

3 *The motoring organizations.* The Automobile Association or the Royal Automobile Club may make the arrangements for you.

4 *A bank.* Banks sometimes offer motor insurance, though it is not their usual work.

Give your instructions clearly and precisely to whoever you ask to act for you, or to the company, if you are dealing directly with it yourself.

Whoever is acting for you may come up with a number of quotations. *Do not leap automatically for the lowest one you are offered. Make some enquiries first.* You will want to know the attitude of the insurer to claims, for the chances are that some time in your driving life you will make at least one claim. When you do you will want it settled quickly, without fuss, and in full. So choose the quote which best balances price and service.

If you have any problems later on, you are entitled to the benefits of the Policy Holders Protection Act. Details of what can be done to help you are available from the Policy Holders Protection Board, Aldermary House, Queen Street, London EC4.

EXTRA INSURANCES

Motor insurance need not necessarily end with a fully comprehensive policy. You can take out a variety of other insurances to give yourself even more protection:

1   If you travel a lot and leave your car out in the street for some considerable time, you might choose to take out an additional policy to cover any personal belongings that you might leave in it. Approach your own insurance company for this. Your claims under such a policy should not affect the no-claims bonus on the motoring policy, and you can insure quite cheaply for losses of high value.

2   If you can never manage without a car, it is worth taking out extra insurance to cover the cost of hiring a car any time when you do not have access to your own, either because it is being repaired after an accident or because it has been stolen.

You can insure yourself against the cost of hiring even if an accident happens though your own fault, but if the accident is someone else's you may be able to claim from them in any case.

Occasionally this type of insurance may be included in your overall policy, but check to be sure.

3   You can take out extra insurance against your car being written off or stolen. This will mean that you will get a guaranteed sum of money and will not have to face the almost inevitable arguments under your basic policy about how much you are entitled to.

4   You can insure yourself against being disqualified from driving. This insurance allows you to hire a driver for up to a year, if you are disqualified under the drink and driving laws, or if you have three speeding offences.

It is not cheap, so do not take it out unnecessarily; it will cost between £15 and £60 a year. Far better to use one of your family to drive you about if the worst happens. You can get up-to-date details of these policies from St Christopher Motorists' Security Association, Cheltenham (telephone 0242 20471).

5   There are various policies to cover you if your vehicle breaks down and needs to be towed a long distance – the motoring organizations also provide a service for their members. Details from National Breakdown Recovery Club, 21a Claremont, Bradford, Yorkshire BD1 BB.

6   If you do not think that the warranty on your car is good enough, write to Autoplan (Insurance Services) Ltd., Mont Cantel House, 146 Wellington Road, Bilston, West Midlands WV14 6AZ.

7   If you are towing a caravan or a boat you may need extra insurance. It is unlikely that your car policy will need to be amended, but check to be on the safe side. Then ask your insurers to give you extra cover for the caravan, if it is your own. For details of caravan rental and its implications, move on to chapter 18 of this section on holidays. You will also find information there about taking your car abroad.

Chapter 17

CUTTING THE COST OF YOUR TRAVEL

TRAVELLING WITHIN THE U.K.

We have already looked at travel by car and seen that it is likely to cost you 12p a mile, taking into account all the running costs as well as petrol. It has always been more expensive than public transport and will remain so, even though increases in public transport fares sometimes narrow the gap for a time.

So far as public transport is concerned, buses are always the cheapest method of travelling – though not of course as cheap as actually walking, or, as is becoming increasingly popular again, cycling. Trains are dearer, but if you have to commute to work they are the only practical means of travelling in the time available. In London the same is true of the underground, which is dearer than the buses.

1 *Walking.* If you do not have far to go this is certainly the cheapest way to travel. Only your shoe leather gets worn and the exercise is good for you.

2 *Cycling.* A new bicycle today can easily cost you £70, though you can still get second-hand ones cheaply. The new small-wheeled bikes are good for towns, but unsuitable if you are a serious cyclist and want to cover a fair distance.

3 *By bus.* Buses are useful for short journeys in town and for longer ones outside. Prices vary enormously depending where in the country you live.

If you are a regular bus user get a season ticket, if they are available in your area. Not only do they save money, but they save fiddling about for change every time you use a bus. If you are retired see if you are entitled to concessionary fares. Your local authority may allow you to travel free all the time, or at least outside the rush hour. Or there may be a reduced fare for pensioners. Children are also entitled to reduced fares. Those under five years old travel free. Half-fares are available up to fourteen or sixteen, depending on where you live. Students with student cards can travel for half-fare on the railways. Airlines vary: check the position.

4 *By train.* Commuter trains are often relatively expensive per mile, and certainly far more expensive than buses, but they save time – and time means money to many people. Cost per mile differs depending on

where you live. In Greater London, for example, the cost is two-thirds dearer than in Scotland. British Rail say that the average fare per mile is 2.26p.

Wherever you live, *get a season ticket, if you use the train regularly*. This will almost always save you money, unless you can travel off-peak for all or most of the time. Let's take the man living in Brighton who travels to London and back every weekday, a total of 100 miles a day. He has the choice of a variety of fares:

1st class ordinary return	£7.50
1st class cheap day return	£4.25
1st class season ticket:	
weekly	£18.60
monthly	£70.65
quarterly	£201.45
six-monthly	£402.90
annual	£733.50
2nd class ordinary return	£5.00
2nd class cheap day return	£2.85
2nd class season ticket	
weekly	£12.40
monthly	£47.10
quarterly	£134.30
six-monthly	£268.60
annual	£489.00

Rail savings become available immediately if you are able to travel after the cheap day concession comes in at 9.30 a.m. or if you buy a season ticket. For instance, five first class returns would cost you £37.50 a week, whereas a weekly season (which incidentally allows you to travel on Saturday and Sunday as well) costs only £18.60. The saving becomes greater the longer you buy the season for. An annual first class season costs £733, as against £1,950 for separate first class returns for 260 working days in a year.

Most people travel second class, however, and the savings there are just as good. Your second class ordinary return costs you £5 a day, or £20 a week, and a weekly season £12.40. By the time you reach an annual ticket (and remember there may well be a fare increase meanwhile which you won't have to pay), the figure comes out at £1,300 for separate daily tickets and only £489 for an annual season.

Even if you allow for a month's holiday and so bring down your daily ticket total by £80 (or £150 if you travel first class) there is still a vast gap between the two costs. Buying a season can make all the difference between being able to live out of town if you wish and being forced to move closer to your work.

All very well, you may say, but I cannot pay out £489 in one go, let alone £733.50. This is where your bank comes in. For this reason, if no other, it is worth considering opening a budget account (see chapter 6 in this section). If you do, you will be able to pay out these sorts of sums before you actually put the money into your account each month. Ask your bank. Wherever you live, a season ticket will save money. Ask at your local railway station for details.

If you travel irregularly you should try to travel in the off-peak period; cheap day returns can save you up to 35p in the pound. Ask at your railway station about any discount fares for two people travelling together, and any special excursions. British Rail also offers weekend returns for journeys over seventy miles one way. These run from Friday to Monday. There are also a variety of longer period mid-week returns worth considering.

If you are retired you can get a special pass which allows you to travel half-fare. For £3 you can travel for half-fare on day returns only, for £6 anywhere at any time. It is worth considering buying this pass, even if you only make a few journeys a year, now that train fares are so high.

Advance booking may also save you money.

5   *By car.* The Brighton-London-Brighton drive would cost you a minimum of £22 a week in the smallest car, nearly twice as much as you would pay for a second class weekly return on the train.

The petrol, of course, would be only a small part of this cost, so you might not be aware of the full cost as you drive. It would also take you longer than the train, be more tiring and is really not worth doing unless you have four people in your car who can contribute. Even then you should have special insurance cover, and your passengers are likely to want to contribute only towards the petrol used and not towards the other costs which mean nothing to them.

It makes sense as a rule to leave your car at home.

6   *By air.* If you are travelling a fair distance between towns which are both served by airports you can fly. The flight generally takes a much shorter time than the train ride, but you must add on the drive to and from the airports, and the waiting time at each end. You may then find that from city centre to city centre there is not much to choose between train and plane as far as time goes. The plane costs more than the train and the train costs more than a coach. Let's look at the London – Manchester run (one way). You can go three ways:

air	£21.10
train: first class	£13.50
second class	£9.00
coach	£4.95

If you have plenty of time you can obviously save a great deal of money going by coach, but it is slow, particularly in comparison with the inter-city trains now running. You may find, however, that the best and most convenient of these are first class only with a 'pullman supplement' on each journey.

AIR TRAVEL OUTSIDE THE U.K.

The further you go, of course, the greater the advantage of air travel in terms of both cost and time. If you fly outside the U.K., there are many ways of cutting the cost, not only because there are a variety of fares on any one route, but also because on some routes advance booking charters bring down the cost substantially.

Take the London to Paris return:

Type	Cost	Conditions
first class	£104	
economy	£69	
IPEX	£40	(must be booked after 2 p.m. the day before flying)
night excursion	£48-50	(must stay at least four days, with one month maximum)
weekend excursion	£40	(for travel only on Saturday or Sunday, with one month maximum stay)
inclusive tour	£varies	(must be part of a package which includes accommodation. Passenger must stay at least until the Sunday following the outward travel. Maximum one month)

You can see that by timing your journey properly you can save a considerable amount of money, whatever the current level of air fares. Insist that the airline gives you details of all its possible fares. And there is no point in flying first class to Paris, except for the snob appeal. The flight only lasts forty minutes, hardly time to need the extra space for stretching out or the free champagne, which are what first class air travel gives you.

But Paris is not too far away. You can get there in just over eight hours if you use the Hoverlloyd coach-hovercraft-coach service, which costs about £21. This is about the cheapest way to go, and takes less time than the rail-ferry-rail service. There are, however, various combinations of different modes of travel at varying prices which you might consider. Consult a travel agent who will know about them all.

171

Now, what about longer distances. London-New York-London is a good example.

Type	Cost	Conditions
first class	£675	
economy	£322-£392	
14-21 day excursion	£278-£324	
22-45 day excursion	£240.50-£302	
APEX*	£153-£192.50	(minimum stay 22 days, book and pay two months ahead)
ABC*	£126-£172	(minimum stay 14 days, book and pay 67 days ahead)
Youth fare	£243-£276	(full-time students 12-24 years only)
Concorde	£866	(only British Airways from London to Washington. Approx. £50 first class return Washington-New York)
Laker Airways	£140	walk-on
	£126-£134	pre-booked

*There is a supplement of £6 each way if you travel at the weekends.

There is a discount of about 10 per cent for children between two and twelve on everything but the youth fare. Infant fares are about 10 per cent of the full fare, though this is not always exact.

You can see that there are even more options for travelling to New York than Paris. You can do particularly well if you are able to travel by APEX or ABC. These are charter companies and require that you book *and pay* some time in advance. The snag is that you cannot change your mind afterwards, and if you find you cannot go after all you do not get your money back. As with most things, you can insure yourself against this eventuality. It costs about £2.

British Airways have now introduced this kind of booking to some parts of Europe, including Spain, Italy and Greece. It has had the effect of cutting economy return fares by almost half, and bringing Europe that much more within the scope of the ordinary family holiday. You have to book and pay one month in advance.

You can also book on other kinds of charters through various 'clubs'. Some of these are genuine, some not. Those that are not genuine have come to be described as 'bucket shop' flights. They are very cheap indeed, but not always reliable. If you lose your money you have no one to blame but yourself. If you think it is worth the chance, the fares are less than one-half of the ordinary economy return.

One comfort: air fares are likely to come down in price over the years, one of the few things which will in this period of inflation. The ordinary first class and economy fares will probably continue to rise for those who have no option but to book at the last minute, but more and more 'deals' can be expected for those who have time to plan.

When you are travelling try to make a total flight plan. If, for example, you are going to America, make all your reservations at one time as this may save you money. There are all kinds of discounts – fares are anyway much cheaper in America than in Europe – covering wives and families.

Some European airlines offer these sorts of discounts too. Where this is the case, fly with that airline rather than any other. Planning takes time, but it can cut the cost of your travel by up to 50 per cent, or more if you are travelling in a group.

Chapter 18

GETTING THE MOST OUT OF YOUR HOLIDAY

Just over half of the population of Britain take a holiday each year away from their homes. As a general rule, this annual break is taken during the summer, and most people stay in another part of the U.K., though a growing proportion go abroad each year. There are hiccups from time to time in the increase in foreign travel, but they are minor and the clear trend is upwards. Very few people take a winter holiday as their main break, and those who do mainly go skiing. The travel business has developed enormously over the past twenty years, and a trend towards two holidays – a main one in the summer and another shorter break during the winter months – is beginning.

Holidays may be one of the first things to be abandoned when the family budget becomes too tight. Yet the travel industry has so far suffered very little, if at all, from our economic crises, which shows how it has kept its prices within the pocket of the ordinary family.

In many cases, travel today is much cheaper than it has ever been. The development of the commercial airlines has brought foreign travel to many who previously could never have afforded it. Tour operators have been able to get extremely cheap flights because they have been able to guarantee a certain number of seats to the airlines. As a result they have been able to offer all-in 'packages' of flights and accommodation at prices which are often only marginally higher than the price of buying the airline ticket on its own.

Just as important as the growth in air travel has been the increase in car ownership. This has enabled families to travel together in a reasonably economical way.

Depending on the amount of money you have available, there are enormous holiday opportunities to suit every pocket, from camping and caravanning to staying at boarding houses, private hotels or the large licensed hotels.

Let's see first how the travel market breaks down. As I said, most people still take their holidays in the U.K. Out of 127,000,000 holidays taken in 1975, 116,000,000 were spent in Britain. Of the 11,000,000 trips abroad, an estimated 77 per cent were on business, not holiday. Therefore, despite their enormous increase in recent years, foreign holidays are still very much in a minority as far as British holidaymakers are concerned.

This table shows where people stay both in Britain and abroad:

	Britain	*abroad*
	%	%
licensed hotel	16	5
unlicensed hotel or guest house	8	9
holiday camp	3	1
camping	4	7
towed caravan	4	3
fixed caravan	9	1
rented flat	2	2
other rented	3	4
paying guest in private house	2	1
with friend or relative	50	20
second home	1	1
others, or in transit	4	9

Note. These columns need not necessarily add up to 100 per cent, because many people use several kinds of accommodation in one trip. Figures are from the British Tourist Authority.

One-week holidays taken in Britain cost on average less than £28 a head for accommodation. If holidays are taken with friends or relatives, accommodation is free, so the average, where accommodation is paid for, is around £37. Even so, this is not a large sum of money when related to the average wage of £3,482 a year (1977), which on average supports four people – husband, wife and two children.

If you go abroad the average cost immediately rises to £104 per head. Most package holidays come within this price range, and, of course, include flights or other transport.

It would seem from these figures that most of us could afford at least one short break a year, even if there is no convenient friend or relative to stay with.

Of course, accommodation is not all. You will certainly spend more on food, unless you are staying with friends, camping or caravanning, or staying in rented accommodation which enables you to do your own catering. You will probably drink more and spend more on general entertainment than you do in an average week at home. And you will almost certainly have invested in special holiday clothes (if you are sensible you will have bought these at sales).

All in all, a holiday may become a very substantial item in an overall budget. Plan your holiday spending just as carefully as any other spending.

WHERE TO SPEND YOUR HOLIDAY

There are two main factors you must consider:

* The money you can spend.
* Your interests.

Money is of course all important, but it would be foolish to have a very cheap holiday skiing if you hate skiing, or a week lying in the sun doing nothing when what you like is plenty of activity. To make sure you have enough money to do what you want, try to make holiday saving a normal part of your monthly budget.

When you have got your money together you must then decide whether you will take your holiday at home, elsewhere in the U.K., or abroad.

At home, or elsewhere in the U.K.?

The only thing to be said for staying at home is that it's cheap. The chances are that you will not have a holiday at all, but will simply be at home instead of at work. If you really do not mind this, fine. But if you really want to benefit from your holiday, you need a change of scene.

Do not assume that by staying in the U.K. you will necessarily spend less than going abroad. The only advantage may be that you can actually work out your costs fairly accurately before you go away.

Abroad

When you go abroad there may be all sorts of expenses you have not thought about. You should never assume that prices abroad are the same as, or lower than, in Britain. Before you go, try to find out the general level of prices from your travel agent. If he is a good agent, he should know this sort of thing.

You can take it now, for example, that London is one of the cheapest capital cities in the world. Almost everywhere else in Western Europe

175

and North America is dearer. And what goes for capital cities tends to go for the rest of the country. Do not think either that journeying to some little, rather undeveloped spot will automatically be cheaper. The amenities which are available may be costly.

Read as much as you can about the place you choose, and write for any information you need to the travel office of the country concerned. These offices exist to help you; you are going to spend money in their countries, and in return they should provide all the relevant information you need.

Here are just a few of the things you need to know:

1 The price of food or restaurant meals compared with Britain.
2 The price of drinks.
3 Any extras, like transport to beaches, towns, etc.; any special taxes.
4 Whether you are covered by reciprocal health arrangements.
5 The kind of clothes you will need.
6 What facilities are available for children.

You will have your own individual preferences, so ask if what you want is available. For example, it is no use going to a 'dry' country if you like drinking.

Most people want value for money when they go abroad. This used to be quite possible. The pound was worth a great deal in many foreign countries, so prices were at bargain levels. Sadly, this is no longer true: the value of the pound has slumped, and today you will find most places relatively expensive compared with Britain.

The cheapest place to go is probably Gibraltar, which has the added advantage of using sterling, so there is no currency problem. The next cheapest holiday places are Spain, Italy, Turkey, Greece and Yugoslavia. You will not find these countries much, if at all, cheaper than the U.K., but bargains are available if you shop around.

On the other hand, some countries are much more expensive than Britain. These include Germany, France, Holland, Scandinavia, Austria and Belgium, and outside Europe, the U.S.A., Canada, Australia and New Zealand.

You may be tempted by the newer holidays offered by tour operators in faraway places. The basic packages are relatively cheap, but when you get there you will find that anything you have to buy is extremely expensive. Even in countries where living costs are relatively low, prices to tourists for drinks, food and souvenirs may be very high indeed. If you are going to the Caribbean, for instance, you should allow a minimum of £1.25 for every drink, soft or alcoholic (1977).

Making sure that you are acquainted with the level of prices in the area you are going to can do much to make your holiday budgeting satisfactory and therefore your holiday more enjoyable.

WHERE TO STAY

It is likely that the cheapest holiday you can take at home or abroad will be with a friend or relative. Here in ascending order of expensiveness, are the other sorts of holiday you could consider:

1   *Camping.* This is cheap, but is really only suitable for families with children, or the unusually active.

If you take your own equipment – which can cost as much or as little as you please – you can either use the general facilities of a camping ground, which will cost only a few pounds a week, or you can camp for nothing, if you can find a convenient field.

There are also camping sites with fixed tents where everything is provided. These are dearer, but even so you should manage a holiday for four in the U.K. for £10-£20 for your site a fortnight, or a little more if you go to Europe. The actual cost depends on the facilities available. Some camps are quite luxurious, particularly as you get nearer to the Mediterranean. Take great care that you know where you are going and exactly what facilities are available before you set out.

2   *Caravanning.* Basically the choice is the same as in camping. Later in the chapter I will go into the costs and insurance aspects of towing a caravan.

3   *Staying in a holiday camp.* These are particularly popular in Britain, though there are some (including a few British-owned ones) abroad. Below is a list of 1977 weekly prices, as published by the *Daily Mirror*.

	BUTLINS	LADBROKE	PONTIN	WARNER
number of centres	17	11	12	15
total capacity	80,000	35,000	53,000	10,000
number last year	1,250,000	450,000	800,000	150,000
number expected this year	1,300,000	500,000	850,000	160,000
self-catering (depending on time of year)	£21-£53.50 (Minehead, suite for four)	£28-£83 (Caister, chalet up to six people) £20-£64 (Chalet up to three)	£28-£67 (Prestatyn, N.Wales, flatlet for three people. Additional people up to seven £6-£12)	£35-£80 (South Bay, Brixham, chalet for six) £21.50-£47 (chalet for four) £23-£51.50 (caravan for six) (£3 charge for cots)
full board (depending on time of year)	£21.50-£46 (Minehead) children under 14 £11.75-£33.50	£23-£39 (Caister) children under 14 £14-£39	£26-£50 (Prestatyn, N.Wales) children under 12 £14-£24	£39-£59 (Sinah Warren, Hayling Island) children under 13 £23-£36
	under 9 £9.75-£26.50 under 2 £6.50-£15	under 9 £13-£23 under 5 £9-£18 under 2 £7-£9	under 9 £12-£22 under 6 £12-£20 under 2 £6-£11	under 3 £9.50-£12

They provide a means for a family to go away together, but then to get away from one another once they have arrived. They probably provide the easiest and cheapest babysitting facilities for those with small children, for instance.

4   *Staying in a hotel*. This ranges from bed and breakfast in a private house to full board in a de luxe hotel. You must decide what you can afford. This of course also applies to renting a house or flat. And having made a price, stick to it. If you allow yourself to go over your budget early in your holiday, you can end up ruining the rest of it.

Once you have booked into a hotel you have entered into a contract with the proprietor. This has certain implications.

If you do not turn up, you will be liable to pay for the room, less a suitable amount for electricity, laundry, cleaning and food. All a hotel has to do to claim money from you is to show that it has done all it could to let the room. If you do have to cancel a booking, give the hotel as much notice as you possibly can. However, if the hotel has a lot of rooms empty you may still have to pay, regardless of how long before you cancelled your booking.

On the other hand, if the room is not ready when you arrive, or the hotel fails to provide you with it, you can·claim damages for general inconvenience. This would include any amount it costs you to find and go to another hotel, the difference between the prices of the two rooms, if the substitute hotel is more expensive.

The hotel can keep your luggage (though not your car), if you cannot pay the bill. But the proprietor or manager cannot hold you in the hotel, unless he has reason to believe that you are guilty of fraud and calls the police. After six weeks, if the bill has still not been paid, he can auction your luggage to offset the cost.

In law hotels are bound to provide travellers with food and drink at any time of the night, but you may find that you have to be satisfied with a few sandwiches. If you think a hotel has been unreasonable in refusing to provide you with food, you can take action and they may be liable for a fine.

Nor can a hotel refuse to give you a room, if it has any vacant, unless you are clearly undesirable. Court cases are rare, but it might be worth insisting on your legal rights in an emergency. This ruling does not apply to boarding houses or pubs.

If you travel in a 'package', however, you are likely to get better accommodation cheaper than if you travel independently. So let's have a look now at package tours.

PACKAGE HOLIDAYS

When you book a package holiday, look carefully at the small print, because if you are forced to cancel it for any reason you may find that it costs you almost as much as going. The simplest way to safeguard yourself against this is to insure yourself in the event of cancellation. Normally, however, you will not have to pay the full cost; most booking forms lay down a sliding scale of charges which must be paid on cancellation. The nearer you are to the departure date, the more you will have to pay. If you find you do have to cancel, do so without delay. The more reliable the firm you choose, the more likely they are to refund your money.

In 1974 several package tour companies went bust and many holiday-makers found that through no fault of their own they had lost not only their holiday but also their money. Following these failures steps were taken to see that this situation did not recur; now, if a firm who belongs to the Association of British Travel Agents fails, those who have booked with them get their money back. As a safeguard for travellers, ABTA makes a tour operator lodge up to 8 per cent of the value of its total bookings with ABTA.

This protects the holidaymaker. To protect the tour operator, ABTA have also tightened up the final dates by which the full money for a tour must be paid. You will now be expected to pay up at least six weeks before departure and cancel after that for only the most extreme reasons – say, that war breaks out. If you book less than six weeks before you are due to go, you will have to pay in full immediately.

Remember that packages can be taken anywhere. They are available in Britain as well as abroad. Remember, too, that not all packages mean that you travel in an enormous group. Package tours can be quite individual, and you may well not be aware that you are one. Admittedly this applies mostly to the dearer packages, but not always. No matter how well off you are it is worth considering a package; you will certainly be travelling at a very heavy discount compared with the independent traveller.

Some rules for package holidays

1 Shop around. Otherwise you may spend more than you need. Tour operators, using exactly the same flights and the same hotels, rarely charge exactly the same price.

    Each operator will have done its own special deal with the hotel, and depending on the numbers he can guarantee the operator will be set an individual price for each room used. Some tour operators have 'loss leaders', and for a period will offer very favourable terms in an area they are trying to build up.

2 When you have chosen, check that the package is exactly what it says it is. If it claims the hotel is near the sea, make sure it is. A sea

179

view should be a real view, not a distant glimpse. Go over the package detail again and again before paying your deposit.

3   Check what you will get in the basic price. Is it bed and breakfast, breakfast and one meal (half-pension) or full board? This can make a lot of difference to the final overall cost of your holiday. Does the basic price include excursions?

4   Does the package give a guarantee that the price you pay will not change, no matter what happens to the value of the pound? More and more tour operators now guarantee that there will be no surcharges to pay, whatever happens to sterling. You will be wise to stick to one that does. Some packages in the past two years have increased in price by as much as 50 per cent between the time of booking and the departure date. Increases like these would cut your spending money drastically.

Getting your money back

If something goes wrong on your holiday and you are dissatisfied, you may be entitled to your money back. Remember, though, that if your package deal turns out to be disappointing, it may be simply because you did not read the brochure properly and expected something that you were not in fact offered.

The contract you sign sets out the conditions under which you travel. Tour operators may say that they do not accept that the holidaymaker has any right to compensation if anything goes wrong, but in law it is not possible for an operator to protect himself against any misleading statements in a brochure which promises that a holiday will be better than it actually turns out to be.

If you feel you have a case you can take it to the county court under the Misrepresentation Act of 1967, or complain to the trading standards officer under the Trade Descriptions Act of 1968 (see section VI, chapter 2). If you win your case, the court can order the operator to pay you compensation.

It is better, however, to see if you can get your money back without resorting to legal action. You should write setting out your complaints and make a request for compensation. Give the firm time to reply. If the company is at all reliable, they will investigate your complaint and write back to you. If you have heard nothing after ten days, write again saying you intend to take action, preferably under the Trade Descriptions Act. Once the trading standards officer is informed, he will investigate your complaint.

Always write, never telephone. Preferably send your letters by recorded delivery. Then you have proof that they arrived.

You have a year in which to bring your complaint if you have dealt with the firm in writing, but if you *have* complained over the telephone you must take legal action within six months. Obviously the quicker you write on your return – or even while still on holiday – the more chance you are likely to have of settling the matter without going to court. If you decide to take legal action, be sure of your case; it is often very difficult to prove. Consult a solicitor.

TAKING YOUR CAR ABROAD

As your car costs you such a lot of money just standing in your garage, it is a good idea to make the most of it by using it as your main form of transport on holiday. This is one time when the car is likely to be full and therefore used as economically as possible. This is particularly true if you are going abroad.

Before you take it, however, there are some things that you must bear in mind.

Car Insurance

Will your normal insurance cover your car when you are abroad? If your insurance does not cover foreign trips, ask for a 'topping up' insurance for the period, or go to one of the companies which specializes in this form of insurance.

You will almost certainly need more cover than your insurance policy automatically gives you, and it is highly unlikely that your continental cover will be as full as the cover for the car when it is in the U.K. The best plan is to arrange with your insurers to have full cover extended for the time that the car will be on the continent. You will have to pay an extra premium for this. There is no standard charge for the extension of your insurance. The cost will depend on where you are going, how long for, and sometimes the model of your car.

Your insurers may give you a European Accident Statement, which they advise you to sign if you are involved in an accident. *Signing it is not a confession of guilt (which you should never make)*. Completing the form is not compulsory, but is encouraged; the form should then be sent to the insurers with any completed claim form or accident report form. Whoever you bump into should also have a form in his or her own language.

As a rule, when the cover for your car is extended, it will also cover any journey you have to make by sea which takes up to sixty-five hours by a recognized route. This includes hovercraft ferries, as well as boats.

If you are travelling for more than sixty-five hours – which is unlikely – you will have to pay an additional premium. This ferry cover does not extend to taking your car by air, but the carrier normally makes himself responsible for any damage which might occur while the car is in the air. To be on the safe side check before you go.

181

Green cards

The 'green card' is the most convenient way of proving that you are adequately insured to travel abroad. You no longer need one when you are driving on many parts of the continent – E.E.C. member states, Austria, Czechoslovakia, Finland, the G.D.R, Hungary, Norway, Sweden and Switzerland – but it is still a very good idea to have one, as it is the quickest and best way of proving, if you are involved in an accident, that you are adequately covered by insurance. It is still essential in those countries where a British insurance policy does not automatically give the minimum cover required by law in whatever country you are driving in. Anyone in the group who is planning to drive should sign the green card.

If you decide that you do want a green card, apply for it at least three weeks before you leave. Tell your insurers the date of your trip, the countries that you are visiting, and any others that you may have to cross in an emergency. Some countries do not accept green cards, so check before leaving. When this is the case your insurance company may not be prepared to extend your insurance and you may have to go to an insurance broker to get the sort of cover you need.

Spain

There are special rules for motoring in Spain. If you are driving there, you will need a bail bond as well as your green card, and this will cost extra. The reason for this is that under Spanish law a car and its driver may be detained by the authorities following an accident, no matter how trivial.

If you want to get the car and yourself released you must insure yourself against the possibility of any civil or criminal action against you from which damages may arise. You will also have to guarantee your presence or legal representation at any proceedings which may follow.

This costs money – far more money than you will be able to take with you under exchange control regulations from Britain. So you buy a bail bond, which is acceptable to the Spanish authorities. It will cost you about £1.50 for cover of 150,000 pesetas (£1,220) and £3 for 400,000 pesetas. Your company may offer you only a £500 limit. This is most certainly not enough. Get at least £1,500.

Caravans

You may also want to take a caravan abroad. If you buy one and use it for all your holidays, it is certainly a good investment and will pay for itself eventually. Indeed, caravan prices have been rising so sharply that if you keep your caravan in good order you may be able to sell it at a profit later.

A fortnight's holiday at caravan sites in Britain may cost you as little as £10; petrol costs, of course, depend on how far you go. Abroad caravan sites are rather more sophisticated, providing all kinds of amenities, including, sometimes, restaurants. They cost rather more, but even so a fortnight's holiday should not cost more than £50-£70, depending on the site. Beach sites, not surprisingly, are the most expensive. As you are unlikely to get even the cheapest room in the simplest hotel for less than £2 per person per night now, the saving for a family of four can be enormous.

You can also hire caravans on a weekly basis if you want to stay put. Fully equipped they will cost a minimum this year (1977) of about £25 at home or abroad. You can also hire a caravan to take on the continent or touring. This will cost an extra few pounds a week. For a fifteen-foot caravan, it is not likely to be more than an extra £2 a week or so, though the hirer will want a £15 or £20 hire insurance deposit to cover himself in the event of damage to the caravan. This will be returned in full if the caravan is returned undamaged.

Insurance for your caravan

You should tell your car insurers that you propose to pull a caravan. Your policy may cover this, but check to be on the safe side. If it does not, there will be a small extra premium to pay. Then, if you own the caravan or it is not fully insured by its owners, ask for extra cover on your car policy to cover that too.

If you have a green card, make sure it shows you are towing a caravan. If you borrow a caravan from a friend or relative, it is even more important to see that you are fully covered by insurance. The same applies if you are towing a boat.

It will cost you about £100 to get a fourteen-foot car plus a caravan plus a family of four across the channel and back. But prices vary enormously with routes, so check this.

YOUR FOREIGN CURRENCY

When you go outside the U.K. you cannot spend sterling. You will have to take foreign bank notes, travellers cheques, or – a relatively new development – your cheque book and bank cheque card. You will have to take enough foreign currency with you to cover all your spending once you get abroad, if you are travelling privately, and anything over and above the accommodation and food you get if you are on a 'package'.

The first rule is to be realistic about what you need. There is no point in ruining your holiday by worrying about money all the time. Work out what you will need in the currency of the country you are visiting and then work back to the equivalent amount in sterling.

Your first question will naturally be what happens if the value of the pound falls while you are away, so that your money does not go as far as you estimated. To avoid this, you can exchange your money before you go. Of course the pound could rise in value, so that you would lose out by getting your currency before leaving Britain. You can't have it both ways; it is up to you to decide which risk you want to take.

Officially, you can take up to £300 in foreign currency or travellers cheques out of the United Kingdom every time you go on holiday abroad, but today there is in fact virtually no limit on what you can take as you can use your cheque book or credit cards as well – though your bank is required to inform the Bank of England if you do so. In addition you can take £25 in bank notes. All this money must be used for your holiday. You cannot use it to put down the deposit on a house, for example; there are special rules about that (see section V, chapter 7, on buying property abroad).

You get foreign currency through a bank, even if you are not a customer of that particular bank, or do not have an account at all. Give the bank a few days' notice, especially if the currency you want is rather unusual. It is against Bank of England regulations to get your foreign currency more than four weeks before you go abroad.

There are various ways of taking money abroad:

1   *Cash:* You can decide to get all your foreign currency in cash before you leave, providing the bank has enough to cover your needs. This is another reason for giving the bank some notice. You may also find that the country you are going to puts a limit on what you can take in, so you may not be able to take all your currency in cash. Italy, for instance, will not allow you to import more than 35,000 lire (about £23), and Greece no more than £11 in drachma. But Spain will allow you to take in £400 in pesetas. In any case you must take some of your funds in cash to cope with your arrival. Cash has the *advantage* of making sure you don't lose by a fall in sterling, but the *disadvantages* that if it is stolen you have no means of recouping the money, and that you won't profit by any increase in the value of sterling.

2   *Sterling travellers cheques.* These can be purchased from any bank. You can cash them for local currency when you arrive at your destination. They are issued in denominations of £2, £5, £10, £20 and £50. The rate of exchange you get depends on the level fixed in the local area that day. Sterling travellers cheques have the *advantage* that you are protected from loss. The bank keeps a note of the numbers of the cheques. You sign the cheques when you receive them and countersign when you cash them, which makes fraud difficult. But there is the *disadvantage* that if the pound falls between the time you buy the cheques and the time you cash them, you will get less for your money than you expected. You will find, too, that you get less for them in shops and hotels than you do if you cash them in a bank.

3   *Foreign currency travellers cheques.* These are probably the best means of carrying foreign currency. They are protected in the same way

as sterling cheques, but have the added *advantage* of fixing the amount of foreign currency you will have available at the time you buy them. Their only *disadvantage* compared with cash is that you are dependent on banks being open to cash them, and in some countries they can only be cashed at a branch of the bank which issued them. Foreign currency travellers cheques are also not available in all currencies.

4 *Your cheque book.* You can now cash a cheque for £30 once a day at any bank in Europe which displays the Eurocard symbol. You must also have your cheque card, which also carries the symbol. This has the *advantage* of providing 'topping up' money if you run out of currency despite all your precautions, and the *disadvantage* that the bank where you cash the cheque may charge you a percentage fee. The service is only available in Europe so far.

5 *Currency transfer.* You can buy currency at home and have it lodged in a bank abroad in your name and draw it when you arrive. This is an excellent way to transfer your money. It has the *advantage* of being safe and easy to withdraw as long as you can prove your identity satisfactorily, but the *disadvantage* that it is really only appropriate if you are staying in one place. It takes time to transfer money, so if you are doing it this way, give the bank plenty of notice.

6 *Credit cards.* These cannot be used to get cash, but they can be used to pay many of your bills in shops, restaurants and hotels. They have the *advantage* of being just as – sometimes even more – acceptable as cash or travellers cheques, but the *disadvantage* that they are not universally accepted. Also, the card company will charge you in sterling at the rate of exchange prevailing when they pay out the bill, not when you use the card, so you never know exactly what rate you are paying. If you use American Express or Diners Club you will pay two lots of currency exchange, first into dollars and then out of them into sterling.

If all these means fail and you still run out of money on holiday, your bank will usually send you more money if you cable them and give them the name and address of the bank where you want to collect the money.

All in all, it's difficult to find yourself completely stranded abroad without money today. If it does happen, contact the local British consulate or embassy. They will provide you with enough money to get home. You will have to repay it later.

Travellers cheques

All the banks advise their customers on how to protect their travellers cheques. National Westminster, for example, suggest that you:

* Carry your passport and travellers cheques in a safe place – not just flung in a beach bag.
* Fill in the detachable slip you will find in your travellers cheque

185

book, and keep this record of your cheque numbers in a safe and
separate place.
* *Don't* countersign unless in the presence of the person who is
cashing the cheque.

They also advise:

* *Do* check rates of exchange when you cash your cheques.
* *Don't* ever get into the awful position of finding yourself abroad
and flat broke. Do use travellers cheques.
* *Don't* exchange travellers cheques or cash with street traders.
There is always the chance that you will get forged notes in
exchange, and in some countries you will be committing a
criminal offence.

Remember, it is common practice abroad for the encashing agent to
call for some proof of identity when accepting travellers cheques. Take
your passport with you when you want to cash money.

Returning from abroad

1 Pay attention to the foreign currency regulations in the countries
you visit. Britain is not the only one with restrictions. Many
countries restrict the amount of actual cash you can take out.
2 Bring back as few coins as possible, as you will probably not be
able to change them at the bank when you get back. If you can, the
rate will be very poor.
3 You must re-exchange cash within one month of your return. But
you are allowed six months to return any travellers cheques.

DUTY-FREE ALLOWANCES

We are all tempted by the words 'duty-free', particularly when applied
to alcohol or cigarettes, living as we do in a country which taxes both
very heavily. And it is true that *sometimes* up to 50 per cent of the price
can be saved by purchasing 'duty-frees. But there are snags.

First of all you are severely limited in the amounts you are allowed to
bring back. The allowances change from time to time, and should
eventually disappear altogether for countries in the Common Market as
E.E.C. duties and taxes become more uniform. The table opposite
shows how they stood at June 1977.

Many people go into a duty-free shop and expect massive bargains.
The things are indeed duty-free but they are not profit-free, and
sometimes the mark-up is enormously high. You may well be better off

goods bought in ordinary (not duty-free) shops in E.E.C. countries		goods bought outside the E.E.C., or in a duty-free shop inside it, or on the plane
	Tobacco	
300	cigarettes	200
150	cigarillos	100
75	cigars	50
400 grams	tobacco	250 grams
	Alcohol	
1½ litres	over 36.8° proof (22.2% alcohol) (generally spirits)	1 litre
3 litres	not over 36.8° proof, or fortified or sparkling wine	2 litres
	plus	
3 litres	still table wine	2 litres
	Perfume	
3 fluid oz. (75 gram)		2 fluid oz. (50 grams)
	Toilet water	
13 fluid oz. (375 cc.)		9 fluid oz. (250 cc.)
	Other goods	
£50 worth		£10 worth

shopping outside where the choice will be wider and prices lower because of the greater competition.

Remember, if you go over your duty-free allowance *you must declare the goods to the customs.* You will have to pay duty on them – and sometimes this is heavy. The penalties for not declaring are severe. It is simply not worth trying to slip something through undeclared.

HOLIDAY INSURANCE

Things can go wrong on holiday, wherever you go. Most things do not matter very much, but sometimes they can cost money – money which you can ill afford. It is only sensible to take out some kind of insurance against the most likely mishaps, particularly if you are going abroad.

This should include:

1 *Medical insurance.* It does not matter where you are taken ill in the British Isles, medical treatment is available, and available free. This is not the case in most countries, though members of the E.E.C. have some reciprocal agreements with one another for emergency medical treatment.

Such agreements, however, do not apply to the self-employed, and you may find anyway that you have to pay and then reclaim the money later on, on form E. 111, which you must make sure you have before you go. Getting this money can be a long and laborious process. You may feel it is not worth it and that you would be better off taking out insurance.

If so, then you must:

* Make sure it is enough. You will need a great deal of cover if you are going to the U.S.A. or Canada. It does not take long to run up a bill of £1,000. Certainly any less than £500 cover will be totally inadequate. Ask your insurer how much you will need where you are going. Skiing accidents which result in a broken leg, for example, are always costly.
* Tell the insurer about any medical condition you suffer from, which may recur at any time. Otherwise you will not be covered for it while you are away.
* If you are sent to hospital, give them details of your cover. The officials will check directly with your company.
* Keep all bills and receipts, even for prescriptions at the chemist.

2 *Car insurance.* Apart from extending your ordinary insurance cover, if you take your car abroad you should consider getting cover for the following extras:

* Hiring a car, if your own breaks down, is useless because of an accident, or is stolen.
* Transport costs for all your party, if you are unable to drive home.
* The cost of bringing the car back to Britain, if it proves impossible to repair abroad.
* The freight costs of flying out spare parts for your car, if that is necessary.
* Customs charges which you may incur if your car is either stolen or completely destroyed by fire or accident while you are abroad. The A.A. S-Star and R.A.C. Cordon Bleu policies cover these items.

3 *Cover for yourself and your belongings.* This is important. You may be involved in an accident. You may lose your luggage or have it stolen.

188

You may lose your money, your travellers cheques, or your tickets.

If any of these things happen, report it immediately – at the airport, hotel or wherever you are. Do not forget also to inform the local police and make them confirm in writing that you have reported the loss to them. Make sure you have a copy of their confirmation. It will probably be a condition of your policy that you report any loss within twenty-four hours. *It is not always possible to report back to Britain in that time, so make sure you lose no time locally.*

You can also insure for rather more unusual things. For instance, people used to insure themselves against the possibility of rain spoiling their holiday. This is less fashionable now, following a few good summers, but you can still do it. You can also insure yourself against being hijacked: this gives cover for injury to yourself, loss of your belongings and accommodation and repatriation expenses.

Holiday insurance is not expensive, and a few pounds spent can make all the difference to your enjoyment.

What you must remember

Before you go:

1 When you take out the policy, be sure it covers the full period that you are away and a little extra in case of delay. Make sure it covers all the countries you may visit.
2 Be realistic about how much cover you need.
3 Check that the age limits cover your whole party.
4 Make a list of the contents of your suitcase.

On holiday:

1 Do not forget to take the policy with you.
2 Keep receipts of all medical bills.
3 Report any losses immediately.
4 Tell the police, as well as airport/railway/hotel officials, wherever you are, of any loss.
5 Ask for confirmation in writing that you have reported the loss.

On your return:

1 Fill in your claim form and produce all receipts and written reports.
2 Give a list of contents of your suitcase, or of the numbers of your travellers cheques if they are lost or stolen.

If you are travelling on a package tour, you may not have to do any of this. Some carriers take out insurance for the whole party and charge an extra fee for it. But check: not all operators do this.

Your Money and Your Job

Chapter 1

CHOOSING YOUR CAREER

The career you choose will have an impact not only on your own standard of living, but on that of your family as well. So choose your career carefully.

If you are a parent, make sure your child is properly advised. If the school does not do this properly, use all the official resources which are available through your local Department of Employment. Try to guide your children into careers with a future. Steer them away from declining industries. Persuade them to avoid the low-paid professions if possible. (Note that this is a book about money not careers. There are many excellent books available to help you choose a career which will satisfy you both in terms of personal enjoyment and in terms of financial security.)

If you are in your thirties, these are the sorts of salaries you can expect to get in the following jobs at the present time (1977):

	£ per annum
company directors	5,000 plus
general managers	5,000-8,000
computer managers	4,550-7,000
marketing managers	4,250-6,300
economists and statisticians	4,200-5,300
company secretaries	4,150-6,550

	£ per annum
systems analysts	4,000–5,500
sales managers	4,000–5,500
chemical engineers	4,000–5,000
physicists	3,900–5,000
civil engineers	3,900–5,300
personnel managers	3,800–5,200
electrical engineers	3,800–5,150
production and mechanical engineers	3,700–4,900
accountants and lawyers	3,600–5,600
chemists	3,300–4,500
press officers	3,300–5,000
draughtsmen	3,250–4,400
sales representatives	3,000–5,000
computer programmers	3,000–5,000

Source: The *Financial Times*

From this you can measure just how well or badly you are doing if you are in one of these jobs. Whatever your job, check on average salary levels and make sure you are being paid what you are worth.

In recent years the position of professional managers has got worse in comparison with those who have gone into the civil service and local authorities. Salaries there are often much higher than they are in comparable jobs in private industry. It is not difficult to increase your salary by as much as 20 per cent simply by moving to the public sector. There, too, jobs are more secure and pensions higher, usually geared to the rate of inflation.

More and more people, who in the past would have chosen to work in the private sector, are today choosing the public sector. Things could change, however. Should the British economy revive and start to grow, it seems certain that the private sector will recover and begin to catch up again.

Think very carefully before you decide on your career. High salaries at the beginning do not automatically mean you will not fall back later in your career. Try to make sure that your earnings are on par with others. At present (June 1977) the average per week is £66.97. You should aim to beat that average, not fall below it.

Here are some of the jobs to avoid where people are earning well below – in fact less than half – the average, as I write:

	£ per week
hairdressers	23.35
London waiters	23.77
shop staff	27.45–33.50

	£ per week
fur coat makers	27.50
laundry workers	27.90
clothing industry workers	27.90–29.70
Toy makers	28.80
Scottish soft drink workers	34.35
flax and hemp workers	34.78
agricultural workers	36.50

You can see from this list why waiters and hairdressers rely on tips to bring their wages up to a living level. Notice, too, how many of the jobs employ mainly women workers. Try to get a job outside these areas if you can. The first step is to get some qualification.

What your contract of employment should tell you

By the time you have been working for thirteen weeks, you should have received a written notice from your employer setting out the terms of your employment. This should tell you:

1 The date you began working.
2 How you will be paid – weekly or monthly.
3 The starting level of your wages or salary.
4 Terms and conditions of hours of work.
5 Holiday entitlement.
6 Terms upon which sick pay is paid.
7 Pension.
8 The length of notice required on either side.
9 Any job title.
10 Any previous employment which counts as part of continuous employment.
11 Disciplinary rules, and grievance procedure, if one exists.
12 The date of expiry of the contract, if the term of employment is fixed.

You may not receive this notice if you work for sixteen hours a week or less, or if you already have a written contract of employment which includes all these details.

Chapter 2

IF YOU ARE UNEMPLOYED

WHAT YOU ARE ENTITLED TO

Most people today are eligible for benefit if they become unemployed. To make a successful claim you must:

* Have no work.
* Be able and willing to take up another job.
* Have paid a minimum of twenty-six Class 1 national insurance contributions.

To get the standard rate of benefit you must have been paid or credited with, in the relevant tax year, Class 1 contributions of at least fifty times the lower earnings limit (£15 a week for the 1977-8 tax year) for that year. If you do not meet this requirement your benefit will be less.

Leaflet NI.12 issued by the Department of Health and Social Security, sets out all the rules in great detail and in simple language which is easy to follow.

At present there are two rates of benefit, one for men, single women and widows, and one for married women. At the time of writing the single person's allowance is £12.90 a week. A married woman can also get benefit at this level if her husband is getting an invalidity pension, retirement pension or any unemployment allowances; if the wife is living permanently apart from her husband; or if she is making a claim for any period after 5 April 1978, if she is paying at the full rate. After that, no newly married women will be allowed to opt out of paying the full contribution.

Further claims can be made for dependents. As a general rule these will be for a wife and children. The married man's weekly rate is £20.90, £8 a week more than the single person's benefit. An additional £3.05 is given for the first child and £2.55 for the second and any subsequent children.

There are further allowances for adult dependents. These could include male relatives who live with you and are incapable of supporting themselves, if you pay for at least half their keep, and female relatives in the same circumstances, but who are also earning no more than the standard amount of an increase for an adult dependent (at present £8 a week), which is shown in the D.H.S.S. leaflet NI.196. In certain circumstances, too, there is an allowance for women with child dependants.

The current figures mean that the 'average' family consisting of husband, wife and two children will get a basic total unemployment benefit, on the husband's qualifications, of £26.50. At current prices this is often clearly not enough to support a family. If you do become unemployed you should visit your local D.H.S.S. office to find out what other benefits you may be entitled to. I have spelled these out in some detail in section III, chapter 4.

You may also be entitled to earnings-related supplement. This is a weekly addition to your basic benefit based upon the amount you earned when you were last employed. You will be entitled to a small payment if you earned more than £500 a year, and a ceiling is reached when your flat-rate benefit and your earnings-related benefit together equal 85 per cent of the current average weekly earnings.

Your benefit may be affected if:

* You get any lump sum from a former employer.
* You still work part-time.
* You have an award from an industrial tribunal under the Employment Protection Act of 1975.

And you may lose your benefit altogether if:

1 You put restrictions on the kind of work you are prepared to do to such an extent that you make it virtually impossible for the Employment Service Agency to find you another post. This means that you will have to be flexible in your demands, and sometimes be prepared to take work which is unfamiliar to you.
2 You leave your previous employment voluntarily without just cause. It is up to you to show 'just cause' for leaving.
3 You have been forced to leave your job because of misconduct. In this case, however, it is up to your former employer to prove 'misconduct' which can range from failure to carry out instructions to dishonesty.

If you repeatedly turn down or fail to apply for jobs which are offered, you may be disqualified from receiving benefit for up to six weeks. This will most often occur when you are offered 'suitable employment', which generally means your usual occupation – though if you are unskilled it would cover a wider range of jobs.

How to claim

You must go to your local unemployment office on the first day that you are unemployed. At the same time you should register that you are available for new employment at the local office of the Employment Service Agency (the old Labour Exchange). When you go, remember to take your P.45 (which your employer will give you when you leave) or a note of your national insurance number with you.

If you do not claim on the first day you are unemployed you may lose some of your benefit, so this is very important.

Payment of benefit

You will usually get your unemployment benefit sent to you as a Giro cheque through the post. Benefit, which includes earnings-related supplement if applicable, will be paid to you for up to 312 days of unemployment (not counting Sundays) in any one period of uninterrupted unemployment.

Once you have had the 312 days' benefit you cannot qualify again for unemployment benefit until you have been back to work for at least thirteen weeks and have worked a minimum of twenty-one hours for each of those weeks.

If you are still unemployed after 312 days you will have to apply for the kind of benefits which I have set out in section III, chapter 4.

Chapter 3

REDUNDANCY AND DISMISSAL

REDUNDANCY

Industries flourish then falter, new technology may require less labour, economies boom and slump. These are just some of the reasons why you could find yourself made redundant. Redundancy comes as a shock to many people, and can change their lives radically.

Periods of notice

Over the years, government-sponsored protection for employees has

195

increased, and, although no one can be completely cushioned against redundancy, dismissal which is not through one's own fault, there are now strict rules which employers must follow when dismissing employees. Employers, too, have corresponding rights; they are entitled, for example, to have proper notice given to them when an employee wants to leave.

Employer and employee can come to an agreement themselves over periods of notice, but the periods set must be as long as or longer than the legal minima. When there is no such agreement the minimum periods of notice are:

length of employment	*period of notice*
4 weeks–2 years	1 week
2 years–12 years	1 week for each year
over 12 years	not less than 12 weeks

In all cases the employee must give at least one week's notice.

This law only applies if the employment has been continuous. You are allowed to be ill for periods of up to twenty-six weeks without affecting your entitlement, and those weeks are included as if you had been working.

Periods when you have been on strike do not break the continuity of your employment, but they are taken off when the full period is calculated. If you happen to have been with the same firm before and after a period in the armed forces, your continuity is not broken, but the time served does not count as part of the full period of employment. *Employees always have the option of taking cash payments in lieu of notice, if they are made redundant.*

Redundancy payments

When dismissed as 'redundant', an employee has the right to go to an industrial tribunal for compensation, as long as he has been employed with the firm for a minimum of two years.

Many companies today have special redundancy agreements of their own, particularly if the industry is running down or the technology is changing, in an attempt to persuade people to leave the industry voluntarily. These voluntary agreements usually give better financial terms than the legal minima, which are:

for each year of employment between the ages of	*employees' minimum payments*
18 and 21	half a week's pay

21 and 40	1 week's pay
40 and 65 (men)	1½ week's pay
40 and 60 (women)	1½ week's pay

The maximum number of years counted is twenty and the maximum pay is £80 a week.

These terms recognize that the older you get the less likely you are to be able to transfer to a new job which pays as well as the old one. If you are offered redundancy you should consider the matter carefully before accepting or rejecting it.

If there is no special redundancy scheme in your company the maximum payment you can get is £20 (for twenty years) x £120 (1½ weeks' pay), or £2,400. Such a sum might be quite useful to someone of forty who was fairly certain of getting another job; redundancy might then seem rather attractive. But to a man of sixty with five years to go to retirement it is not such an attractive proposition. Redundancy payments are tax-free, so the maximum of £2,400 is equal to £3,240 before tax at the current standard rate of 35 per cent.

Privately arranged redundancy schemes often set no limits either on the time worked or on the amount earned. In a scheme which gives, say, one week's pay for every year worked, a man who is made redundant after forty years' service when earning £5,000 a year, or about £100 a week, could end up with £4,000.

Redundancy is clearly something you must think about carefully, if you are offered voluntary redundancy as is usually the case in private schemes.

Defining redundancy

Employers only have to make compensatory payments when employees are dismissed for redundancy. It is therefore vital to the employee that he should be able to prove that he has been made redundant.

You will get his redundancy pay:

1 If your employer declares you redundant.
2 If your employer's conduct justifies you in leaving, for example if you are demoted for no reason, – very rarely – if your wages are not paid.
3 If there is a lay-off or a period of short-time working of four consecutive weeks, or of any six weeks out of thirteen, you can claim redundancy pay. It will only be disallowed if your employer can prove that full-time working will recommence within four weeks.
4 If an employer refuses to renew a fixed-term contract when it expires.

197

You will not be able to prove redundancy, however, if your employer has made a written offer of suitable alternative employment and you have rejected it unreasonably. But no tribunal will regard your decision to reject as unreasonable if you are offered a much lower position, or a job which is quite outside your capabilities. Conflict is inevitable in some cases, however.

If you find that you cannot reach an agreement with your employer you may have to go to a tribunal. You may well prove your point if your employer is known to be running down or closing his business, or if a particular part of it is being run down or closed.

Where a firm is moving headquarters, so that continued employment with that firm requires an employee to move house, it is normal for companies to work out special 'one-off' redundancy agreements. There are many reasons why employees may not wish or be able to move, and their employment cannot simply be terminated without compensation simply because they are unable to move. You may feel that it will be difficult for you to claim redundancy if your employer resists, but remember that the onus is always on the employer, not the employee, to prove his case at the tribunal hearing. (When employees go to the new area, they are usually helped with removal costs.)

Claiming redundancy pay

You must follow special rules when making your claim, otherwise it may not be allowed by the tribunal.

The most important requirement is that within six months you must either have agreed and received your redundancy money (after that, except in very special circumstances, it is too late to put in a claim), or have made a claim to your employer in writing, or have already referred the claim to an industrial tribunal.

Some exceptions may be made to these rules in certain cases. If you have left your claim too long it may still be considered by the tribunal.

In some cases an employee may find new work before the period of notice runs out. This does not necessarily mean he or she will not be entitled to redundancy money.

UNFAIR AND WRONGFUL DISMISSAL

Occasionally employers sack workers and staff for no good reason. When this happens, as long as the person involved has been employed for more than twenty-six weeks, he can take action against the employer and claim compensation. At the outset it is important to distinguish between *unfair dismissal*, where there is a statutory right under the Industrial Relations Act of 1971 for every employee who feels that he has been unfairly dismissed to go to an industrial tribunal for compensa-

198

tion, and *wrongful dismissal* when an employee feels that there has been a breach of contract, which can lead to a common law action in the civil courts.

Unfair dismissal

If you feel you have been unfairly dismissed, or are not getting redundancy money to which you are legally entitled, you should make your claim on a form which is available from the offices of the Department of Employment.

Once the claim has been made, it is up to the employer to prove that the dismissal was fair and justified. If he makes no such claim the tribunal will award compensation to the employee.

Find out what the employer is required to prove; then you can work out how good a chance you have of succeeding in your claim. He must show one of the following:

1   The qualifications and capability of the employee were inadequate for his job.
2   The conduct of the employee was such that the dismissal was justified.
3   The employee was redundant (in which case he is entitled to redundancy pay).
4   The employee could not carry on working where he was, without either the employee or the employer contravening some statutory restriction or duty.

If the employer proves his case and is held to have 'reasonable' grounds for dismissing the employee, the claim will fail. What is held to be 'reasonable' is a matter for each industrial tribunal to decide. If the case goes against the employee there is a right of appeal. If he wins, the tribunal will ask the employer to take the employee back. If the employer refuses, he will be given compensation.

This will consist of a 'basic award', calculated in almost the same way as a redundancy payment, and an additional 'compensatory award' decided by the tribunal. This latter will take into account such things as:

*   The extent to which the conduct of the claimant led to the dismissal.
*   The loss of earnings which has resulted and the prospects for new employment.
*   And, recently, some award for 'hurt feelings'.

The maximum award is £5,000 and the payment is tax-free.

It is rarely in anyone's interest to go to the tribunal if it can be avoided. If you feel that you have been unfairly dismissed, either talk to your employer yourself to see what he is prepared to pay you to leave without taking further legal action, or, if you cannot do this yourself, get a solicitor to act for you.

If you are extremely lucky your employer may give you £5,000 and agree to pay your legal fees to the solicitor. In such a case you may well feel content, as this is the most you could have achieved at the tribunal. Usually, however, an offer is likely to be somewhere between nothing and £5,000.

What ever it is, you must then think very carefully. Just how strong is your case? Is the compensation you may get at the tribunal likely to be more or less than the offer you already have? Remember, a large company will often have better legal advice than an employee. And though you will not have to pay anything for your application to be heard by the tribunal, you will of course have to pay a solicitor if you want legal advice.

If you find yourself in this situation, do not turn down a reasonable offer simply through greed, or because you wish at all costs to meet your employers publicly at the tribunal (you can conduct your case yourself if you wish). You must be very sure of your case and the evidence you can produce, or you may find that you get nothing at all in the end.

Remember, too, that you cannot be dismissed on grounds of sex, race or marital status. For example, you can no longer be sacked automatically because you marry, as often used to happen to women. There are few occupations today which can legally be limited to one sex. If you think you have been acted against illegally on these grounds, get in touch with the Commission for Racial Equality, which enforces the Race Relations Act, or the Equal Opportunities Commission, which deals with the Sex Discrimination Act.

Wrongful dismissal

This applies when an employee feels that the conditions of his contract of employment have not been observed in the manner of any dismissal – though the dismissal itself may have been 'fair'. You might claim that you have not had proper notice as set out in law, or, if you have a fixed contract, that you were dismissed before the end of the term.

If the case is proved, compensation will be given only to the level of the lost earnings which have resulted. In some cases damages may be awarded for any potential earnings lost. These damages look only to the future and not at the existing situation. You cannot, for instance, get damages because you feel that your reputation has been damaged by the dismissal. In these cases the employer can cite the behaviour of the employee as a contributing factor to the dismissal. If he proves this, the employee may lose the case, even though this is a wrongful, not an unfair, dismissal case.

Legitimate dismissal

Not all dismissals are unfair or wrongful. There are quite legitimate reasons for even summary dismissal. These include theft, gross incompetence, negligence and insubordination. Of course it is possible to argue about some of these. Though it would be difficult to disprove dishonesty if you were caught in the act, cases of alleged insubordination or negligence have been taken up.

If you find, for instance, that you were sacked for one isolated act of mild 'insubordination', you would probably have a good case for wrongful dismissal. If you were persistently rude or persistently disobeyed instructions from your superiors, you would find your case much more difficult to uphold.

Chapter 4

IF YOU ARE SELF-EMPLOYED

As you read through this book you will see that the self-employed are disadvantaged in many ways, particularly when it comes to the social services and pensions. For example, they will not be eligible for the new 'earnings-related' part of the Castle pension scheme which starts in April 1978 (see section V, chapter 9). And even to get the flat-rate pension they have to pay a much higher national insurance contribution that those who are employed (at present £2.66 for a man and £2.55 for a woman), because they have no employer to make a contribution parallel to their own. It is vital, therefore, for the self-employed to take care of their retirement adequately themselves and to supplement the flat-rate pension. They are also disadvantaged over unemployment pay and sickness benefit (see chapter 1 of this section, and section I, chapter 14).

Before you decide to be self-employed, you should consult your bank manager, an accountant and a solicitor. There are many practical difficulties and pitfalls which may beset you. The National Federation of Self-Employed Limited may be useful to you; their address is 32 St Annes Road West, Lytham-St-Annes, Lancashire, FY8 1NY (telephone 0253 727075). It operates a service for the self-employed, which includes the issuing of a number of booklets discussing the practical problems of being self-employed and listing sources of funds for small businesses. You may also find the Small Firms Information Centre very helpful. It exists to help companies with a turnover of up to £50,000 or so, or those employing about 200 people. Its address is Peter House, Oxford Street, Manchester, M1 5AN (telephone 061-323 5282). It has a 24-hour answering service.

Despite the possible problems, being self-employed can be very rewarding personally. You will have to remember, however, that you will need capital not only to develop and expand your business but also to provide for your family in case you hit a sticky patch (for sickness insurance see section I, chapter 14) or have a long period of illness. Remember, too, that you will need a dedication and purposefulness which you do not always need if you are employed by someone else. There is no one for you to fall back on, if you are trying to develop your business alone.

Chapter 5

SETTING UP A PARTNERSHIP

You may decide to set up a partnership. Be very clear in your mind what the differences are between operating alone, in partnership or through a company.

If you operate alone you carry all the responsibility for the business – its successes, failures, profits and losses.

In a company the liability of the owners is limited to the stake they have in the company.

In a partnership you have the advantage of the use of the various skills of the partners. All the profits can be shared out among members of the partnership, but at the same time the partners are totally liable for losses. This means that if a partnership fails with heavy debts, each partner is liable up to the limit of all his or her personal assets and possessions.

There may also be 'sleeping partners', who put up money for the business and get a share of the profit, but take no part in the running of the business. They are liable only for the amount of money they have put into the partnership. This kind of limited partnership must be registered at the Companies Registry, at the addresses given in the next chapter.

Most small self-employed people choose to operate alone. Few form companies. Some choose the partnership way. This is particularly popular in professions like stockbroking or jobbing, law and accountancy, where a number of individuals get together to run a business. In fact partnerships are rather more popular than they used to be. Until 1967 private companies were allowed to keep their accounts private. Now they cannot. Limited partnerships are the only option open to anyone who wants to keep his financial affairs secret at the same time as limiting his liability. The most famous example of a limited partnership is C. & A., the well-known clothing retailers. It was a private limited company until the 1967 Act was passed, and then became a limited partnership. This means that even today no one has any idea of the profit levels of this group.

In theory every partner can be limited, but the business would then have to be run by paid managers.

HOW PARTNERSHIPS WORK

When a partnership is set up, it is covered by the Partnership Act of 1890, unless a specifically different separate agreement is made. It is a contractual arrangement which runs for a certain length of time.

Ending a partnership. You can choose to set a date on when the partnership will end. If you do this you can always set up again, if you wish. But most partnerships are what is known as 'at will', and continue until a partner either gives notice that he is leaving or dies.

This notice must be given in writing, and if it is not so given the other partners are entitled to assume that the person is still a partner with the same rights and responsibilities as everyone else in the partnership. If a partner acts in a way which damages the partnership's business, the other partners are not protected against his actions and must take responsibility for them.

The rights of partners. Unless there is a special agreement to the contrary, they must all have:

* Access to the partnership books.
* A share in the profits or losses, either on an equal basis with all the other partners or in a way specified in the partnership agreement.
* Voting rights. Again these may be equal or in proportions laid down in the partnership agreement. Senior partners sometimes have veto rights.

Partners cannot be dismissed because the partnership contract is for a fixed period, unless there are special powers written into the agreement.

Similarly, a new partner may not be taken on unless all the existing partners agree.

Partnership agreements. These cover points such as whether partners may have other business interests outside the partnership and how directly they can go into competition with their previous partners if they decide to leave.

These rules must not be too strict, otherwise they would be difficult to enforce. If would be difficult, if not impossible, for example, to enforce an agreement which said that former partners could not operate in their particular line of business for a considerable number of years. However, it might be easier to enforce one which limits partners' future activities to outside the area – which must be clearly defined – where the partnership does most of its business. Even this might be regarded as too strict in, say, the broking business in London, where most partnerships do their business in the City.

As you can see, there are complications in forming a partnership. You must be very aware of the risks and responsibilities you carry as a partner. Seek legal and financial advice before you make a decision to go ahead. *Never draw up the partnership agreement yourself without the help of a solicitor and an accountant.* If you do so, you could be storing up a great deal of trouble for yourself.

Chapter 6

FORMING A COMPANY

If you are self-employed the chances are that at some time you will consider setting up a company. The stage at which this becomes desirable will vary, depending on the nature of your business, but once it becomes at all complicated it is well worth taking some advice on forming a company.

The overriding advantage of having a company is that you can limit your liability for business debts. If you are in business alone – what is known as a 'sole trader' – or with a business partner, you are responsible for any debts you may incur. In contrast, a company has a legal identity of its own, quite separate from that of its owners, and their personal liability is limited to the value of the shares they have in it.

Since the war there have been two main Companies Acts, in 1947 and

1967, and these apply to all companies registered in Scotland, England and Wales (a separate law applies in Northern Ireland). These Acts distinguish between two forms of companies, public and private, but all limited companies have to file what is called an annual return at the Companies Registry. All returns have to include a balance sheet, of which more in the next chapter. A new Companies Act is being considered at the moment. It will probably tighten up regulations, particularly those covering fraud.

THE PRIVATE COMPANY

It is highly unlikely that your first step will be to form a public company. It is far more usual to begin as a private limited company. The basic difference between the two is that private companies are not allowed to offer their shares to the public; the Acts insist on strict control over the transfer of their shares. Also:

1 There must be at least two shareholders and not more than fifty, excluding any employees. There is of course nothing against employees being shareholders.
2 There must be at least one director and a company secretary.

It is clear that if you are operating a business completely on your own you will have to bring in at least one other person and give or sell them a share, however small, in the business before you can set up a company.

Having thought over the pros and cons, if you want to go ahead, go to a solicitor and ask him to help you prepare the company's Memorandum of Association and Articles of Association and some other statutory declarations and certificates. The Memorandum of Association is a kind of charter which sets out the activities of the company. The law states that it must include:

* The full name of the company with 'Limited' as the last word.
* A description of the objects for which the company was formed.
* The address of the registered office of the company.
* Details of the capital structure of the company, including the category, number and denomination of the shares.
* A statement that the liabilities of the members are limited.

The Articles of Association set out the rules by which the company is managed. By law they must include:

* The rights of the shareholders.
* The rights and duties of the directors, including their borrowing powers.

A company can either draw up its own articles or adopt the ones laid down in Schedule 1, Table A, of the 1948 Companies Act. Before you can go ahead three more statements must be drawn up. They are:

* A declaration by the solicitor involved in forming the company, or the company secretary, or a director, stating that all the requirements of the two Companies Acts have been met.
* A notice of the location of the company's registered office which need not and often is not the same as the main place where the business is operated.
* A statement of the nominal capital of the company.

When you have all these documents you are ready to register your company. It costs £50 to register a new limited company and £40 to register a change of name. All individuals or companies trading under names which are not their own must register the name of the business at Companies House, 55-71 City Road, London, EC1 1BB.

You will also have to pay a capital duty of £1 per £100 on the nominal capital. This means £1 for a company with £100 capital, £10 for £1,000, and so on.

The documents and the money should now be lodged with the Registrar of Companies at:

* For companies in England and Wales:
    The Registrar of Companies,
    Companies Registration Office,
    Crown Way, Maindy, Cardiff CF4 3UZ.
* For companies in Scotland:
    The Registrar of Companies,
    Exchequer Chambers,
    102 George Street, Edinburgh EH2 2DJ
* For companies in Northern Ireland:
    The Registrar of Companies and Commerce,
    Law Courts Building,
    May Street, Belfast BT1 4XJ.

You can do all this yourself, but you will find the whole process much easier if you use a solicitor.

You can start trading as a private company as soon as the Registrar has studied all the documents and found them satisfactory. He will then issue a Certificate of Incorporation and you are in business.

THE PUBLIC COMPANY

The Certificate of Incorporation does not entitle you to trade as a public company. To do that another document, a Trading Certificate, is also essential. As I have said, it is highly unlikely that from being a partnership or a sole trader you will become a public company. But this step may come in time, so it is worth considering a few of the differences between the private and the public company.

A private company may decide to go public for a number of reasons: to release the original capital invested in the business to the people who started the business; to pay for death duties; to finance expansion by selling shares to outsiders; to establish a public value for the shares of the company. To have securities and shares publicly quoted, it is necessary to 'go public'. These shares, whatever type they are (see section V, chapter 1), are then 'traded' – that is bought and sold on a recognized stock exchange.

The first visible step comes when a company offers its shares to the general public by issuing a prospectus; this is also run as an advertisement in a newspaper, with a coupon for anyone wishing to buy the shares. If more want to buy than there are shares available, the applications are all scaled down, and when a great number of people want a small number of shares there is in effect a raffle.

A lot of effort goes into preparing a prospectus, and there is no way of doing this without professional help. Anyway, Stock Exchange regulations require that a public issue of shares is made through a recognized 'issuing house'. Most of the merchant banks have a subsidiary for this kind of business, and there are some independent specialist firms too.

This is a very technical subject and requires expert advice. There are a few points to consider, however, before you spend money 'going public'. The Federation of Stock Exchanges has very firm rules about what companies it will allow to have their shares quoted publicly:

1 The total market value of the securities quoted must be at least £500,000, and if more than one kind of share is issued any one kind must have a market value of £200,000. So a company must be of some size before going public.

2 Though you do not have to sell off all your shares – you can keep some, even the majority, for yourself and your family – you will be expected to issue at least 35 per cent to the public. There are some exceptions to this, but not many.

3 You will have to produce a balance sheet and a profits record for some years back – at least five is insisted upon at the moment. Companies with profits of less than £100,000 before tax are not especially liked.

Once you have become a public company you are free to raise money in a variety of ways. But you will of course have to comply with all the stock exchange rules concerning disclosure of details of your business. These include half-yearly figures, total sales and profits figures, and a number of other business details which on balance you may prefer to keep secret. There are of course legal requirements which apply to *all* companies. If this is the case you should not set up a company. There are other ways of raising money to finance expansion, as we will see in chapter 8 of this section.

Chapter 7

YOUR COMPANY'S ANNUAL ACCOUNTS

If you set up a company you will have to produce accounts once a year. You must draw up a balance sheet showing what assets the company has and what liabilities, if any. You must also produce a profit and loss account, showing what income you have had during a particular period and what outgoings – the balance between the two indicating whether you have made a profit or a loss in your business.

Making up your own accounts is important, and vital to your business. But reading other companies' accounts is important to investors and businessmen. By a careful study of two years' figures, you can discover what has been happening in a company above and beyond the simple statement of profits.

THE BALANCE SHEET

This tells you what your total assets and liabilities are at a particular moment in time. It should be worked out in what is called the 'double entry' system of book-keeping. This means that total assets will always equal total liabilities.

Let's take an example. Our company A.B.C. Ltd. is set up on 1 January. Its share capital is £10,000, which has been put up by its directors. As it begins to trade its balance sheet will look very simple, with liabilities on the left and assets on the right:

Liabilities	*Assets*
Ordinary shares 10,000	Cash £10,000

This, very simply, is the double entry system. The company has £10,000 in its bank account to finance its business – its sole asset; this money is owed to the shareholders who put the money up – its sole liability.

On its first day of trading our company buys new machinery costing £2,000 and raw materials costing another £2,000. It pays cash for the raw materials, but buys the machinery on credit. If it were to draw up a balance sheet then it would look like this:

Liabilities		*Assets*	
Long-term		*Fixed*	
Ordinary shares	£10,000	Machinery	£2,000
Current		*Current*	
Creditors	£2,000	Raw materials	£2,000
		Cash	£8,000
	———		———
	£12,000		£12,000
	———		———

Notice that the assets have become divided into *fixed* and *current*. Fixed assets are those which are unlikely to be changed except over a long period, like land, buildings and machinery. Current assets are either cash or assets which can be changed quickly into cash. Liabilities in turn are divided into *current* and *long-term*. Current will include anything owed to people outside the business – the bank, suppliers or the taxman. Long-term will include the money owed to the shareholders of the business and mortgages.

This picture of the business will change with every day that the company operates. To see what it will look like at the end of the first year's trading, let's suppose these transactions have taken place:

* You buy £20,000 worth of raw materials in the first year, but use only £15,000 for the goods you produce during the same period. The £5,000 left over will be shown as stock and work-in-progress in your balance sheet.
* You buy your factory premises, paying £3,000 cash and taking out a £7,000 mortgage.
* You rent a showroom after nine months and pay one year's rent of £1,600 in advance, so that you have nine months' rent in hand at the end of the year (£1,200).
* As you have not paid for all your raw materials, you still owe money to your creditors (£8,300) and to your bank (£1,300). These are shown under liabilities.
* Not everyone has paid you for the products you have sold to them, so a figure for your debtors (£12,000) will appear under assets in your balance sheet. You prudently assume that you may not always get payment in full, so you allow something (£500) for bad debts, giving a net debtors' figure of £11,500.

* You have been using your £2,000 worth of machinery for a year, and you reckon that it will last for twenty years, so you make an allowance for depreciation (£100).
* You make a profit of £5,000 which is owned by your shareholders.

All these transactions must appear in one form or another *on both* sides of your balance sheet. This will probably be drawn up for you by an accountant, whose calculations will then be checked by an auditor, who is there to see that accounts are properly drawn up. Remember, every asset will be reflected in a liability. A balance sheet is not a profit and loss account; it simply shows the distribution of your assets and liabilities. Your balance sheet will look like this:

A.B.C. Ltd.

Balance sheet after one year

Liabilities		Assets	
Long-term		*Fixed*	
Ordinary shares	£10,000	Factory	£10,000
From profit and loss account	£5,000	Machinery (£2,000 at cost, less £100 depreciation)	£1,900
Mortgage loan	£7,000		
Current		*Current*	
Creditors	£8,300	Stock and work-in-progress	£5,000
Bank overdraft	£1,300	Debtors £12,000, less £500 provision for bad debts	£11,500
		Cash at bank	£2,000
		Advance payments	£1,200
Total	£31,600	Total	£31,600

This is of course a very simple balance sheet, nothing is allowed for wages, for example. The situation will become more complicated with each year. There are certain points you should bear in mind when looking at any balance sheet, however:

1 It only shows what is happening to a company at a *particular specified moment*. The situation can change rapidly, and it is not unknown for a company to manipulate its invoicing to show the company in the most favourable light. This is a bad thing to do and is difficult to keep repeating.

2 It shows only the financial situation. Only in the broadest way will it indicate how a business is doing – the state of the company's bank account, the stock situation, the level of debtors, and things like that.

3 It will not always set down assets at their current market value. Stocks may be valued at their original purchase price, so too may machines and factories. It doesn't really matter how you do your valuation, so long as you are constant from year to year.

THE PROFIT AND LOSS ACCOUNT

This is much simpler to prepare than your balance sheet. You simply tot up all your receipts and all your costs and the difference is your profit or loss.

Depending on the nature of your business and the size of it, the costs can be very varied. You must include not only the costs of your raw materials and labour, but also any bank interest or promotion and distribution costs, for example.

Chapter 8

HELP WITH BUSINESS EXPANSION

If your partnership or company is doing well and you want to expand, it is possible that you will have to look outside for at least some of the money for that expansion.

First of all, work out exactly how much money you will need and how long you will want it for. Then draw up a plan to show the potential lenders. Be thoroughly familiar with this plan, so that you can answer any questions which may come up.

Lenders regard anything up to one year as short-term, between one and ten as medium-term and anything over that as long-term. If you make the wrong decision at the start about how long you want money for you can get into a mess. If you get only short-term money, you may have to borrow later on penal terms to pay off your loan. On the other hand, you could tie up too many of your company's assets in long-term borrowing. *Take professional advice from your accountant right from the start.*

GETTING A SHORT-TERM LOAN

The bank

Your automatic first choice for short-term finance will be your bank. The best and cheapest way of borrowing from a bank is to have an overdraft facility which you can use when and how you wish as long as you keep within the limit you are given. It is usually relatively easy to renew the facility at the end of the agreed period, as long as your business prospects remain good.

The bank may also make you a 'term loan', at a fixed rate of interest for a fixed period of time, though generally they like these to be for more than a year.

Trade credit

It can be extremely helpful for the small businessman if his supplier will allow him to pay over a period. This kind of loan does not carry interest rates as such; in effect the rate is the difference between what is paid over a period and the discount which will be offered to anyone who pays cash within, say, one month of delivery.

Discounts vary but they are usually around 2½ per cent, which means that in effect you pay 30 per cent a year for the credit. This is far more than you would pay a bank, but it is nevertheless a popular means of getting credit and may suit a great number of businesses.

Bills of exchange and acceptance credits

These are provided by the discount houses and the merchant banks, which you can read about briefly in section 1, chapter 2. They have been operating this type of credit for many years. A bill of exchange is a written promise to pay for goods received now at a later specified date. This date is normally three months in the future. The bills can, however, be bought and sold (i.e. are negotiable), so that the person who is owed the money need not wait the full three months for the payment; he can offer the bill to a bank or a discount house as security for a loan.

The bill can either be held by the purchaser until payment is due, in which case it is called a 'trade bill', or sold to the bank in which case it is known as a 'bank bill'. Acceptance credits come in when a bank agrees to accept bills regularly from a particular company, for which the company pays the bank a commission charge. These are 'prime bank bills', and are bought – discounted – at the most favourable rates. Before an accepting house takes you on it will investigate your credit-worthiness.

When bills are due for payment, whoever holds them gets the money in full and receives the amount of the discount as income. Discounts vary and are linked to interest rates, but they are a fairly cheap form of financing.

Factoring

A new service has grown up in recent years to help businesses over their short-term financial problems. It is called factoring, and it involves the allowing of credit against the invoices which a company sends to people who have bought its products. The factor gives money to the company in exchange for the invoices, usually about 80-90 per cent of their total value. This means that if the factor manages to collect all the debts he will make a good profit, while the businessman will pay up to 20 per cent for the service. That may seem a lot, but the businessman is then rid of all the problems of chasing people for money, and the saving in administrative costs can often make up for the percentage lost.

Besides, the factor is taking all the risk. Some companies do not like their customers to know they use a factor, because before taking on an invoice the factor will want to investigate the credit-worthiness of the customer. Some customers may resent this. It also costs money, and the factor's client may find he is paying up to 25 per cent in the early stages of the service. This charge falls as the relationship is established.

You are likely to need an annual turnover of £100,000 and an average invoice value of £100 before a factor will take you on, so it is a limited but useful form of financial help. You can have confidential invoice factoring, whereby the customer does not know you use a factor, but to maintain confidentiality a great deal of the administration will remain in your own hands and may be more costly in the end, even though the initial cost of the service may be lower.

Factoring companies offer a wide range of services; you will see advertisements in the paper. Write to them if you are interested.

MEDIUM- AND LONG-TERM FINANCE

Though some sources of finance are limited to either medium or long-term loans, it is as well to put these together: the basis of the arrangement is similar whatever length of time you are seeking the loan for. The exception to this is the raising of equity capital, which means bringing outside partners into your business, which you do through the Stock Market or by private arrangement.

The bank

It is unlikely that you will be offered a long-term overdraft, and if you wish to borrow for longer than a year you will have more chance if you go to a merchant bank rather than a clearing bank (see section I, chapter 2) – though the latter are lending more and more to businesses for medium- and long-term finance.

Before you get any advance at all from any bank you will be expected to show that lending money to you is a good business proposition. This does not simply mean showing your past record and reasonable estimates for future business, but also that you run your business in a proper manner with proper financial control.

Even if all that is satisfactory, you may still not get a loan, because the banks prefer a few reasonably large borrowers to a greater number of small ones. Most banks have a minimum, which will be at least as high as £50,000.

Hire purchase and leasing arrangements

If your company is very small, these may be your best bet. Hire purchase is offered in exactly the same way as to individuals, but tends to be for rather larger amounts. Certain companies specialize in this kind of business, including some of the factoring companies mentioned earlier. Finance companies also handle this type of business.

You can also lease rather than buy equipment, though there can be tax disadvantages in doing this. If you buy on H.P. you will be treated by the taxman as if you were the owner of the equipment and will be entitled to any investment grants or allowances which may be available. If you lease it is the person doing the leasing who gets any such allowances.

There may be problems, in any case, if you are very small. The lessor companies may be unwilling to do business with you, so you will have to be very persuasive. Make sure, too, that you know exactly what rates of interest you are being charged.

Mortgages

You can get these for any length of time, but they are most useful as a way of getting long-term finance. They work like any mortgage, with a repayment date and a rate of interest. You will be able to raise up to 70 or 75 per cent of the valuation put upon the fixed assets of the business, and as values rise you may be able to extend the loan.

Insurance companies and pension funds are the main lenders of mortgages to businesses. The building societies are severely restricted when it comes to lending to industry. Again, your whole operation will

214

be looked at; it is not enough just to have sound premises. And again you may find it difficult to borrow less than £50,000.

Sale and lease-back

This is in some ways the same as getting a mortgage, except that you give up your right to the freehold of any premises which are covered by such an operation. You sell the freehold for a sum of money and then take out a lease – usually a long one – on the same premises, so that you can continue to run your business from them. After that, a rent is paid to the freeholder. The rent includes an interest charge, which fluctuates with interest rates. Sale and lease-back arrangements may be available to anyone with premises worth more than £25,000, generally from insurance companies and property companies.

OTHER SOURCES OF FINANCE

These are the usual ways of raising capital for business expansion, but there are other sources of money, some financed from government sources and some private.

If you have a new and experimental product you may get help from two sources, both part of the government sector.

These are Technical Development Capital (T.D.C.), which is mainly concerned with production and marketing, and the National Research Development Corporation, which finances initial research and development. The organizations are separate, but liaise closely together. In exchange for money, they may ask for a share in the ownership of the company (an equity stake), a seat on the board of directors or a levy on sales, or they may simply give you a straightforward loan with the usual interest terms. They are useful if you cannot get money from anywhere else, particularly because about one fifth of the deals they do are for amounts less than £10,000. T.D.C. has various branches around the country, and does not turn down more than a quarter of the serious applications it receives. This kind of money is known as 'venture capital', and is also available outside the government sector. Most merchant banks, some clearing banks and a variety of other financial institutions have a subsidiary which deals with applications for venture capital.

You can also go to Finance for Industry (F.F.I.), which was set up in 1973 by the merger of the Industrial and Commercial Finance Corporation (I.C.F.C.) and the Finance Corporation for Industry (F.C.I.), both of which were set up by the government in 1945 to help with postwar reconstruction.

Both of these are carrying on as they did before the merger, but they now have the benefit of more capital, because F.F.I. takes deposits from the public (see section I, chapter 3). I.C.F.C. provides small amounts of money, below the level the banks are willing to lend, usually for ten years or more. It exists particularly to help smaller companies, though today its average loan is about £75,000. F.C.I. is involved in much larger projects, like North Sea oil and developments in the E.E.C. It is not really for the small businessman.

There are also many smaller private organizations which are prepared to lend money. Charterhouse and the Small Business Capital Fund are the best known among these. Your bank manager should be able to give you information about these two and others.

In addition, money can be raised by 'going public' (see chapter 6 in this section). And in the case of finance for exports money can be raised through the British Export Houses Association. Finance for exports is a risky business and interest is charged accordingly. A third of the money provided in this way comes from a government department, the Export Credits Guarantee Department.

If you are very large you may be able to get finance from the government-sponsored National Enterprise Board. But this is not for smaller businesses.

The government of the day also provides direct help to industry. The extent of this will depend on where you operate from: the poorer the region, the better chance there is of getting funds, as the government wishes to encourage development in certain areas. It has divided the country into Special Development Areas (S.D.A.s), Development Areas, Intermediate Areas, and the rest. The S.D.A.s are regarded as needing help most, and there are grants – note, grants not loans – available to help set up manufacturing industry, so as to encourage the relocation of labour to depressed areas.

The level of support and the number of areas affected changes from time to time; you should write to your local office of the Department of Trade and Industry to see what is currently available. This is only the most general outline of the help which may be available to you in the maintenance and extension of your business. Here are some useful addresses for further information, listed alphabetically, with telephone numbers in parentheses:

Accepting Houses Committee,
    Roman Wall House, 1-2 Crutched Friars, London EC3N 2NT
    (01-481-1896)
Banking Information Service,
    10 Lombard Street, London EC3V 9AR
    (01-626 8486)
British Bankers Association,
    10 Lombard Street, London EC3V 9AP
    (01-623 5511)

British Export Houses Association,
  69-75 Cannon Street, London EC4N 5AB
  (01-248 4444)
British Overseas and Commonwealth Banks Association,
  10 Clement Lane, London EC4N 7AB
  (01-623 7500)
British Overseas Trade Board,
  1 Victoria Street, London SW1H 0ET
  (01-222 7877)
Charterhouse Investment Trust Ltd.,
  1 Paternoster Row, London EC4M 7DH
  (01-248 3999)
Council for Small Industries in Rural Areas,
  11 Cowley Street, London SW1P 3NR
  (01-930 7134)
Department of Trade and Industry (Head Office),
  Millbank Tower, Millbank, London SE1P HQN
  (01-834 2255)
European Investment Bank,
  2 Place de Metz, Luxembourg
  (Luxembourg 435011)
Export Credits Guarantee Department
  Aldermanbury House, Aldermanbury,
  London EC2P 2EL
  (01-606 6699)
Finance for Industry Limited,
(including Industrial and Commercial Finance Corporation Limited,
Finance Corporation for Industry Limited, and
  subsidiaries)
  Piercy House, 7 Copthall Avenue,
  London EC2R 7DD
  (01-628 4040)
Finance Houses Association,
  14 Queen Annes Gate, London SW1H 9AG
  (01-930 3391)
Foreign Banks and Affiliates Association,
  16 St Helens Place, London EC3A 6BT
  (01-283 1080)
I.C.F.C.,
  91 Waterloo Road, London SE1 8XP
  (01-928 7822)
  (There are also some local offices)
Issuing Houses Association,
  Roman Wall House, 1-2 Crutched Friars, London EC3N 2NT
  (01-481 1896)

217

National Research Development Corporation,
  P.O. Box 236, Kingsgate House,
  66-74 Victoria Street, London SW1E 6SL
  (01-828 3400)
Small Business Capital Fund,
  88 Baker Street, London W1M 1DC
  (01-486 5021)

Chapter 9

WOMEN AT WORK

There is no reason today why a woman should expect to do less well in her career or accept less money for the same work than a man, just because she is a woman. The Sex Discrimination and Equal Pay Acts have seen to that.

EQUAL PAY

You may still find, however, that your employer will try to pay you less than a man for doing 'broadly similar work'. If this happens, you can now insist – and back your insistence with legal action – on being paid the same money. And you cannot be given the sack for taking action.

The Equal Pay Acts says you are entitled to the *same rate of pay and other terms of employment as a man* if:

1 You are doing the same or broadly similar work.
2 If your job has been given the same value as a man's under a job evaluation scheme.

This applies to all work, manual and non-manual, full- and part-time, in factories, shops, offices and anywhere else. But as a rule you can only compare your work with a man working in the same establishment or for the same employer (though there are exceptions).

Taking action

If you think you have a case, the first step is to try to settle the matter with your employer, either personally, through your trade union if you are a member, or through the official arbitration body, A.C.A.S. (Advisory Conciliation and Arbitration Service).

If this fails, you can go to an industrial tribunal which will settle the matter, and you can appeal if you think the tribunal has been unfair. Tribunals cost nothing. They are not frightening, and you can represent yourself or use a lawyer. *It is better to have a lawyer, but make sure the lawyer has experience of tribunals.*

You can also seek the advice of the Equal Opportunities Commission, Overseas House, Quay Street, Manchester M3 3HN, before taking action. They may decide to back you officially.

JOB OPPORTUNITIES

The Sex Discrimination Act, which the Equal Opportunities Commission also monitors, deals with those cases where people feel they are losing out in their jobs, or have been refused jobs, just because of their sex. This Act applies *equally to both sexes,* though it is women who more often encounter discrimination.

Discrimination has been defined in five ways:

1 *Direct sex discrimination.* This means treating a man or woman less favourably at work just because of their sex. This includes passing someone over for promotion or refusing them a job, simply because of their sex.

2 *Indirect sex discrimination.* An example of this is demanding a qualification for a job which is not really relevant, but which only one sex is likely to have: for example, insisting that a hotel receptionist has an O-level in domestic science, a subject which girls rather than boys usually take, or that a trainee manager in a shop has an O-level in woodwork, a subject which almost only boys study at the moment.

3 *Direct marriage discrimination.* This means treating a person less favourably because he or she is married. This includes sacking someone because they have got married.

4 *Indirect marriage discrimination.* This includes making conditions of employment which make it more difficult for married people to apply. This could arise, for example, if an employer refused to take on anyone with children.

5 *Victimization.* If an employee was treated less favourably than other employees because he or she had asserted rights under the Equal Pay Act, or the Sex Discrimination Act, this would be victimization.

It is obvious that this Act is particularly important for women. It opened up the whole area of job opportunities for women. Better jobs mean more money and an increase in the economic power of women.

Taking action

As in disputes over equal pay, you can take your complaint to an industrial tribunal, but common sense dictates that you try to settle the matter with your employer before taking this step. Again, it is worth getting in touch with the Equal Opportunities Commission before taking action.

WORKING WOMEN

If you are a woman, the chances are that there are different considerations for you in choosing a job than there are for a man.

If you are single or your children are grown up, you probably do not differ much from a man – though the chances are you will still have some extra domestic responsibilities. You should choose your job taking account of these.

Remember that going out to work will probably mean that your housekeeping will cost more. You will have less time for cooking and therefore be less able to take advantage of, say, cheaper cuts of meat, which need long cooking; you may need a cleaner; you may need someone to take care of your children after school before you get home, or even full-time if they are less than school age.

Your wages may push your family income into the higher tax brackets (read the section on tax and married people), and you may have to take a job which allows you to take time off in case of family illness, which may effectively rule out a lot of jobs.

These are just a few of the things most women have to think about when they take jobs. Unless you are very dedicated, the chances are you will not want a job which means that you actually lose money after you have paid out the extras. So sit down and work out just what financial benefit you and your family will get from your working and ask yourself whether it is worthwhile.

I'm not suggesting that women with domestic responsibilities shouldn't go out to work – I have always worked myself – but the hidden costs make the real contribution to improving the family's standard of living far less than it appears when you just consider the salary you are offered.

You should try to ensure that there is some 'tiredness money' left over from your wages for yourself – money for little extras which can give you a lift and make you feel that your extra effort is worthwhile. This could be money for the hairdresser, a few extra clothes, or an extra treat or holiday for the family which you all enjoy and which saves you doing the chores. These are all important in keeping your family contented and keeping yourself happy at work.

220

Family Finance

Chapter 1

THE WEDDING

WHO PAYS FOR WHAT AT THE WEDDING

Fashions in marriage change and today it is less common for a father to 'splash out' in a big way for his daughter's wedding. But some still do, and anyway most couples plan some kind of celebration to go with their marriage ceremony, whether it takes place in a church, chapel, synagogue or registry office.

One decision where money should not be a consideration is whether to have a religious ceremony or a registry office wedding. One expense which is quite unavoidable in either is the marriage licence. If you want to get married quickly – that is, within twenty-four hours – you will need a 'special licence' which costs £14.25, but if you are prepared to wait three weeks or more you will pay £6.25 for a marriage certificate for those couples who live in the same district or £8.25 for those who do not.

The registry office ceremony is usually cheaper than the religious ceremony, but that is obviously not the point. Those who are religious will automatically choose a wedding in church. A simple church ceremony is not expensive, but as you add an organist, a choir, extra flowers and church bells the bill rises accordingly. In most churches the officiating minister, vicar, priest, or rabbi must be paid a fee, often according to what the couple feel they can afford. It may be waived if the couple has strong church connections. Apart from this fee all costs are optional.

It will not come as a surprise to many people that the average wedding and reception usually end up costing far more than was budgeted. The problem is remembering everything and very often a significant item is overlooked until the last minute.

It isn't very romantic, I know, but it is best to sit down and work out all the possible costs before you embark on an elaborate wedding. Tradition has it that the major expenses are borne by the bride's family, a remnant of the old dowry tradition. More and more today, however, the bride and bridegroom's family share them – a trend which is only common sense when women work and make a contribution to the family budget after the marriage.

The first decision to be made is how big the reception should be. If a big wedding reception is going to mean, say, not enough for a deposit on a house, sensible couples are going to think twice and ask for the money instead. However, weddings are very often not really for the benefit of the couple involved but for their families and friends. So rule number one is try not to upset anyone, but don't give into pressure, particularly if you are going to be paying for it for years, when the memory of the day will have dimmed and other more mundane but essential items of living have had to be sacrificed.

If you decide to go ahead and have a reception:

Just as in any other transaction, get several estimates for the reception. Check the cost carefully – are the charges for food, drinks and service all included. Is V.A.T. included? Does the estimate leave you open to any extra unforseen charges?

Do not pay more than about a quarter of your total budget on the bride's, bridesmaids' and bride's mother's outfits.

Make sure you know the cost of the invitations, any announcements, special transportation. Get several estimates for the cost of photographs.

Remember, formal dress for everyone including the bride can be hired.

Add about 25 per cent to your budget for the things you haven't thought about.

If the costs are being borne in the traditional way, by far the biggest bill goes to the bride's family. Here are the items the bride usually pays for:

The church fees (the officiating minister, organist, choir, bell-ringers, etc).

The flowers in the church.

The cost of the reception.

Presents for the bridesmaids.

Bridesmaids' clothes.
Invitations.
Announcements.
Transport.
Photographers.

The groom pays for:

The bride's engagement and wedding rings.
The marriage licence.
The stag night dinner.
The bride's flowers, any flowers for the mothers and buttonholes for the men.
Presents for the best man and the ushers.
The honeymoon.

Engagement and wedding rings

This is a tricky one. You can save money, but you must ask yourself whether an economy in this area will get you off to a bad start with a reputation for being stingy. A way out is to get the bride's view by some window-shopping beforehand, deciding jointly on the price range, and sticking to it. Then:

1 Choose a reputable jeweller.
2 Tell him the sort of price you want to pay.
3 Try to pay cash.
4 Insure the ring.

Incidentally, having a wedding ring is only a custom, it is not essential, and today some people do without one altogether. In contrast, many men wear wedding rings today. The rules are the same and the bride pays.

Saving on your wedding and honeymoon

1 Have the reception at home. Make it simple. Do the catering yourself. Without looking mean you can control how much drink you need buy.
2 Have a buffet or even just cocktail snacks rather than a meal. Many guests prefer the informality.
3 Buy a wedding dress you can wear again. The same goes for the bridesmaids' outfits.
4 Plan your honeymoon well ahead. This may well be the one time you don't want a package tour with other people, but individual

223

packages can be arranged by reputable travel companies and by booking ahead you can save money on individual air tickets (see section 1, chapter 17).

WEDDING PRESENTS

Wedding presents are often a headache – and not just for those buying them. Ending up with twenty-five toast racks or twelve pepper mills is no joke, and a quantity of household linen that does not match your colour scheme is disappointing. And it's just as disappointing for the giver if his gift is not appreciated.

The couple must make the first move and produce a wedding present list, which can be left with a department store or stores. This should be as detailed as possible, indicating preferred brands, designs, colours and quantity. It should also cover a wide price range to cater for all pockets. If no list is available then:

1 Decide how much you want to spend. Don't be competitive with other guests when you can't afford it. It doesn't impress anyone.
2 If you know the couple well, try to match their tastes, not your own.
3 Try to fit your gift to the way they will live. Sophisticated designs are wasted on those who live a rural life, or garden implements on flat dwellers.
4 Don't give money, unless you are a very close relative. It's in bad taste.
5 If you are really stuck, give a gift voucher from a reputable store with a wide range of goods. These are always appreciated to fill in gaps among gifts.

A second wedding, incidentally, is usually much cheaper. It is quieter, clothes are less elaborate and receptions smaller. Very often the couple will say that they do not want presents.

Chapter 2

HOME AND FAMILY

SETTING UP AND RUNNING A HOME

The build-up to marriage, the ceremony itself and the honeymoon are often the most exciting period in our lives. But the setting up of a home and the starting of a family soon brings realism, and many couples find that the early years of married life are financially the most difficult they ever face. The pooling of resources can bring a pleasant feeling of financial security, but it may not be long before the considerable expense involved in setting up and running a home begins to be felt, particularly if the couple is suddenly reduced to living on one wage with an (expensive) addition to the family. Let's look at some of the costs facing a young couple living in, say, the north-east of England.

1 *The house.* If you buy one at or around the current average price for a new house of £13,307, you will probably have to find at least £1,330 deposit (10 per cent) before you can go ahead with the purchase. It is a good idea, if possible, to try to get this money together before marrying. If you can start off in your own home, the financial strains and stresses will be less than otherwise, and you will always have an asset which can be cashed in in case of emergencies. The building society will fix the maximum loan they are prepared to offer you, but it is only sensible to try to keep your repayments to no more than one quarter of your gross income before tax.

2 *Rates, gas, electricity, telephone, water rates.* It is impossible to set a figure for these, for they will vary with every house. But work them out properly for your own home and take care not to underestimate. You should be able to find out what the rates are from the estate agents who are selling you the house. Each house has a rateable value of £X; the rates due are expressed as Yp in the £1. The Y element may change annually. Your Local 'Authority' will give you the rate.

3 *Travelling costs to work.* Is it cheaper by car? Can you both use it?

4 A house is not a home without *furniture and essential fittings,* and you should set out to buy these carefully (see section I, chapter 11). But it is very difficult today to find even the bare essentials for a house or flat for less than £1,000. Of course, you can always buy some things on hire purchase, but remember that you are probably already buying your

225

house in this way, so take great care not to over-extend yourself. You can always save by buying second-hand.

5 You may decide you want to start *a family* straightaway, or this may happen without any planning. Even if you have decided to wait a year or two, try to work out your budget to allow for the arrival of a child.

To make sure that your marriage gets off to a good financial start you should both be entirely honest with one another about your wages or salary. Those marriages where husband or wife refuses to tell their partner what they earn, cannot start off in an atmosphere of mutual trust. I do not suggest you pool all your resources (see sectionI, chapter 6 on bank accounts), but that you pool a certain amount, keeping back agreed amounts for your own private spending. When you marry you will have to follow the rules for personal budgeting far more closely than you did when you were single. If you begin sensibly, quarrels about money need never arise.

Wives and children are entitled to be maintained by a husband or father, but they have no entitlement in law to a specific amount from him. When working out the areas of responsibility as far as payments go the husband ought to make sure his wife has enough to cover hers, and for him to adjust payments upwards as bills increase, or circumstances change. Wherever possible some small personal allowance should be included; there is nothing worse for a wife who does not work than to have absolutely nothing for her personal spending. Wage and salary increases should be shared out properly as well. Too many wives face a 'wages freeze' long after the husband has received a rise.

FAMILY PLANNING

The possibility of planning the maximum size of our families lies within the reach of all of us today. Gone are the days when contraceptives were costly. Every kind of contraception is free under the National Health Service if your doctor supplies the service, apart from the condom which varies in price.

If you join your local Family Planning Association office and pay your subscription, you will be able to get the condom free there as well.

If you have decided that you absolutely do not want any more children under *any* circumstances, you can consider the possibility of sterilization. Male sterilization is free on the N.H.S. There is a waiting list of about six to nine months for a vasectomy, as the male form of sterilization is called. You can also have the operation done privately if you wish. The cost will vary to some extent depending on how quickly you wish to have it done. It ranges between £25 and £50 as a general rule.

Female sterilization is also possible, but, unlike vasectomy, is not often recommended and your doctor will usually only agree if there is a sound medical reason for performing the operation, or extreme social pressures. Again, where it is desirable, it can be done free on the N.H.S.

ABORTION

Sometimes all the precautions fail and you find you are going to have a baby which you have not planned for and do not want. When this happens most women, especially if they are married, decide to make the best of it and go ahead and have the baby. In some cases, however, for a variety of reasons, the woman involved, with the agreement of her husband if she is married, may feel that under no circumstances can she face the prospect of a child.

Today the law allows abortion in certain conditions on the National Health Service. In these cases it is free. But there are conditions. It is not enough in this country simply to want an abortion. We do not have abortion on demand. It is necessary for two doctors to agree that there are sound medical grounds for performing an abortion. These need not be strictly physical grounds, however, and include cases where the two doctors judge there are or could be serious emotional as well as physical risks to the mother and the baby, or to the family into which the baby would arrive.

Abortions on the N.H.S. can sometimes be delayed, in certain parts of Britain, for so long that there would be a serious physical risk to the mother if one was performed. This can also happen if a woman does not discover she is pregnant for a couple of months. In cases like these, where the grounds for an abortion can be proved, it is possible to get an abortion more quickly in the private sector of medicine. Charities like the Pregnancy Advisory Service will perform abortions for around £50, but the cost may be £150 or even £200 from a private clinic. Don't think that by paying for an abortion the operation is any safer than under the National Health. So, if you do want an abortion, try to get one on the N.H.S.

THE COST OF HAVING A BABY

Fortunately the arrival of a baby is a joyous event for most people. The vast majority of babies, planned or unplanned, are welcomed into the family unit. Nevertheless, now that people do have a choice about how many children they want to have, they tend to have fewer than the average family of the past. Many parents today prefer to have fewer children and cater for them all adequately rather than have more and have to make serious sacrifices to maintain them properly.

The ideal family size is something we all have our own views on, and the best way to bring up children is the subject of as many divergent opinions as there are families. Some may feel that it is important for a

227

family to be limited, so that the children can live in a house rather than a flat, be educated privately, go on annual holidays and have plenty of clothes. Others feel that material possessions are not so important and that the love of a large family more than makes up for a few sacrifices. Whatever your own view, it is a good idea to look at just what a child can cost you in money terms from when it is born till it reaches the school-leaving age of sixteen.

In 1976 the *Sun* newspaper carried out a survey from which it concluded that the total cost of raising a child from pregnancy to the age of sixteen was £7,958, taking into account all the state benefits like maternity grants, tax allowances and child benefits. Without these, it reckoned, the total cost would be nearer £10,000.

The *Sun* took its information from the Department of Health and Social Security and a variety of child and family organizations. Its average child – and remember no one is actually average – had a state education, first at a primary school and then at a comprehensive after the age of eleven. At the comprehensive it was assumed it had three sets of school uniform and games kit.

Let's start first of all with the pregnancy. All treatment for pregnancy including the confinement and after-care is free on the N.H.S. Prescriptions for pregnant women are free, and this concession continues until the baby is one year old. Dental treatment for the mother is also free for the same length of time. Milk is also available free to pregnant women who already have two children under the age of five.

Think carefully before embarking on private treatment in pregnancy. All too often you will be paying out unnecessarily.

Private confinements

You can of course choose to have your baby outside the National Health Service and there will always be some people who prefer to do this, particularly as it is increasingly difficult today to persuade doctors to let you have your baby in the privacy of your own home, as many women would prefer.

First of all, remember that pregnancy and childbirth are not illnesses, but a perfectly natural condition which is assisted as needs be by doctors and midwives. There is no need to pay for expensive medical services which will almost certainly not be needed. The only reasonable case for private treatment is for those mothers who want privacy desperately, and this can sometimes be secured even on the N.H.S. Amenity beds are available in some hospitals at a small cost of £2 a day for a single room, or £1 a day for a bed in a small ward with two or three others. Check with your local hospital before you consider private treatment.

If you do decide to go privately the consultant's fees will cost between £100 and £200. This does not include blood tests, X-rays or anaesthetist's fees if you turn out to need a Caesarian delivery, or an epidural injection – a local anaesthetic designed to ease discomfort. It does include your post-natal examination.

If private beds are available in National Health hospitals they can cost from £16.10 a day in an ordinary district hospital to £18.90 in a teaching hospital, if you have your own consultant. A nursing home can cost anything up to £50 a day, but a fee between £12 and £35 is usual for a private room, or £11 upwards for a bed in a small ward. Some nursing homes operate a scheme whereby you pay for your bed and put down an extra £10 or so, should you need a consultant at the birth. The length of time you will stay in hospital varies. Some hospitals and homes will let you go home in little more than twenty-four hours, if there are no complications, others insist you stay a week or ten days, so the cost could be anything between £25 and around £350. Your N.H.S. family doctor can supervise the birth in a nursing home and is not permitted to charge a fee, but if he is unable to attend and you use the nursing home doctor he will be acting on a private basis and you will have to pay.

Medical insurance policies do not normally cover childbirth, but some do include emergency treatment like Caesarians. Check this point if you have private medical insurance.

Pregnancy and birth

A great deal can be free if you so choose during pregnancy, but there are nevertheless some unavoidable costs, mainly for clothes. The *Sun* made these estimates:

nighties (two at £2.50)	£5.00
support bras (two at £1.50 each)	£3.00
support tights (two packs of 2 at 90p each)	£1.80
maternity slips (two at £2.25 each)	£4.50
maternity dresses (three at £6 each)	£18.00

This list is clearly a basic minimum, but even so the total comes to £32.30. And we haven't yet thought about the baby. Here is a basic list for him or her:

basic layette (clothes, nappies, etc)	£30.95
extra clothing (rompers, nighties, stretch suit)	£16.90
cot and mattress	£30.75
sleeping bag	£2.65
blankets	£4.05
pram	£55.00
carry-cot	£5.45
high chair	£18.50
playpen	£14.00
potty	£0.70

baby bath	£1.75
bottle pack	£4.25
bouncer cradle	£3.90
toys, rattles, etc	£15.00

This brings us to a grand total of £209.15, so far: not a meagre sum.

The government has recognized that having a baby can break the family budget, so it has devised several allowances to help parents out. First there is the maternity grant. At the present time this is a lump sum of £25 and goes to everyone, provided that either the mother or the husband has paid at least twenty-six flat-rate national insurance contributions in the preceding year.

But this is only a small contribution to the total cost. There is a further allowance to women who have worked and paid fifty weeks' full stamps in the twelve months ending fourteen weeks before the baby is due. The allowance is paid for a maximum of eighteen weeks starting eleven weeks before the expected date of birth. At present the rate is £11.10 a week, so if paid in full the allowance is worth a total of £199.80, but for every week that the prospective mother works after the tenth week before the birth she loses a week's allowance. If you wish to apply you should get in touch with your local office of the Department of Health and Social Security or clinic. To collect either benefit you will have to produce a Certificate of Expected Confinement, which your doctor or hospital will provide.

MATERNITY LEAVE

You may decide that you want to go on working after your baby is born. In recent years women's rights at work have improved a great deal and it is now forbidden by law to dismiss a woman simply because she is pregnant, whether she is married or not.

It is also the law that women are entitled to return to their jobs any time within twenty-nine weeks of the date of confinement. And even this period may sometimes be extended by four weeks, if the mother or baby requires it.

If you are pregnant and you want your job back after having your baby, you must have had the job for two years and stay at work at least until the beginning of the eleventh week before you expect the baby. You must also tell your employer that you wish to return at least three weeks before you leave. If you don't do this and then change your mind, it is too late; you have surrendered your rights.

* *This means that a woman can quite legally take 39 weeks away from work to have a baby without risking getting the sack, or not getting back the same job she previously held.*

230

Many companies today have special arrangements about maternity leave and pay during this period, but the legal minimum payable is six weeks' money at nine-tenths of normal salary, minus the maximum current maternity allowance.

THE COST OF BRINGING UP A CHILD

From birth to five years

By now the baby has arrived, and if you have received the full maternity allowances from the government you will only have spent a net sum of £14.35. It is with the birth that the expenses really start though many couples find that friends and relatives are generous in their presents, especially for first babies.

By the time your child is five, you can reckon on having spent something like the following, assuming that in all health matters you use the National Health Service.

food (£5 a week)	£1,300
clothing (£80 a year)	£400
nursery heating	£104
bed (after two years)	£14
holidays (£20 a year)	£100
toys, books, presents (£1 a week)	£260

Your outlay has now reached a net total of £2,192.25. If this seems a lot, look at the individual items. You will see that they are not extravagant; indeed, you could very easily spend more, though the average cost per baby will come down with each new arrival, as clothes, prams, nappies, baby equipment and toys can be passed from one baby to another.

From five to eleven

The child is now ready for school. The food bill goes down slightly if the child is having school dinners, but the clothing bill goes up and items like pocket money begin to appear. I will discuss how to work out allowances for children later on. Here is what the bill may look like between the ages of five and eleven:

food (£4.90 a week)	£1,274
clothing (£135 a year)	£675
pocket money (average of 50p a week)	£130
school meals, holidays, other school expenses	£468
bicycle	£35
toys, presents, books, etc.	£250

231

This means that by the time the child goes on to secondary school, he or she has cost the parents a net £5,024.25.

From eleven to sixteen

During the years from eleven to sixteen the child gradually gets more expensive. All children differ in their interests, but a common pattern goes like this:

food (£6.50 a week)	£2,028
clothing (£3 a week)	£936
school uniform, games gear (three changes)	£135
fares (a year)	£240
pocket money (average £1 a week)	£312
holidays, school trips, projects	£480
bicycle	£60
books, presents, etc.	£450
musical instruments and tuition	£284

This is the kind of overall picture you will see, if you are educating your children through the state system and using the National Health Service. The situation is quite different – and much more expensive – if you decide to educate your children privately.

Tax allowances

The sums above are a bit pessimistic because they don't take into account the fact that parents will have been getting a tax allowance for the child. This allowance is given for the whole of the financial year in which the child is born. This means that if a child is born on 4 April, the last day of the financial year, an allowance can be claimed right back to the previous 5 April. If either the father, or – more rarely – the mother is paying at the standard rate of 35 per cent, the allowance will have been worth a total of £754.60, at the 1977-8 level of 35 per cent, by the time the child is eleven.

The tax allowance goes up for children over eleven. It is now raised to £231.00. This means that the saving between the ages of eleven and sixteen amounts to £404.25.

I have worked out the tax allowances on the levels for 1977-8 as if they will be unchanged from the time the baby is born until he or she is sixteen years old. Of course, this will not happen, and allowances in whatever form they are paid, either in tax allowances, generally to the father or in cash benefits to the mother, will increase with the years. This is likely to be more than balanced out, however, by increases in costs, which will probably rise by at least 10 per cent a year.

Child benefits

The child benefit scheme, which was introduced in April 1977, is the first stage in abandoning the old concept of family allowances. These were given to families for all children after the first at the rate of £1.50 a week. The new system is quite different from the old because it provides a cash benefit, which goes to the mother or the person directly caring for the child, whereas family allowance was taxable and had to be included in the husband's tax return. This meant that it was technically *his* income – though the mother normally collected. The ¡child benefit system will not be fully developed until 1980, but this is how it works:

1　It replaces family allowances, but not totally yet. It will eventually replace the tax allowance which parents get at present for their children. It means that eventually there will be no tax allowances for children, but mothers will get a cash payment which will not be liable for any tax.
2　It includes first children as well as others, unlike Family Allowances.
3　It has been fixed to begin with at £1 per week for the first child for 1977-8, and no doubt like other allowances will rise with inflation. The benefit remains at the old family allowance rate of £1.50 for all children after the first.

All told the net cost has now reached £7,958.40. Of course the cost of any one child will never be exactly the same as that outlined above. You can do your own breakdown according to the needs and interests of your children. You will be surprised how large a proportion of your money they absorb.

EDUCATING YOUR CHILD PRIVATELY

Many parents set the private education of their children above very many other aims they have in life. It is a tremendous commitment, particularly if a couple has more than one child, and quite severe financial sacrifices may be called for. The private education of one child can add up to well over £10,000 more to the cost of bringing up a child. And that will only include straight fees to the end of compulsory education at the age of sixteen; it does not allow for school uniform, and travelling costs if your child is at boarding school.

Private schooling is still popular despite rising school fees. At present (1977) parents of more than 300,000 children are choosing to send them to one of the 1,000 plus independent schools in the country. The fees may seem high, but they are not as high as they might be, because most of them are charitable trusts and so are eligible for tax relief. Should their status as trusts change, fees are likely to rise sharply.

School fees generally rise by about 10 per cent a year, though between 1975 and 1976 they increased by as much as a third in some cases, and there is no guarantee that rises like these will not recur. At the beginning of 1977 the average fee looked like this:

London day schools (provinces a little cheaper)		£800
preparatory schools		£1,000
smaller independent schools	boarding	£1,500
larger independent schools		£1,600

These are only averages, and some boarding schools are now charging almost £3,000 a year in fees alone. Not all pupils pay the full school fees, however. Quite apart from scholarships and bursaries awarded by some of the school themselves, places at some public schools are paid for by central government and local authorities. For most families, nevertheless, school fees are a real burden, but there are some ways of minimizing them.

1 Take out an *insurance policy* as soon as the child is born. Such policies work quite simply, and the terms vary depending on how much money you are trying to raise. What usually happens is that you pay a certain premium until the child reaches school age, or the age at which you wish to send him or her to an independent school. This entitles you to a sum of money for a set number of years which must be used for schooling. Once you start to draw the money, the premium goes up. The problem is to decide just how much help you will need. In any case, the chances are that in addition to the money from the policy you will have to dip into your own pocket as well before the child's school days are over.

When you take out the policy make some enquiries about the current level of fees at two or three schools you would like your child to attend. Add 10 per cent on to the fees for each year before the child starts school to get more or less the starting fee for your child. Then work out the total cost over the years, adding a further 10 per cent for each year, and try to get a policy which will give you an annual sum which is an average of that. You draw the amount you need each year. The premiums will be quite high, but a policy like this spreads the cost of schooling over, say, fifteen years and is much easier to bear. Take out the policy as soon as possible after the child is born. The later you leave it the more you will pay, and you may find that you are still paying the higher premiums long after your child has left school. You may be able to switch it from one child to another, and if you do not draw the money as school fees it works like an ordinary endowment policy.

2 *A covenant*. You may have an elderly relative who wishes to help you with school fees. He or she can arrange for a payment to be made to you on behalf of the child. Covenants can be made for a variety of

234

purposes and last for seven years (see section IV, chapter 5). It is unlikely that a covenant will cover all your education costs, but it can be a considerable help.

3   Try to get a contribution to the fees from your company if your job is such that you have to have your children educated at boarding school. This applies to people who have to travel a lot, or get overseas postings to places which are unsuitable for children at school or where educational standards are very low.

School fees when you are educating privately are only the beginning. Fare concessions to teenagers who are above the half-fare age limit (14 or 16 depending on the area) but still at school are not allowed for children who are being educated privately. If your child is at boarding school, his travelling expenses and your own for visits to the school are becoming increasingly expensive. School uniforms are usually more extensive and expensive than for children in the state sector. All these items can add a further few hundred pounds to your total annual school bill. Do not forget them when making your calculations of the total cost.

Advice about schools, help with fees

If you are undecided about which school to send your child to, the Independent Schools Information Service, Albany Mansions, Victoria Street, London S.W.1. (telephone 01-222 7353), may be able to help you. *The Public and Preparatory Schools Year Book* and *The Girls Schools Year Book,* both published by A. & C. Black, may also be useful. These set out some details about the independent schools, but not their fees, which can change from term to term. You can usually find the books in the reference section of your local library.

Crises arise in all our lives, and school fees which have been managed on the family budget can suddenly become a great burden. This can happen in cases of redundancy, divorce or death. You need not despair, however, as some help is available through charitable trusts. The Educational Grant Advisory Service, founded in 1862, deals with about 3,000 applicants a year and grants some form of help to all but about 500 of them. It operates from 26 Bedford Way, London W.C.1 (telephone 01-636 4066). This is probably the biggest, but there are other smaller foundations which may also be able to help you. Here are just a few, in alphabetical order:

Buttle Trust,
   Alderley House, Vauxhall Bridge Road, London S.W.1.
Gabbitas-Thring Educational Trust,
   6 Sackville Street, London W.1.
Professional Classes Aid Council,
   10 St Christopher's Place, London W.1.

School Fees Insurance Association Educational Trust,
  10 Queen Street, Maidenhead, Berkshire.
Thornton-Smith Young People's Trust,
  4 St Mary's Road, Patrixbourne, near Canterbury, Kent.

EDUCATION AFTER SIXTEEN

If your children stay on at school after the age of sixteen they may be eligible for a grant from the government, via your local authority, to help them financially during their extended schooling. The level of the grant depends on the amount of parental income and the system works broadly as follows.

In order to qualify for a grant the person applying for the grant must have been resident in the United Kingdom for the three years preceding the proposed course of study. If the applicant has been living with parents who are working abroad or in the British Forces overseas, the right to a grant is not affected, but it might be if he had taken a year out of schooling to work abroad or even taken a long holiday.

Discretionary or mandatory grants

Grants are divided into two kinds, discretionary and mandatory. Local education authorities have considerable powers over the granting of discretionary awards.

Discretionary awards are usually given for courses lower than degree standard and go mainly to sixteen to eighteen year olds and mature students. They cover a very wide range of courses, for example drama, music and chiropody, but they are also available for some professional examinations like the Law Society and accountancy exams. As many of these courses are taken by women and only discretionary grants are available, women and girls often find it more difficult to get their qualifications than men, if they are not able to support themselves during their studies. If you fail to get a grant on your first application, it is well worth trying again.

Mandatory awards, that is, those which are automatic, are given for designated courses which are degree or degree equivalent. Those who receive them normally have at least 2 'A' levels or their equivalent, and the grant will be for at least three years. At the beginning of 1977 maximum mandatory grants were running at the following levels:

postgraduate students away from home in London	£1,655
postgraduate students away from home outside London	£1,475
postgraduate students at home	£1,075

undergraduates away from home in London	£1,145
undergraduates away from home outside London	£1,010
undergraduates at home	£785

Basically, these maximum grants go to anyone whose parental qualifying income is £3,200 or less. This is equal to about £3,900 gross. After that the grant decreases gradually until by a qualifying level of £10,000 the student gets only a basic £80 grant which goes to everyone. The assumption is that the rest of the money a student needs will be provided by his or her family. There is, however, no law which obliges parents to pay the money out and some of the 'poorest' students today come from families where the income may be relatively high, but very little of it is reaching the student. Any money earned during a vacation does not affect the amount of the grant.

This is how the 'qualifying income' is worked out. You take the gross income before tax of the husband and wife for the previous financial year and set against it the following allowances:

1 Mortgage interest and other interest payments allowed for tax purposes.

2 Dependent children: age under 11   £425
            11–16   £435
            17 and over   £545

3 Other adult dependents, but not spouse   £545

4 Domestic assistance if eligible   £435

5 A parent who holds a statutory award   £215
(i.e. is already getting a grant)

6 Superannuation (not national insurance contributions) and life insurance payments to a maximum of 15 per cent of gross income.

This table shows what parents are expected to contribute towards the student's living expenses at sample levels:

Residual Income £	1976-77 contribution £	1977-78 contribution £
3,100	110	—
3,200	130	20
3,300	150	40
3,400	170	60
3,700	230	120
4,000	290	180
4,300	340	240
4,600	370	300
4,900	400	350

7,000	610	550
10,000	910	823
13,000	1,210	1,096

Scale continues at £1 per £11 of additional income.

If you come from a family where the qualifying income is high, it is worth seeing whether you qualify for independant status. This means that your grant is not assessed on parental income and is always therefore the maximum.

To qualify you must fulfil one of the following conditions:

1 You must have supported yourself out of earnings for at least three years before your course begins. You are allowed up to six months' unemployment in this period, and for married students time spent at home looking after children is counted. Or,
2 You must have reached the age of twenty-five.

If you are over twenty-six when you begin your course you may be eligible for a further annual payment which is related to your age. It starts at £68 at twenty-six and moves to £400 if you are 29 or over. There is also a 'two homes allowance' if you live in college during term time and also maintain a home for your dependents somewhere else.

There are other grants, including some for dependents, and it is worth enquiring about them. There are also additional allowances for divorced and separated students. For example, you may also be allowed £30, for special equipment, if you are taking such courses as music, medicine, veterinary science, ophthalmic optics, architecture, landscape architecture, town and country planning, art and design, physical education or domestic sciences.

If you have to study abroad, your local authority may, at their discretion, contribute up to £100 if you are going to a 'high cost' country. These include most of Europe, except Italy, Japan and the U.S.A. Local authorities will refund the cost of medical insurance a student studying abroad needs to take out.

CHILDREN'S ALLOWANCES

Only foolish parents do not give their children an allowance each week. A child needs to learn to manage money and this cannot start too soon. The parent who indulges a child's every whim and supplies him with money on demand will eventually find himself with an adult who will never learn proper money management.

Family circumstances vary, but regardless of how much you can afford there are some general rules which will help both parents and children:

* Give a child an allowance as soon as he realizes that money can be used to buy the things he wants.
* Make it clear what the allowance covers. The older children get, the more responsibility they can have over their spending, until by the time they leave school they have experience of running a mini-budget.
* Take into account the allowances the child's friends get. There is nothing worse than being given less money than one's friends, but those who have far more than their friends may find things equally difficult.
* Give advice when asked for it about how an allowance should be spent, but *never* give instructions. Be flexible. There is no point in spoiling a child's enjoyment by refusing *ever* to make an advance on the following week's allowance.
* Review the level of the allowance from time to time, annually if possible. When deciding to increase an allowance explain your decision and give the child a chance to put his own views forward.
* At the start you may have to give a small child a little of the total weekly allowance every day. Later you can move to a week and then longer periods. If your child is likely to be a student getting a grant three times a year, try, if you can manage it, to do the same thing.
* Try not to make an allowance dependent on a child doing 'jobs', or at least give them a basic, plus extras for any tasks you agree.

Children and bank accounts

Most children enjoy having money in the post office or in a bank. The post office is more visible, easier to use, and more suitable for children who have little money. A child can deposit as little as 25p at a time. Some children are ready for this kind of account by the age of seven.

A current bank account is another matter. The teenager who can control his money properly is fairly rare. Only the parent can judge such cases as these, but if a child has shown consistent common sense by the time he is fifteen I think it is worth a try. When children are under age the bank will usually insist that an account is joint with one of its parents, so that the parent can see the statement and keep a tactful check on how the account is managed, retiring gracefully once the child becomes a wage earner.

Credit cards are a different matter and only in very exceptional cases would I advise a parent to underwrite them. Some parents, however, may trust their children enough to allow them to use their (the parents') own accounts.

Chapter 3

WHEN MARRIAGES GO WRONG

DIVORCE

Not all couples live happily ever after. As many as three out of ten of all marriages end in divorce and the younger you are when you marry the greater the chances are that your marriage will end not in death, but in divorce. In marriages where one or both partners are less than twenty, for example, there is a fifty-fifty chance that they will eventually divorce.

This book is only concerned with the financial aspects of the breakdown of a marriage, but money becomes interwoven with emotions when there is a separation or a divorce. The first consideration, then, is to think clearly and not allow feelings of anger, revenge or outright vindictiveness to influence you in coming to a proper financial arrangement.

To some extent these arrangements are covered by law. No court will order a man to pay so much in maintenance that he finds it difficult to live. No court will turn a woman out of her home just because her marriage has broken up and her husband, or ex-husband, wishes to sell the house, except in very rare circumstances where there would be no hardship.

Let's look first at the current cost of a divorce:

1 The basic cost of filing a suit for divorce is £16.
2 Filing fees for any application for financial support are £10.
3 Taking confession statements in cases of adultery costs about £10.

These are the legal charges, but the major cost you will probably face is that of a solicitor, and possibly a barrister. Solicitors' charges vary enormously. They are unlikely to charge you less than £4 an hour for the work they do for you and you may pay anything up to £20. About £8 to £10 is average. So clearly, the more a couple can reach agreement between themselves before going to solicitors the more money they will save. It is no use being vindictive and letting the costs run away with themselves, because you expect your husband or wife to be saddled with them. The more a divorce costs the less money there is available in any

240

settlement, and you cannot always be sure to get your costs paid by the other side, even if you are the 'innocent' party.

A barrister will usually charge about £15 to represent you at a simple undefended divorce hearing. But if you start to disagree on, say, custody of children or financial matters and he is asked to give an 'opinion', he will charge you much more. Try to find out before you embark on a divorce what the solicitors' fee will be and what he will be doing for that fee. Ask about possible extras. If the divorce goes through quickly and easily you should know the extent of your bill roughly before you start, but a solicitor cannot estimate in advance for any unforeseen problems which may arise and which could put the bill up.

You can do a divorce yourself in certain circumstances, but it is sensible to try this only when no problems are likely to arise. That way you can bring the costs of the divorce down to the £16 filing fee plus about 50p for the forms you must fill in. You can even get a divorce by post and neither of you need appear in court. If a couple can agree about this, a great deal of money can be saved. There are several excellent books which explain how you should go about it. If you have children under the age of eighteen you will have to appear in court in any case, so that the court can be satisfied that their welfare is assured.

Order for costs

In most simple divorce cases the petitioner, particularly if it is the wife, will ask for an order for costs to be made against the respondent. This will usually be granted. There are cases, however, where no order for costs is made or where the petitioner and respondent are each ordered to pay their own costs. This would happen if the court felt that the petitioner had acted in such a way as to make the divorce far more expensive than it otherwise need have been. In divorces by post the cost works out at only around £8.25 each, a sum hardly worth bothering about. If you decide on legal separation instead of divorce, the financial rules are the same.

If you think your lawyer has charged you too much, you can ask for an itemized breakdown of the bill. If it still seems too high when you have looked at it, get your solicitor to obtain a certificate of reasonableness of his costs from the Law Society. If, when you see the certificate, you are still not satisfied, you should contact The Law Society, 113 Chancery Lane, London WC21 1PL, or if you live in Scotland, contact The Administrative Secretary, The Law Society of Scotland, 27 Drumsleigh Gardens, Edinburgh EH3 7YR. If you have a low income or are not working, you may qualify for legal aid (see section VI, chapter 1). You may get some reduction in your costs this way.

The 'best' way to divorce

Divorce is always a sad business, but it does happen and should be faced sensibly. The 'best' way to divorce is either to do it by post, if you have no children under eighteen, or, if not, by consent after two years' separation with all questions of maintenance and custody worked out with your solicitors before the divorce hearing. That way you can both save thousands – and I mean thousands – of pounds and your divorce should not cost more than a few hundred pounds at the most.

MAINTENANCE

It is obviously best if a couple can agree on the level of maintenance, which the man usually pays to support his former wife and children – though today a woman can, theoretically at least, be made to support a former husband.

It is advisable, too, to give this agreement legal standing as soon as possible, because there are financial advantages for both husband and wife. While a husband is paying maintenance voluntarily, he gets no tax relief apart from the normal allowances for a wife and children, depending on the children's ages. As soon as the agreement becomes a legal one, i.e. accepted by the Court, he is able to pay maintenance net of tax at the standard rate, while the wife is usually able to reclaim part of the tax he has paid.

If a husband finds that a wife is unwilling to come to a legal agreement – and sometimes this happens even though the financial advantages are clear – it may be best for the husband to apply immediately to the court to sort the matter out, or force his wife to go to Court herself by withholding maintenance. This may sound extreme, but the sooner these financial matters can be settled the sooner any other problems will sort themselves out.

The sensible wife will apply to the court for maintenance for herself and for the children of the marriage, which will last until the children either leave home or go out to work. She can go back to the court if her husband is either not paying enough, or not regularly enough. In the majority of cases this matter is settled fairly amicably between the couple, and the court will merely be rubber-stamping their agreement when the divorce suit goes through.

Maintenance levels

The most important thing to remember when you are getting divorced is that the overwhelming probability is that both husband and wife will have to accept a lower standard of living, at least temporarily. If you do

242

not accept this, the chances are that you will go on squabbling about money at (sometimes) enormous cost to both.

If previously only the husband was working and supporting the family, his salary will now have to keep up two separate homes, until his wife either remarries or gets a job. The wife will be trying to live on a much smaller proportion of her ex-husband's income, unless she takes a job to supplement the amount she gets from him. If he remarries, she may find that getting any 'extras' over the basic maintenance for the children becomes virtually impossible.

All rights to maintenance for the spouse cease as soon as an ex-wife (or ex-husband if the wife is maintaining him) remarries, but rights to maintenance for the children continue until the child or children have completed full-time education, or reached the age of seventeen. There are no absolute rules in deciding the level of maintenance, but as a general guide the court will start with the life-long provision of about one-third of the husband's income before tax for the wife, plus up to one fifth for each child. Obviously the provision for children is only a guide: were it at a fixed rate, a man with three children, for example, would have nothing left from his salary to live on himself. Sometimes, where the husband gives up all rights to the matrimonial home, the Court may order him to pay less maintenance to his former wife as a compensation for giving up his only capital asset.

If the wife was also working, the one-third rule applies not just to the husband's income, but to their total gross income added together.

Here are a few examples to show you how it works.

husband's income	£4,500
wife's income	nil
total income	£4,500
one-third to wife	£1,500
maintenance order	£1,500
husbands's income	£4,500
wife's income	£3,000
total income	£7,500
one-third	£2,500
wife already has	£3,000
maintenance order	nil

243

husband's income	£12,000
wife's income	£3,000
total income	£15,000
one-third	£5,000
wife already has	£3,000
maintenance order	£2,000

As you can see, the husband benefits from his estranged or ex-wife working. It may be a temptation for this reason for a wife not to work, even where she is able. This is a mistake, not only for financial but also for personal reasons. It is a good idea to get out into the world to make new friends and achieve some financial independence after a marriage ends.

Where a husband's income is very large or very small, the one-third rule may not be followed, and in marriages which have lasted only a very short time, particularly where there are no children, the court may award a former wife no maintenance at all.

When you are trying to work out maintenance levels remember that if you are unable to settle and have to go to court the two factors which will be taken into consideration are, first, the wife's standard of living before the break-up, which the court will seek to maintain as far as possible, and, second, the husband's income and ability to pay, which may be affected if he decides to remarry. Obviously, unless a man is very wealthy or very poor these two aims may be incompatible. Settle for the best you can reasonably expect. The level of payments can of course be modified by the court if circumstances change. The husband may earn more, or lose his job; the wife may start or stop working.

Maintenance payments are usually paid at regular intervals, but occasionally a couple will agree that a once-and-for-all lump sum should be paid to the wife. This can be paid in instalments, but once agreed it cannot be varied. The same applies if a lump sum is ordered for children. Clearly if a woman is planning to remarry quickly the payment of a lump sum is more attractive than periodic maintenance payments. Lump sums may also be more attractive to the working wife. If the couple did not own their own house, a lump sum can be the deposit for a new house and, therefore, a prospect of long-term financial security, or it can be used to start a business. Think carefully before you make your claim and discuss all the possibilities with your bank manager or solicitor. Check too on any pension rights you may have after a divorce.

Children

Maintenance for children is a very thorny area financially, and children are involved in 75 per cent of divorce cases. Maintenance payments for children usually end on the birthday following the age limit for compulsory schooling. At present that is sixteen, so payments will normally end on the seventeenth birthday. If the child continues in full-time schooling, or is unable to work for any physical or mental reason, the payments may continue. A couple should try to work out a sensible arrangement for the maintenance of children. It is no use taking so much money away from the man that he is unable to spend any money himself on his children, over and above the payments to his ex-wife. The man will have his children at least for some weekends and holidays and that will cost him money. Although there is the vague one-fifth rule, the court will usually order a husband to pay at least £5 a week for a child, if his income justifies it. He may or may not continue to receive the child allowance for tax purposes.

Short marriages

For a woman marriage used to be a passport to financial security for life. This is no longer so. Maintenance is now often more generous than in the past, but the court pays attention also to the particular circumstances of each marriage. One which has only lasted a few years, where the couple are still young, and there are no children, is now often simply dissolved by the court with no order for maintenance to an able-bodied wife who is quite capable of getting a job.

The court may make a nominal order of 'one shilling a year' in certain cases. This order is designed to cope with changed circumstances, for an order, once made, even for a 'shilling', can be varied. At a later date, should an ex-wife become incapacitated or without an income for any reason, she can go back to the court and ask for the order to be varied. Sometimes a lump sum, though smaller than after a longer marriage, may be paid to the ex-wife.

In a marriage where a wife has always worked and there are no children and the marriage has lasted only a few years, there is no good reason why the husband should be bound in any way to maintain an ex-wife. A solicitor would advise potential ex-husband's to resist any maintenance claim, however small it may seem. You don't want to be remarried for twenty years with four children, only to find an ex-wife turning up with a new claim.

Getting your maintenance

One big worry after divorce can be actually getting the maintenance you have been awarded. To make this as sure as possible:

1   Keep proper records of all payments and when they arrive.

2   If you think your ex-husband or wife may not pay, you can ask the court to have the payments registered in the Magistrates' Court. When this happens the payments go first to the court, which then passes them on to the recipient.
3   Try to make sure you know where your ex-spouse is living and working. If he or she has disappeared, there *may* be no official help forthcoming to locate him or her.
4   You can sometimes get an attachment of earnings. Under this section the employer withholds the amount of the order from (usually) the husband's salary and sends it to the wife.
5   If arrears have built up you can go to the court, which will either issue an attachment of earnings or a committal order. The maximum for which the ex-spouse can be committed to prison for contempt of a court order is six weeks. The threat of committal is usually enough to make most people pay up. The procedure for getting arrears differs depending on whether you go to the magistrates' court or the county court; your solicitor will advise you as to which court you should go.
6   Apply for social security. Then the local office *will* help you to trace a missing ex-spouse.
7   If you feel that your maintenance is insufficient and the salary of your ex-spouse has risen sharply, you can apply to the court for more money. If your husband's (or wife's) salary has fallen, however, he can similarly apply to have the amount reduced.
8   If your ex-spouse has gone abroad and fails to continue payments, check to see whether Britain has a reciprocal arrangement with the country involved to collect maintenance payments.

DIVISION OF ASSETS

The matrimonial home

When a marriage breaks up there are assets which must be divided fairly between the couple. The most important of these is normally the matrimonial home. If the home is held in joint names, both are entitled to live in it, until the matter is settled by the court, or the couple reach an agreement. Obviously in most cases it will be the wife who stays, or at least the partner who is caring for the children, and this will usually be the woman. The house cannot be sold by either party without the agreement of the other.

If the house is in the name of only the husband, or the wife, the situation is more complicated. Many women fear that their husbands could force them out of the house, or sell it from beneath them. This is not the case, and under the Matrimonial Homes Act of 1967 both husband and wife have the right not to be evicted, or excluded from any part of the matrimonial home, unless the Court decrees it. Nor can the house be sold without a court order. A spouse with no proprietorial right to the house can register a claim to his or her occupation rights. This claim is filed at the Land Registry, so that any prospective buyer will know that a person other than the owner has the right to live in the house – a right which takes precedence over the rights of any other person who may buy the house. Do not forget to register this claim; without registering you cannot claim your rights.

The law has changed considerably over the years to give women financial rights to their homes, even if they are not joint owners, or do not go out to work, so that the financial contribution they can have made to the home is minimal or non-existent. The Matrimonial Proceedings and Property Act, 1970, set out for the first time that a wife does have some financial rights, and it recognized her contribution to the home as a home-maker caring for a family.

What happens varies in each case. The Court may instruct a husband to turn the house over to his wife or ex-wife. Alternatively it may allow him to maintain an interest, but state that the home must remain intact while the children are being educated. It may then decide that once the children are grown up the house must be sold and the proceeds divided. Obviously it is best for the wife if she can secure absolute ownership of the house; her maintenance will allow for the mortgage payments. In a case like this, if she remarries and decides to sell the house, she will be entitled to all the proceeds. A Court does not normally consider the remarriage prospects, unless these are stated when maintenance is being decided. In law the husband can make the same claims in similar circumstances.

The only problem then, as far as occupation goes, is the building society or insurance company where there is a mortgage outstanding on the house. If the payments are not kept up, the building society will eventually simply repossess the house and the Land Registry filing then becomes irrelevant. This can be a problem for many wives, who will have to find some way of keeping up the payments if the husband fails to do so. This is yet another reason for making a legal agreement as soon as possible. Building societies are not monsters, and if they are informed of the situation they will do all they can to help, even altering the terms of the mortgage in some cases, to bring down the monthly repayments, or suspending them for a time until a wife has been to Court or got herself a job which enables her to meet payments. If all efforts fail and the house is sold, the wife (or indeed the husband) can claim a right to part of the proceeds. *It is advisable not to let things go this far.*

This is roughly the situation for owner-occupiers. A solicitor will describe the rules in more detail for you, and there are also several excellent books to help you which are on sale at most large bookshops.

The same sort of protection goes to husbands and wives who live in rented property and whose home is covered by the Rent Act (see section V, chapter 7). A court can order that the tenancy be transferred to the other spouse, whether it is private rented property or council housing. This is very important for women, because unlike in owner-occupied houses where joint ownership is now the rule rather than the exception, tenancy agreements are usually between the owner and one spouse, that one generally being the husband. If a tenancy is transferred all the rights and responsibilities go with it, the responsibility for paying the rent, the responsibility for maintaining the property (if the lease stipulates it) and the right to continue living in it.

Other assets

Most people today have assets other than their home. To begin with there are the contents of the house. Normally these will go to the wife, or whoever is taking care of the children, with the exception of personal belongings, such as family paintings, antiques, or other things which one partner has brought into the marriage. These do not become joint property, so it is no use a wife hanging on to her husband's personal belongings, or a husband on to his wife's. He or she can sue for them under section 17 of the Matrimonial Property Act, and there is no way a wife or husband can claim something which does not belong to him or her. Wedding presents are held to be joint property, unless specifically given to one partner, a rather unusual occurrence. This is a very tricky area, and a couple should try to sort this out amicably, but be warned, it is often the sticking point in an otherwise fairly amicable agreement.

LIVING TOGETHER

Although marriage has never been more popular, the moral attitude to it has changed and many couples live together at least for a period before marrying. Many other couples live together happily for many years, for one reason or another. Maybe one partner is already married and has not been prepared to push an unwilling spouse into a divorce, usually on religious grounds. Some of these relationships are successful and life-lasting; others, just like marriages, founder.

If you are living with someone, you should remember that it is not exactly like being married to them. There is no marriage contract and therefore none of the financial rights that go with marriage. Nevertheless, although the law does not recognize the so-called 'common-law wife', the courts today are taking a much more sympathetic attitude, particularly towards the woman, in cases like these. If there are any children, a woman will certainly be awarded maintenance for them on very much the same terms as for the children of a marriage. If a couple has lived in a house or run a business which the woman can prove she has

248

contributed to, a court may award her a share in it. If you are living with someone the best way to protect yourself is to have a legal share in everything. Then if the relationship breaks up you will at least be guaranteed your share in the home and its contents.

SINGLE-PARENT FAMILIES

In the vast majority of divorce cases, one partner ends up with the main responsibility for the day-to-day care of any children of the marriage. There are more than 1,375,000 single parent families in Britain, and in 1,123,000 of them it is the mother who is caring for the children.

Most couples who divorce usually manage in the end to sort out their financial affairs, but there are always a few cases where the mother may find it exceedingly difficult to get any money out of her ex-husband, even where there has been a legal agreement. Endless forays into the Court to collect arrears or secure an attachment of earnings to ensure payment can be a costly and wearing business. In some cases it is not possible to find out where a former husband is.

When this happens there is almost inevitably financial hardship for the family. Very often they are entitled to the sort of government benefits which go to all poor families and which I have outlined in the next chapter. But these are not enough to ensure a good standard of living, and in order to achieve this the mother often has to return to work. This step will be easier if she has a proper career to go to in which she already has experience or training. If you are a woman and marrying – although it sounds unromantic – try to make sure:

1 That you have some basic skills which you can always use if you are widowed or divorced, or your husband is unable to work for any reason.
2 That you have some experience in your career before giving it up. This will make it easier for you to return to it later.
3 If you have a sound and flourishing career, that you consider very carefully before giving it up when you have children. The legal maternity leave is now generous and you may find it worthwhile to continue working, even when your children are small.
4 That you try to stay in touch with developments in your particular field, so that you do not get rusty.

Bear these things in mind, then if you suddenly find you have to go out to work again, it will be far easier to re-start than if you have been cocooned in your home for years.

There are some organizations which exist to help single-parent families, both emotionally, and, where possible, financially:

They are, alphabetically:

GINGERBREAD
   9 Poland Street, London W1V 3DG
Membership is free and the organization is open to both sexes. It
welcomes voluntary contributions.
FAMILIES NEED FATHERS
   23 Holmes Road, London N.W.5 (01-485 4226) open afternoons
   only, 2-6 p.m.
Formed to help men who feel they are not getting proper access to their
children. Both men and women may join.
THE NATIONAL COUNCIL FOR ONE-PARENT FAMILIES
   255 Kentish Town Road, London NW5 2LX
Gives advice either by post or in person.
THE NATIONAL FEDERATION OF CLUBS FOR THE DIVORCED AND SEPARATED
   13 High Street, Little Shelford, Cambridge.
   Represents clubs throughout Britain, and gives advice on housing,
finance, problems with children, etc.
SINGLE-HANDED LIMITED
   68 Lewes Road, Haywards Heath, Sussex.
This organization tries to find resident housekeeping jobs for single
mothers in the homes of single fathers. It will also bring together two
women both with children who would like to share responsibilities.
There is a fee for these services.

Chapter 4

HELP FOR POORER FAMILIES

Over the years, as the welfare state has developed, state benefits have
been introduced to assist those whose income is temporarily or permanently below certain levels. The income levels at which these benefits
are made available are revised upwards from time to time, as are the
rates of benefit. Announcements can be made at any time, but as a rule
the major changes are announced by the Chancellor of the Exchequer in
his annual Budget in late March or April, with the new rates of payment
starting in the following autumn.

FAMILY INCOME SUPPLEMENT

Family Income Supplement (F.I.S.) is designed for people in full-time employment who have at least one dependent child and whose normal gross weekly income (that is, before tax and national insurance contributions) is below a certain level set by Parliament.

As I write, this is set at £41.50 for a family with one child. The amount goes up by £3.50 for each additional child. Full-time work means that you must be working for more than thirty hours a week. Anyone can apply, but where a couple is involved it must be the man who is in full-time work and it does not matter whether you are employed by someone else or self-employed. All your children under sixteen are included and any over that age who are still at school, if they are living with you. The qualifying level of income is the same whether you are single or married. There are some things which are not taken into account when assessing your income, which will normally include a husband's and his wife's earnings. They are:

children's income
the first £2 of a war disablement pension
the whole of any attendance allowance
rent allowances
payments for children boarded out with you

What you get

The amount you will be granted is half the difference between your family's total income and the level of income set by the government for your family size. The maximum payment is £8 for families with one child £9 for families with two children and so on, going up by 50p for each additional child. Here is an example, using weekly payment figures:

income level below which you qualify	£41.50
man's earnings before deductions	£26.50
family allowances (second child)	£1.50
total family income	£28.00
difference	£8.00
family income supplement payable (half of £8)	£4.00

This second example shows how the maximum can be less than half the difference. This usually happens with a single woman with dependent children:

income level below which you qualify	£41.50
total income	£20.00
difference	£21.50
family income supplement payable (maximum payment)	£8.00

If you get F.I.S., other benefits also go along with it when you are in need. These are:

Free school meals for children at school
Legal aid, with certain limits
The refund of fares for members of your family attending hospital
Free prescriptions, dental treatment and glasses on the N.H.S.

Claiming

Get form FIS.1 which is available at all social security offices. Fill it in and send it to the Department of Health and Social Security, Family Income Supplements, Poulton-le-Fylde, Blackpool FY 8NW. Post offices and social security offices keep the forms and will also supply you with a stamped addressed envelope. All applications are treated confidentially. You must send either five weekly pay slips or two monthly ones. If you are self-employed, you must send your last profit and loss account.

If your claim is allowed, you will be sent a book of orders which can be cashed each week at the post office of your choice. As a rule the book will cover fifty-two weeks and is not affected if your circumstances change during that time.

CHILD'S SPECIAL ALLOWANCE

This allowance goes to those divorced women whose ex-husbands have died, if they have any children and the husband was contributing, or had been ordered to contribute, at least 25p a week towards the support of the children. The allowance, which is not paid if the woman remarries, is at present £6.45 for the first child and £5.95 for any other children. As the child benefit is at present (June 1977) £1 for the first child and £1.50 for subsequent children this means the total weekly amount, including family allowances, is £7.45 for the first child and £7.45 for the others. Any claim must be made within three months of the former husband's death or some benefit may be lost, and it is based on his national insurance contribution record. Leaflet NI.93, available at post offices or social security offices, will tell you all about it.

GETTING IT FREE

Under the National Health Service basic treatment is free, but there are charges for prescriptions, glasses and dental treatment. Certain people are exempt from these charges, mainly the young, the elderly and people who are receiving state benefits of some kind.

Prescriptions. The following are exempt:

1 Children under sixteen.
2 Men over sixty-five and women over sixty.

Also people who have exemption certificates:

1 Expectant and nursing mothers.
2 People who suffer from certain medical conditions.
3 War or service disablement pensioners.
4 People and their dependents who are receiving supplementary benefit or family income supplement.

Prescriptions can also be free on the grounds of low income. Leaflet PC.11, which is available at most post offices and local social security offices, explains the arrangements and also includes a claim form. Income is assessed in more or less the same way as in claims for supplementary benefits, except that the first £4 of any earnings is disregarded. You can also get leaflet FP.91/EC.91 at post offices. This describes the arrangements for exemption certificates.

Dental treatment. The following are exempt:

1 Children under sixteen.
2 Those over sixteen who are still at school full-time; there is no upper age limit. School here does not mean any college of further education.
3 Anyone between sixteen and twenty-one who has left school.
4 Expectant mothers.
5 Women who have had a child in the previous twelve months.
6 People and their dependents who are getting supplementary pension, benefits—family income supplement or any other state allowance.
7 Anyone, and their dependents, who is exempt on grounds of low income (Leaflet PC.11 explains this).

The same applies for *glasses* with standard National Health frames and lenses, except that expectant and nursing mothers are excluded and so are young people over sixteen, unless they are still at school full-time.

Milk and vitamins. Seven pints of milk a week (or one 20 oz. packet of National Dried milk) and vitamin A, D and C drops and tablets are available free to:

1 Expectant mothers and all their children under school age in families which are already receiving supplementary benefits or family income supplement, or have special needs because of low incomes.
2 Any expectant mother who already has two children under school age. Income is irrelevant here.
3 All but the first two children under school age in a family with three or more children under school age, again regardless of income.

Free milk also goes to handicapped children between the ages of five and sixteen who are not registered pupils at an ordinary school or special school, and also to all children at an approved day nursery or playgroup.

Drugs and appliances supplied by hospitals. Drugs, elastic hosiery, wigs and fabric supports are usually charged for by hospitals. Drugs and elastic hosiery are exempt to the same people who qualify for free prescriptions. Wigs and fabric supports also go free to anyone over sixteen in full-time attendance at school.

HELP FOR SCHOOL CHILDREN

Free school meals are available to children of poorer families, generally those who are already getting benefits of some kind. Qualifying incomes are worked out by taking gross income and subtracting expenses like rent, rates, mortgage repayments, income tax, national insurance contributions, trade union subscriptions, superannuation and fares to work. The first £2 of a mother's earnings is also disregarded. These are the present rates, but remember that as with all state benefits they change from time to time:

Number of children in family including those under school age	*Number of children who receive free school meals when net weekly income is less than the amount shown*					
	1	2	3	4	5	6
1	£23.90					
2	£29.30	£28.55				
3	£34.70	£33.95	£33.20			
4	£40.10	£39.35	£38.60	£37.85		
5	£45.50	£44.75	£44.00	£43.25	£42.50	
6	£50.90	£50.15	£49.40	£48.65	£47.90	£47.15

Free school milk goes to all children under seven who are at a state school. Those between seven and twelve may also get free milk, if it is recommended on health grounds by the school medical officer.

Local authorities may also help with clothing and sports gear; the decision is at their discretion. Your local education office or education welfare officer will give you details.

SUPPLEMENTARY BENEFITS

Supplementary benefits are rather different from most social security payments. They are designed to provide income on a non-contributory basis for people who are not working full-time. You will get a supplementary benefit if your income, whether it comes from part-time work or social security, is judged not enough to meet your requirements. 'Scale rates' are worked out by. the Department of Health and Social

Security and individuals' requirements are worked out according to these rates, with additional allowances for rent and any special items. Whatever you are earning is then deducted from this total. The difference is made up by the supplementary benefit. You may qualify for Family Income Supplements as well.

For the purposes of calculation, family income is lumped together and only the husband can claim. Couples who are living together, but not married, are usually treated as if they were married. This means that a woman who is living with a man as if they were married is likely to lose any benefits she would have got on her own account. If you are receiving supplementary benefits, you will also be entitled to free school meals, prescriptions, dental treatment, etc. These are the present rates:

Weekly scales		*Ordinary scale*	*Long-term scales**	
			Claimant (and wife) under 80	*Claimant or wife 80 or over*
Married couple		£17.75	£21.55	£21.80
Single householder		£10.90	£13.70	£13.95
Any other person				
18 or over		£8.70	£11.00	£11.25
16 to 17		£6.70	—	—
Dependent child	13 to 15	£5.60	—	—
	11 to 12	£4.60	—	—
	5 to 10	£3.75	—	—
	under 5	£3.10	—	—
Blind people				
married couple	one blind	£19.00	£22.80	£23.05
	both blind	£19.80	£23.60	£23.85
single person	18 or over	£12.15	£14.95	£15.20
	16 to 17	£7.60	—	—

*The long-term scale rates apply to (a) supplementary pensioners and (b) people under pension age, except the unemployed, who have received supplementary benefit for a continuous period of two years or more. These higher scale rates include a margin of 50p (75p for the over 80 rate) towards special expenses

Source: Department of Health and Social Security.

RATE REBATES

Rate rebates are available to some owner occupiers and tenants; you do not have to be getting supplementary benefits to claim. On p. 256 are the current (1977) broad rates. If your family circumstances are different to those listed below contact your Local Authority. There arc no income limits.

The size of your family	Your weekly income	Your weekly rates				
		£1.00	£1.50	£2.00	£3.00	£3.50
		Weekly rebate				
One person	£12	£1.00	£1.50	£1.92	£2.52	£2.82
	£16	£1.00	£1.30	£1.60	£2.20	£2.50
	£20	£0.68	£0.98	£1.28	£1.88	£2.18
	£24	£0.42	£0.72	£1.02	£1.62	£1.92
	£30	£0.06	£0.36	£0.66	£1.26	£1.56
	£40	—	—	£0.06	£0.66	£0.96
Couple	£16	£1.00	£1.50	£2.00	£2.88	£3.00
	£20	£1.00	£1.50	£1.96	£2.56	£2.86
	£25	£0.96	£1.26	£1.56	£2.16	£2.46
	£30	£0.57	£0.87	£1.17	£1.77	£2.07
	£35	£0.27	£0.57	£0.87	£1.47	£1.77
	£50	—	—	—	£0.57	£0.87
Couple (or one parent) and one child	£20	£1.00	£1.50	£2.00	£2.92	£3.00
	£25	£1.00	£1.50	£1.92	£2.52	£2.82
	£30	£0.92	£1.22	£1.52	£2.12	£2.42
	£35	£0.54	£0.84	£1.14	£1.74	£2.04
	£45	—	£0.24	£0.54	£1.14	£1.44
	£55	—	—	—	£0.54	£0.84
Couple (or one parent) and two children	£25	£1.00	£1.50	£2.00	£2.89	£3.00
	£30	£1.00	£1.50	£1.89	£2.49	£2.79
	£35	£0.89	£1.19	£1.49	£2.09	£2.39
	£40	£0.52	£0.82	£1.12	£1.72	£2.02
	£50	—	£0.22	£0.52	£1.12	£1.42
	£60	—	—	—	£0.52	£0.82
Couple (or one parent) and three children	£25	£1.00	£1.50	£2.00	£3.00	£3.00
	£30	£1.00	£1.50	£2.00	£2.86	£3.00
	£35	£1.00	£1.50	£1.86	£2.46	£2.76
	£40	£0.86	£1.16	£1.46	£2.06	£2.36
	£50	£0.19	£0.49	£0.79	£1.39	£1.69
	£60	—	—	£0.19	£0.79	£1.09

Source: Department of the Environment.

RENT REBATES

Rent rebates or allowances are also available in some cases to tenants of furnished or unfurnished accommodation (business and service tenants do not qualify). The table opposite is a model for the current (1977) rates. Again, if your circumstances are different to those listed, contact your Local Authority.

256

The size of your family	Your weekly income	Your rent (per week, after taking off rates, etc.)							
		£2.00 or less	£3.00	£3.50	£4.00	£4.50	£5.00	£6.00	£8.00 or more
	£	up to			Your rebate or allowance (£)				at least
One person	12	2.00	3.00	3.50	4.00	4.50	5.00	6.00	7.56*
	16	2.00	3.00	3.50	4.00	4.46	4.76	5.36	6.56*
	20	1.76	2.56	2.86	3.16	3.46	3.76	4.36	5.56
	25	0.67	1.47	1.77	2.07	2.37	2.67	3.27	4.47
	30	—	0.62	0.92	1.22	1.52	1.82	2.42	3.62
	35	—	—	—	0.37	0.67	0.97	1.57	2.77
Couple	18	2.00	3.00	3.50	4.00	4.50	5.00	6.00	8.00*
	25	2.00	3.00	3.50	4.00	4.50	4.94	5.54	6.74*
	30	1.69	2.49	2.79	3.09	3.39	3.69	4.29	5.49
	35	0.62	1.42	1.72	2.02	2.32	2.62	3.22	4.42
	40	—	0.57	0.87	1.17	1.47	1.77	2.37	3.57
	45	—	—	—	0.32	0.62	0.92	1.52	2.72
Couple (or single parent) and one dependent child	25	2.00	3.00	3.50	4.00	4.50	5.00	6.00	8.00*
	30	2.00	3.00	3.50	4.00	4.50	5.00	5.62	6.82*
	35	1.77	2.57	2.87	3.17	3.47	3.77	4.37	5.57
	40	0.68	1.48	1.78	2.08	2.38	2.68	3.28	4.48
	45	—	0.63	0.93	1.23	1.53	1.83	2.43	3.63
	50	—	—	—	0.38	0.68	0.98	1.58	2.78
Couple (or single parent) and two dependent children	30	2.00	3.00	3.50	4.00	4.50	5.00	6.00	8.00*
	35	2.00	3.00	3.50	4.00	4.50	5.00	5.71	6.91*
	40	1.86	2.66	2.96	3.26	3.56	3.86	4.46	5.66
	45	0.74	1.54	1.84	2.14	2.44	2.74	3.34	4.54
	50	—	0.69	0.99	1.29	1.59	1.89	2.49	3.69
	55	—	—	—	0.44	0.74	1.04	1.64	2.84
Couple (or single parent) and three dependent children	35	2.00	3.00	3.50	4.00	4.50	5.00	6.00	8.00*
	45	1.95	2.75	3.05	3.35	3.65	3.95	4.55	5.75
	50	0.80	1.60	1.90	2.20	2.50	2.80	3.40	4.60
	55	—	0.75	1.05	1.35	1.65	1.95	2.55	3.75
	60	—	—	0.20	0.50	0.80	1.10	1.70	2.90
	65	—	—	—	—	—	0.25	0.85	2.05

*The most you can normally get off your rent is £6.50 a week, or £8.00 a week if you live in London.

Source: Department of the Environment.

1 *The size of your family:* 'Dependent child' means anyone under 16, or someone over 16 who is at school, college, university or in an apprenticeship.

'One person' means anyone who is not living at home with a husband or wife and without any dependent children. Other adults living at home could reduce your rebate or allowance.

2 *Your income:* 'Your weekly income' means average weekly pay before tax and other deductions (including a wife's pay less £5) plus regular overtime, pensions and superannuation, sickness or unemployment benefit, interest on savings and investments (but not the savings themselves), Family Allowance and Family Income Supplement, etc.

3   *Your rent:* 'Your rent' means what you pay for a week's rent after taking off anything you pay for rates, water rates, heating and lighting, furniture and most services.

For details of other state benefits turn to the following chapters:

Unemployment pay   section II, chapter 2
Child benefit scheme   section III, chapter 2
Pensions   section V, chapter 9
Supplementary benefits for the aged   section V, chapter 9

Chapter 5

CARING FOR YOUR DEPENDENTS

MAKING A WILL

If you make a will then when you die your assets will be transferred to your dependents in the way you choose; you must appoint an executor to see that your wishes are carried out.

Not everyone makes a will; many people are quite superstitious about it, taking the view that if they make a will they are in some way signing their death warrant. You should approach making your will in a positive way, however. It is likely that as your life develops your situation will change, and you will make not one will in the course of your life but several. Just one example: you will want to protect your children in totally different ways when they are small and when they are older with independent lives of their own.

The longer you delay in making your will the more difficult it will become. Death is nearer the older we get, and thinking about a will can become very hard. Do it while you are relatively young and healthy. That way it will be part of your financial thinking for many years.

Intestacy

If you die without making a will you are said to have died intestate. This is an irresponsible thing to do, even if you do not have a great deal of money. For example, where a married couple have a joint bank account and the bank does not allow the wife to draw on the account in the event of her husband's death. Where there is no will the process of releasing the money can take a very long time. Eventually the spouse will get the chattels, then the first £55,000 and half of what is left if there are no children. The rest goes to other blood relatives. Where there are children £25,000 goes to the spouse, with half of what is left going to the children and the income on the other half goes to the spouse for his or her lifetime, reverting to the children on his or her death.

Six good reasons for making a will

1 Your money and other assets will go where you want them to when you die.
2 You can choose the people who will administer your estate. They are called your executors. Decide on them carefully and do not always pick a relative, as this can lead to quarrels. If your estate is at all complicated, have more than one executor.
3 You can give your executors wider powers of investment than they normally get under the law. This way you can help your family and other people or organizations to whom you leave legacies improve and secure their financial future.
4 You can arrange a particular financial plan to suit your family's special needs.
5 The business of looking after your estate is cheaper than if you leave no will.
6 You can save your beneficiaries money. With the help of professional advice you can arrange your affairs so as to make provision for your dependents while you are still alive, and lessen capital transfer tax (see p. 264) which will be due on your estate when you die. You can also adjust any other taxes for which you may be liable.

In contrast, there are *no* good reasons for not making a will.

Using a solicitor

There is no need to use a solicitor when you are making a will. As long as you state your wishes and find two witnesses to your signature at the end of it, it will be perfectly valid. But not using a solicitor may be a false economy. There are many legal rules and regulations, and what you write down does not always mean exactly what you intended, so the actual phrasing of the will is quite important.

A solicitor is useful because he will not only help you to draw up your will correctly, so that you are sure that your wishes will be carried out in the way you want, but – especially if he is a family solicitor who knows your circumstances well – he may be able to point out things which have escaped your notice. He will point out, for instance, that you cannot have as witnesses to your signature any person who will benefit under your will.

Doing it yourself

If you decide that you really do not wish to pay the rather modest fee a solicitor charges and you feel that your affairs are so simple that you do not need one, at least buy and read a book on will-making before you go ahead and make a will yourself. If you just fill in one of the will forms which are on sale in many stationers without guidance, you could make a mistake. Obviously these forms have a particular set formula, and this could result in you not expressing your wishes as clearly as you want to. It is much better to follow the instructions in a book and, if you reach a point where you have any doubts at all about whether you are expressing your wishes properly, get in touch with a solicitor.

If there are no problems, draw up the final version of your will and get your witnesses to verify your signature. You need not show them the will; it is your signature they are witnessing, not the contents of your will.

After your death, details of your will are available to the public. If you do not wish anyone except the beneficiaries to know what you have left, you can leave special instructions. But this really does need the help of a solicitor. The taxman will have to know the details, of course.

Choosing your executors

Your will must state who you have made your executor, or executors. You may think you are flattering someone by making them your executor, but it is not always an easy task. It may require a lot of work, as we will see later on, so the choice must be made with care. It is no use, for instance, making your husband or wife one of your executors, and then choosing another one with whom you know they will find it difficult to agree. As a courtesy, consult the person or people you have chosen. You need not do this, but unless prior consultation has taken place he or she need not take on the job. If a person you have chosen as executor dies you will have to find a replacement immediately.

Five suggestions for choosing your executor
1   One of the tasks of an executor is to arrange the funeral. For this reason, even if you choose at least one professional executor, it is useful to have someone else as well who is close to your family and will find the personal dealings with them easier at this time.

2   One's husband or wife is a reasonable choice. They will normally be the chief beneficiary of the estate and will want – and should have – some say in how it is administered. But we all get older and some husbands and wives would welcome a co-executor. If your children have grown up they could make a good second choice, provided your will is fairly simple.

3   You may prefer, however, not to burden your spouse with the problems of sorting out your will. In that case choose a family friend you can trust and who has some experience in legal or accounting fields. If you cannot think of anyone suitable, use a solicitor. Solicitors are quite used to dealing with this kind of work and will charge you an additional fee. As you will see later, when a will is proved it is usually necessary to use a solicitor; this 'charging fee', as it is called, is not usually a particularly heavy extra burden on your estate.

4   If none of the above are suitable, you can go to people who specialize in this kind of work. Most of the big banks have executor and trustee departments. Most bank branches have booklets on display which set out the sort of services they can provide. This is a more expensive way of operating, however, because the bank will charge a fee in addition to the fee charged by the solicitor employed by the bank. But there is a lot to be said for banks. They do not die, so that you get continuing service from them at any time.

5   You can go or write to the Public Trustee, who operates from Kingsway, London, WC2. This office was set up by the government many years ago, and if you name him in your will he will act as executor, administrator or trustee of your estate. He is particularly useful for people with small estates, but the banks charge relatively less the bigger the estate. On an estate over £50,000 it is cheaper to go to a bank.

THE TASKS OF AN EXECUTOR

At some time in our lives many of us will be asked by one or other of our friends or relatives to be their 'executor'. What this means is that on that person's death you become his or her legal representative, taking on all legal rights and responsibilities, and carrying out the wishes of the *testator* – the person who made the will. Before agreeing to become an executor make sure you understand exactly what it means. Sometimes the task is an enormous one. You will have to collect together all the assets of the estate, pay all debts, which incidentally include tax, and then distribute what is left in accordance with the will.

First of all, before the work of settling the estate can begin, you must get probate. Probate is the process required by law before the Court accepts the will as valid and empowers the executor to set about his work (see below).

The responsibility of an executor starts at the moment of death, and any delay in getting probate can cause problems for relatives. Insurance companies, for example, won't pay up on policies, and banks sometimes limit access to a bank account until probate is granted. It is not unusual for widows and dependents to find that they have no money for day-to-day expenses – a problem which is not automatically solved by couples having a joint bank account (see section I, chapter 6).

How to get probate

1 *Prepare an Inland Revenue affidavit.* This is a statement of all assets and debts at the time of death. Changes afterwards do not usually count, though you can charge funeral expenses against the estate. If you think there will be capital transfer tax to pay, (see later in this chapter) get a professional valuation done as soon as possible. The Inland Revenue officer may refuse to accept the valuation and ask for another one if he thinks the assets have been undervalued. And even if he does accept it, the matter can be reopened if some asset is sold at any time for more than the valuation price, unless a 'clearance certificate' has been issued.

Don't try to be too clever, however, particularly in dealing with an estate inherited by a married person. The tax on estates starts much later for them than for other people, and what is saved in transfer tax may turn up again as a gains tax if an asset is sold for much more than the original valuation, and more tax may be paid in the end. Take advice if you are not a professional on whether a *higher* probate value may not be best.

At this stage the affidavit is signed but not sworn. But this doesn't mean that you are not responsible for making a full disclosure. You may not be able to discover all the tax liabilities immediately, but allowance is made for that.

2 *Swear the Executor's Oath.* You go to a Commissioner for Oaths or a solicitor to swear the oath. This is vitally important.

3 After swearing the oath, *lodge the original will and probate papers at the Probate Registry,* together with two cheques, one for a fee based on the asset value and the other for any capital transfer tax required. Then, all being well, probate will be granted in a few weeks.

Many executors leave the probate process to their solicitors. If you decide to do it yourself, you will be charged an additional fee because of the extra work involved. About one in seven executors prove the will themselves through the Personal Application Department of the Probate Registry. Local probate registry offices are in the telephone book. The principal office is in London and is now called the Principal Registry of the Family Division of the High Court.

There can be upsets. For example, the validity of a will may be challenged. You can avoid this to some extent by not touching the will once it is found. Don't remove any papers attached to it, but don't add any either. You may have to swear that the will is in the same state as when you first received it.

Though delay is rare, executors should remember that the heirs cannot receive their legacies and that monies, insurance policies, etc., remain frozen until probate is granted. Delay can cause hardship, therefore, and should be avoided.

Dividing up the estate

With the granting of probate you are ready to start on the next stage, supervising the execution of the wishes of the testator. Points to notice are:

* There is no reason why you should not benefit in any will where you are an executor. It is witnesses to wills who cannot benefit.
* If a will is simple and you are a friend you may do the executor's work for nothing. But professionals will charge a fee.

The actual task of dividing up the estate varies enormously. It may be simple and just a matter of transferring a family house and money to the heirs, but it can be very complicated indeed. *Do not take the job on unless you are sure you can carry it out properly.*

ACTING AS A TRUSTEE

You may find, particularly where there are children, that you are not only executor but also *trustee*. This will prolong your involvement with the estate for many years. There are two common ways in which a trust may arise:

1 A husband or wife may not leave his or her estate outright to the widow or widower, but only the right to any income from capital for life, with the capital sum going to the children. It is more common when a man dies first. He may not trust his wife with total access to capital which he wants to go to his children eventually, or he may simply not want his widow to have the bother of managing the estate.
2 A trust may be set up for the benefit of children who have not yet grown up. The income, and sometimes part of the capital, is used for their upbringing and schooling, and the capital reverts to them either when they come of age, at eighteen, or sometimes later. Twenty-five is popular.

The trustee can find himself with a thankless task trying to balance the needs of the widow – the *tenant* of the trust – and the children – the *remaindermen*. The aim is to keep the money intact, or even to make it grow, for the eventual benefit of the remaindermen, but at the same time to ensure that the tenant has adequate and increasing money to live on, in a period of inflation. Friction can arise in cases where the trustee is allowed to give some capital to the tenant from time to time. This reduces what is left for the heirs and can upset even happy families. It can happen, of course, that the tenant and the remaindermen are not close, or even related; it is not rare for disputes to end up in court. The trustee will then need all the tact he can muster.

A will should state how wide the powers of the trustees are. It can stipulate that they can invest in whatever they like, but if it makes no stipulation the investments are covered by the Trustee Investments Act, 1961.

Broadly, this Act allows up to half of the trust fund to be invested in the ordinary shares of companies quoted on the stock exchange. These are generally limited to the large companies and unit trusts and a certain dividend record is required. The rest has to go into fixed interest stocks which are mainly government and local authority issues.

You can give up your trusteeship, but only if you leave behind at least two other trustees, or a trust company. If you can't find anyone to take over from you, a solicitor or professional trustee will usually agree to act in your place. He will charge a fee, so make sure that the will allows you to pay him out of the estate.

As you can see, being a trustee or executor can be an enormous task. Think carefully before you agree to act. It is often a job for professionals.

CAPITAL TRANSFER TAX

Once you have decided where you want your money to go after your death, and who your executors will be, the next most important thing is to look at the implications of capital transfer tax. Even in death we do not escape taxes, and anyone with more than £15,000 or married with more than £30,000 needs to consider this tax. Here I will be looking at it only from the point of view of someone making a will, though it has to be paid on all transfers of capital, with certain exceptions, whether these take place before or after death.

Capital transfer tax, sometimes called the 'gifts tax', replaced the old Estate Duty in 1975. If you have a will outstanding which is based on the old estate duty provisions, take professional advice. It is highly likely that it will have to be changed, or your heirs will suffer.

For the purposes of this tax, capital means all your assets, not just money. It means that when a business changes hands after death a transfer tax must be paid if the value of the business is more than £15,000. It means that when agricultural land changes hands tax may have to be paid. Similarly with a work of art. The implications of this are clear. Where the asset is not actual cash, the person who inherits may have difficulty in finding the money. Estates may have to be broken up and other things sold to find the money.

This all means that you must try to leave your assets in such a way that the problems of raising the tax will be minimised. First of all let's look at the rates of the tax as it is charged on death:

slice of cumulative chargeable transfers £	C.T.T. rate %	aggregate C.T.T. payable at top of slice £
0 – 15,000	nil	nil
15 – 20,000	10	500
20 – 25,000	15	1,250
25 – 30,000	20	2,250
30 – 40,000	25	4,750
40 – 50,000	30	7,750
50 – 60,000	35	11,250
60 – 80,000	40	19,250
80 – 100,000	45	28,250
100 – 120,000	50	38,250
120 – 150,000	55	54,750
150 – 200,000	60	84,750
200 – 250,000	60	114,750
250 – 300,000	60	144,750
300 – 500,000	60	264,750
500 – 1,000,000	65	589,750
1,000 – 2,000,000	70	1,289,750
2,000,000 and over	75	

This table gives you an idea of the sort of amount of money which will have to be found for the taxman when you die. If you do not have the minimum amount of £15,000 you can ignore the tax, but if you are just a little above, consider the exemptions, which may well bring you back below the starting level again. The starting level is likely to rise as inflation continues. Here again I am looking only at what happens on death.

1 All your debts must be paid before the net value of your estate is assessed.

2 The first £15,000 is not subject to capital transfer tax.

3 All transfers between a husband or wife are exempt from the tax. This means that anything which one leaves to the other is liable for tax only when the surviving partner dies.

4 Unlimited gifts to charities or political parties are exempt if they are made more than one year before death, and similar gifts not exceeding £100,000 made on death or within one year of death are also exempt.

5 There is a complicated formula to help farmers, but it only covers working farmers who are wholly employed on the farm. Get your adviser to explain it to you.

6 If you have inherited a property less than four years after its previous owner received it and tax was paid the previous time, you will get 80 per cent relief from capital transfer tax in the first year, moving down to 20 per cent in the fourth year and nothing in the fifth year.

SETTING A WILL ASIDE

Think carefully about what you are doing when you make your will, because it may be set aside by a court, even if it is perfectly valid and made in the proper manner. This can happen if someone who expected to inherit did not, or did not inherit as much as they felt they were entitled to. The most common case of this is when a man cuts his wife out of his will, or, less often, leaves nothing to his children.

Until 1939 there was nothing a family could do, in England and Wales at least, if a man died and it was found that he had left all his money to a cats' home, or perhaps a mistress his family knew nothing about. All that changed with the Inheritance (Family Provision) Acts of 1939 and 1975. Under this, certain members of a person's family can apply to the executors and the court for a reasonable provision to be made for them from the deceased's estate. The relatives who are protected in this way are a husband or wife, a son under eighteen, an unmarried daughter of any age, and any children of the marriage who are not capable of taking care of themselves because of some physical or mental disability. The lesson, then, is to consider all the proper claims upon your money when you are making a will, and to be as fair as possible to all claimants.

If you live in Scotland the position is different from that in England and Wales. You must check the situation with a solicitor. For example, you cannot cut your husband or wife out of your will. The spouse and the children have 'legal rights' over at least part of your estate. You cannot ignore these rights when making a will, and the matter will be set right by the courts if you fail to provide for your family. This means, of course, that people in Scotland have less freedom than in England and Wales in deciding what to do with their money.

A will can be revoked for other reasons as well, basically because it is held to be invalid. This can occur, for example, when:

1 It is claimed and subsequently proved in court that the person making the will – the testator – was of unsound mind at the time he or she made the will. Such claims will normally only be made when the testator was exceedingly old or seriously ill when making a final will, and probably when there had been several previous wills making very different bequests. Old people have been known to cut off their families suddenly and leave all their money to a charity. In such a case the family (in England and Wales) will probably be awarded something from the estate by the court. It has sometimes been claimed that the testator was under the influence of some person to such an extent that he or she left the estate to them. This has sometimes happened with family servants, who may have come into the life of the testator when he or she was getting old.

2 A will fails to comply with the formal requirements. The most common reason for this is incorrect witnessing. This is yet another reason for using a solicitor.

3 It can be proved that a will has been forged.

WHEN YOU SHOULD MAKE A NEW WILL

It is clear that as your life changes, and your responsibilities along with it, you will need to make a new will. This happens if you have a new child, or children, if one of your legatees dies, or when your children grow up and become independent. All these are important reasons for making a new will, but overriding all is the need to make a new will if you marry. Marriage automatically revokes any previous will, so a new one must be made, except in the very rare circumstances when a new will has been made in the expectation of marriage. This is particularly important for anyone who is divorced and is contemplating remarriage. You may wish to make sure that you protect the children of an earlier marriage, and possibly even an ex-wife, or husband. Unless you make a new will making this clear after your remarriage, your new spouse will inherit everything and your children will automatically be disinherited. A divorce, on the other hand, does not invalidate a will.

Anyone found guilty of murder or manslaughter cannot benefit under the will of the person killed.

This chapter has dealt only with making a will. An important part of looking after your dependents is making proper provision for them by means of a pension, part of which survives after your death. I have dealt with this in section V, chapter 9.

Chapter 6

THE COST OF DYING

In the end we all die and a funeral has to be paid for. It is best, if possible, to make arrangements to meet the cost yourself beforehand, so that there is no problem for your relatives. The government assists by a death grant which is usually paid to the executor, who will be arranging the funeral.

You can claim the grant by signing the back of the special certificate which you will receive from the Registrar of Births, Marriages and Deaths, when you report the death. Send this to your local social security office and they will send a claim form. Alternatively you can call at the office. The grant varies according to the age of the person who has died. At present the grant is:

Under 3	£9
3-5 inclusive	£15
6-17 inclusive	£22.50
man aged 18 or over (born after 5 July 1893)	£30
woman aged 18 or over (born after 5 July 1893)	£30
man born on or after 5 July 1883, but before 1893	£15
Woman born on or after 5 July 1883, but before 1893	£15

It is highly unlikely that the grant will cover the full cost of a funeral – though some local authorities do manage to dispose of unclaimed bodies for that price.

If you or your family have been receiving supplementary benefits, however, the Department of Health and Social Security will give considerable help towards the cost of a funeral – but not an elaborate one!

The National Association of Funeral Directors passed a resolution at its annual conference in 1976 that it would not set down recommended scales of fees for funerals, so it is very difficult to estimate exact costs. You may find that you can get a basic funeral for around £115, but the average is somewhat higher, around £160-£190.

In the latter half of 1976 there was a sharp increase in cemetery and crematorium fees and from the beginning of 1977 church fees went up sharply. If you wish a minister of religion to be present at the crematorium (if you are not having a church ceremony), this will cost an extra £7 or so. The only items which vary significantly in price are the coffin and the headstone, if you want one. A coffin will cost a minimum of £35-£40, and the price of headstones varies enormously. You should get an estimate from a monumental mason, who will probably also be able to tell you what kind of headstone is permitted in a particular cemetery. Rules on this vary; some churches, for example, do not permit statues to be part of a headstone.

The cheapest funeral is a local one, and the cost will include an inexpensive coffin, a hearse, one limousine, four bearers, the use of a Chapel of Rest from death until the funeral and all other arrangements. You may incur extra expense if the death takes place unexpectedly away from home, or at night. Like anyone else, undertakers charge extra for night working.

Most funeral directors belong to the National Association of Funeral Directors, 57 Doughty Street, London W.C.1 (telephone 01-242 9388). Its members deal with about 420,000 of the half a million or so funerals in the United Kingdom each year. It has a Code of Conduct, and if you think you have been overcharged your complaint can be investigated by a committee which can recommend, though not insist on, a cut in the bill.

When arranging a funeral do not forget the optional extras which will bring the price up. Apart from those mentioned above, there is also a further fee for embalming, and death notices in newspapers must be paid for. No one wants to appear mean when arranging a funeral, but if you can bring yourself to do it, ring up two or three firms for estimates of the cost.

If you are making the arrangements yourself before you die, you can stipulate what sort of funeral you want. The cheapest way of disposing of your body is not to have a funeral at all, but to leave it to your local hospital. The only problem is that sometimes hospitals have a surplus of bodies and may refuse to take yours.

Taxation

Throughout this section the standard rate of tax is assumed to be 35 per cent. Whatever the standard rate, the principles remain the same: a 1 per cent increase or decrease in the rate means a 1p loss or gain respectively for every £1 of taxable income.

Chapter 1

WHEN WE PAY TAX

Taxation is involved in many parts of our financial life. It is the prime means whereby the government raises money to run the country. The payment of tax is compulsory whenever it is assessed, whether by a company or an individual. Failure to pay your taxes can result in severe penalties.

Although the tax inspector and collector spread their tentacles into many parts of our daily lives, I will deal here only with the most common aspects of taxation which affect most people. You will need the help of an accountant who specializes in tax with the more complicated areas of taxation. I have indicated where these areas lie in chapter 5 of this section.

DIRECT AND INDIRECT TAX

The taxes individuals and companies pay are divided into direct and indirect:

Direct taxes are paid directly to the Inland Revenue by the tax payer. There are four varieties:

1   Unified income tax, which most of us pay through Pay As You Earn (P.A.Y.E.) each week or month, or twice a year if you are self-employed.

2 Investment income surcharge, which is payable on all unearned income above £1,500.

3 Capital gains tax, which you pay if you make a profit on the sale of certain things, including shares, a second house, paintings and antiques.

4 Capital transfer tax, which is paid when you give your money or assets away either during your lifetime or after your death.

5 Corporation tax, which is paid by companies on their profits.

Indirect taxes are included in the price of many things that we buy and services that we use. These taxes are principally Value Added Tax (V.A.T.), customs and excise duties, which are paid on imports and stamp duties which apply on certain contracts. (I have dealt in more detail with V.A.T. 'in chapter 3 of this section.)

The level at which we pay these taxes is announced for each financial year by the Chancellor of the Exchequer in his annual Budget. In this he sets out the rules for the country as a whole, just as every person should do for himself. Tax rates do not automatically change from year to year; they may be held at the same rate for several years – though it is unusual for there to be no change at all either in the rate of tax or in the personal allowances which can be set against income for tax purposes.

The tax year runs from 6 April to the following 5 April. Remember these dates, because they can affect the amount of tax you pay in some areas.

Unified income tax and the investment income surcharge

Unified income tax is the tax which affects most of us, as it applies to anyone at work and earning more than £805 (1977-8). It is called unified because it combines what used to be two separate forms of tax, standard income tax and surtax. Collection has been simplified by putting them together and collecting both standard rate income tax, which is 35 per cent on the first £6,000 of taxable income, and the higher rates, mostly under P.A.Y.E. for people who are employees.

Tax allowances
If you look at your pay slip you will see that you are not paying 35 per cent. This is because we all have certain tax allowances which we can set against our income before we reach the part which is taxed. At present (June 1977) these allowances are:

personal (which everyone gets)	£805
married man's	£1,225
wife's earned income relief (if she is working)	£805

	1st child	2nd and subsequent children
children – under 11 at the start of the tax year	£196	£170
11 to 16	£231	£205
16 plus and studying full-time	£261	£235
housekeeper (for widow or widower only)	£100	
dependent relative – of man	£100	
of woman	£145	
person looking after children (for working widow or widower or divorcee only)	£100	
additional personal allowance for children (only if housekeeper allowance not claimed)	£420	
blind person's – if either husband or wife are blind	£180	
if both are blind	£360	
allowance for daughter who looks after you (not son, and only if you are old or infirm and maintain your daughter)	£55	
age allowance for 65s and over – single	£1,080	
married	£1,695	
mortgage interest	all interest on principal residence allowed up to mortgage limit of £25,000	
insurance premiums	$17\frac{1}{2}$% up to $\frac{1}{6}$th taxable income	
earnings from work overseas which involves 30 or more days' work abroad in any one tax year	25% of foreign earnings tax-free	

You can see from this that the most highly taxed people are single people with no dependents who have no mortgages or life insurance. Those who get taxed least are married men with several children, a mortgage on their house, some life insurance and an aged relative or two to support.

Earned and unearned income

Income has been divided into two kinds for tax purposes – earned and unearned. Broadly, earned income is treated more favourably than unearned, which includes anything which does not come directly from employment.

Earned income is:

Your wages or salary. This will include any 'fringe' benefits like a company car, which will be partly taxable.

Any income from your business, profession, partnership or company.

Any money you get from an invention. This would include income from books and songwriting.

Any 'golden handshake' you get when leaving your job – but you pay tax only on any excess over £5,000, in most cases.

Any state pension or private pension or the income portion of an annuity.

272

Unearned income, on the other hand, is money which comes in without your having to work for it – even though you may have worked to obtain the investment in the first place (and paid tax on the money which you then saved). It includes:

National savings interest (in ordinary accounts the first £70 interest is tax-free).

Interest on clearing bank deposit accounts.

Building society interest, which is tax-free if you are only paying standard rate tax.

Interest on company dividends and government or local authority stock.

Rents from any property you may let out.

Income from any trusts in your favour.

How much tax will you pay?

If you know the tax charged at various levels, you can work out how much tax you will pay after your allowances. The current rates of tax payable on taxable income are:

	taxable income	rate of tax	total taxable income	total tax payable
The first	£6,000	35%	£6,000	£2,100
The next	£1,000	40%	£7,000	£2,500
	£1,000	45%	£8,000	£2,950
	£1,000	50%	£9,000	£3,450
	£1,000	55%	£10,000	£4,000
	£2,000	60%	£12,000	£5,200
	£2,000	65%	£14,000	£6,500
	£2,000	70%	£16,000	£7,900
	£5,000	75%	£21,000	£11,650
The rest		83%		

You may be wondering why earned and unearned income are separated. This is because there is a *special investment surcharge* on anyone who has more than £1,500 in investment income.

This is levied at the rate of 10 per cent for any unearned income between £1,500 and £2,000, and 15 per cent over that. If you have a taxable income of £4,000 which includes £200 from interest and dividends, you will simply pay tax at the standard rate. This will add up to £1,400. But if your earned income is £2,000 and you have £2,000 in investment income, you will pay £1,400 plus 10 per cent surcharge on £500 of your unearned income, making a total tax bill of £1,450. The richer you are, of course, the more you pay; the highest investment income rate is 83 per cent plus 15 per cent surcharge, making 98 per cent, which means on the top slice of income you could pay as much as £98 in tax out of every £100 income. Very few people pay at this level.

Irregular incomes

Some people do not have a regular income. Actors, writers and composers, for example, get paid for the work they do as they go along. The Inland Revenue has devised a formula which enables them to spread out their earnings over a period, so that they avoid having to face massive tax bills in one year and then nothing another year. You will need expert advice on how to do this, so get an accountant. His fees will be allowed as an expense against your earnings.

Tax-free income

Certain kinds of income are generally not liable for tax. You will already know of some of these if you have read section I, chapter 3, on savings. Here is a longer – though not complete – list:

The first £50 interest on ordinary National Savings Bank accounts.
Interest on National Savings Certificates.
Bonuses on Save As You Earn schemes, Defence Bonds, British Savings Bonds and National Development Bonds.
Interest on post-war credits (government stock issued to help the war effort).
Prizes on premium bonds.
Any gambling wins.
Most social security benefits.
Education grants or money which is a reward for passing an examination, if it comes from your employer.
Severance payments (often called 'golden handshakes') or capital sums on retirement, if they are less than £5,000, and gratuities for extra service in the army, navy or air force.
Wounds and disability pensions.
The capital part of an annuity.
Housing improvement grants from local authorities.

Capital gains tax

This tax is paid on anything on which there is a 'chargeable gain'. A gain of this sort arises when you buy something at one price and sell it at a higher one.

For instance, you might buy shares for £5,000 and sell them when they are worth £6,500. Your chargeable gain would then be £1,500, less the costs of buying and selling as outlined in section V, chapter 2. Gains tax, like income tax is charged in years from 6 April to the following 5 April. Anyone is liable to it if they are resident in Britain, or if they have a business here and make a profit on the assets of the business.

Exemptions

But capital gains is not chargeable on everything. There are certain exceptions:

1 The profit on the sale of your own home. If you have two houses you will have to decide which is your principal private residence and you will pay capital gains on the other if you sell it.
2 The sale of your own car. If you are a dealer, however, you will have to pay tax on your profits in the normal way.
3 Bonuses on National Saving Certificates, Defence Bonds, Save As You Earn and National Development Bonds.
4 Any foreign currency which you take abroad for your personal use.
5 Gambling wins.
6 Compensation for damages.
7 Gilt-edged stock, but you must have held this for over a year or inherited it.
8 Money gained when an assurance policy matures.
9 Anything which is sold for less than £1,000, including the profit, or when your total disposals are not more than £1,000 in any one year.
10 Anything you give to the nation – paintings, sculptures, or your house if it is of historic interest, for example.
11 Charities and gifts to charities.

How much do you have to pay?

At present the normal rate of capital gains tax is 30 per cent, but there is an alternative way of being taxed which may reduce it. If your total gains are not more than £5,000 in any one year, you have the option of paying tax at your top rate of income tax, but on half the gain only.

Let's see how these alternatives work. Supposing you make a gain of £2,000, when you are already paying tax at the rate of 40 per cent, and have used up half that rate. Normal capital gains tax at 30 per cent would amount to £600. On the other hand, if half the gain is exempt from tax, and the balance of £1,000 is taxable as income, you would pay £425 (£500 at 40 per cent = £200; £500 at 45 per cent = £225). You therefore save £175 by using the alternative method.

Points to remember

1 You may charge any losses against your gains. Losses can also be carried forward for relief in future, not backwards to past years.

2   You cannot offset income tax allowances against capital gains. So even if you are living on a pension and paying no tax because your income is too low, you could still find yourself paying capital gains tax.

3   Gains are charged after all expenses are allowed.

4   You do not have a gain, until the asset is actually disposed of.

5   Gains tax is payable three months after the end of the tax year in which the gain is made, or thirty days after the inspector has assessed the tax, if this is later.

6   On investment trusts and unit trusts, you are allowed to deduct 17½ per cent from the gains tax rate (see section V, chapter 5). This means that you only pay 12½ per cent.

Capital transfer tax

Capital transfer tax (C.T.T.) is very complicated. If you have considerable capital you will need the advice of an accountant. Here I will set out only the aspects of the tax which will affect a lot of people.

Many people have not even heard of C.T.T. – though they may have heard of estate duty, which used to be payable when a person died. C.T.T. has replaced estate duty – with an important difference: it applies not only when people die, but also when they make gifts over a certain value during their lifetime. It does not mean that if you give a child pocket money you will have to pay C.T.T. on it – even if the money is rather more, for example when you maintain a student at university away from home. It is charged only on a gift.

C.T.T. is payable on the cumulative total of all the lifetime transfers you make after 26 March 1974 and on any assets which go to someone else on your death. I have already dealt with tax on transfers after death in section III, chapter 5, so here we will look only at transfers made during your lifetime.

The rates chargeable on lifetime transfers are lower than those at death, and at present are as follows:

cumulative transfers		% on slice
up to	£15,000	nil
the next	£5,000	5
	£5,000	7.5
	£5,000	10
	£10,000	12.5
	£10,000	15
	£10,000	17.5
	£20,000	20
	£20,000	22.5

£20,000	27.5
£30,000	35
£50,000	42.5
£50,000	50
£50,000	55
£200,000	60
£500,000	65
£1,000,000	70
the rest	75

C.T.T. is usually payable by the donor, that is, the person making the gift, and it is his responsibility to declare any gifts and disposals he has made to the Inland Revenue. Donors may, however, make it a condition of a gift that the recipient must pay tax, so, if you receive a gift, check to see if the C.T.T. is also being paid, or if you will be liable.

Exemptions

C.T.T. is not payable on all lifetime transfers. The following are all exempt:

1 Any transfers between husband and wife in life and after death. This means that only one lot of C.T.T. need be paid on the assets of a married couple. If a man gives all his money to his wife and then she happens to die first, it can all come back to him – if she has left it to him in her will – without being liable for C.T.T.
2 Total transfers in any one year of up to £2,000. You can carry any unused part forward for one year only.
3 Small gifts of up to £100 each to any recipient can be made in addition to this £2,000.
4 Gifts in consideration of marriage. A parent can give up to £5,000, a grandparent or great-grandparent £2,500, and anyone else £1,000.
5 Normal expenditure out of your income, including gifts.
6 Gifts to charities. There is no limit on these if they are made more than one year before death. After death the limit is £100,000.
7 Gifts to the nation, such as pictures and sculptures, are exempt if they go to museums, art galleries or universities.
8 Gifts for public benefit. The donor cannot decide what comes under this exemption; it is up to the Treasury. In some cases they have refused gifts of historic homes, for example, because the upkeep is too expensive.
9 Gifts to political parties. The same rules apply as for charities. To qualify, a political party must have at least two members sitting in Parliament, or one member and a total vote of at least 150,000. It is no use, therefore, thinking you can make C.T.T. exempt gifts to

the small fringe parties which spring up from time to time, but whose total votes only number a few thousand.

Apart from these exemptions, there are certain other concessions. There are special concessions for agricultural land and woodlands, and where an asset is transferred upon a death very soon after it was transferred to the person who has died, there is some relief, up to a maximum qualifying period of four years.

Remember: you can reduce your liability for C.T.T. by carefully disposing of your assets during your lifetime.

HOW DIRECT TAXES ARE ASSESSED AND COLLECTED

When the Chancellor of the Exchequer sets out his tax proposals in the Budget in March or early April, long debates follow and there may be some amendments to his original proposals. When this process is finished the Finance Act is passed, and it is then the business of the Board of the Inland Revenue to publish the new rates of tax. They then collect the new taxes, basing their assessments of how much we should pay on the details of income we send to them in our 'tax return'.

The Chief Inspector of Taxes

The 'assessment' of tax, as it is called, is the responsibility of the Chief Inspector of Taxes, who operates from Somerset House in the Strand in London. The detailed work is done by offices around the country. There are more than 700 local offices, each under the control of a district inspector and two or more tax inspectors.

If you live in London, you may have to send your return to Manchester. If you live in Manchester, it may be Newcastle-upon-Tyne. It has been a deliberate policy of the government to spread its offices around the country to lessen the concentration of government business in London.

Your local tax office will check your return and work out all your allowances, finally issuing you with a 'code', which is a number related to your allowances. This is also sent to your employer, who can then work out how much tax to deduct from your wages or salary each week or month. The inspectors will also deal with any enquiries you may make about your tax affairs.

These codings only relate to Pay As You Earn. If there are any discrepancies at the end of the year, you will receive a rebate if you have overpaid and a bill if you have underpaid.

The Accountant and Comptroller General

The collection of taxes is dealt with by the office of the Accountant and Comptroller General. Its head office is in Worthing, with offices around the country to send out the bills, and local offices to chivvy those who are dilatory in paying.

When the assessment is ready the collector of taxes is notified. If you do not pay on time he will add interest, usually at the rate of 9 per cent a year, until the bill is paid, so it is a good idea to pay at once.

On the other hand, if the taxman owes you money and does not pay quickly you are entitled to interest from him from the day the tax becomes due for repayment.

If you think your tax bill is wrong it is no use writing or phoning to complain to the collector; his job is merely to collect. You must send any queries to the inspector at the office which deals with your tax. After agreement has been reached he will pass the details on to the collector, who will send you an amended bill.

THE TAX SCHEDULES

Taxation in this country is so complicated that the government has set out details of the various taxes in the Tax Acts, in six sections, known as 'Schedules'.

Schedule A deals with any kind of rent you get from property, which can be either buildings (unless it is furnished, when it comes under Schedule D), or land. You reach a net income figure after offsetting any expenses in maintaining the property. You cannot invent a figure for these: you will have to produce receipts for both materials and labour. Expenses may include repairs, any insurance premiums protecting the property; general rates and water rates if you pay them; any services which you provide which are not paid for, for example the upkeep of gardens and private roads. There are also certain other permissible expenses but these usually apply only to large property owners.

Schedule B deals with income from woodlands, but only when these are run as a business.

Schedule C deals with any income from local government stocks or gilt-edged, and foreign dividends on which interest is payable in the U.K.

Schedule D covers all income from savings or investments in companies; income from the letting of furnished property (expenses are again allowed); income from any trade or profession or any freelance earnings; any income from abroad unless it is earned income; and anything which is not covered in the other schedules.

Schedule E is the one we all know about. It deals with all income from employment, including, if you are a married man, your wife's income,

279

unless you have chosen separate assessment or separate taxation (see chapter 4 in this section). It includes income from full-time and part-time work, tips, anything you get in kind (except luncheon vouchers worth 15p or less), and any pensions, including widow's benefits and some social security payments. Sickness and unemployment benefit, supplementary allowances, student grants, maternity grants and allowances, and the death grant are exempt from tax. Some pensions, like wounds and disability payments, are also exempt.

Schedule F deals with the distribution of dividends by Companies.

An enormous number of items are dealt with in most of these schedules, far too many to enumerate here. But details of most of them are included in the tax return, which we all have to make if we have any income, earned or unearned.

Chapter 2

YOUR TAX RETURN

FILLING IN YOUR TAX RETURN

There are a few general rules about filling in tax returns:

All your income must go in.

Where you have no income from a particular source like interest or dividends from shares write 'none'.

Claim all your expenses – though some, like travelling expenses to and from work, are not allowable against tax.

When you have finished your return,check through it again to see that you have left nothing out.

Then sign it with the date. You are signing a declaration which states: 'To the best of my knowledge and belief the particulars given on this form are correct and complete.' *This is most important. There are severe penalties if you lie to the inspector*. He will find out in the end, because anyone who pays you money will have to supply details to him. I have outlined the penalties later on.

Always keep a copy of your return, because if there is something the inspector wants to query you will then have it in front of you.

Here are some of the expenses you can claim:

1 The use of your car for business purposes. You will be allowed money for petrol and something towards wear and tear. You must tell the inspector how much you use the car on business and how much for your personal private use, giving mileages for each. He will then calculate your allowance.
2 Subscriptions to a professional organization, if it is essential to your work.
3 Superannuation contributions, unless they are to a trade union.
4 Special clothes or tools which are necessary to your trade and which you have to buy yourself if they are not supplied by your company.

Under the Taxes Management Act of 1970 every person who has any income earned or unearned, is required to make a 'return' of his or her income to the Inspector of Taxes.

The return is a form which asks for details of all your income. There is also space for you to set down what allowances you think you are entitled to. You do not put down the tax allowances set out in the Budget, but give details of your children, dependent relatives, etc. If you have any expenses which are incurred in the course of your work, put these down too, and the inspector will decide whether they are allowable or not.

From the details you give him the inspector will work out your coding. If your circumstances change during the year – say, you get married, have a child or take out a new mortgage – you must inform your tax inspector and he will change your coding accordingly.

There are three different types of return:

1 *P1.* This goes to people who are employed by someone else and have a very simple income. If you are single and have no dependents you simply sign the form and give the name and address of your employer. It is not even necessary to give details of your income, because your employer will already have supplied them. Your allowance will simply be £805, the single person's allowance. Your employer will receive the appropriate coding and deduct tax from your wages accordingly. It is unlikely that you will receive a tax return form the following year or possibly even the year after that. Simple returns are only required every two or three years.

2 *11P.* This form is designed for those with more complicated incomes. A person who receives this form will quite likely have some income from employment and some freelance earnings, perhaps from the sale of his own painting or writing or from private jobs which he does in his own time, and will be entitled to a variety of allowances. The form is basically the same as P1, but rather more detail is asked for. You will, for instance, have to show your income. This will be the gross amount

which your employer will tell you each year on a form called a P.60. If you are in a private pension scheme, the amount you pay in contributions will be deducted from your gross salary to show you the amount that is taxable before allowances.

3 *11*. This form is for the self-employed, and will probably include rather more in expenses than for those who are employees.

If you are married, and you and your wife are being taxed in the normal way – that is, all her income is 'deemed' to be her husband's for tax purposes – her income must be included on the husband's return. It is possible for husbands and wives to be taxed separately, and I will come to that in chapter 4 of this section. If you are taxed together your wife will be able to earn up to £805 without her income attracting any tax. This figure is the same as the single person's allowance.

To help you fill in your return I have invented a family. Mr X is fifty and is a factory safety engineer earning £4,500 a year. He uses his car for his trips to various factories. Mrs X is a schoolteacher working part-time for £2,500 a year. They have three children, one aged twenty studying at university, one aged eighteen out at work and the third aged fifteen still at school. Mr X's widowed mother lives with them and has only her state pension, but Mr X's father left him a house on which he made a profit of £2,625 when he sold it, in this tax year. Mrs X keeps some savings in an ordinary account in the National Savings Bank, which brings in £26 interest a year, and more in a building society, which earns £45 interest a year. Mr and Mrs X live in a house which they are buying on a mortgage on which interest payments amount to £220 a year. Mr X also has life insurance premiums which cost £40 a year and bank borrowings of £200. He has been married before, has another child who is now twenty-seven, and pays £800 a year alimony to his ex-wife.

He now has to fill in his return, probably a 11P, because his affairs are quite complicated. He and his wife have decided to be taxed together, with his wife's income being considered his for tax purposes, because their joint incomes are below the level where it pays to be taxed separately.

The return covers six pages, providing space for all the details of his income, expenses and any allowances which may be set against it. A sample tax return is produced at the end of this chapter.

Page One is very important, because it is here that the tax payer signs his name declaring that the information on the other pages is true. There is also a space where you enter your date of birth and that of your wife, if you were born before 6 April 1918. If this is the case make sure you fill this part in, because otherwise you will not get the extra personal allowance which is available to the elderly. This is £1,080 if you are a single person or a widow or widower, and £1,695 for a married couple. Mr and Mrs X in my example do not qualify, so they will leave this part empty.

282

Income

Page Two. The first section asks for details of your occupation and the name and address of your employer. Anything you pay into a private company pension scheme is deducted from your gross earnings to reach your taxable income. Mr X is not in a pension fund, so his employer will already have told the inspector that he earned £4,500.

When it comes to his wife's earnings, Mr X must put in all details of what she earns. He takes her gross salary and makes any deductions for pension contributions; the resulting figure is £2,375 – £2,500 minus £125.

Now here is an interesting anomaly. Mr X must provide this figure, but there is no law which states that a wife must tell her husband what she earns. The inspector will eventually find out from her employer, but if she wishes not to tell her husband (even if she sees the return she may not know what he earns, because his earnings need not go in), the consequences are not particularly severe. The husband will just have to send an explanatory note.

Mr X gets no expenses, so he leaves that part blank. Nor has he had any compensation for loss of his job or any leaving payment. It is best to write 'none' rather than leave a blank, because then the situation is quite clear. Nor does he work abroad, so there is nothing to enter here.

The next section deals with pensions and social security benefits. This does not affect Mr and Mrs X yet, but those who do have them should fill in details of their state pensions. If the wife has paid full national insurance contributions and is therefore entitled to a pension in her own right (see section V, chapter 9), an X is entered in a square provided.

The following benefits are taxable:

widow's pension
widowed mother's allowance
guardian's allowance
child's special allowance
mobility allowance

But the following are not taxable and need not be entered on the return:

sickness benefit
invalidity benefit
unemployment benefit
maternity benefit
death grant
attendance allowance
family income supplement
industrial injury benefits
supplementary benefits
non-contributory invalidity pension

If you are a woman and receive alimony payments, enter them here. Your divorced or separated husband will already have deducted tax at the standard rate of 35 per cent before sending the payments to you, but you should write in the gross amount and the Inland Revenue will make any adjustment necessary.

We then come to private pensions, which will include any company pension you receive and, if you are self-employed, any pension you have bought for yourself. If for any reason you have a pension from abroad that should also be entered.

The next section deals with rents from any property you may let out. This is divided into furnished and unfurnished property. You should also enter any income you may get from ground rents or land. Provide a separate list if there is not enough room on the form. You will need to indicate which properties belong to the husband and which to the wife.

You can set your expenses against any income you receive from property. These will include any rent or rates you yourself have to pay on the premises; upkeep of furniture; maintenance and repairs; the cost of providing services for tenants; insurance premiums; any fees you pay an agent for letting the premises, and management expenses. You must remember to keep all your bills, and if you have made a loss, which is not all that unusual, you will be entitled to relief.

Page Three. The first section asks for details of any dividends you have received from British companies, or any tax credits from unit trusts. You must give a full description of each holding – the number of shares you hold, the name of the company, and the amount of the dividend. Again, there are separate sections for husband and wife. You must also include in this section details of any unit trusts you hold, the amount of any dividend, and details where the income has been reinvested in new units.

Then there follows a section where you enter any other dividends, interest, trust income, or annuities which have been paid to you after tax has been deducted. Again, full details of the source should be given in each case, and the amount of the *gross* (pre-tax) dividend, even though you have received it net. Nothing here for Mr and Mrs X, but in the next section Mrs X's £26 interest from her National Savings Bank ordinary account must go in the appropriate column – even though this will not be taxed because it is below the £50 allowed before tax becomes payable.

The next section also asks for details of any other bank interest (which is taxable) and of income from any other source, including War Loan, Defence Bonds, National Development Bonds, British Savings Bonds, and loans to private individuals.

Next comes untaxed income from abroad. This affects relatively few people.

Now we come to any interest received from a building society, and here Mr X must enter his wife's £45 a year. As Mr X is paying tax only at the standard rate of 35 per cent, there will not be any tax to pay on this interest, but it must nevertheless be included.

Then, just to make sure that you have told all, there is another section for any other income or profits. This could include something like commission. The final section on income asks if there have been any changes in your untaxed income or outgoings since the end of the previous financial year.

Outgoings

Page Four of the return brings us to outgoings. First of all come expenses incurred in your employment. These can include the replacing or maintaining of tools or special working clothes. Mr X does not have any of these, but he does use his car when he travels from factory to factory.

The Inland Revenue will not allow him all the maintenance and running costs of the car. It will make a deduction for his private use and will not make any allowance for travel between his home and principal workplace. In Mr X's case this will be the headquarters of his company.

I will suppose here that Mr X can claim that one-sixth of the use of his car goes on travel from factory to factory, and that the car costs £12 a week to run and maintain. This is £624 a year, and one-sixth is £104. The inspector will give you further details of this allowance if you write and ask him, and he may have further queries to make to substantiate your claim.

Expenses can also include any compulsory payments which you may have to make to a professional body in order to work. You must state the name of the body and the amount involved. Mr X does not have any unavoidable expenses like this. You cannot claim for professional entertaining, unless it is reasonable entertaining for an overseas customer. However, most people who have to entertain professionally have an agreement with their firm that their expenses will be recovered on production of the relevant bill.

But Mr X is involved in the next section, which deals with interest on loans for the purchase or improvement of property. He has a mortgage on which he pays £220 in *interest*, in addition to the capital repayments, and he has a bank borrowing of £200.

As his mortgage is with a building society, it gives the Inland Revenue details of the interest paid – as would a local authority. Nevertheless, include it here.

If you have borrowed money from any other source – say your bank or an insurance company or a private lender – you will have to get a certificate of interest paid from the lender and send it to the tax office.

Mr X's bank borrowing is divided into two parts. He has an overdraft of £100 towards new furniture and a loan of £100 to build a garage. The first £100 is not tax-deductible, because only loans for houses or house improvements are, but the £100 for the garage is allowed against his tax. The bank will furnish him with the details of the interest, which he can then relay to the inspector. Improvement means more than just decoration.

You can only claim tax relief on a mortgage or mortgages attached to your 'main residence', and the limit on that mortgage is £25,000 (see section I, chapter 8). Once again, husband and wife are treated as one person and cannot have two main residences.

There are exceptions, however. You are also allowed tax relief on mortgage interest on a house occupied by a relative who is incapacitated by old age or infirmity, as long as he or she does not pay you any rent. There is an exception, too, for divorced or separated husbands. They are allowed two mortgages, one on their own home and the other on that of their divorced or separated wife. Mr X has been divorced, but he paid off the mortgage on his first wife's house many years ago.

If you have sold your house and have a bridging loan for a period, you will be allowed tax relief on that interest, but you must consult the inspector. Bridging loan relief does not go on forever. The Inland Revenue usually feels that twelve months is long enough for you to sell your house. Interest paid on option mortgages is not allowed against tax; that is already allowed for in the lower interest rate payable on such mortgages (see section I, chapter 8).

Next comes interest on any other loans. There are relatively few of these, so this section affects a limited number of people. It includes some loans taken out before 27 March 1974 when tax relief on overdrafts and other loans ceased. Some, however, are still eligible for residual relief.

The last section asks for details of other outgoings and includes any covenants and settlements you may have made. You must give details of the covenant, stating the name of the charity or person who will be benefiting from it. You should enter the gross amount, although you have paid it out net. If it is for £100 a year for the seven-year period, write in £100, but you pay the recipient only £65, that is, £100 net of income tax at the standard rate. The recipient will later be able to reclaim the tax deducted, as long as he is not liable for tax.

This section also includes alimony payments, and here Mr X inserts the £800 he pays to his ex-wife under a court order. It is important, for, if the agreement is voluntary, no tax will be allowed on it. Again, the gross amount has been entered, although Mr X will actually have paid out £520, that is, the amount of the order less 35 per cent standard rate tax. He will later have to make good the 35 per cent to the Inland Revenue, and the Inland Revenue has a formula for adjusting his coding. If for any reason the payment is made gross, this should be stated on the form.

You may also pay rents to someone abroad. If you do, write these down gross, but deduct standard rate tax before making the payments.

Capital gains

We now come to capital gains, which I have already discussed earlier in chapter 1 of this section. Basically, you pay at a maximum rate of 30 per cent, with 17½ per cent deduction in the case of unit trusts and investment trusts, as we have seen there is an alternative way of paying which may reduce your liability.

Mr X made a gain this year on the sale of the house his mother lived in and which his father signed over to him many years ago. He must give details of the disposal of the house and of the amount of the gain, compared with the value of the house when it was given to him. So he puts down £2,200. This is the £2,500 profit he made less his selling expenses of £300.

Husbands' and wives' gains are aggregated as if they were one person. Gains can arise in all sorts of ways, the most common being sales of property, shares, unit trusts and land.

If you have sold a total of assets worth less than £1,000 in any one year, you will not be taxed, so write disposals not exceeding £1,000. Write 'none' if you have made no gains. Remember to charge all your expenses against your gains. That includes any losses you may have made. You must separate out each gain, including development gains you may make from land.

The person making the tax return must also set down any 'chargeable' assets he has acquired. If you have acquired a valuable painting, for example, you should put down details of it and its value, so that the gains tax – if any – can be calculated should you ever sell it.

Allowances

Pages Five and Six. On these pages you set out what allowances you think you are entitled to. The inspector will automatically deal with the single person's allowance. But if you are married, and either living with your wife or wholly maintaining her on a voluntary basis, you must put that down. You give her christian or other forename, followed by the date of your marriage if you got married after 5 April 1975, and then her maiden name.

If you are maintaining a separated or divorced wife (or husband) under a court order, you can ignore these first sections, as you will already have entered your alimony payments as one of your outgoings. So Mr X here puts only the name of his second wife.

Next, if you and/or your wife were born before 6 April 1913, there is a space for an 'X'. Do not forget this or you will not get the extra age allowance to which those over sixty-five are entitled. There is a leaflet available from your tax office, 'Income Tax and the Elderly', which you may find helpful.

Now we come to your children. You can claim for any child at any age as long as they are in full-time education and their total income is only £115 a year or less, apart from any educational grant they may get, which does not count. The allowance is reduced by £1 for every £1 of the child's income in excess of £115 and you must state what their income is. If more than one person claims for a child – for example, if divorced parents both claim – the allowance will be split and you must show the proportion you are claiming.

If your children are adopted, or maintained by you even if they are not adopted, or step-children, you may claim for them but you must give details. As soon as a child goes out to work, he will get his own tax return and should not be included in yours.

Our Mr X therefore enters details of his child who is studying at university full-time and of the fifteen-year-old who is still at school. He gets no relief for the eighteen-year-old who is working.

Anyone claiming for a child but only themselves getting the single person's allowance may also be entitled to an additional personal allowance. The same applies to a married man whose wife is totally incapacitated throughout the financial year. In the latter case the additional allowance is to provide for someone to come in and take care of the incapacitated wife.

The opposite does not apply. A wife with a totally incapacitated husband cannot apply for this relief, even if she goes out to work and maintains the family and is therefore unable to be at home to look after him. The Inland Revenue is concerned only that there is a woman in the house who could look after her husband. In cases like this, some women who would prefer to work are forced to claim social security, or have to pay someone to look after their husbands but get no corresponding tax relief.

Next comes the housekeeper allowance; you cannot get this as well as the additional personal allowance. If you are making this claim, details of the person for whom the claim is made, her marital status, her residence, her relationship to you, if any, and how, whether and how much she contributes herself to her keep.

We have now reached page six. First, dependent relatives. You may claim if a relative (or one of your wife's if you are married) is unable to work because of incapacity or old age. Similarly you may claim if your mother (or your wife's) is a widow, separated or divorced, and dependent on you. So here Mr X can claim for his mother, who is living with him on a state pension and nothing else.

You must fill in the name and address of any dependents, their relationship to you, details of any pension they receive, how much you give them and whether they live with you. You must also state whether another relative helps to maintain the person and give the dependent's date of birth and the nature of the infirmity if there is one. You are not limited to helping to maintain only one relative, though Mr X will claim only for his mother.

Next comes the allowance which is permitted if you have to depend on a daughter's services. This applies if she lives with you to take care of you, or your wife, because you are old or infirm. But you must be maintaining her, and the allowance is the smallest that is available. Similar details must be given as with other dependent relatives.

You qualify for the blind person's allowance only if you (or your wife) are registered as blind. It is not enough, for example, to be extremely short-sighted. The allowance is reduced if you get any other tax-free allowances for your disability. You cannot get this allowance and the daughter's services allowance, so if you qualify for both claim the blind person's: it is more than three times as much as the daughter's services.

Next come death and superannuation benefits. If you are simply in a private pension scheme, you will normally put nothing here because your employer will already have deducted your contributions from the total earnings he sent to the Inland Revenue.

But two kinds of schemes are not included. First, superannuation schemes which provide benefits for a widow or orphans, when relief is given as if it were a life insurance policy.

And second, superannuation or death benefit schemes run by trade unions, in which a proportion of the contribution goes towards a superannuation payment after retirement. Again relief is given as if it were a life policy. The proportion of the contribution has been agreed with many trade unions. If you are a member of a union, ask them about any schemes they may have.

The usual details are required: the name of the scheme, the full contribution, and the proportion which goes towards death or superannuation benefits.

You must also include here any retirement annuity payments. Give details of employer or insurance company as appropriate, the number of the scheme, and the amount you will pay in the tax year.

Lastly, your life insurance. You must enter separately the details of each policy, whether it is on your own or your wife's, the date of the policy if it was taken out after April, any capital sum which will be paid out if you die before the policy matures, the amount of the premiums, and the date of the final premium if it is paid before 6 April 1979. Mr X fills in here the details of the policy he has.

That's it. Check through your form, sign it and send it off. It is not as difficult as it sounds. You will be entitled to some allowances but not all of them. Take the form slowly. If you make a mistake, the tax office will query it, but no action will be taken against you if it is a genuine mistake – though if you deliberately mislead the inspector you may find yourself suffering quite stringent penalties (see chapter 5 of this section). All being well – and it usually is – you will eventually get a detailed coding sent to you from the office. A copy of the code will also go to your employer.

Check the coding: the inspector can make mistakes as well. Your coding will have a number, and an H after it if you are a married man; otherwise it will be L. If, however, you do not wish your employer to know whether you are married or not, ask the tax office to designate your code with a T.

Mrs X should not forget to claim child benefit for her student child and the fifteen-year-old. This is £1 for the first child and £1.50 for subsequent children. Family allowances have now been replaced by child benefit. The allowances were regarded as part of the husband's income and taxed accordingly, but child benefit goes directly to the mother or person caring for the child and does not come into the tax return at all. Child allowances have been reduced to make up for this. The aim is that by April 1979 child allowances will disappear altogether and be replaced by bigger child benefits, which will go to the mother as of right.

A last point for women: if you are filling in a tax return on your own account, use the column marked 'self', not 'wife', even if you are married. If you are a married woman being taxed with your husband, you must obey the instruction on the form which reads: 'If you are a married woman please pass this form on to your husband.' This may not please you, so go on to chapter 4 of this section which deals with the separation of married people's earnings.

A sample tax return is reproduced on the following pages. The form is Crown Copyright and is reproduced with the permission of the Controller of Her Majesty's Stationery Office.

District
H.M. Inspector of Taxes,

London Provincial 13 District,
Duckworth House,
Talbot Road,
Stretford,
MANCHESTER, M32 .0EU.

Date of issue

In any enquiry please quote:

908

908
SPECIMEN

TAX RETURN

Income tax year 1977-78

You are required to fill in this form, sign the declaration below and send it back to me within 30 days.

It is recommended that you read the introduction to the enclosed Guide before you start to fill in the return.

H.M. Inspector of Taxes

DECLARATION
False statements can result in prosecution

To the best of my knowledge and belief the particulars given on this form are correct and complete.

Signature.. Date.........................197......
(A woman should state after her signature whether she is single, married, widowed, separated or divorced)

Private address
(Use BLOCK letters and include postcode, if any)

If you make the return as Executor, Trustee, Receiver, etc.. state in what capacity and for whom made:

If you and/or your wife were born before 6 April 1918, please enter date(s) of birth ▶

Self	
Wife	

11P(1977)

INCOME: Year ended 5 April 1977

	See Note	Details		Amount for year Self £	Wife £
Employments or offices	2		Occupation Employers' names and addresses		
	4–6	Earnings, (including fees, bonus, commission, tips, etc.)			
	7–8	Benefits, expense allowances			
	9	Leaving payments and compensation			
	10	DUTIES PERFORMED WHOLLY ABROAD	Employment concerned		
	10		Deduction claimed (enter "X") A [ ] one quarter [ ] B [ ] the whole [ ] Dates of absence		
Trade, profession or vocation	2 11–13	Nature Business name and address		£	£
	14	Balancing charges			
	14	Deduction for capital allowances	Self £ Wife £		
	15	If exceptionally your profits for Class 4 National Insurance contributions purposes are affected by interest paid, certain capital allowances or losses not given in the assessment, give details on a separate sheet and enter "X" here ▶ [ ]			
Social Security Pensions and Benefits	16	Retirement pension or old person's pension	If wife's pension paid by virtue of her own contributions enter "X" here ▶ [ ]	Self £	Wife £
	17	Widow's and other benefits Nature of benefit .... (see identity page of Order Book)			
	18	Family allowances/Child interim benefit .... per week			
Other Pensions	19–20	Pension from former employer and other pensions (including War Widow's pension)	Payer's name Address		

	1	Please also state the current weekly/monthly rate of each Social Security or other pension you receive	Nature of pension	Self £	Wife £	State "Weekly" or "Monthly"

Property			Address	Gross income including premiums £	Expenses (enclose statement) £	Self £	Wife £
	21	Unfurnished lettings					
	21	Furnished lettings					
	22	Ground rents or Feu duties					
	23	Land					

Page 2

292

INCOME : Year ended 5 April 1977

	See Note	*Details*	Amount for year	
Dividends from United Kingdom companies and tax credits	24	Name of United Kingdom company Self .... Wife	Amount of dividend £	Amount of tax credit £
Other dividends, interest, trust income, annuities, etc., already taxed	25–28	Source *(show each separately)* *Enter the gross amount for each holding, trust, etc.*	Self £	Wife £
Interest not taxed before receipt	29	*Enter ALL the interest from each account* National Savings Bank { *Including any exempt amount (see note 29)* { Ordinary account ► Investment account ► Trustee Savings Bank { Ordinary account ► Investment account ►	Self £	Wife £
	30	Other banks *(enter name of bank)*		
	31	Other sources (including War Loan, British Savings Bonds and loans to private individuals)		
Untaxed income from abroad	32		Self £	Wife £
Interest from United Kingdom Building Societies	33	Name of society	Self £	Wife £
Any other profits or income	34–44	*INCLUDE INCOME FROM SETTLEMENTS, ESTATES OF DECEASED PERSONS AND TRANSFERS TO BE TREATED AS YOUR INCOME*	Self £	Wife £

Alterations in untaxed income or outgoings since 5 April 1976

	45	

Attach a separate sheet if there is not enough space in a section

OUTGOINGS: Year ended 5 April 1977

	See Note	Details	Amount for year Self £	Wife £
Expenses in employment	46			
	47	Fees or subscriptions to professional bodies *Name of professional body*		
Interest on loans *(Excluding Bank overdrafts)* **for purchase or improvement of property**	48–50	**Only or main residence** *Name of lender* *Account number* Interest payable	£	£
		— To a building society or local authority		
		— To any other person including a bank		
	51	**Let property** — no. of weeks let ☐ *Enclose certificates*		
		— address		
	52	**Other property** where loan incurred before 27 March 1974		
	50	**Option mortgage** (if any) — amount outstanding at 5 April 1977 £..................................		
Interest on other loans *(Excluding Bank overdrafts)*	48, 53	*Name of lender* Qualifying loans	£	£
	54	Any other loans incurred before 27 March 1974 *Enclose certificates*		
Other outgoings	55	Covenants, bonds of annuity and settlements	£	£
	56	Alimony, aliment or maintenance		
	57	U.K. property rents or yearly interest paid to persons abroad		

CAPITAL GAINS and Development Gains: Year ended 5 April 1977

	See Note	Details		Self	Wife
Chargeable assets disposed of	58–70	Date of disposal	Description	Amount of gain for year *(Distinguish Development gains)* £	£
		Unit Trust units and shares in Investment Trusts			
		Other assets			
Chargeable assets acquired	71	Date of acquisition	Description	Cost or acquisition value £	£

Page 4.

294

ALLOWANCES: Claim for Year ending 5 April 1978

See Note	Before making any claim read the appropriate note
A	**Married man living with wife or wholly maintaining her** Wife's Christian or other forenames

<table>
<tr><td></td><td>If you married after 5 April 1976 please state—</td><td>(a) date of marriage</td><td>(b) Wife's former surname</td></tr>
</table>

B   **Age allowance for persons born before 6 April 1913**
If you and/or your wife were born before 6 April 1913, enter "X" here ▶ ☐

C   **Children**

Children Full names of child (Surname first)	Child's date of birth Day : Month : Year	Child's earnings and other income				Child 16 or over on 6 April 1977 Name of university, college or school or nature of training
		Year ended 5 April 1977		Year ending 5 April 1978 (estimated)		
		Earnings	Other income	Earn-ings	Other income	
		£	£	£	£	

If this is your first claim for a stepchild or adopted child, please say so

Children for whom you claimed an allowance for 1976–77 but are not claiming for 1977–78

	YEAR ENDED 5 APRIL 1977
Full name	Earnings £...................... Other income £.........................

D   **Additional personal allowance for children**

Does the child on whom you base your claim live with you?	If your wife is incapacitated	
	What is the nature of the incapacity?	Is it likely to continue throughout the year ending 5 April 1978?

If the amount of a child's income alone prevents a claim for child allowance and additional personal allowance is claimed state—

Full names of child *(surname first)*	Child's date of birth Day : Month : Year	Child 16 or over on 6 April 1977, name of university, college or school, or nature of training

E   **Housekeeper or person looking after children**

Surname of housekeeper	Status of housekeeper (Single, married, separated, divorced or widowed)	Is she resident with you?	Relationship (if any)	If she is a relative, 1 Does any other person contribute to her maintenance? 2 If so, what is the weekly amount?
Christian or other forenames				1. 2.

ALLOWANCES (continued)

See Note	Before making any claim read the appropriate note

F — Dependent relatives

Name and address of dependant	Relationship to you (or to your wife) If "mother" state whether widowed, separated or divorced	Dependant's annual income excluding voluntary contributions			If not resident with you, the weekly amount you contribute	1 Does any other relative contribute? ('Yes' or 'No') 2 If 'Yes', enter the weekly amount	Dependant's date of birth	Nature of infirmity (if any)
		National Insurance pension or benefit	Other pension	Other income				
		£	£	£	£	1 ___ 2 £		

G — Daughter on whose services you are compelled to depend

Daughter's surname / Christian or other forenames	Status of daughter (single, married, separated, divorced or widowed)	1 Is she resident with you? 2 Do you maintain her?	Which of you is aged or infirm, (yourself or your wife)?	If aged, enter date of birth (Day / Month / Year)	If infirm enter nature of infirmity
		1 ___ 2			

H — Blind person's allowance

Self or Wife	Local authority with which registered	Date of registration	Tax free blindness disability payments receivable in the year ending 5 April 1978 Description	Amount
				£

J — Death and Superannuation Benefits

Name of Scheme or Trade Union	Full contribution for the year	Portion of contribution for Death or Superannuation benefits
	£	

K — Retirement annuity payments

Occupation in which non-pensionable earnings arise: enter name of employer if a non-pensionable employment or office	Name of Insurance Company, etc. or Trust Scheme	Contract number or Scheme membership number	Amount to be paid in year to 5 April 1978	If a special form is required, put 'X' here ▼
			£	

L — Life insurance

Name of Company	On whose life ('Self' or 'Wife')?	Date of Policy or contract if after 5 April 1976	Capital sum payable on death	Premiums to be paid in the year ending 5 April 1978	Date final premium payable (if before 6 April 1979)
			£	£	

Do not forget to sign the Declaration on page 1

Chapter 3

VALUE ADDED TAX

Value Added Tax, or V.A.T. as it is called for short, was introduced in Britain on 1 April 1973 to replace the old purchase and selective employment taxes. It was brought in to bring our indirect taxes into line with other members of the E.E.C., as they all have some kind of V.A.T., though it differs in detail from country to country. In Britain it is levied on a wide range of goods and services at the rate of 8 per cent, with some products attracting a higher rate. These change from time to time, so check the rate on anything you are buying.

V.A.T. is a completely new departure in taxation policy in Britain and has caused a lot of headaches. This is not because it is particularly complicated – it isn't – but because the Customs and Excise language of the instructions has confused many people and – most unusual in Britain – those responsible for paying the tax have to act as their own tax assessors to some extent, rather than having that side of the work done for them completely by tax inspectors.

Fortunately, though we all pay V.A.T. in some form or another, we don't all have the bother of working it out. If you are buying something you can forget about V.A.T. The trader will have worked it out and incorporated it in his price to you. Prices usually include V.A.T., though some traders prefer to show it separately so that you know exactly what you are paying in tax. It can also fool you into thinking the price is lower than it is, so watch out for this.

WHO IS LIABLE FOR V.A.T.?

The operative factor here is whether you have a 'business'. If you have, you may be liable for V.A.T. The Inland Revenue defines a business as any trade, profession or vocation. Clubs and associations, such as sports clubs and members' clubs, are also included, but not trade unions.

All businesses under this definition which have supplies coming in worth more than £7,500 a year must register themselves for V.A.T. with the Customs and Excise department. Supplies in this case can be in the form of money (an author's earnings or a restaurant's takings, for example), or specific goods.

If you don't have this amount coming in you can register voluntarily.

297

Taxation

If you are not registered you will not have to charge V.A.T. to any of your customers but you will not get any allowance on any V.A.T. you have paid to someone else in the course of your business.

If you have not registered, but then find your supplies are more than £2,625, £4,500 or £6,375 by the first, second and third quarters of any year, respectively, you must tell the Customs and Excise. They will then register you, unless you can prove that your total supplies will not be more than £7,500 for the full year. This can happen quite often – for example with authors, or seasonal businesses.

Take advice if you are not sure. If you do the wrong thing, your problems with the 'Vatman' may go on for years.

WHAT IS LIABLE FOR V.A.T.?

V.A.T. is levied on all imported goods and on a wide variety of products made and services rendered in the United Kingdom itself. Another whole range of goods and services is *zero-rated*, as opposed to exempt. This means the V.A.T. rate is nil per cent, but this could be changed at any time.

It is important to know the difference between exempt and zero-rated goods, because if you are selling zero-rated articles you can claim a refund for any V.A.T. which you have paid to other people, whereas if you sell things which are exempt you cannot.

Here is a list of zero-rated and exempt items. You will notice that they are quite different in character.

zero-rated
food – but not pet food, alcohol, soft drinks, ice cream or potato crisps
water – but not distilled and bottled water
books – but not stationery and diaries
talking books and wirelesses for the blind
newspaper advertisements – but not radio or television advertisements
heating fuel and power – but not petrol and derv
construction of buildings – but not repairs, sales by a builders' merchant, or architects' and surveyors' fees
transport – but not taxis and hired cars, or pleasure boats
large caravans – but only caravans longer than 22.9 feet or 7.5 feet wide
gold – but not coins or jewellery, only bullion
bank notes
drugs, medicines, medical and surgical appliances – but only if purchased on a prescription from a registered pharmacist

298

charities – but only donated goods sold for the relief of distress. Other business supplies are treated normally

clothing and footwear – but only young children's protective clothing and crash helmets

Exports

exempt

land – leasing and hiring out of land, but not hotels, holiday accommodation, camping sites, parking space, timber, mooring and sporting rights

insurance – all types

postal services – except telegrams, telephones and telex

betting, gaming and lotteries – but not admission charges or club subscriptions

finance – but not brokers' commissions or unit trust management fees or consultancy fees

education – but not correspondence schools or secretarial colleges

health – but not health farms, beauty clinics, etc.

burial and cremation

From time to time the government puts a higher rate of V.A.T. on some products as part of its economic policy, either to cut down consumer demand or to raise extra revenue. These are usually what are regarded as luxuries, though you may not regard them as such. Domestic appliances, which most women would regard as essential, are a favourite target for government action. At the time of writing the following items carry V.A.T. at 12½ per cent:

domestic appliances – but not cookers, space heaters, immersion heaters or light fittings

radio and T.V. sets – but records and tapes carry the ordinary rate

boats and aircraft – but boat hire for holidays is normally taxed

photographic equipment – but films are standard-rated

furs

jewellery

petrol

HOW DOES V.A.T. WORK?

If you are registered for V.A.T., you will have to make returns every three months. The account you return for any three months must be made within one month of the end of the period, and the tax must be paid at the same time.

This is what you have to do:

299

1   Total all the tax invoices you have received.
2   Total all vouchers for tax on imports.
3   Total all outputs.

The sum will then look like this:

total outputs	£20,000	
V.A.T. allotted		£2,500
total invoices and vouchers	£8,000	
V.A.T. paid out		£1,000
balance to be paid to the Customs and Excise		£1,500

You can see that if you keep all your receipts and bills the process is quite simple, but you must keep your records in order.

To show how the tax is added on a single item, let's look at a product which the retailer finally sells to the customer for a price of £200, excluding V.A.T.

	price	V.A.T.	Customs and Excise receives
Raw materials imported by the manufacturer	£10	80p	
Manufacturer sends tax on import to Customs and Excise			80p
Manufacturer sells product to wholesaler	£50	£4	
Manufacturer sends V.A.T.			£3.20
Wholesaler sells product to retailer	£100	£8	
Wholesaler sends V.A.T.			£4
Retailer sells to customer	£200	£16	
Retailer sends V.A.T.			£8
Customer pays V.A.T.			£16

The total price to the customer, then, is £216, of which the Customs and Excise gets £16. You will see that the amount of V.A.T. sent to the Customs and Excise at each stage is adjusted according to the amount already paid.

300

Points to notice:

1 A group of companies can opt to be treated as a single business and inter-company trading is then ignored for V.A.T. purposes. Alternatively, divisions can be registered separately.

2 V.A.T. must be paid on the purchase of second-hand goods, but in some cases – antiques, works of art, cars, boats and a few other things – it is only chargeable on the dealers' mark-up. There are other special rules which apply to cars.

3 If you are buying on H.P. the V.A.T. is payable when the contract is signed.

4 You cannot recoup V.A.T. on business entertaining, unless it is for overseas visitors.

If you want more details there are a series of Notices on every aspect issued by the Customs and Excise department. These are free from any Customs and Excise office, as listed in the phone book.

Chapter 4

MARRIAGE AND TAXATION

SEPARATE ASSESSMENT

In most of the major decisions affecting our lives, the taxman is involved. Marriage is no exception. Contrary to rumour, two cannot live as cheaply as one. The costs of marriage and a family, which I discussed in section III, chapter 2, can be formidable. For once, the tax system does something to help, and the married man is given extra allowances for his wife and children.

Briefly, the law says that financially husband and wife are to be treated as one person – that one being the husband. This means that only he makes a tax return to the Inland Revenue, and he includes his wife's income along with his own. This is known as aggregation of income. He gets all the relief for children, mortgage, etc. He pays any tax underpaid by his wife as well as himself, and gets any rebate, even if it applies to his wife's income only.

This law has been relaxed over the years giving women more control over their money. Some couples, when both are working, opt for what is known as separate assessment of earnings. This does not change the amount of tax paid, but divides the allowances in such a way that husband and wife pay their share of tax according to their income. Doing this can stop a good many family rows about money, but there is no tax advantage. All that happens is that the total tax is calculated and divided between husband and wife in proportion to their incomes. Reliefs are divided like this:

* Life insurance relief goes to the one who pays the premiums.
* Relief for dependent relatives and children not of the marriage goes to the one who supports them.
* Other allowances are split in proportion to their incomes.
* The tax allowance to the wife must not be less than the single person's allowance.

In the table opposite the column on the left shows how the tax bill works out for a husband and wife who are taxed together. They earn £8,000 a year between them and have an investment income of £3,000; they have one child under eleven and the wife maintains her widowed mother. The two columns on the right show what happens when they are separately assessed, with the husband earning £5,500 and the wife £2,500 (last two columns on the right). The table shows how the total tax is the same either way.

Separate assessment solves some problems, but not those of higher earning couples who find themselves penalized in the tax they pay in comparison with two single people on the same salary. Two wages added together reach the higher levels of tax far sooner than two separate incomes.

SEPARATE TAXATION

In the 1971 Finance Act the government went some but not all the way to solving their problems when it allowed separate taxation (not separate assessment) for married women on their *earned* income only. They realized that many women found it was simply not worth their while going out to work. After paying someone to replace themselves at home and paying tax they were out of pocket, and many valuable workers were lost.

When you have a progressive tax system as we do in Britain, if you aggregate married couples' incomes, you eventually penalize people for being married. The way the system works makes a jointly taxed (aggregated) couple better off until their total income reaches something over £9,000, depending on individual circumstances, because the husband gets an extra allowance for his wife in addition to her own personal earned income allowance.

After £9,000 being married actually costs money in tax terms, unless a

	Mr X (£)	Mr X (£)	Mrs X (£)
earned income	8,000	5,500	2,500
investment income	3,000	1,500	1,500
	11,000	7,000	4,000
income tax at the different rates			
£6,000 at 35%	2,100		
£1,000 at 40%	400		
£1,000 at 45%	450		
£1,000 at 50%	500		
£1,000 at 55%	550		
£1,000 at 60%	600		
£11,000 (split 7:4)	4,600	2,927	1,673
additional rate on £1,500 investment income			
£500 at 10%	50		
£1,000 at 15%	150		
(split 50/50)	200	100	100
total tax before allowances	4,800	3,027	1,773
allowances: personal (married man)	1,225		
additional personal (wife's)	805		
child relief (under 11)	196	1,417	809
	2,226	1,480	846
dependent relative relief	100	—	100
total allowances	2,326	1,417	909
Tax equivalent of allowances (at 60%, 55%, and 50%)	1,313.00	835.55	477.45
total tax payable	3,487.00	2,191.45	1,295.55
		3,487.00	

couple elect for separate taxation. And joint incomes at that level are not exceptional these days. Working husbands and wives should consider each financial year whether they are in effect paying a 'morality tax', and if they are do something about it.

A couple must 'elect' for separate taxation. The request must be made by both husband and wife not earlier than twelve months before the start of the financial year in question and not later than twelve months after the end of the financial year.

Inland Revenue leaflet No 13, 'Taxation of Wife's Earnings', explains the whole process in detail and updates the figures each year to show where separate taxation starts to be favourable.

If a couple elect for separate taxation they are treated as single people as far as their *earned* income is concerned. (Unearned income from rents, savings, dividends, etc., is still regarded as the husband's income, even if the wife owns the property, shares, or whatever). Each then makes their own tax return, the husband including in his any unearned income of his wife's.

'Earnings' for the wife include everything she gets from paid employment, but not:

* Child benefit.
* Any national insurance benefits she may get which do not result from her own insurance.
* Any pension or other allowances given in respect of her husband's past employment.

Tax reliefs are then allocated like this:

* The husband loses the allowance he gets for his wife and receives – as she does – the single person's allowance.
* The husband gets all the child relief for his own children, but not, for instance, for those of his wife from a previous marriage.
* The individual can only offset such items as trading losses, deeds of covenant and interest against his or her own income and not that of the other.
* Some allowances are lost, including age allowance.

Other reliefs are allocated as if the couple were not married. This means, for instance, that husbands and wives would each get relief on the premiums insuring their own lives. If a husband has been getting relief for premiums paid on his wife's policy, he will lose it if the couple decide to be taxed separately. Mortgage relief can be divided.

Opposite are two simple examples of how separate taxation works. In the first example the couple earn £11,000, divided equally between them.

	taxed together	taxed separately	
	Mr Y	Mr Y	Mrs Y
	(£)	(£)	(£)
earned income	11,000	5,500	5,500
married man's allowance	1,225	—	—
wife's earned income allowance	805	—	—
single person's allowance	—	805	805
total relief	2,030	805	805
taxable income	8,970	4,695	4,695
first £6,000 at 35%	2,100	1,643	1,643
next £1,000 at 40%	400	—	—
£1,000 at 45%	450	—	—
£970 at 50%	485	—	—
total tax	3,435		
		3,286	

They would save £149 a year by being taxed separately.

In contrast, a couple earning less than £9,000 would suffer from being taxed separately. This couple earn £7,000 a year, divided equally between them.

	taxed together	taxed separately	
	Mr Y	Mr Y	Mrs Y
	(£)	(£)	(£)
earned income	7,000	3,500	3,500
married man's allowance	1,225	—	—
wife's earned income allowance	805	—	—
single person's allowance	—	805	805
total taxable income	4,970	2,695	2,695
all taxed at 35%	1,735.50	943.25	943.25
		1,886.50	

If they were taxed separately they would lose £151 a year.

The starting level and the sums work out differently in different circumstances. The closer together the two incomes, the greater the saving. Again, the smaller proportion of unearned income in the total the greater the saving. Where a dependent relative is supported by the wife (for revenue purposes she cannot support her husband's relatives while he is alive and working) the allowance rises from £100 to £145. This increased allowance is only permitted in cases of separate taxation, *not* separate assessment and it is one of the few ways in which women have an advantage in the tax system.

If you are close to the level where you will benefit from being taxed separately, particularly if you are recently married, it may be best if you opt for separate taxation from the word go. This breeds an attitude of self-reliance and independence early on, and means, particularly if you are a woman, that you will always be able to cope with your financial affairs. It would be foolish, however, to throw money away just for the sake of being independent.

When a couple are taxed together, the husband is liable for all tax, and although it's nice when you get a rebate, it's sometimes difficult to persuade a wife who may feel she's already paid enough tax on P.A.Y.E. to hand the extra money over if she has underpaid.

Remember all this only applies to earned income. A husband must give details of their joint dividends and interest on his tax return. There is, however, no law which says that a wife must tell her husband about her income, earned or unearned – though the Inland Revenue will always catch up with you in time.

Chapter 5

WHEN YOU NEED AN ACCOUNTANT

Most people can fill in their own tax return without using an accountant to help. You cannot charge your accountant's fees against your income tax as an outgoing if all he does for you is fill in the return. It is for the more complicated business accounting that an accountant does that fees are allowed against tax. Most people who are employed by someone else and do not have family complications should be able to manage their return themselves. If there is any inaccuracy the inspector will probably spot it and query the matter with you.

But once you get into the realms of, for example, covenants, divorce, property leases, fringe benefits, golden handshakes, your domicile and residence, overseas income and double tax relief agreements, or tax due from a company you own or a partnership of which you are a member, you should seek the advice of an accountant.

It is not simply a matter of filling in the return, but of knowing when and what allowances can be set against your tax and the most efficient way to do it. Accountants are, or should be, highly skilled in making sure that you pay the minimum tax without infringing the law (see the last chapter in this section).

To discourage you from trying to deal with these matters yourself, I will set out here just the briefest details of the tax implications of the following:

COVENANTS

These (and gifts and settlements) can help you and the recipient save tax. A covenant must cover at least seven years and cannot be made by you to your children. You can make one to other people's children, however. Many people make them to grandchildren or god-children, to charities, and to old people on low incomes. The money is paid by the donor after standard rate tax, but if the recipient is not liable for tax it can be reclaimed. Remember, though, if you make a covenant to a child which is more than £115 a year, the father will have his child allowance reduced or eliminated altogether.

DIVORCE AND SEPARATION

It pays everyone involved to have a court settlement. This means that the husband (or nowadays it could be the wife) will be able to deduct any alimony paid from his taxable income, and in turn the wife or husband (though this is much rarer) may be able to reclaim some of the tax paid. It is always foolish to delay coming to a legal agreement, for as a rule everyone is better off, and there are means of saving money on both sides in the way that the payment is divided between the separated or divorced spouse and any children of the marriage.

PROPERTY LEASES

If you have any major dealings in the leasing of property, you must discuss these with an accountant, or you may lose money, in addition to losing any right to repossession of your premises.

FRINGE BENEFITS

These must all be declared. I have already mentioned cars and any

307

luncheon vouchers over 15p, but there are many other fringe benefits which must by law be declared. These include:

* Rent-free accommodation close to your work.
* The use at home of a television set paid for by your company. This will be taxed at 10 per cent of its annual value.
* Cash vouchers.
* If you get a loan for any purpose other than to buy your home, either interest-free or at a much lower rate than most people have to pay, you will be taxed on the 'benefit' you receive between that and the official rate, which is fixed by the Treasury. There are some rules about this, and some exceptions, so you will need the advice of an accountant.

GOLDEN HANDSHAKES

These are payments made to people either as compensation for loss of their job before their contract or notice expires or as a reward for so many years' service with a company. They are called 'golden' because they used to be completely tax-free, but today they are partly liable for tax. The first £5,000 is usually ignored, then depending on the particular situation the tax is worked out in various ways. You will need the advice both of a solicitor and of an accountant to get the best deal you can, from the point of view of both the amount you will get and the tax you will pay on it.

An accountant could well get you a rebate on the tax charged. He might, for instance, be able to get the payment divided over six years, in which case it would be liable for less tax. If you are made redundant there are minimum official agreements, but it may be possible for you to get more.

DOMICILE AND RESIDENCE

You may not actually live in this country, but you will be liable for full tax here unless you take certain steps to make sure that the Inland Revenue knows you are no longer resident. This has an effect on the U.K. income, capital gains and capital transfer tax that you will have to pay.

Your domicile is the place you regard as your natural home. You can only have one domicile, unlike nationality where you can sometimes have two. Most people are domiciled in the country where they were born. But you can have a domicile of origin, of choice, or of dependency.

Residence is different, and is fixed from year to year depending on where you are, and you can be regarded as being resident in two countries at the same time. This depends mainly on where you spend most of the year, or where your 'place of abode' is. Residency applies not only to individuals but also to companies.

All these questions are very complicated, so if you contemplate living abroad or keeping one home here and another one abroad consult an accountant to ensure that you do not pay too much tax. If you wish to live abroad permanently, here are some of the ways of proving that you are doing so:

* Live there.
* Buy a house there, or rent one on a lease.
* Start a business there.
* Marry someone from there.
* Change your will to fit in with the law of the country to which you have moved.
* Arrange for your family to live with you.
* Buy yourself a burial plot there.

There are many other things you could do. For instance, you could change your nationality, which would fix it once and for all – but that is not necessary. What you must do is prove to the satisfaction of the Inland Revenue that you live in your new country for all practical purposes.

TAX ON FOREIGN INCOME AND DOUBLE TAX RELIEF

This is an arrangement which the U.K. has with many other countries to try to ensure that people do not pay tax twice over. For instance, you may get a dividend from one country which is already taxed, then have to pay tax all over again in the U.K.

Various arrangements have been devised, and before you even think of investing overseas you should explore the situation with an accountant. Quite apart from anything else there are certain rules for assessing what overseas remittances (income) actually are, what allowances you can deduct, and how much you can leave abroad. All these questions need special knowledge which is rarely available to the ordinary person who suddenly finds that he has some income from overseas, perhaps from a long-lost uncle.

Overleaf is a list of the countries which currently have double tax relief arrangements with the U.K. These agreements are rarely cancelled, but they are altered slightly from time to time, so ask your accountant precisely what the particular agreement is with the country in which you are interested.

In addition to these there are many more limited agreements which apply only to certain businesses. These mostly just cover profits on shipping and air transport and include Argentina, Brazil, Lebanon, the

U.S.S.R. and Portugal. Agreements with Iceland only cover shipping profits and those with Iran and Spain only cover air transport profits.

Double tax relief arrangements exist with the following countries:

Antigua	Grenada	Norway
Australia	Guernsey	Pakistan
Austria	Indonesia	Portugal
Barbados	Irish Republic	Rhodesia
Belgium	Isle of Man	St Christopher
Belize	Israel	and Nevis
Botswana	Italy	St Lucia
British Soloman Is.	Jamaica	St Vincent
Brunei	Japan	Seychelles
Burma	Jersey	Sierra Leone
Canada	Kenya	Singapore
Cyprus	Lesotho	South Africa
Denmark	Luxembourg	S.W.A. (Nambia)
Dominica	Malawi	Swaziland
Falkland Is.	Malaysia	Sweden
Faroe Is.	Malta	Switzerland
Fiji	Mauritius	Tanzania
Finland	Montserrat	Trinidad and Tobago
France	Netherlands	Uganda
Gambia	Netherlands Antilles	U.S.A.
Ghana	NewZealand	West Germany
Gilbert and Ellice Is.	Nigeria	Zambia
Greece		

In his 1977 Budget the Chancellor of the Exchequer introduced a new concession for employees who are resident in the U.K., but whose work takes them abroad now and again. If you have to spend thirty or more days out of Britain on business – they need not be consecutive days – you are now allowed complete relief from taxes on 25 per cent of that part of your income for that year which relates to foreign employment.

CORPORATION TAX

Corporation tax is paid by companies not individuals. Most companies have their own accountant, and rightly so. If you have just set up a company you may feel that doing without an accountant is an economy you can make. This is always a mistake.

At present corporation tax is charged at the rate of 52 per cent for each accounting year. Companies do not keep to the country's financial year ending on 5 April; they can at present choose any date on which to end their accountancy year – though all new companies are being encouraged to choose 31 March, for the sake of uniformity.

The system of corporation tax is called the 'imputation system'. What happens is that the company pays dividends to its shareholders and then pays tax to the Inland Revenue of 35/65ths of these dividends. This is called 'Advanced Corporation Tax' (A.C.T.), which is then deducted from the final corporation tax bill, so that in fact the full 52 per cent is not paid at the end of the year. Small companies pay at a reduced rate on profits which do not exceed a certain amount. This amount varies from tax year to tax year, and an accountant is needed to work out at what level of profit the company will pay what tax.

If a company makes losses for some years, these can be offset against profits that are made later. Such a situation is quite common among new companies, and later on the relief can be useful. Losses can also be offset against corporation tax already paid; the result is then a tax repayment.

If you are a 'close' company, that is, a company which is controlled by five or fewer people and what are called their 'associates', which broadly means close relatives, there are special tax provisions. You are *not* a close company, however, if your shares are quoted on the stock exchange and at least 35 per cent of the shares are owned by outsiders. Check to see what your situation is.

PARTNERSHIP TAXES

Partnerships (see section II, chapter 5) are not taxed in the same way as individuals either. How do you know that you are in partnership – because there need not necessarily be a written agreement? To find out you must ask yourself a lot of questions. Here are just a few of them:

Is there a written agreement?
Are the partners responsible for all debts?
Has a business name been registered?
How are the profits divided?

The senior partner, who is known in law as the 'precedent partner', must make the return of the income and the outgoings of the partnership as a whole. The gross income is split between the various partners, sometimes in equal shares, sometimes not, and they are then responsible for income tax in the usual way, each making their own individual return.

If they show a loss, that is shared out in just the same way as a profit, and each partner can use this loss in several ways to offset his profits from other years. When partnerships are simple, the partners may be able to manage without an accountant, but in more complicated ones they would be well advised to call one in to help assess their income and outgoings in a satisfactory manner.

Chapter 6

KEEPING YOUR TAXES TO A MINIMUM

TAX EVASION

Only the very poor escape taxes in this country, and to many people the amount they pay seems excessive. But taxes are compulsory. There is no way out of paying taxes which are levied by law, and anyone who does not pay tax for which he is liable is breaking the law. This is called *tax evasion,* and it carries quite severe penalties. This is not just a matter of not paying your tax bill, but extends to not telling the Inland Revenue the truth and the whole truth about your income. If you don't tell the Inland Revenue that you have a bit of money tucked away in a bank account earning taxable interest, for example, you could find yourself paying a fine of £100, *when* – not *if* – they catch up with you, as they always do in the end. Even a failure to fill in and send back your annual tax return can land you with a fine of £50.

Here are a few of the penalities which the Inland Revenue has thought up for us, though they will accept less sometimes if they think there are extenuating circumstances and you have made a genuine mistake:

If you	*you may be fined*
send an incorrect return	£50 plus any additional tax, or, in the case of fraud, £50 plus *twice* the additional tax.
help someone to prepare an incorrect return	£500
give wrong information to the Inland Revenue	£500 if you are convicted of fraud; otherwise £250
do not tell the Inland Revenue that you are liable for tax	£100

TAX AVOIDANCE

This is quite another matter. There is no law which says you must not arrange your financial affairs in such a way that you pay as little tax as is

312

legally possible. That is just part of sensible money management. There are some rules about tax avoidance as well, but these are mainly to do with overseas income and investments and don't affect the majority of us.

Remember a tax accountant is a tax payer's best friend. Go to a proper one – don't take advice from just anyone. As with so many things, many people think they know more than they do. Your accountant knows the rules and regulations and where savings can be made. You will have to pay him according to the amount of work he does for you, but if your affairs are at all complicated the Inland Revenue will probably let you charge his fees as an expense against your tax – though, as I have already said (chapter 5 in this section), they won't if all the accountant does for you is fill in a simple tax return.

Since income tax affects more of us than any other form of tax, let's look at that first to see where you can make savings, or at least to make sure you are getting all the allowances and reliefs you are entitled to. But there are also ways of avoiding paying unnecessary capital gains or capital transfer tax.

Personal reliefs and allowances. It goes almost without saying that you should claim all your allowances as soon as you are entitled to them, for example when you marry, or take out a mortgage.

Child allowances. I can't suggest that you time all your children to arrive in the first few days of April, but if they do you will get the full child allowance for the whole year, up to 6 April, in which the child is born. You used to get tax relief for the whole of the year in which you married as well, but the married man's allowance can now only be claimed from the month in which you marry. The rule which gave a woman two lots of allowances in the year she got married has also gone.

Married people's earnings. Ask yourself whether you wouldn't be better off taxed separately, or if you are already taxed separately whether aggregation wouldn't suit you better. Many couples find that as their circumstances change old patterns of payment no longer keep the joint tax bill to a minimum, so think about this every new tax year.

Wife's earnings. If you are in business and it's at all possible, pay your wife a wage. She can then claim her earned income allowance. But don't try to pay her more than the job is worth; the Inland Revenue will not allow it.

Employees' fringe benefits. Get as much as you can paid in a tax-free form. Payments like this range from luncheon vouchers up to 15p, through company cars to interest-free loans and pension schemes. Employers should make sure they provide these things and, if they can, accommodation for their employees. Make severance payments in the form of 'golden handshakes', which save tax for the employee.

Business expenses can be offset against income tax. There's a wide variety of these, from the normal costs of business, to the use of a car for business or even fees to a professional body. If in any doubt, check with an accountant.

New businesses. Time the start of your business to keep down your tax bill for the first few years. You'll need an accountant's advice on this.

Overseas income. If you have money abroad take the advice of an accountant. He may be able to save you a lot of tax.

House purchase. I've been over the rent or buy debate earlier. If you decide to buy take advice as to which kind of mortgage will save you most tax. Pay close attention to the life of the mortgage, and try to get the most relief at the time of your maximum earnings.

Life assurance. You can usually deduct 17½ per cent of any qualifying premiums from your tax bill. Take out as much insurance as you can afford, but don't overload yourself. Some forms of insurance do not qualify for tax relief.

Self-employed annuity contracts. These provide an excellent way of saving tax if you work for yourself, and relief ranges up to 83 per cent for high incomes.

Deeds of covenant. These can save money over a seven-year period. Payments are made by the covenanter after deducting tax at the basic rate, which can then be reclaimed by the beneficiary if he is not a tax payer (see chapter 5 of this section).

Capital gains tax. Try to keep your taxable disposals below £1,000 each year. Towards the end of the tax year look carefully at any investments you have in case you can set some losses against gains. Work out the most favourable way for you to be treated for gains tax.

Capital transfer tax. Give away as much as you can within the limits while you are alive. The amount you are allowed to give varies each tax year. If you are married leave as much as you can to your spouse.

Repayment of tax. The Inland Revenue is notoriously slow at paying back overpaid tax, so get your claim in as quickly as possible.

Here are four rules for tax planning:

1 Never make yourself miserable trying to save tax. Probably the ultimate in this is emigrating when you know it would make you and your family unhappy.
2 Never cut off your nose to spite your face. There is no point in losing money in a business just to save tax – though if you did you wouldn't be the first to do so.
3 Never impoverish yourself. Don't give away all your money to save capital transfer tax. The law may change anyway, and it is the law on the date of your death which counts.
4 Never go in for long-term tax saving schemes. The law may change and you may be stuck with them. Always be flexible and review your planning from time to time.

314

Investing

Chapter 1

INVESTING IN THE STOCK MARKET

TAKING A RISK

If you have pursued a sensible financial policy, you may eventually find that you have as much money as you want in reserve for a rainy day, that you have a reasonable income coming in from your savings, and that you still have some capital left over.

Even if you have not reached this desirable state, if you are young and without responsibilities, you may feel that you can afford to do something a little more exciting than saving in a bank or building society with your spare cash.

In either case, this is the time for you to turn to investing rather than saving. Basically, both amount to the same thing; the aim behind both is to increase your wealth. But while regular saving should mean that your capital is secure and growing and that you are gaining the maximum income from it, investing can give rather more. The aim of investment is to increase the value of your capital and your income rather more than you would do by saving. To do this, you must take a risk.

You can invest in many different ways – by buying shares in the country's biggest companies; by buying properties to rent out, or to improve and sell; by buying antiques, silver, precious stones and the like, which you hope will eventually increase in value; by putting some money by in a pension fund to secure a better income in your old age.

All these ways of trying to increase your wealth have one thing in

315

common: they all involve some risk. The degree of the risk varies, depending on what sort of investment you choose, but it is always there to some extent. The company in which you invest could double its profits and thus the value of your investment; alternatively it could go bankrupt and you would lose all your money. The value of the painting or antique you bought could increase sharply, or it could become unfashionable. In the latter case, if you try to sell, you would be lucky to get back the price you paid for it originally. Changes in the law relating to renting and security of tenure for tenants could depress the value of the property you bought, or, in contrast, a sudden change in renting policy on the part of the government could dramatically increase the value of your property. All your pension plans could come to nothing, because you are taking a risk on how long you will live and you may not reach pensionable age before you die. On the other hand, you could live so long that you get far more in pension than you ever put into the fund.

In any one of these areas you can make a profit and increase your wealth, stay exactly where you are, or lose some, if not all, of your money. This is the essence of investment – *you take a risk when you start out for the chance of making a better than average profit*. The purpose of this section is to help you minimize the risk of loss and maximize your chances of profit.

Only the individual can decide whether he is ready to take a risk. You must look at your total financial situation. How secure are your sources of money? Is there any danger of losing your job? Have you responsibilities towards others which will not allow you to take risks? Have you the temperament to take a risk?

This last is rather important. All the preconditions for investment may be there, but if worry over them is going to ruin your life, stick to things which are safe and secure. Go back to section I, chapter 3, and look for secure havens for your savings.

Now, assuming that you fully appreciate the risk you are taking, let's start with the stock exchange and investment in shares.

WHY STOCKS AND SHARES?

Buying stocks and shares is a favoured way of investing for several reasons. First, if you have shares in a company you are one of the owners with certain rights to its profits and assets – though unless you are actually running the company these rights may be somewhat remote.

Second, many people believe that as the economy generally expands the profits of individual companies will also grow and that dividends will rise with them. As a result share prices will rise, bringing a profit to shareholders.

Third, dividends are now usually declared and paid twice a year. The first payment is called the interim dividend and the second, the final one, making a particular total for a company's financial year, so the investor can be assured of an income which will offer a certain return at the price he paid for the shares, regardless of how the share price moves up and down.

There are disadvantages in buying stocks and shares, however. Companies have liabilities as well as assets and they are therefore not so clear-cut an inflation hedge as are objects and articles. At certain times the liabilities of a company may assume greater weight and depress the share value. However, in sound companies at least, such setbacks are followed by a rebound in values as it may also be expected that the profits of most companies will rise with inflation; this must eventually work through to shareholders. But you may buy shares in a company which does badly no matter how much the economy generally expands.

The Stock Exchange

The Stock Exchange is the marketplace used by the public to buy shares in British industry and commerce. Many of Britain's larger companies have only grown to the size they have by issuing some of their shares on the open market to raise money for expansion. For most people, the Stock Exchange offers as much opportunity for investment as they need, without going to other sources which may be more risky.

There are several branches of the Stock Exchange around the country, the London one being easily the biggest. Until 1973 these were all separate, with their own rules, and the exchanges outside London concentrated mainly on local shares and the very large country wide British companies – though of course they could always get a share for you which was quoted only in London. Then, in 1973, the exchanges amalgamated themselves to form one body, which is simply called the Stock Exchange. The regional centres have stayed open and the local stockbroking firms in those areas have also remained. Its operations are scrutinized by the Stock Exchange Council which is made up of elected partners from broking and jobbing offices.

If you want to buy shares you will have to operate through one of these stockbroking firms. You cannot go to the Exchange like going to a shop, or write up for shares. You must use a stockbroker, and he in turn buys shares from a (stock) jobber, who keeps a number of shares in hand for buying and selling. If you do not have a stockbroker, you can buy shares through your bank, which will have its own stockbroker who deals for the bank. On the whole it is better to have your own stockbroker and to try to build up a relationship with him. He should be highly knowledgeable and able to advise you about the best times for buying and selling, or whether to buy and sell at all.

If you are new to investing it is probable that you do not know a stockbroker. At one time the only way to find one was by introduction.

Today, however, the Stock Exchange issues a list of brokers who are prepared to act for small and unknown investors. You may also see an advertisement, but not many stockbrokers do much advertising, except occasionally for prestige purposes. In fact they have only been allowed to advertise for the past few years, and not many have taken the opportunity. Here are the addresses of the various stock exchanges round the country that you can write to for advice:

Birmingham: The Secretary, The Stock Exchange, Birmingham B3 3JL

Liverpool: The Secretary, The Stock Exchange, Exchange Street East, Liverpool L2 3PB

London: The Public Relations Officer, The Stock Exchange, London EC2N 1HP

Northern Ireland: The Secretary, The Stock Exchange, 10 High Street, Belfast BT1 2BP.

Scotland: The Public Relations Officer, The Stock Exchange, 227 Ingram Street, Glasgow G2 1BU

York: The Secretary, The Stock Exchange, 3 St Sampson's Square, York YO1 2RL

Before you think about investing start to read the financial pages of your newspaper. As you get more interested, try reading one of the many excellent books on investing. The trick here is always to buy the latest book or the latest edition. The investing world changes rapidly, and you need to keep up-to-date with the best opportunities. Learn as much as you can, but until you really feel confident always take the advice of your stockbroker or bank manager.

All the advice and all the reading in the world will not make you an investment expert immediately. That will only come with experience.

Shares

A share is just what it says. When you buy one – or, rather, usually a fair number – you are buying a share in the company and become one of the owners of the company.

Each company has what is called an authorized capital. This is the total value of the shares it can issue at any one time to the public. The shares which have actually been issued make up the issued capital. The issued capital may be as much as the authorized capital or it may be less.

This capital can all be divided into the same kind of shares or into different kinds. However it is done, every share will have what is called a par value. This is the nominal value and can be any amount, 10p, 25p, 50p and £1 being the most common – though it can be higher or lower, as low, say, as 1p. It is highly unlikely that the price the investor pays –

318

the market price – will be the same as the par value. This is used only for the purpose of declaring a dividend – the name used to describe the interest paid on each share. Dividends are announced today both in percentages and in cash. A 10 per cent dividend on a £1 share will be 10p; on a 25p share it will be 2.5p, and so on.

The Stock Exchange does not only sell shares in companies, it also sells government stock. These are debts which the British Government owes to the private investors who buy the stock. They have their uses, which I will come to later. It also buys and sells the shares of some of the major foreign companies and some foreign government stock, but these are only suitable for the professional or very knowledgeable investor, so we can ignore them at this point.

Loans and debentures

You are not likely to come into much contact with these in the early stages of investing, unless perhaps you inherit some. Strictly speaking they are not shares; they are given the name 'stock', and are the debts of the company. In the event of liquidation (the term used to describe a firm going bust) stockholders have the first claim on any money which is to be shared out. They carry a fixed rate of dividend, which is normally paid twice a year, and are usually issued in £100 lots.

They may be simply a general loan to the company, or they may be what is called 'secured' on a particular piece of the company's property, just as a house mortgage is secured to the house itself. They are then called debentures. Where there is no security they are called loans. Debentures come first in the money shareout.

Debentures and loans may have a date attached to them. This is the date at which the company must pay off the loan (we will see this again with government stocks). In the case of debentures, it may mean that the holder can exchange them at a future date, or dates, for shares in the company.

The prices of loans and debentures vary depending on demand, and the return rises and falls with interest rates. An offer for sale may be at a fixed price, or investors may be asked to tender for the shares at whatever price they choose. The shares then go first to the highest bidders. Tenders are not very frequent.

Preference shares

These are part of the true share capital of the company. The preference shares, sometimes still called stock, is a special class which comes before ordinary shares (see next section) when the company goes into liquidation. They are what is known as 'fixed interest' stock. No matter how well the company does, you will never get more than this fixed interest, though of course if the company does badly you are

319

safer with your fixed interest than you would be had you bought ordinary shares where the dividend rate varies.

Prices may go up and down, their level being influenced almost as much by interest rates generally as by how the particular company is faring. When interest rates are rising, prices fall, so that the return on shares is equal to general interest rates; conversely, when rates are falling, share prices rise. Obviously with the interest fixed it is not possible to make great profits on preference shares, but they have a useful place in an investment 'portfolio' – all the shares that you may hold at any one time.

Many older preference shares have a low fixed return, and their prices have fallen below the par value, which is always possible for any type of share. Say interest rates generally are around 9 per cent, and your preference shares carry a 5 per cent dividend. If the par value is £1, it is highly likely that the price will be around 56p, which gives you a 9 per cent yield. This formula can be set out as follows:

$$\frac{\text{par value x dividend}}{\text{market price}} \quad \frac{100 \times 5}{56} \ = \ 8.9 \text{ per cent}$$

If you want to be doubly sure of your dividend you can always buy Cumulative Preference shares. With these, if a company has done so badly that it has not even been able to pay a dividend on its preference shares, all arrears will be paid up as it recovers.

If a company goes bust, the preference shareholders will be paid back before equity holders, but not until after any holders of debentures and loan stock. Preference shares do not constitute a 'debt' in the same way, and holders have no legal status as debtors.

Since corporation tax was introduced (see section IV, chapter 5), the dividends of preference shares have had to be declared *net* of tax. This means that the old designation of dividend entitlement, such as 10 per cent Preference, where this implied the gross payment, would now be 6½ per cent *net* (after 35 per cent standard rate tax).

Equity shares

This is where the real risk comes in investing and also where the real profits can be made. Ordinary shares or equities are at the end of the line as far as security goes; holders of equity take the most risks, so their rewards and their downfalls will be the greatest. They may be called *ordinary shares,* or stock units. It does not matter; there is no real difference.

Again, equity shares all have a par value, but it is their market price which matters. The holders of ordinary shares are part owners of the company, and are entitled to a share in its assets and profits, after all the fixed charges have been paid.

Voting and non-voting shares. Equity holders are usually entitled to vote on matters affecting the company. If you do not like the way a company is run, you can tell the directors at the annual general meeting, and if you are really displeased you can vote against the acceptance of the annual report, which must be made and presented to the shareholders once a year.

There are also non-voting shares, which carry all the rights of the voting shares, apart from the vote. The dividend will be the same on both types of share. The non-voting shares are often called the *'A' shares,* and in some very large companies they are more often quoted than the ordinary shares. In a large company it often does not matter whether you have a vote or not.

The issuing of non-voting shares has been very useful for some companies, especially those where the original family is still strong. They have offered a means of raising money to expand without losing any control over the business.

The non-voting are often a few pence cheaper than the voting shares, so you get an effectively higher yield on them. But – and it is a big but – you have no control over the company's affairs at all. In a takeover situation, for example, the bidder need not offer as much for non-voting as for voting shares. It is power he is after, not just quantity of shares, and there is no power in non-voting stock. Occasionally – though it is more frequent in America than in the U.K. – groups of small shareholders have gathered together enough support to change the course of a company or, say, sack one of the directors, or the entire board.

In general the Stock Exchange disapproves of non-voting shares and would be unlikely to permit the issue of new ones. It seems probable that they will eventually disappear. When 'A' shares are given a vote, holders of the ordinary shares are usually compensated by the issue of a few extra shares.

Ordinary and 'A' ordinary are the most common varieties of equities, but there are others as well. Some shares are called *Deferred* or *Deferred Ordinary*. These are quite rare, and usually have some sort of restriction on them. Holders may not get a dividend until after the holders of ordinary shares, for example, or may not be entitled to a full share in the assets of the company.

The market price. If you look on the financial pages of most newspapers you will see that each day they give the market price of the different shares. The market price is the amount people are prepared to buy or sell shares for. If a company is doing well and investors expect that it will pay a bigger dividend soon, the price of the shares will probably rise – unless everyone is very depressed and prices generally are falling. Similarly, if a company is thought to be doing badly, prices will fall, unless the setback is thought to be only very temporary.

The price of the shares is different depending on whether you want to buy or sell. You pay more if you are buying and get less if you are selling. The difference between the two prices is called the 'jobber's turn', and is the profit he makes for the service he provides. The price given in the newspapers is usually a 'middle price'. Depending on how 'active' the shares are – that is, how many people want to buy or sell them – you will have to take a few pence or more off if you are selling and add a few on if you are buying. The more active the shares the nearer the actual price will be to the quoted 'middle' one.

Your true interest. It is the market value of the share which is important to you, not its par value, because it is that which tells you what return you will get on your investment. If your £1 shares carry a dividend of 20 per cent, but the price you pay – the market price – is £2, your true interest – this is called the yield – is 10 per cent, not 20 per cent, because you have paid twice the par value for the shares. You can work out the true yield on any share at any price by using a simple formula:

$$\frac{\text{par value x dividend}}{\text{market price}}$$

Take a 50p share standing at a market price of 89p, paying a 12 per cent dividend:

$$\frac{50 \times 12}{89} = 6.74$$

Your yield will then be £6.74 for every £100 you have invested, not 12 per cent which is the dividend. Work out a few more examples until you understand the principle properly.

Dividends must now be declared in cash amounts, and *net* of income tax. You always need to know whether a dividend is being spoken of in gross or net terms. Yields are always worked out on the gross dividend.

New issues

New shares are also created when Convertible Debenture stockholders exercise their option to change the stock into ordinary shares, shares from a company already quoted, or shares of a foreign company.

When a completely new share comes on to the market, it may be issued in a variety of ways:

1 *A public issue.* This invites investors to apply for stated amounts of shares or fixed interest stock.

2 *An offer for sale.* This is broadly the same as a public issue, but it

will have been 'underwritten' by an issuing house. This means that the issuing house will already have bought all the shares at a lower price than the one asked from the public. If the shares are all sold, the issuing house makes a profit; if not, they have to keep them and perhaps sell at a loss. When this happens it is called 'leaving the shares with the underwriters'. Whatever happens the company selling the shares is assured of its money. When times are good, offers for sale are often 'oversubscribed', and those lucky enough to get the shares may be able to sell at an immediate profit as soon as dealings start on the stock market.

3   *An introduction.* This is not often used for equities. It is a means of establishing an official open market in shares where there are enough investors already existing to justify a market. It does not work in the same way as an offer for sale – though some of the shareholders may say that they are prepared to sell some or all their holdings at stated prices.

4   *A placing.* This is just what it sounds like. Shares are placed at a fixed price with financial institutions and price investors. A quotation will only be granted by the Stock Exchange if enough shares will be made available to create a reasonably free market in the shares when dealing starts.

5   *A rights issue.* Sometimes a company may need money for expansion and decide not to do it through borrowing, but by raising it from the shareholders, who are then given the right to subscribe to new shares in a certain proportion to their shareholding.

This is how it works. Suppose a company's shares are standing in the market at £2.60 and the directors decide to offer rights in the proportion of one new share to every two already held at a price of £1.40. After the issue, if the shareholder takes up the rights, for each two shares he held previously he will have three shares worth a total of £6.60, or £2.20 each. This is the price that all the shares would be quoted at immediately the new shares are released on to the stock market. The new share will be selling at 80p above the price offered to shareholders. This is called the premium. Of course, theoretically the price of the existing shares will come down, but there is rarely a complete adjustment, because most companies use the capital they raise sensibly and so add to the profits and assets of the company

If you are offered a rights issue take it up if you can, because if you do not you will effectively have a smaller share in the company than you had before, as well as foregoing the possible profit. This is called 'watering your equity'. If you really do not want to put up extra money you can always sell your 'rights' to the shares at the premium before the money is due to be paid. If you ignore the offer altogether you may lose money, as the price of your existing shares may come down.

6   *Scrip issues.* A lot of fuss is made about these issues, because they are a 'free' issue of shares, but in fact they mean nothing. A scrip issue is made when a company thinks that its reserves are getting out of line with

its issued capital, so it makes an issue of shares to make them more equal. The scrip may come in any ratio, one for one, one for three, one for ten or even two for one. Say it is a one-for-one issue. After you have received the new shares the share price will fall by half, so the value of your total investment is unchanged. Dividends, too, will be adjusted to take account of the increase in the number of shares.

You may make a profit after a scrip issue, however, when investors think the company is doing well – and companies rarely make scrip issues if they are on the verge of bankruptcy. As a result the market price may not adjust totally and the new shares in say a one-for-one issue will be quoted at a little more than half the old price. The price will soon come into line again if the company fails to produce higher profits and an effectively higher dividend.

7 *Share splits.* Like scrip issues they mean nothing as far as the value of your investment goes. A company may decide that the price of its shares is so high that it puts investors off and limits the market in them. If a £1 share is standing at £8.40, the company may consider that by splitting the shares into four 25p units at £2.10 each a better market might be created in them. Alternatively, the opposite process can take place and shares can be consolidated.

8 *Takeover bids.* When there is a successful takeover of one company by another the deal may be done in cash or in shares. Bids may be a straight cash sum, or shares in the bidder company may be offered to shareholder in place of their old ones, or sometimes a combination of the two, or an option. Takeovers are governed by a code of conduct which is administered by a Panel on Takeovers and Mergers which sees that all bidders behave properly, especially when two or more are in competition with one another for the same firm. Do not accept a takeover bid for your shares until the last minute, in case a better offer comes along.

New shares are also created when Convertible Debenture stockholders exercise their option to change the stock into ordinary shares, and sometimes when executives and directors exercise stock options which they have been offered by their companies.

Chapter 2

BUYING AND SELLING STOCKS AND SHARES

THE COSTS

Broker's commission

You already know that a stockbroker will buy and sell shares for you. For this service he will charge a commission, and this will be the biggest item in your costs, apart from the cost of the shares themselves, if you are buying. The minimum commission is 1.5 per cent, the value of the shares you are buying or selling – known as the 'bargain' – is over £470. On very large bargains commission rates fall, but on bargains below the £470 figure the commission charge is relatively very high, because the official minimum charge is £7 – which on a £100 bargain is 7 per cent.

In fact brokers are allowed 'discretion' on bargains worth less than £200, but it is unlikely that you will get away with paying less than £4. It simply is not worth the broker's time and the administrative costs involved. This means that buying shares in small amounts is expensive, so skill will be needed in your choice, if you are to make any money.

Remember that commission is also payable when you sell, so if a broker charged you the minimum £7 each time on £100 worth of shares, you would have to make a profit of £14, or 14 per cent, to cover his commission alone. It is not always easy to make such a large profit, at least in the short term.

Commission on debentures and loans is less than on preference shares or equities. They are usually bought in larger amounts anyway. The commission is 0.75 per cent on the first £5,000, and less on larger amounts. I will deal with commission on gilt-edged stocks later.

Transfer stamp duty

In addition to the broker's commission you will have to pay what is called transfer stamp duty when you buy – though not when you sell. This is levied at the rate of 2 per cent, rising in steps at certain levels. You do not have to pay it on gilt-edged stocks, or on new issues which are being quoted in the stock market for the first time. Nor do you have to pay it on debentures.

The steps in transfer stamp duty are small up to £100, then they widen to 40p for each £20 until you reach £300, and after that to £1 for every £50 or part of £50.

The contract stamp

This is a very small charge, and does not arise at all until the bargain is worth £100. Then it is 10p up to £500, 30p from £500 to £1,500, and 60p over £1,500.

The total costs for a bargain at the £470 threshold will come to just over 3½ per cent. Below that costs can more than double, but the more the bargain is worth the less will be the charges.

THE PROCESS

What you do

Assume a stockbroker has accepted you as a client, or that you are happy for your bank to make the order for you. You can then give your instructions by telephone. You must be very clear what you want to do, for the stockbroker will do exactly as you tell him – though, of course, he may advise you to wait before buying or selling, or not to buy or sell those particular shares at all. You can ignore that advice and he will then put the bargain through for you, but think carefully before you do.

You should tell him exactly how many shares you wish to buy or sell. If you are sensible, you will also say what price you are prepared to pay or accept. You may, for instance, have read in your paper that morning that Bloggs and Company have got a tremendous new order from the Middle East, and you may then think that at the price they are quoted the shares look cheap. Say they are 135p each. What you have to remember is that other people can read too, and that particularly includes stockbrokers and jobbers when it comes to share prices.

The jobber may have gone to the Exchange that morning thinking that at last night's price the shares are too cheap and that he must set a price of 138p to begin with to see what the demand is like. If it is heavy and he wants to encourage people to sell so that he can meet the demand he may put the price up even further.

By the time you ring with your instructions, the price could have reached 145p. At this level the shares may not be such a bargain, so tell the broker what your price limits are. The same goes for selling; you must tell the broker the lowest price you are prepared to accept.

The broker will carry through your instructions, as will the bank through its broker, even though they are not written down. The Stock Exchange motto is 'my word is my bond', and that is how both jobbers and brokers operate. Only leave open the price at which you will buy or sell if you are convinced that the price of the shares you are buying will go on rising or the shares you are selling will go on falling. You can never be sure of either of these things, and that is where the risk comes in.

The next day you should receive the 'contract note' through the post. This will give you details of your bargain. If you wish, your stockbroker will always telephone you to confirm after he has done the deal. The contract will tell you the price at which you have bought or sold and the total value of the deal, plus the costs of contract stamp, transfer stamp duty, commission and the V.A.T. which must be paid on the commission. The contract note will look like this:

1 To buy

800 Jones and Company Stores Ltd at 89p	£712.00
Add	
Transfer Stamp	£15.00
Contract Stamp	30
Commission at 1.5 per cent	£10.68
V.A.T. at 8 per cent	85
	£738.83

2 To sell [in a later account]

800 Jones and Company shares at 96p	£768.00
Less	
Contract stamp	30
Commission at 1.5 per cent	£11.54
V.A.T. at 8 per cent	92
	£780.76

You can see from these two examples that although there was a profit of £56 if you take only the buying and the selling prices of the shares the true profit after all charges is a mere £41.93 on this transaction.

The stock exchanges are officially open from 9.30 in the morning until 3.30 in the afternoon, but if you are anxious to comple a deal on one particular day your broker can always deal 'after hours' until about 5.30. After hours dealing is done on the telephone.

What the broker does

You telephone the broker. He then gets in touch – either himself or through one of his partners, who may be 'dealing' on the 'floor' of the Stock Exchange – with the jobber, to try to buy the shares within the limits you have stated. The 'jobber' will be holding supplies of the shares and is constantly trying to balance supply and demand.

The dealer will not say whether he is buying or selling and the jobber will quote two prices, the 'offer' and the 'bid'. The former is the price at which he will sell to you as the buyer, the latter the one he will buy from you as the seller. If the price is within the limits ordered, the dealer will then clinch the bargain. If it is not, he will come back for further instructions.

He may think the price of the shares you were going to buy will go on rising and that you may want to think again about your price limit or if you are selling he may think the price is going to fall further and that you should get out at whatever price you can. On the other hand, he may advise you not to buy or sell at all on that particular day. *Listen to the advice your broker gives you, even if in the end you decide not to take it. After all, you are paying for it.*

PAYING FOR YOUR SHARES

You do not have to pay up immediately the broker sends you details of the transaction. The Stock Exchange works on a series of what are called 'accounts'. Each account is usually of two weeks' duration, starting on a Monday and finishing on a Friday – though sometimes when it covers a bank holiday it may be longer.

You will get a bill covering whatever purchases or sales you have made during the period of the account. The bill will tell you your balance. You will get a cheque for the balance if you have made an overall profit; if you have lost you will be asked for a cheque. If you buy and sell the same shares within one account there is only one lot of commission, not two, to pay, so you need less apparent profit to make a real one than if the transactions take place in two different accounts.

The bill will come to you a few days before the 'account day', which is the day on which either you must settle your bill or you must receive a cheque. Account day is always the second Tuesday after the end of the 'accounts'. Each account is usually of two weeks' duration, starting on a arrangements and for the broker to do the paper work. You must pay by then, because it is also the day that the broker and the jobber settle their books and all Stock Exchange companies balance up with one another.

To show you how it works, opposite is the account calendar for November and December 1977. You will notice that as well as showing all the accounts and account days, it shows what are called 'new time dealings'. These are usually (bank holidays excepted) the Thursday and the Friday before an account begins when you can deal as if it were the new account. You have to pay something extra for this privilege.

Sunday		6	13	20	27
Monday		7	14★	21	28★
Tuesday	1	8§	15	22§	29
Wednesday	2	9	16	23	30
Thursday	3	10 †	17	24 †	
Friday	4	11 ‡	18	25 ‡	
Saturday	5	12	19	26	

December, 1977

Sunday		4	11	18	25
Monday		5	12★	19	26
Tuesday		6§	13	20§	27
Wednesday		7	14	21	28
Thursday	1	8 †	15	22	29 †
Friday	2	9‡	16	23	30 ‡
Saturday	3	10	17	24	31

★ Dealings start   ‡ Dealings end
† New time dealings   § Account days

You will notice that because of the Christmas break there is only one full account in December, starting on Monday 12 December.

You do not own the shares from the time you pay for them. They are yours from the moment the broker has done the deal for you. This means that you are entitled to any dividends or new issues, which are declared, and that in the event of a takeover bid the offer will be to you. It takes some time, however, for all the formalities to be gone through, and it can happen that these things are sent initially to the former shareholder. The two brokers involved will make sure that you eventually get them, wherever they have gone in the first place.

It may not be convenient for you to have dividends sent to you, and if you wish you can have them sent to your bank. You simply inform the registrar of the company. This is useful in some circumstances. You may move and forget to tell the company of your new address. If dividends go to your bank, this will not matter for some time.

TAXATION ON DIVIDENDS

When you receive your dividend it will not be the amount which has been declared by the company. Before it pays you, the company is directed by the government to deduct tax at the standard rate (35 per cent at present).

Say you were expecting £100 – a 10p dividend on 1,000 shares of £1 par value – this will arrive as £65, that is, £100 less 35 per cent. This does not apply to all stocks; some gilt-edged are different (see next chapter).

If you do not pay tax, as may happen when you are retired or unemployed, you must then reclaim the tax which has been paid. If, on the other hand, you pay tax at a higher rate than 35 per cent, as many investors do, you will have to pay the extra. It is clearly easier for the government to collect tax in this way rather than having to chase each shareholder for it.

CAPITAL GAINS TAX

You will be taxed on any profits you may make on your stocks and shares. At the moment it is levied at the rate of 30 per cent. Paying this is a matter between you and your tax inspector. You will be expected to declare your gains – and, of course, your broker will have a record of your transactions. The inspector can go to him if he wishes, so it is not a good idea not to declare your gains.

You balance up any losses you may have had against any gains – you only make a loss or a gain if you have actually sold, not if the price of the shares has simply gone up or down – and you are taxed on the net gain you have made, if any. Net gains are calculated not on the actual profit, but after all the charges like commission, transfer stamp duty and contract stamp have been deducted.

By carefully weeding out your investments at the end of the financial year you can minimize the amount of capital gains tax you have to pay. If you have a net loss one year you can carry it forward to offset any gains you may make in the future, but you cannot carry losses backwards to offset earlier gains.

If the total value of your sales is less than £1,000 you need not record your gain for the inspector. This can be useful in some cases. You may also choose to be taxed on half your gain only, at the top income tax rate you pay. But if your gains are more than £5,000, the excess will be charged at your full income rate if you take this option. (see section IV, chapter 1).

There are some tax concessions for holders of unit trusts and investment trusts, however, and you do not have to pay gains tax on any gains from gilt-edged stock, unless you buy and sell within a year.

The timing of your investments is as important as the shares you choose. Even the prices of the best shares fluctuate. If you buy at the wrong time you can lose money even on the shares with the best market performance.

Chapter 3

INVESTING IN GILT-EDGED

The government owes the public a lot of money. Some of this comes from the money deposited in the various government-controlled savings schemes and some from what are called gilt-edged stocks. These are the debts of the government to the private investors who buy the stock.

Stock is always dealt in £100 units, but there are well over fifty kinds of stock available – including straight loans to the government, stocks issued when industries were nationalized, corporation and county stocks, and some Commonwealth and Colonial loans.

The gilt-edged market is one of the means used by the government to run the economy. The various forms of taxation provide the other major means. It buys and sells in the market and whatever it does can influence interest rates. The government operates through its own broker, but the broker's actions are always stealthy so that no one ever knows whether it is buying or selling at any one time. If the government buys, it tends to put market prices up; if it sells, the reverse happens.

Private investors are interested in the gilt-edged market because its price levels reflect the levels of interest rates. If a member of the public thinks, for example, that interest rates will fall, he may be tempted into gilt-edged because prices will rise. If interest rates are very high, however, the price of gilt-edged will be very depressed. As prices rise, the government can get rid of some of its holdings and control to some extent the amount of the rise.

Gilt-edged stock is very easy to buy and sell. Stockbrokers charge less commission on it than they do on other deals. On the first £2,000 worth you pay only 0.625 per cent, compared with 1.5 per cent for ordinary shares. On the next £12,000 it falls to 0.25 per cent for stock which has ten years to go before it is redeemed – that is, before the government pays back the principal. For shorter-dated stocks the rates are rather different. There is also no transfer stamp duty on transactions in gilt-edged, nor any capital gains tax to pay.

DIFFERENT KINDS OF STOCK

It can be very important to understand the difference between the various kinds of stock:

1 *Short-dated stock.* These stocks are due to be redeemed within five years of your purchase. They are unlikely to change much in value and are 'safe' because their value will move slowly towards the level of the repayment price.

2 *Medium-dated stock.* These have a life of between five and fifteen years when you purchase them. They will fluctuate rather more than 'shorts', but may have better tax-free redemption profits, especially if they carry a low rate of interest.

3 *Long-dated stock.* These have a life of more than fifteen years and their prices will be influenced by the general level of interest rates. When interest rates are rising their prices will be falling, and vice versa.

4 *Irredeemable or undated stock.* These stocks need not and probably will not ever be redeemed. Their prices are totally geared to interest rates. There are not many of these and they will either have no redemption dates stated at all, or they may be said to be redeemable after a certain date. The most well-known are War Loan 3½ per cent, which date from the 1914-18 War, and Consols 2½ per cent, which were introduced after the last war.

There is no point in buying these except for income, and at certain times they have very high yields indeed. War Loan has been down to £18, at which price the yield was 19.4 per cent. Do not buy them thinking there will be a change of heart by the government and the stock will be repaid. This is such a long shot as to be virtually out of the question, though groups get together from time time to pressure the authorities. The price will move with interest rates, and for no other reason.

Gilt-edged can be very useful to those on low incomes. Interest on some of the stocks is paid gross without the deduction of income tax; so there is no bother of reclaiming. It is also easy to buy. You can use a stockbroker in the ordinary way, but some of the stocks can be bought through the National Savings Stock Register.

The following list shows the securities which may be bought in this way:

Description of Securities   Interest payable

Description of Securities	Interest payable	
2½% Consols	5 January	5 April
	5 July	5 October
2½% Annuities	5 January	5 April
	5 July	5 October
2½% Treasury Stock 1975 or after	1 April	1 October
2¾% Annuities	5 January	5 April
	5 July	5 October
3% Guaranteed Stock	1 January	1 July
3% British Transport Stock 1978–1988	1 January	1 July
3% Redemption Stock 1986–1996	1 April	1 October
3% Treasury Stock 1977	15 May	15 November
3% Treasury Stock 1979	17 March	17 September

3½%	War Stock	1 June	1 December
3½%	Conversion Stock	1 April	1 October
3½%	Treasury Stock 1977–1980	15 June	15 December
3½%	Treasury Stock 1979–1981	15 February	15 August
3½%	Funding Stock 1999–2004	14 January	14 July
4%	British Transport Stock 1972–1977	20 June	20 December
4%	Consols	1 February	1 August
5%	Exchequer Loan 1976–1978	26 March	26 September
5%	Treasury Stock 1986–1989	15 April	15 October
5¼%	Funding Loan 1978–1980	15 June	15 December
5½%	Funding Stock 1982–1984	15 January	15 July
5½%	Treasury Stock 2008–2012	10 March	10 September
5¾%	Funding Loan 1987–1991	5 April	5 October
6%	Funding Loan 1993	15 March	15 September
6½%	Funding Loan 1985–1987	1 May	1 November
6¾%	Treasury Loan 1995–1998	1 May	1 November
7¾%	Treasury Stock 1985–1988	26 January	26 July
7¾%	Treasury Stock 2012–2015	26 January	26 July
8%	Treasury Stock 2002–2006	5 April	5 October
8¼%	Treasury Stock 1987–1990	15 June	15 December
8½%	Treasury Loan 1980–1982	15 January	15 July
8½%	Treasury Loan 1984–1986	10 January	10 July
8¾%	Treasury Loan 1997	1 March	1 September
9%	Treasury Loan 1994	17 May	17 November
9%	Treasury Loan 1992–1996	15 March	15 September
9%	Treasury Stock 1978	15 March	15 September
9%	Treasury Convertible Stock 1980	3 March	3 September
9½%	Treasury Stock 1999	15 January	15 July
10½%	Treasury Stock 1976	14 June	14 December
10½%	Treasury Stock 1978	14 January	14 July
10½%	Treasury Stock 1979	1 May	1 November
11½%	Treasury Stock 1977	26 March	26 September
11½%	Treasury Stock 1979	9 March	9 September
12%	Treasury Stock 1983	17 March	17 September
12¾%	Treasury Stock 1995	15 May	15 November
13%	Treasury Stock 1990	15 January	15 July
13¼%	Treasury Stock 1997	22 January	22 July

The list is subject to variation from time to time as securities are repaid or new securities included. An up-to-date list may be obtained on application to The Director, Bonds and Stock Office, Lytham St Annes, Lancs. FY0 1YN.

The charges you pay are only 25p for every nominal amount of stock of £100 then 5p for every further £50 of nominal stock. The National Debt Commissioners do the dealing for you and the price is based upon the one ruling in the stock market at the time when you apply.

REDEMPTION YIELDS

If you are interested in gilt-edged stock, you will hear a lot about redemption yields. With all stock, except the undated, you have a guarantee that you will get your money back as long as you hold the stock until the redemption date, when it will be paid back at par, £100.

The nearer you are to redemption, of course, the smaller will be the guaranteed profit. The further away redemption is the less you will pay for the stock and the greater will be the eventual profit. Each year you get an ordinary dividend yield, as on a share, but you also get a little bit added to the price each year as you move towards redemption year. A formula has been worked out – you can get it from the Stock Exchange – so that you can find out not only the flat or running yield but also the 'redemption yield'. Unlike with equities, where the yields are always flat yields, the redemption yield on gilt-edged is higher, because it actually allows for your income to grow. But you will have to hold the stock to redemption to get the full benefit of this. Here is how some flat and redemption yields compare:

stock	redemption date	market price	flat yield %	redemption yield%
Treasury 9%	1978	£97½	9.22	11.34
Treasury 9%	1980	£93	9.68	11.79
Treasury 15½%	1998	£110½	14.66	14.60
War Loan 3½%	undated	£28¾	12.41	—

From this you can see how redemption yields and flat yields vary. In the case of Treasury 15½%, the redemption yield is actually less than the flat yield because the price is more than par, £100, and will come down the nearer redemption day gets. War Loan 3½% of course has no redemption yield, as it has no date for repayment.

Chapter 4

WORKING OUT YOUR INVESTMENT POLICY

UNDERSTANDING THE STOCK MARKET

Once you know the mechanics of investing, you will be eager to go on to learn how to invest wisely with the minimal risk.

It will take a long time for you to understand how the market works, however. First of all you must appreciate that share prices can go up or down. The following table show how the *Financial Times* industrial share index of thirty shares has moved in the past ten years. (The index is produced by averaging out the prices of active shares from (usually) large companies whose share price movements are thought to reflect the general movement in the market as a whole.)

Year	index high	date	index low	date
1967	420.7	16 November	308.6	28 February
1968	521.9	19 September	385.0	2 January
1969	520.1	15 January	357.4	28 July
1970	423.4	14 January	315.6	15 June
1971	474.0	29 December	305.3	2 March
1972	543.6	19 May	461.6	28 September
1973	509.5	10 January	305.9	14 December
1974	339.3	2 January	150.0	12 December
1975	377.8	19 November	146.0	6 January
1976	400.8	4 May	265.3	27 October
1977*	477.4	18 May	357.6	1 January

*To mid-July.

You can see from this table that stock market prices fluctuate widely. In 1975, for example, they dropped back close to the levels last reached in 1954.

The picture given by The *Financial Times* Ordinary Share Index alone is somewhat misleading, however, since many investors will have portfolios of shares which have grown much more over the last ten years than is shown by just this one indicator.

Moreover, growth in income, when added to the capital sums involved, alters the 'total return' on investment considerably. It produces, very roughly, a doubling in the value of a representative fund between 1967 and 1977. Even so the crash on the stock markets in 1974 was a frightening phenomenon, and the fluctuations since then still illustrate the importance of timing. Share prices do not automatically rise with inflation like other prices. The factor which affects stock market prices uniquely is sentiment. This is the view that investors take not only of a company's prospects but also of the country's. As a rule, market specialists are looking nine months to a year ahead. Everything may look rosy in the economy, but if the forecasts are not good share prices will begin to fall. On the other hand, they are likely to start recovering before there is any real evidence of economic recovery.

It is most important to learn to understand stock market 'sentiment'. Without it you can buy or sell just at the wrong time. Even if you have made a very sound investment in a company that is doing well, it cannot fail to be affected to some degree by general market sentiment.

Interest rates also affect share prices. If they are high, then investors will be looking for higher yields on their stocks and prices will come down. If interest rates start falling, then prices will begin to rise and yields to fall.

There are many other factors which affect stock market prices but you can only learn these by experience. You can best begin the process of learning by reading and using your own experience to help you work out what may be good investments.

Picking out promising companies

Choosing good investments is not simply a matter of working out what industries seem likely to grow and become more profitable. That would be comparatively easy.

We have all seen the growth in electronics in recent years, and the enormous orders coming in for equipment to bring North Sea gas and oil ashore. Then there are the companies with interests in the gas and oil resources. Does this make all of them a good investment? In contrast, there are companies which operate in countries overseas where there is some risk that they might lose all their assets for political reasons. Does this make all of them a bad investment?

The answer to both these questions is, not necessarily. There is far more to investing than choosing a home-based, expanding industry. Some will do better than others; some, even in the most flourishing trade, go bankrupt.

How do you sort the good from the bad? After a while you will begin to pick out companies which seem more promising than others. If you read the papers – and read the industrial as well as the financial news – you will slowly gather information about companies which will stick in your mind. But this takes a long time and to begin with you will have to rely on certain indicators like the yield or the company's prospects. The newspapers can be a great help here. Some of those which take investing seriously will tell you not only the price of shares but also their yields.

Yields can be important for the beginner. If one company's shares offer a rather higher yield than similar shares of other companies, there must be a reason for it. The company may be doing badly, its shares may be tightly controlled, or it may – and this does happen – not have been noticed. If this is the case it will eventually come to the fore and its price will move to the correct level. If you are one of those who spotted it first, you could make a good profit eventually.

On the other hand, the yield on a certain company's shares may be lower than with similar companies. Again, there could be several reasons. The company may be doing, and may be known to be doing, much better than its competitors (of course, it may not be, in which case, when the results of the year's trading are announced the price will come sharply back into line). Investors may be expecting a bid for the company and the price will already have risen to around the level of the expected bid price. Or it may just be one of the 'glamour stocks' where a great growth is forecast for the future, without any basis in current trading.

Sometimes investment in these sorts of companies comes off, sometimes it does not, but they are dangerous for the new, inexperienced investor, especially if he does not have much capital.

Just looking at the prices in the newspapers can therefore suggest a lot. You can take your investigations from there. The *Financial Times* has the best share prices service. Here is an extract from one of its lists to show you what it looks like:

high/low this year	Company	middle price	change on day	dividend	times covered	yield	price/ earnings ratio
228 134	Gt. Universal	195 xd	+5	§6.66	3.0	5.3	9.7
224 123	Do. 'A' Ordinary	188 xd	+3	§6.66	3.0	5.4	9.3
25 14	Gre.Milletts 10p	19	—	§1.0	2.8	8.1	6.7
11 7	Hall & Earl 5p	9	+½	0.54	4.3	9.8	3.6
44 24	Hardy (Furn.)	28	—	2.37	1.3	13.0	8.8
44 22	Do. 'A' N.V.	27½	+½	2.37	1.3	13.2	8.6
12 6½	Helene Lon. 10p	8¾	—	0.57	5.4	10.0	2.9
53 34	Henderson K. 20p	53	+5	1.98	6.4	5.7	3.9
32 14	Henriques A. 10p	16	+1	1.67	2.5	16.1	3.8
46 23	Hepw'th 'B' 10p	35	+2	2.08	1.3	9.1	12.7
12 3	Highlight Sp. 10p	4	—	—	—	—	—
95 49	Homecharm 10p	69	+1	§2.95	3.1	6.6	7.4
95 41	House of Fraser	80	+1	§3.88	1.8	7.5	11.4
55 38	House of Lerose	45	—	§3.51	2.8	12.0	4.1

§ Interim since increased
xd See para. 2 below.
Many other footnotes are also given in the *Financial Times* each day.

All these figures will tell you something:
1 *Highs and lows*. This shows you how much the price has moved about this year and how close to either extreme the current price is.
2 *The middle price*. This is neither the buying nor the selling price but lies mid-way between them. If there is 'xd' by the price this means that account has been taken of a recently declared dividend in the quoted price.
3 *Changes on the day*. This tells you whether the price has moved and how far up or down, and is also some indication of whether the

shares are active. But you can only get a true indication of this from the *Stock Exchange Daily* official list, which shows numbers of 'bargains' and tells you what prices shares have been bought and sold at during the day. It comes out each evening.

4   *The dividend.* This is given in pence per share.

5   *Times covered.* This tells you how safe your dividend is. Total earnings (another name for after-tax profits) are divided by the total amount of the dividend to all shareholders. If the total dividend is £100,000 and earnings are £450,000 the sum is £450,000 ÷ £100,000 = 4.5, so the dividend is 'covered' four and a half times by profits. In such a case a company can stand a quite sharp fall in profits without having to cut its dividend. In contrast, say the dividend costs £100,000 and earnings are only £120,000, the dividend is only covered 1.2 times. This does not give much leeway, so quite a small fall in profits could mean a cut in the dividend. Not all companies cut their dividends even if profits fall below the cost of the dividend. They may have built up reserves for a rainy day, or judge that the setback is only temporary.

6   *Dividend yield.* This tells you in percentage terms what income you can expect for every £100 you have invested in the shares. It is expressed gross before tax, so if you are a tax payer you must net it down to allow for tax at your personal rate.

7   *Net price/earnings ratio.* It is very useful to understand this, as it shows you how many years of profits are reflected in the current market price. Say net earnings (profits) are 60p a share and the share price is 10p, you are buying six years' profits at that price. The P/E ratio indicates what investors generally are thinking about the company.

If investors expect profits to be static or to move only slowly upwards, they will not be prepared to buy at a price which shows a high P/E ratio. If, on the other hand, they think profits are going to rise sharply, they will be prepared to buy on a high P/E ratio, because increasing profits will bring that level down at their own particular purchase price. For example, if you buy on a P/E ratio of twelve and profits rise by one-third in the following year, the ratio will drop to eight at your purchase price.

These lists appear in the *Financial Times* every day but Monday, as the market is closed on Saturday and Sunday. On Monday the months in which the dividends on each share are due are given in place of the highs and lows and the change on the day.

The financial pages of newspapers

If you are a real beginner, you will probably start by reading the newspapers. Let's see what you can expect them to do for you.

Newspapers gear their writing to their readership. This means that in the case of financial news or comment they differ greatly. It does not mean that one is better than the other; it simply means that what you will read in a particular paper is pitched to the general level of the reader. It would be no use a complete beginner with no knowledge of finance starting off with the *Financial Times*. Most newspapers are very successful at finding their right market.

No preferences, so here are the daily papers in alphabetical order to help you find the best one for your needs:

The *Daily Express* has a financial page every day. It covers the main events of the news and is written in a way which can be easily understood by the layman. On Saturdays it carries some family financial advice on such matters as mortgages, insurance policies, savings plans and the like. The main share prices are quoted daily.

The *Daily Mail* also has a daily page, which is well liked by people who work in the financial business. It also has a very useful financial supplement called 'Money Mail' each Wednesday. This covers a variety of financial subjects in a simple straightforward way, which is helpful even for those who are quite advanced. Rather more share prices are quoted daily.

The *Daily Mirror* sticks to things which affect everyone, like savings and mortgages. It also deals with industrial and financial events which may affect us all in a broad way. The share prices quoted are limited.

The *Daily Telegraph* is the paper of the middle classes, and it caters for them. Its financial pages are substantial, and each Saturday it carries a family finance section which is of great help in planning your savings and investment.

The *Financial Times* is really for the professionals, those involved in the business of money. It has the most extensive list of stock market prices and the most detail on them. It also has various indexes which show the movement of share prices generally, commodity prices, foreign exchange rates, and major share prices in foreign countries, as well as many articles on investment and news from different companies. Each Saturday it has advice for investors and gives general financial and legal advice.

The *Guardian* has a daily financial page in a business and industrial section and a Saturday family finance section. It serves people who are less affluent than the *Telegraph* readers and its articles are easy to follow with sound advice. It sometimes takes a 'social' rather than a financial approach to money matters.

The Times has the most extensive coverage of business, industrial and financial news after the *Financial Times* and produces a full page of the main share prices every day. Its Saturday section tends to discuss the more unusual facets of the financial world, rather than giving simple advice. It is for the more sophisticated investor who does not feel that he need take a totally specialist paper.

So much for the dailies. Then there are the Sundays. Of these the *Sunday Telegraph* is most concerned with the needs of the private investor, the *Sunday Express* gives share tips, and the *Observer,* which has been expanding its business coverage, combines news stories from the business world with share tips and easy-to-follow financial advice. *The Sunday Times* has a complete business section, the 'Business News'; this covers industry, commerce and the economy, but rarely gives straight investment advice. The rest of the Sundays cover finance when it is news, rather than having regular columns of advice each week.

There are also several financial weeklies, the most important of these being the *Investors' Chronicle,* which as its name suggests exists for the private investor and the professionals. You will need to understand financial terms to read it, but when you do, if you are serious about investing, it is almost a must.

Company accounts

Understanding company accounts is important to the investor. They can tell him a lot about the company, and as two years' figures are always given the investor will also know whether the company has done well or badly compared with the previous year. This, together with the chairman's report, which may come with the accounts or may be saved until the annual general meeting, can help him decide whether to keep the shares or not.

Section III, chapter 7, shows you how company accounts are drawn up. It gives a very simple form of accounts, but no matter how big the company the principles remain the same.

You will be able to see some things about a company just by glancing at the two sets of figures – the balance sheet and the profit and loss account. You can also work out more complicated ratios, which will help you see how the company has done in comparison with recent years.

Even if you do not work out these figures yourself, newspapers and investment magazines will refer to them, so it is a good idea to understand what they mean. Here are the definitions of a few of the more usual ones. I have not included any we have already talked about:

Profits. These may be gross profits – that is, sales less costs. Mostly, however, pre-tax profits are chosen as the main indicator of how a company is faring. These are total profits less costs and any items which may be exceptional to a particular year's trading, except for tax. Tax is not included as it is a charge which is outside the control of the company, a variable item depending on government policy.

Net earnings. These are net profits, after all charges such as tax, minority interests and any preference dividends have been subtracted. Surplus Advance Corporation Tax is regarded as part of the tax charge.

Net assets per share. This is the value of the company assets which correspond to each ordinary share in the company. The figure is worked out by taking the book value of all the assets of the company, taking things off which are difficult to measure like good will, and dividing the result by the number of shares.

Asset value may matter or it may not. It shows the underlying value of the shares, but this is of more significance in some industries than others. Oil and heavy engineering companies, for example, tend to produce high asset values for their shares because they are industries which need a lot of assets in order to operate. Shares in service industries like retailing, on the other hand, tend not to have very high asset values.

Return on assets. This shows how much money is made on the company's assets. It is worked out by taking pre-tax profit figures plus loan stock interest and expressing it as a percentage of issued capital, loan capital (but not intangible assets) and reserves. It is one measure of efficiency in a company: the higher the return the more efficient the company seems to be.

But again this is not always the case. Companies with few assets – again the service companies – often produce what looks like an amazingly high return-on-assets figure. This cannot be compared with the return on assets in the heavier industries, however, as these require enormous assets to operate at all. This calculation is sometimes called return on capital employed.

Profit margin. This is pre-tax profits expressed as a percentage of turnover. It is less important than return on assets, because certain industries work on a large profit margin whilst others are forced to operate on low margins and make their profits by massive turnover.

Cash flow. This is profits which are kept back in the business for further development (retained profits) plus depreciation.

Current ratio. Current assets divided by current liabilities.

Many other ratios can be worked out, but these are mainly of interest only to professionals. They include such items as stock turnover, debtor turnover, profits per employee and total wages turnover. But if you manage to understand the above, you have quite enough to enable you to make the most of your investment opportunities.

Getting investment advice

Be quite ruthless in seeking out investment advice; it is after all your money which you are laying on the line when you invest.

1 You can get advice from *newspapers.* Some of them run regular features answering investment queries and problems. This is somewhat hit and miss, however, as most newspapers do not deal with personal enquiries. It is just a matter of luck whether the question you send in will be answered in the feature – and then, of course, the answer will be available to every investor. If it is not, your letter will most likely go unanswered.

This may seem unfair, but it costs money to run an investment advisory service and it is just not a newspaper's basic job. Some of them will answer your letter for a fee. On the whole writing to newspapers is not the best way of getting advice. Newspapers are primarily useful in telling you what is going on in the market; they may suggest that some shares are worth buying and what they have to say will influence your overall investment policy.

2   Ask your *stockbroker*. He should know what is going on in the market and will anyway have a good idea what shares are being favoured by investors generally. As with any profession, the quality of stockbrokers varies, but you will soon find out just how good your broker is at investment advice, or whether he is really only useful for putting your order through. All the training and expertise in the world cannot make up for 'flair'. Try to make sure that you have a stockbroker with that vital quality.

3   Ask your *bank manager*. He is likely to go to the bank's broker to seek the advice you are needing, so do not expect him to come up with advice immediately. His specialization is banking, not broking, but he has sources of information not always available to the ordinary investor.

4   Consult a *merchant bank*. These organizations have developed enormously in the postwar era. They not only carry on their traditional banking and acceptance business, but have also widened out into the field of company management and investment advice.

They are not for the small shareholder as a rule, however, because they will insist on a minimum total value of your investments before working for you. This may be £50,000 or it may be much higher – though they will sometimes make exceptions for favoured customers who put other business their way.

They will charge a fee for their services, but this may be worked out in many different ways. It may be a percentage of the total value of your investments, or an initial fee plus a proportion of any profit they may make for you.

5   There are some *specialized companies* which have grown up in the last twenty years which do nothing but manage investors' portfolios. They are not interested in the very small investor either, but they do not usually set their sights as high as the merchant banks. They like to deal with a minimum of £30,000 to £40,000, but will occasionally take on people with £10,000. After all, if they are successful the small investor may become quite a big one. Their fees are similar to those of the merchant banks, and they may insist that you follow their advice. If you do not, they may well not wish to act for you.

6   There are several more *technical publications* which may help you. The *Stock Exchange Daily* official list is the source for dealings in shares, jobbers produce daily lists and a variety of other information. Most stockbroking firms today issue a monthly newsletter, and some of them are very good indeed. There are also monthly Stock Exchange lists

published by Matheison's and by Straker. These give information on prices, highs and lows, details of dividends and dates when they are payable.

7   One excellent source of information about individual companies is *Extel Statistical Services,* 37/45 Paul Street, London EC2A 4PB. They produce cards on every public company whose shares are quoted and also on some which are not. It has cards covering a variety of foreign companies, some private companies, and various kinds of information on new issues.

Every time there is information from the company, a new news card is issued. There is also a card which shows the position looking back over several years. This is brought up to date at the end of the company's financial year. You can take the whole service, which costs £565 and is unlikely to be needed by the ordinary investor, or you can buy one card in the company in which you are interested. These cost 85p each, with a minimum charge of £1 for the basic card and the current news card.

Some important Stock Exchange terms

These are just a few of the more common expressions used in the financial world of the Stock Exchange. There are many more. If you come across one you do not understand, ask your broker. Its in his interest as much as yours that you thoroughly understand the business.

Account: this is the name given to the periods into which Stock Exchange dealings are divided. It usually lasts two weeks, occasionally three, starting on a Monday and finishing on a Friday.

Account day: the day, eleven days after the end of an account, when you either pay up, or receive your proceeds.

After-hours dealings: these are sales and purchases which are done on the phone after the Stock Exchange closes officially at 3.30 p.m.

Arbitrage: prices can vary in different markets and advantage can sometimes be taken of this by buying in one market and selling in another.

Bargain: any purchase or sale done between a jobber and a broker.

Bid price: the price at which a jobber is prepared to buy.

Bear: this is an individual who 'sells' shares that he does not hold in the hope of buying them at a lower price later and making a profit. He is called a bear because bears hug downwards and the investor is expecting prices to fall.

Blue chip: a share which is thought to be relatively safe from loss. Blue chip companies tend to be the biggest and longest standing industrial groups and financial institutions. They are not, of course, completely risk-free.

Broker: a member of the Stock Exchange who deals directly with the

Investing

public. He buys and sells for his client via the jobber and charges commission for his services.

Bull: the opposite of a bear. The investor buys shares in the hope of a price rise. Called a bull because bulls toss their horns upwards. Sometimes people become 'stale bulls' when prices have not risen as they expect and they are prepared to take a loss.

Call option: this gives you the right to buy shares at *today's* price within a specified period, regardless of how the share price moves.

Cash settlement: most deals are settled on account day which is the eleventh day after the end of the account, but some deals – mostly gilt-edged – are settled immediately.

Closing prices: these are the price levels ruling when the Stock Exchange closes at 3.30 p.m.

Contango: if you do not wish to settle on account day, you can carry the deal over into the next account by paying a rate of interest on the transaction to do so.

Cum: this simply means 'with', and when a share price is quoted in this way it means that whoever buys gets the right to any dividend, rights issues, scrip issues, cash payments, etc., which have been declared recently.

Discount: this is the amount by which a share is quoted below its par value. For instance, a £1 share quoted at 90½p is standing at a 9½p discount.

Dollar premium: this is a certain percentage over normal exchange rates which has to be paid for 'investment dollars' which in turn are required for the purchase of most overseas securities. The rate changes daily and is given in some newspapers.

Equity: the same as an ordinary share. This is the risk capital of the company. All the profits left after dividends have been paid on other classes of shares are theoretically available for equity holders, though companies usually keep some profits to improve their reserves.

Ex: this is the opposite to 'cum'. When a share price is quoted 'ex', this means that dividends or any other benefits have gone to the previous holder.

Final dividend: the dividend declared at the end of the company's financial year.

Funds: the same as gilt-edged.

Gilt-edged: the term used for government and some other fixed interest stocks.

Interim dividend: the payment which is made at any time during the company's financial year, as distinct from the final dividend which is paid when the full year's profits are known.

Jobber: these are the members of the Stock Exchange who hold shares and deal in them on the floor of the Stock Exchange. They do not deal directly with the public.

344

Jobbers' turn: this is the difference between the buying and selling prices quoted by the jobber. The gap represents his profit per share.

Kaffirs: the name given to South African mining shares.

Limit: the buyer or seller can limit his broker to a stated maximum or minimum price.

Limited market: not all shares are freely available. Some of them are difficult to buy or sell because of stock shortages, or other reasons.

Lists closed: this term is used when public offers for shares are fully subscribed. Most lists are open for a specified time, but if the offer is very popular the list may open at 10 a.m. in the morning and close one minute later.

Longs: government stocks with a life of more than fifteen years left.

Making a price: jobbers do this to indicate that they are prepared to deal in a reasonable number of shares. The higher price is the one he will sell at (the investor is buying), the lower one the price at which he will buy (the investor is selling). Brokers do not tell a jobber whether they wish to buy or sell, but simply ask him to make a price and then reveal their intentions.

Marking: details of the price may be entered on a 'marking slip' and the deal will then be recorded in the day's Official List of prices. Marking is not compulsory.

Mediums: government stocks with a life of five to fifteen years.

Middle price: this is the price given in the newspapers each day. It is mid-way between the buying and selling price. The more active the stock the less difference there is likely to be between the buying and selling price, but the middle price on its own will not indicate this.

Money stocks: very short-dated government stocks.

New time: investors can buy for the following account on the last two days of the previous account. This is usually Thursday and Friday.

Nominal price: this is a price the jobber gives which is simply an indication of the approximate price. It is not a price at which he will necessarily conclude a deal.

Offer price: the price at which the jobber is prepared to sell shares.

One way: this means that the jobber cannot buy *and* sell, but can only buy *or* sell.

Opening prices: these are the price levels ruling at the time the Stock Exchange opens. They may not be the same as the previous night's closing prices, particularly if there has been a lot of after-hours dealing or a big item of news which dealers feel affects the stock market situation.

Ordinary shares: the risk capital of the company.

Par value: the nominal value of the shares. This may be anything from 1p to £100.

Premium: the opposite of discount, when a price is quoted above its paid-up or par value.

Put and call option: the right to buy or sell shares under an option.

Investing

Put option: the right to sell shares after the purchase of a put option.

Renunciation: when new issues of shares are made the investor is not forced to accept them and he can renounce his rights. This mostly happens with a 'rights' issue. It would be foolish to turn down a scrip issue as the value of the original investment will fall as prices adjust to the issue.

Scrip issue: this is also known as a 'free' issue. It happens when a company decides to capitalize on its reserves. It is simply a paper transaction designed to bring the company's reserves into line with its issued capital. It neither adds to nor detracts from the company's assets.

Settlement: bargains are usually 'settled' on account day, eleven days after the end of the account.

Shorts: gilt-edged stocks which are due for repayment within five years.

Stag: anyone who applies for a new issue and then sells the shares on the first day they are dealt in – whether they make a loss or profit, though the aim is obviously to make a profit.

Undated stock (irredeemables): government and similar stocks which have no redemption date. The most well known are War Loan 3½ per cent and Consuls 2½ per cent.

Unquoted: shares which are not dealt in officially on the British Stock Exchange. They can be bought and sold under a special rule (Rule 163 (1) (e)). They are usually shares which are quoted on a recognized stock exchange abroad.

RULES FOR INVESTING

In investing you will only learn by trial and error. The more advice you take, the less error there is likely to be and the less the overall risk. Compare the progress of shares you would have bought, had it not been for the advice of your broker or bank manager, against the shares they have recommended. It can be a chastening experience.

Even if you are a beginner, however, you can follow your own counsel and guard against loss by following twelve basic rules for building up a balanced 'portfolio', made up of a variety of investments:

1 Do not put all your eggs in one basket. This means never start off with shares in just one company. Spread your risk. You may not make quite as much money on shares in a range of companies as you would with an investment in a single one if that one does well, but the risk is much smaller. The greater the spread through industries as well as particular companies, the safer for the beginner.

2 If you are really investing for income to live on, spread your investments over different types of shares. Decide how much you

should put into fixed interest stocks to give you a basic income before you go into riskier things.

3 Study all the aspects of every investment before you make it. Avoid declining industries and stick to those which in general will grow. Use your eyes. Many women have made good investments by backing their choice of retailers with an investment.

4 Always be ready to sell if you have made a mistake. Treat your portfolio as a constantly changing thing. If a really good opportunity comes along take it, even if it means selling some of your existing shares at a loss.

5 Keep some cash available all the time to take up opportunities which come along. These may be new issues, perhaps rights issues. Put this money on short-term deposit somewhere you can get hold of it quickly, but where it will earn interest meanwhile. Never invest all your money in case you suddenly need some cash for an emergency, otherwise you may have to sell at an unnecessary loss.

6 If shares in a particular company have increased substantially in value and you would like to make sure of the profit, but not give up your interest entirely, sell some of the shares, perhaps enough to bring your remaining holding down to the cost of the original purchase. This is a good idea, because even if prospects are still good, there can be a danger in overloading your portfolio with shares in one company.

7 There are times when it is worth selling any particular share you have. No shares stay at peak levels, or go on rising without any setback – even if their fall is only in sympathy with a general setback in the market. There have been times when not to sell even the best shares was foolish.

   Go back to the table of highs and lows in the *Financial Times* Index. The really clever investors got out of the market completely in mid-1973 and did not come back until mid-1975. But there were many points in the intervening period when it was possible to sell and buy back at lower price levels later.

8 Keep a careful watch on your portfolio and value it from time to time. Do not assume because shares generally are rising that the value of your portfolio is moving with them. Do not do this every day, or even every week or month, but try to do quarterly valuations and decide what if anything should be sold.

9 In an ideal portfolio dividends will come in at fairly regular intervals throughout the year. But you cannot always achieve this. The vast majority of companies' financial years end on 31 December. The dividend announcement will come any time in the next four months and the payment some time after that. So some bunching of your dividends may be unavoidable. When the

dividend is paid is a point to bear in mind if you are looking at two possible investments which seem equal in all other respects.

10 There is an old adage in the stock market which adjures you to let profits run and cut losses. There is certainly some sense in this when it comes to losses. Recovery always takes some time. It may be better to accept a loss and transfer your money to some other investment where you can recoup much sooner.

11 Taking a loss can also help you with your capital gains tax problems. Net gains are calculated to the end of the financial year, 5 April. It might help you to take a loss around this date to bring your gains tax bill down, and to reinvest somewhere else after the new financial year has started.

12 Finally, decide what your investment policy is and follow it through. Are you looking for income now or for capital gain in the future, with little regard to present yields on the shares? How much risk are you prepared to take? Do you see yourself as a long-term investor, or a speculator? Decide what proportions of your capital you want to put into the more risky investments. Perhaps you will want to put half your money into stocks and shares which will provide you with a good or fixed income, and to take a bit of a gamble with the rest.

Speculation

It is basically a gamble, but a gamble in which you may well not lose your original stake. Speculating is fun. It's fun to see your purchases rise in price and beat the general trend in the market. But it's dangerous too. If you do not have the instincts of a gambler, do not start to speculate. You can lose as much as you gain. But if you want to speculate and still safeguard your money to some extent, here are a few rules to follow:

1 Many speculators buy and sell in the same account. This means that they do not actually have to put any money up: they just pay the difference if the price goes down and get a cheque if it goes up. Try to have sufficient funds so that if your speculation goes wrong you can actually take up the shares, pay for them, and sell later without a loss.

2 Do not fall for any inside information you may be given. Sometimes people do have inside information. When they do, they should not tell anyone nor take advantage of it themselves by dealing. 'Insider' dealing is against the law. Even if the tip is an accurate one, it may turn out to be allowed for in the current price.

3 Check on any company yourself. Even if a tip turns out to be a bad one, is it a good investment anyway?

4 Do not speculate in any shares where the market is not active. You

can get locked in and see all your profit slip away if there are no buyers around and you have to lower your selling price accordingly.

5 Do not be too greedy. Get out when you have made a reasonable profit.
6 If a speculation goes wrong, get out before the price crashes.
7 Know as much as you can about the area in which you choose to speculate. If you know a great deal about the retailing industry, for example, follow your hunches there, rather than buying shares in an area you know nothing about.

Forming an investment club

An investment club can be profitable and fun. It is also a good way of learning more about investment. A group of people get together and each agree to put up a weekly or monthly amount which will go into the purchase of shares. They will need to be people with a reasonable amount of spare cash available which they are willing to put at risk by investing in shares which are chosen collectively. As the costs of investing are so high it is sensible to get together a minimum of £100 for each investment. For ten people – which is manageable size – this would mean an investment of £2.50 a week each, or £10 a month.

The decision on which shares to buy is taken after a general discussion with majority approval. Obviously if you are a person who likes his own way when investing, do not join a club.

You may, of course, have any number of people you wish in an investment club. The more there are the more important it is to draw up proper rules and appoint a treasurer and secretary.

Whatever the size, however, there are a number of basics to be decided upon:

1 The share each person will have in the club, the terms on which he or she can leave, and the notice required. You could, for instance, decide that anyone who left in money for less than a year was entitled only to the money they had put in, or an exact share of the current total assets, whichever is the lower. If the club has lost money overall on its investments, it will be the latter.
2 Proper accounts must be kept, including details of all investments and the time and the price at which they were bought.
3 Decisions must be made on how to deal with taxation and dividends – whether, for example, dividends will be shared out once or twice a year, or reinvested for a period.
4 If you decide that all members need not put in the same amount of money you must divide their voting rights accordingly.
5 You should put some limit on the life of the club. If you wish to

349

extend it you can always do so, but there should be a definite period after which people have the option of taking their original stake and their profits out without penalty.

Investment clubs can work well, but obviously there can be difficulties. Think carefully before you form or join one.

Chapter 5

UNIT AND OTHER TRUSTS

UNIT TRUSTS

You may feel, if you are an absolute beginner, that the whole process of investing is far too daunting: you have no stockbroker, your cash is limited, and you do not like the idea of the high risk involved. Yet you would like to share in the growth of the economy and of the companies in that economy. Well, there is a way you can do that. It is by investing in unit trusts.

When you invest in a unit trust you are putting your faith in professional advisers who make the investment decisions for you. Look at their track record and you can decide whether to back them or not. A unit trust is a means whereby a large number of individuals are able to pool their money into a single fund which is taken care of by professional investment managers.

These managers buy a number of shares, split the total into units of equal value, and offer these units to anyone who wants them. Every unit will have in it a little bit of each share bought. These units are quoted just like shares, with a buying and selling price, but usually they are not actually quoted on the Stock Exchange. The unit trust managers issue a price each day and most of the newspapers carry some, if not all, of them. This price is worked out according to a formula fixed by the Department of Trade and is a direct reflection of the price of each share in the fund.

Unit trusts first developed in the U.S.A., and came to Britain in the early 1930s. It is only in the postwar years that they have really caught on here, however, but they have proved a great help to people who want to build up their capital slowly and without the risk involved in investing in just a few stocks.

Each unit trust is completely separate from any other trusts, but several different ones are run by a few management companies. They are subject to all the same rules as any other trust. They have a trustee – usually a bank – to see that the trust is properly managed. The managers who run the fund are accountable to the trustees and must show that all the money they receive for the fund is used correctly. In the past twenty years unit trusts have grown a great deal, and there are now over 380 trusts in which British investors can put their money.

You can buy almost any number of units – some minimum amount is usually stated, but it is not large – or you can buy units on a monthly plan, whereby you can add to your investment steadily by investing a few pounds each month. You can withdraw your money at any time at the current sale price. Building up your capital in this way has several advantages:

1 *You do not need a lot of money to start off with.* Unit trust managers are content to deal with far lower investments than stockbrokers, because when small orders are added together they make one single big purchase (or sale). This means that each unit trust holder is getting all the advantages available to a big investor.

2 *You spread your risk.* The average unit trust will have shares from at least twenty companies in it – that is a rule for trusts – and some of them many more. This means that if one investment goes wrong the others are still there to maintain the value of the units. This spread of investment means that the prices of unit trusts should not fall as much as an investment in any single company might. Conversely, they are unlikely to rise as much either.

It is important to realize, though, that even in a unit trust you can lose money. If the market goes down like it did in 1974 no one escapes the trend. (We will see on p. 357 how you can use any setback to your benefit.)

But when prices rise,the prices of unit trusts tend to rise slowly and you may feel that this is an unexciting way to invest and that you would rather trust your own judgement and have a go at making a 'killing'. Of course, not all trusts and not all managers are equally successful. It is partly a matter of luck at the beginning which trust and which management group you choose.

3 *The trusts are run by expert managers.* When you invest in a unit trust, it is like having your own professional investment adviser. Of course, the advice you get is going to hundreds of others, too, and there will not be the personal touch. And you will have to follow your own counsel at the beginning. Do you want a trust that overall has a high income, one which is aiming mainly at capital gain, or one which

351

specializes in commodities, North Sea oil, or E.E.C. investment, or companies in other countries?

Whatever you want there will be a trust – indeed many trusts – to suit you. How do you choose your managers? This is a matter of luck to some extent, but you can get some idea, though it is by no means an absolute guide to the future, by looking to see how individual trusts have fared in recent years.

Most newspapers, *The Times*, the *Financial Times* and the *Daily Telegraph* in particular, run regular features, usually on a Saturday, with tables showing which trusts have done what over various periods of time. Every so often the *Investors' Chronicle* does a major survey, and there are also specialist magazines – *The Unit Holder* is one – which can provide useful advice.

Beware, however, of the high fliers of the past. They may not continue to do well. Commodity shares may have exhausted themselves for the time being; maybe there has been a setback in a foreign market which has previously been showing a rise. If you have satisfied yourself that one group of managers seems to have done well – it may even be simply that the price of the units has fallen less than in other trusts in a market setback – then check on the type you have chosen. If interest rates are falling, for instance, a purchase of a high yielding trust now could provide you with some capital gain as well as a good income at the price you paid.

4   *There are tax advantages.* You can avoid a lot of tax problems by investing in unit trusts rather than individual shares.

First, *income tax*: trusts pay income tax on their dividends like anyone else. But the companies in which the trust has invested will already have paid what is called Advance Corporation Tax and so the dividend is subject to a tax credit, which will be equal to the amount of A.C.T. which has been paid. The dividends from the companies in which the trust has invested are passed on to the shareholder twice a year. Of course not all dividends are payable at the same time, but it would be administratively very expensive to keep dishing dividends out to unit holders as soon as they come in. The tax credit covers your income tax liability, so there is no tax for the standard rate tax payer to pay. If you do not pay tax at all, you can reclaim this credit. If, on the other hand, you pay tax at the higher rates, you may have more to pay.

Next, *gains tax:* you will normally pay capital gains tax on any gain you make on individual shares, unless the value of the total investments you sell is under £1,000 in any one year. There is a further concession for unit trust holders, however. The gain on the trust is taxed at 15 per cent less than the investors' normal rate. This means 1½ per cent for those who are taxed at an income tax rate of 35 per cent.

The managers of the trusts will already have paid gains tax on their profits at the rate of 17½ per cent instead of the normal corporation tax rate of 52 per cent. If the unit trust holder sells his shares and there is a profit, this 17½ per cent is deducted from the gains tax due from him. If you are paying 30 per cent on any other gains you will only pay 12½ per cent on sales of your unit trust shares.

You can also get these advantages in *investment trusts*. A word on these is necessary here. These are limited companies, whose business is to invest in a number of companies. They have the same purpose as unit trusts, which is to spread the risk of investment by employing expert management, but they are not 'open-ended' like unit trusts. Unit trusts simply buy more shares the more money they get in, whereas investment trusts are ordinary limited companies and as such are quoted on the Stock Exchange. If they want to raise more money to invest, they must do it with a 'rights issue' in the ordinary way.

The prices of investment trust shares fluctuate far more widely than those of unit trusts. A price of a unit is always the total value of the trust's shares divided by the number of units. Investment trust shares, on the other hand, may be bought or sold below, or above, their asset value – though, of course, if the trust is broken up, the assets will be divided among shareholders at the asset value. In recent years investment trust shares have often tended to be below their asset value; this is known as 'selling at a discount'. It could not happen with a unit trust.

5 *Buying and selling unit trusts is very easy*. You simply fill in a form or write a letter to the fund involved and enclose your cheque. If you are going for one of the monthly plans you either send a cheque each month or arrange a banker's order.

Where to get information

There are well over 300 unit trusts operating in this country, run by some eighty management groups. If you want to find out the range of trusts offered by each group, you will have to write to them. Here are the addresses of the leading unit trust managers (telephone numbers in parentheses):

Abbey Unit Trust Managers Ltd., 72-80 Gatehouse Road, Aylesbury (0296 5941)
Allied Hambro Group, Hambros House, Hutton, Brentwood, Essex (01-588 2851 or 0277 211459)
Ansbacher Unit Management Co Ltd., 1 Noble Street, EC2V 7JH (01-606 4010)
Arbuthnot Securities Ltd., 37 Queen Street, London EC4R 1BY (01-236 5281)
Archway Unit Ltd., 317 High Holborn, London WC1V 7NL (01-831 6233)
Barclays Unicorn Ltd., Unicorn House, 252 Romford Road, London E.7 (01-534 5544) 35 Castle Street, Edinburgh (031-226 5013)
Baring Brothers & Co. Ltd., 88 Leadenhall Street, London E.C.3. (01-588 2830)
Bishopsgate Progressive Management Co., 9 Bishopsgate, London E.C.2. (01-588 6280)
Bridge Fund Managers, King William Street, London EC4R 9AR (01-623 4951)
Britannia Trust Management, 3 London Wall Buildings, London Wall, London EC2M 5QL (01-638 0478/0479)

Investing

British Life Office Ltd., Reliance House, Tunbridge Wells, Kent (0892 22271)

Brown, Shipley & Co. Ltd., Managers, Founders Court, London E.C.2. (01-600 8520)

Canada Life Unit Trust Managers Ltd., 2-6 High Street, Potters Bar, Herts. (Potters Bar 51122)

Capel (James) Management Ltd., 100 Old Broad Street, London EC2N 1BQ (01-588 6010)

Carliol Unit Managers Ltd., Milburn House, Newcastle-upon-Tyne (0623 21165)

Charterhouse Japhet, 1 Paternoster Row, London E.C.4. (01-248 3999)

Chieftan Trust Managers Ltd., 30-31 Queen Street, London EC4R 1BR (01-248 2932)

Confederation Funds Management Ltd., 120 Regent Street, London W1R 6AY (01-437 9040)

Cosmopolitan Fund Managers, Copthall Avenue, London EC2R 7JX (01-628 9222)

Crescent Unit Trust Managers Ltd., 4 Melville Crescent, Edinburgh 3 (031-226 4931)

Discretionary Unit Fund Managers, 22 Bloomfield Street, London EC2M 7AL (01-638 4485)

E.F. Winchester Fund Management Ltd., Old Jewry, London E.C.2 (01-606 2167)

Equitas Securities Ltd., 41 Bishopsgate, London E.C.2 (01-588 2851)

Equity and Law Unit Trust Management, Amersham Road, High Wycombe (0494 33377)

Framlington Unit Management Ltd., 5-7 Ireland Yard, London EC4B 5DH (01-248 6971)

Friend's Provident Unit Trust Managers, Pixham End, Dorking (0306 5055)

G. and A. Trust, 5 Rayleigh Road, Brentwood (0277 227300)

G.T. Unit Managers Ltd., 16 Finsbury Circus, London EC2M 7DD (01-628 8131)

Gartmore Fund Managers, 2 St Mary Axe, London EC3A 8BP (01-283 3531)

Gibbs (Antony) Unit Trust Managers Ltd., 23 Blomfield Street, London EC2M 7NL (01-588 4111)

Govett, John, 77 London Wall, London E.C.2. (01-588 5620)

Grievson Management Co. Ltd., 59 Gresham Street, London EC2P 2DS (01-606 4433)

Guardian Royal Exchange Unit Managers Ltd., Royal Exchange, London EC3P 3DN (01-628 8011)

Henderson Administration, Premier U.T. Administration, Rayleigh Road, Brentwood, Essex (0277 227300)

Hill Samuel Unit Trust Managers, 45 Beech Street, London EC2P 2LX (01-628 8011)

Intel, 15 Christopher Street, London E.C.2. (01-247 7243)

Ionian Unit Trust Management Ltd., 64 Coleman Street, London E.C.2. (01-638 5666)

Key Fund Managers Ltd., 25 Milk Street, London EC2V 8JE (01-606 7070)

Kleinwort Benson Unit Managers, 20 Fenchurch Street, London E.C.3. (01-623 8000)

L. & C. Unit Trust Management Ltd., The Stock Exchange, London EC2N 1HP (01-588 2800)

Lawson Securities Ltd., 63 George Street, Edinburgh EH2 2JG (031-226 3911)

Legal and General Tyndall Fund, 18 Canynge Road, Bristol (0272 32241)

Leonine Administration Ltd., 16 Finsbury Circus, London E.C.2. (01-236 1171)

Lloyds Bank Unit Trust Managers Ltd., Registrar's Department, Goring-by-Sea, Worthing, West Sussex (01-623 1288)

Lloyd's Life Unit Trust Managers Ltd., 72-80 Gatehouse Road, Aylesbury (0296 5941)

London Wall Group, 1 Finsbury Square, London EC2A 1PD (01-606 5811)
unit dealing, 18 Canynge Road, Bristol BS99 7UA (0272 32241)

M. & G. Group, Three Quays, Tower Hill, London EC3R 6BQ (01-626 4588)

Manufacturers Life Management Ltd., P.O. Box 21, Stevenage (0438 56101)

Mercury Fund Managers Ltd., 30 Gresham Street, London EC2P 2EB (01-600 4555)

Midland Bank Group Unit Trust Managers Ltd., Courtwood House, Silver Street Head, Sheffield S1 3RD (0742 79642)

Minster Fund Managers Ltd., Minster House, Arthur Street, London E.C.4 (01-623 1050)

M.L.A. Unit Trust Management Ltd., Old Queen Street, London SW1H 9JG (01-930 7333)

Mutual Unit Trust Managers, 15 Copthall Avenue, London EC2R 7BU (01-606 4803)

National and Commercial, 31 St Andrew Square, Edinburgh (031-556 9151)

National Provident Investment Managers Ltd., 48 Gracechurch Street, London EC3P 3HH (01-623 4200)

National Westminster, 41 Lothbury, London EC2P 2BP (01-837 8044)

N.E.L. Trust Managers Ltd., Milton Court, Dorking, Surrey (0306 5911)

New Court Fund Managers Ltd., 72-80 Gatehouse Road, Aylesbury (0296 5941)

Norwich Union Insurance Group, P.O. Box 4, Norwich NR1 3NG (0603 22200)

Pearl Trust Managers Ltd., 252 High Holborn, London WC1V 7EB (01-405 8441)

Pelican Units Administration Ltd., 1 Fountain Street, Manchester (061-236 5685)

Perpetual Unit Trust Management, 48 Hart Street, Henley-on-Thames (04912 6868)

Piccadilly Unit Trust Managers Ltd., 65 London Wall, London E.C.2 (01-638 0801)

Practical Investment Co. Ltd., 44 Bloomsbury Square, London WC1A 2RA (01-623 8893)

Provincial Life Investment Co. Ltd., 222 Bishopsgate, London E.C.2 (01-247 6533)

Prudential Unit Trust Managers, Holborn Bars, London EC1N 2NH (01-405 9222)

Quilter Management Co. Ltd., The Stock Exchange, London EC2N 1HP (01-600 4177)

Reliance Unit Managers Ltd., Reliance House, Tunbridge Wells, Kent (0892 22271)

Remigium Management Ltd., City-Gate House, Finsbury Square, London E.C.2 (01-606 1066)

Ridgefield Management Ltd., P.O. Box 419, Bank House, Manchester (061-236 8521)

Rothschild & Lowndes Managers Ltd., St Swithin's Lane, London E.C.4 (01-626 4356)

Rowe and Pitman Management Ltd., City-Gate House, Finsbury Square, London E.C.2 (01-606 1066)

Royal Trust of Canada Fund Managers Ltd., 54 Jermyn Street, London S.W.1 (01-629 8252)

Save and Prosper Group, 4 Gt. St Helens, London EC3P 3EP
68-73 Queen Street, Edinburgh EH2 4NX
(dealings: 01-554 8899 or 031-226 7351)

Schroder Wagg, J. Henry, & Co. Ltd., 120 Cheapside, London E.C.2 (01-242 8252)

Scottish Equitable Fund Managers Ltd., 28 St Andrew's Square, Edinburgh (031-556 9101)

Segbag Unit Trust Managers Ltd., P.O. Box 511, Bucklesberry House, London E.C.4 (01-236 5000)

Security Selection Ltd., 8 The Crescent Minories, London EC3N 2LY (01-488 4313)

Stewart Unit Trust Managers Ltd., 45 Charlotte Square, Edinburgh (031-226 3271)

Sun Alliance Fund Management Ltd., Sun Alliance House, Horsham (0403 64141)

Target Trust Managers Ltd., 31 Gresham Street, London E.C.2 (dealings: 0296 5941)

Target Trust Managers (Scotland), 19 Athol Crescent, Edinburgh 3 (031-229 8621/2)

Trades Union Unit Trust Managers, 100 Wood Street, London E.C.2 (01-628 8011)

Transatlantic and General Securities Co., 91-99 New London Road, Chelmsford, Essex (0245 51651)

Trident Trusts Schlesinger Trust Managers Ltd., 140 South Street, Dorking (0306 86441)

T.S.B. Unit Trusts, 21 Chantry Way, Andover, Hants. (0264 62188)

Tyndall Managers Ltd., 18 Canynge Road, Bristol (0272 32241)

Ulster Bank, Waring Street, Belfast (0232 35231)

Unit Trust Account and Management Ltd., King William Street, London EC4R 9AR (01-623 4951)

Wieler Growth Fund, King William Street, London EC4R 9AR (01-623 4951)

How to buy

If you have decided that you like the idea of investing in unit trusts, take your time about deciding which one. Day-to-day fluctuations in the price of unit trusts are small and you are likely to lose very little by delaying your purchase until you are sure which trust you want. Read your newspapers and magazines and base your decision on the following criteria:

1   Is it the kind of trust you want? Does it offer the right sort of income, and good prospects of growth? Is it specialized enough?

2   Is the management record generally good? Is it particularly good in the unit trust you are considering? Do the shares in the portfolio meet with your approval as investments?

3   How big is the trust? It may be as big as £100 million or it may be quite small, £1 million or less. The bigger it is the more 'average' its performance is likely to be. The smaller it is the more chance of gain or loss.

4   How little may you invest, either in a savings plan or in a lump sum? A few trusts will not allow you to invest less than £1,000 (and management costs are lower as a result), and a £100 minimum is quite common. Other trusts may not permit savings schemes.

5   What other services does the trust offer? These can be many and varied. Apart from savings schemes and unit-linked policies (see next section), they may also have share exchange schemes whereby you can swop individual shares you hold for the equivalent value in units. Children's gift plans are quite common, too. These differ to some extent from trust to trust, but basically they allow you to invest on behalf of minors.

Now you have chosen your trust. The next step is to apply for the units. You simply write to the fund you have chosen and enclose your cheque. The price to you will be the offer price ruling on the day your cheque arrives. Like shares, unit trusts have bid and offer prices – the former is the one you sell at, the latter the one you buy at. The gap between them is usually between 5 and 6 per cent. We have already gone into the reasons for this gap. If you are making an outright purchase you will buy an exact number of units and the managers will return the balance. If you are starting a savings plan you buy in units and fractions of units each month.

You will then receive your certificate, which you must not lose as you will need to return it when selling. If you lose it, you will eventually be able to sell, but the process will take longer.

Then you sit back and wait for your dividends. These will arrive twice a year along with a half-yearly report and accounts from the managers. You can buy more units at any time.

Regular saving in a unit trust

This works very simply. You make a straightforward investment of a fixed sum of money each month. This sum buys a number of units (very often including a fraction of a unit). Every six months the managers send you a statement of your account, showing how many units you have bought and at what prices and giving details of the tax credit and any dividend.

You can have this dividend paid out to you or reinvested in more units. It is worth following the latter course to begin with, because the dividend will be scarcely worth having; it is only later on that it will make a significant contribution to your income. Your savings also grow more quickly this way, and the reinvested money will get its share of any gains which come along.

Rules for the minimum you can invest differ from management company to company. Some may allow you to invest as little as £5 a month, but this is becoming rare. A £10 minimum is normal.

When you save in this way you need not be too concerned about fluctuations in price. You are buying each month at the then current price, so if the price falls you will be able to buy more at the lower price and bring down the average cost of your units.

This is called 'pound cost averaging', and works like this:

£10 invested each month	price of units	number bought	average cost per unit
month 1	50p	20	50p
month 2	52p	19.23	50.98p
month 3	48p	20.83	49.95p
month 4	46p	21.74	48.90p
month 5	44p	22.73	47.83p
month 6	47p	21.28	47.69p
month 7	47.3p	21.14	47.64p
month 8	47.5p	21.05	47.61p
month 9	48p	20.83	47.66p
month 10	48.5p	20.62	47.74p
month 11	49.2p	20.32	47.87p
month 12	50p	20	48.04p

At the end of a year you will have invested £120; the number of units bought will be 249.77, at an average price of 48.04p per unit. At the current 50p these will be worth £125.

This means that at the end of one year you have units worth £125

357

compared with £120 invested. Not an especially wonderful result, but remember at one stage the price of the units dropped to 44p and you would have lost money if you sold because the selling price would have been even lower.

The second year might look like this:

£10 invested each month	price of units	number bought	average cost per unit
month 13	51p	19.61	48.26p
month 14	52p	19.23	48.51p
month 15	52p	19.23	48.73p
month 16	52.5p	19.05	48.95p
month 17	52.7p	18.95	49.16p
month 18	53p	18.86	49.36p
month 19	53.5p	18.69	49.56p
month 20	54p	18.52	49.76p
month 21	55p	18.18	49.99p
month 22	55p	18.18	50.19p
month 23	53p	18.86	50.31p
month 24	52p	19.23	50.38p

After two years the total amount invested has reached £240; you will have bought a total of 476.36 units, at an average price of 50.38p; they will now be worth £247.70 at the current price of 52p.

Even now you will not have made any real profit – the units would only fetch about £232 at the current selling price – but you will have learned the most important thing about saving schemes in unit trusts: they are for long-term investment only. It is unusual to make a reasonable profit in less than three years. Not only do unit trust prices move rather more slowly than individual shares, but the gap between buying and selling prices tends to be a little wider than with individual shares.

Let's assume that in the third year the price of the units rises fairly steadily, and you will see how the setback in the first two years is of benefit to you now as the average price of your investment trails behind the rise in the price of your units.

£10 invested each month	price of units	number bought	average cost per unit
month 25	52.1p	19.19	50.45p
month 26	52.5p	19.05	50.52p
month 27	52.3p	19.12	50.59p
month 28	53p	18.86	50.67p
month 29	55p	18.18	50.81p
month 30	55.5p	18.02	50.95p
month 31	56p	17.86	51.10p

month 32	56.2p	17.79	51.25p
month 33	57p	17.54	51.41p
month 34	58p	17.24	51.58p
month 35	58p	17.24	51.75p
month 36	60p	16.67	51.95p

By the end of the third year, then, the average cost of each unit is lagging far behind the current cost. Even when the price reaches 60p you will still have paid an average of less than 52p a unit. Your total investment has now reached £360, with which you have bought 693.03 units, which are worth £415.82 at the current price of 60p. You will just about have a net profit, for the units will probably fetch £391 at a selling price of 56.4p.

Unit-linked life policies

This is basically how pound cost averaging works. You can also take advantage of it in another form of regular saving in unit trusts. This involves not just the simple purchase of units each month, but the linking of that purchase to a life assurance policy. This form of saving has become very popular in recent years, because it protects your investment to some extent.

There are two kinds of unit-linked policies. With the first, the main emphasis is on the life insurance aspect. Part of the money you pay each month is invested in units, but the rest is kept by the insurance company towards a policy which carries similar benefits to the life policies discussed in section I, chapter 13. The amount which goes into the units is quite small to begin with and grows gradually over the period of the policy. There is always a guaranteed minimum paid out at the end of the policy, or on the death of the holder, regardless of the total value of the units which have been bought. The holder gets no income as such from this type of saving. It is kept by the insurance company and is paid out in the form of regular bonuses.

With the second kind the main emphasis is on the investment in units. The insurance company keeps only between 5 and 10 per cent of the total sums paid for insurance purposes. The life cover provided is, of course, correspondingly less – usually the current value of the units, plus an amount equal to the total premiums still to come. The income from the units is usually invested in more units for the policyholder.

There are certain differences in the benefits of this kind of saving, depending on the insurance company you choose. The holder may get insurance cover at least equal in value to the total premiums he has paid in, even if the total value of the units purchased is not that much, but this is not always the case.

The chief advantage of a unit-linked life policy as opposed to ordinary saving is the guarantee, however limited. The main disadvantage is that policies usually have to be taken out for ten years, and failure to complete the period can lead to the sort of penalties usual with insurance policies (see section I, chapter 13).

There are some other points to note:

1   The premiums you pay qualify for tax relief in the normal way. They can be paid monthly, quarterly or annually, but monthly premiums are best, because they give you an investment in units each month. There will be a fixed minimum which you must pay in premiums. This may be as little as £1 a month, but can be £5 or more.

2   From the total amount you pay in each month, something goes to the life cover and the rest into units at the current price on the day you pay your premiums. The money may go into any trust of your choice which permits these schemes.

3   You do not need to take a cash payment immediately the policy matures. Stock market prices may be low and you may prefer to leave the units until there is an improvement, particularly if you do not have the guaranteed minimum payment in your policy.

4   You do not need to go to a unit trust management company for this kind of investment, though there is nothing to stop you doing this. Insurance companies are increasingly setting up their own funds, but these are not 'authorized unit trusts' and therefore do not have to obey the same rules. They can, for instance, invest outside the stock market and they often do, particularly in property. This can be a useful standby when the stock market is having a bad time.

How safe is your money?

Unit trusts are authorized to operate by the Department of Industry and unit holders are protected by law against fraudulent behaviour by management companies. The protection is given by the Prevention of Fraud (Investments) Act (1948), which lays down, among other things:

1   There must be a reasonable amount of money behind the management company.
2   The management company can (and obviously must if it is to continue in business) charge a management fee to unit holders. This is limited to a total of 13½ per cent over a twenty-year period. This is worked out in the following way: there is an initial service charge, which is usually between 3 and 5 per cent, which is included in the selling price of the units. Then there is a half-yearly service charge, usually between 35p and 50p for every £100 invested. This is taken out of the unit holder's dividends.

As these initial charges, as well as stockbroker's commission, buying costs and the jobber's 'turn', are reflected in prices, the gap between buying and selling prices is rather larger with unit trusts than with shares in a single company.

3 The unit trust must have an absolutely independent trustee. This trustee, which must also be a large concern, is there to look after the shareholders' interests, as laid down in the 'trust deed'.

4 Every unit trust must have its own trust deed which lays down the rules as to how the trust is to be run. Trust deeds do not vary much, however, and all must follow certain guidelines issued by the Department of Industry. A trust deed will include the formula according to which the unit prices are calculated, details of the management charges, and some rules for the investment policy of the fund. It may say, for instance, that the trust may not invest more than a certain proportion of its funds in one company. The figure is usually 5 per cent, but it can be higher. Nor is a unit trust allowed to hold more than 10 per cent of the equity of a single company, and it must limit its investments to the securities quoted on the Stock Exchange. Unless a trust obeys the rules of its trust deed, the Department of Industry will not authorize it and it cannot advertise its units to the public.

5 No unit trust is allowed to operate door-to-door selling techniques.

All this means that investors are fairly well protected when it comes to the running of the trust. The only thing they are not protected against is fluctuations in share prices. That is where management skill comes in. The unit trust manager has to try to do better than average when share prices are falling, and at least as well when they are rising.

PROPERTY BONDS AND OTHER FUNDS

Alongside unit trusts you may see the prices of property bonds quoted. These operate in more or less the same way as unit trusts, except that property bond companies invest in property and not shares. They are not authorized, however, as the Department of Industry authorization only goes to trusts which invest in companies quoted in the Stock Exchange. This means that property bonds cannot be advertised to the public in the same way as unit trusts.

The managers of these funds have got round this advertising difficulty by linking the bonds to a life insurance policy, which can be advertised. If you invest in one of these bonds you pay a premium for a single premium life assurance policy, or an insurance bond – hence the name property bond.

Single premium policies do not carry tax relief, and the cover you will get is limited, so although these are assurance policies they should not be part of your total life assurance scheme (see section I, chapter 13).

Investing

The operations of property bond companies are not governed by the same rules as unit trusts, and the rules are a little less stringent. It is still possible for rather unscrupulous people to set themselves up in this field, so if you are interested in property bonds stick to companies which have a wide spread of interests.

Property bonds are useful for people who like the idea of an interest in property, but cannot afford to buy actual properties, but there are snags. With unit trusts you know the exact price of your units every day, but with property it's anybody's guess. Professional valuers make estimates of the value of a property, but they cannot possibly estimate precisely what the property would fetch if it were sold. Again it is far easier to sell shares than property. If people rushed out of property bonds to such an extent that properties actually had to be sold, they might realize less money than they would if the selling process was more leisurely and simply part of the continuing activity of the fund.

To avoid such disasters the fund will keep a certain amount of money in case of emergencies, but if it gets into a really bad way it might still have to delay repayment for some time.

If you think you may need your money suddenly, property bonds are not for you. These bonds do not have the special tax concessions available to the holders of unit trusts either.

This type of single premium life assurance policy can also be used where a fund is invested in equities. This is very useful for high tax payers, who can find they pay less tax as a result of the tax concession which is allowed to the insurance company which manages the funds. Here is an alphabetical list of property bond companies (telephone numbers in parentheses):

Abbey Life Assurance Co Ltd., 1-3 St Paul's Churchyard, London E.C.4 (01-248 9111)
Albany Life Assurance Co. Ltd., 31 Old Burlington Street, London W.1 (01-437 5962)
A.M.E.V. Life Assurance Ltd., Alma House, Alma Road, Reigate (Reigate 40101)
Arrow Life Assurance, 30 Uxbridge Road, London W.12 (01-749 9111)
Barclays Life Assurance Co. Ltd., 252 Romford Road, London E.7 (01-534 5544)
Beehive Life Assurance Co. Ltd., 71 Lombard Street, London E.C. 3 (01-623 1288)
Canada Life Assurance Co., 2-6 High Street, Potters Bar, Herts. (Potters Bar 51122)
Cannon Assurance Ltd., 1 Olympic Way, Wembley HA9 0NB (01-902 8876)
Capital Life Assurance, Coniston House, Chapel Ash, Wolverhampton (0902 28511)
Charterhouse Japhet Life Assurance Co. Ltd., 1 Paternoster Row, London E.C.4 (01-248 3999)
City of Westminster Assurance Co. Ltd., Ringstead House, 6 Whitehorse Road, Croydon CR0 2JA (01-648 9664)
City of Westminster Assurance Society, Ringstead House, 6 Whitehorse Road, Croydon CR0 2JA (01-684 9664)
Commercial Union Group, St Helens, 1 Undershaft, London E.C.3 (01-283 7500)
Confederation Life Insurance Co., 120 Regent Street, London W1R 6AY (01-437 9040)
Cornhill Insurance Co. Ltd., 32 Cornhill, London E.C.3 (01-626 5410)
Credit and Commerce Insurance, 60 Mark Lane, London EC3R 7TN (01-488 1166)
Crescent Life Assurance Co. Ltd., Acre House, Windsor, Berks. (Windsor 62443)

Crusader Insurance Co. Ltd., Vincula House, Tower Place, London E.C.3 (01-626 8031)

Eagle Star Insurance /Midland Assurance, 1 Threadneedle Street, London E.C.2. (01-588 1212)

General Portfolio Life Insurance Co. Ltd., 60 Bartholomew Court, Waltham Cross (Waltham Cross 31971)

Grosvenor Life Assurance Co. Ltd., 65 Grosvenor Street, London W.1 (01-493 1484)

Growth & Securities Life Assurance Society Ltd., United House, London W.11 (01-229 6166)

Guardian Royal Exchange, Royal Exchange, London E.C.3 (01-283 7101)

Hambro Life Assurance Ltd., 7 Old Park Lane, London W.1 (01-499 0031)

Hearts of Oak Benefit Society, Euston Road, London N.W.1 (01-387 5020)

Hill Samuel Life Assurance Ltd., N.L.A. Tower, Addiscombe Road, Croydon (01-686 4355)

Imperial Life Assurance Co. of Canada, Imperial House, Guildford (0483 71255)

Individual Life Insurance Co. Ltd., Enterprise House, Isambard Brunel Road, Portsmouth PO1 2AW (0705 27733)

Irish Life Assurance Co Ltd., 11 Finsbury Square, London E.C.2 (01-628 8253)

King and Shaxson Ltd., 52 Cornhill, London E.C.3 (01-623 5433)

Langham Life Assurance Co. Ltd., Langham House, Holmbrook Drive, London N.W.4 (01-203 5211)

Life Assurance Co. of Pennsylvania, 39-42 New Bond Street, London W1Y 0RQ (01-493 8395)

Lloyds Bank Unit Trust Managers Ltd., 71 Lombard Street, London E.C.3 (01-623 1288)

Lloyd's Life Assurance, 612 Leadenhall Street, London EC3M 7LS (01-623 6621)

London Indemnity and General Insurance Co. Ltd., Northcliffe House, Colston Avenue, Bristol (0272 97281)

M. & G. Group, Three Quays, Tower Hill, London EC3R 6BQ (01-626 4583)

Magna Assurance Co. Ltd., 18 Chequers Street, Uxbridge, Middx. (Uxbridge 52181)

Merchant Investors Assurance, 125 High Street, Croydon (01-686 9171)

N.E.L. Pensions Ltd., Milton Court, Dorking, Surrey (0306 5911)

New Court Property Fund Managers Ltd., St Swithins Lane, London E.C.4 (01-626 4356)

Norwich Union Insurance Group, P.O. Box 4, Norwich NR1 3NG (0603 22200)

N.P.I. Pensions Management Ltd., 48 Gracechurch Street, London EC3P 3HH (01-623 4200)

Phoenix Assurance Co. Ltd., 4-5 King William Street, London EC4P 4HR (01-626 9876)

Property Equity & Life Assurance Co., 119 Crawford Street, London W1H 2AS (01-486 0857)

Property Growth Assurance Co Ltd., Leon House, Croydon CR9 1LU (01-680 0606)

Provincial Life Assurance Co. Ltd., 222 Bishopsgate, London E.C.2 (01-247 6533)

Prudential Pensions Ltd., Holborn Bars, London EC1N 2NH (01-405 9222)

Reliance Mutual, Tunbridge Wells, Kent (0892 22271)

Royal Insurance Group, 1 North John Street, Liverpool (051-236 6622)

Save and Prosper Group, 4 Gt. St Helen's, London EC3P 3EP (01-554 8899)

Schroder Life Group, Enterprise House, Portsmouth (0705 27733)

Scottish Widows' Group, P.O. Box 902, Edinburgh EH16 5BU (031-655 6000)

Solar Life Assurance Ltd., 107 Cheapside, London EC2V 6DU (01-606 0471)

Sun Alliance Fund Management Ltd., Sun Alliance House, Horsham (0403 64141)

Sun Life of Canada (U.K.) Ltd., 2, 3, 4 Cockspur Street, London SW1Y 5BH (01-930 5400)

Target Life Assurance Co. Ltd., Target House, Gatehouse Road, Aylesbury, Bucks. (0296 5941)

Transinternational Life Insurance Co. Ltd., 6 Bream Buildings, London EC4 1NV (01-405 6497)
Trident Life Assurance Co. Ltd., Renslade House, Gloucester (0452 36541)
Tyndall Assurance/Pensions, 18 Canynge Road, Bristol (0272 32241)
Vanbrugh Life Assurance, 41-43 Maddox Street, London W1R 9LA (01-499 4923)
Welfare Insurance Co. Ltd., The Leas, Folkestone, Kent (0303 57333)
Windsor Life Assurance Co. Ltd., 1 High Street, Windsor (Windsor 68144)

MANAGED FUNDS

Recently a new type of fund, called a managed fund, has appeared. This is a combination of a unit trust and a property bond. You make your payment and then the managers invest in property, in equities or sometimes in fixed interest stocks.

The money is moved around from one place to another, depending where the managers think the best opportunities lie at any one time.

The idea is to provide holders with more regular growth than you can expect in a unit trust.

You can also invest in these funds by means of a regular savings plan linked to an assurance policy. Your premium buys shares which are valued regularly and the value of the policy depends on the value of your total units, so that you always know what your policy is worth.

FUNDS FOR FOREIGN INVESTMENT

There are two other kinds of funds which are organized in the same way as unit trusts but which specialize in foreign investments.

The first of these is quite straightforward. The fund is based in the United Kingdom and the shares are bought through the medium of the 'dollar premium' (see the section on buying foreign property in chapter 7 later in this section for an explanation), or by borrowing foreign currency through a technique known as 'back-to-back' loans. Anyone living in Britain can buy a stake in these funds, and the price will reflect the extra cost of the dollar premium.

There are also what are known as 'offshore' funds, which are legally based outside the United Kingdom and are not subject to any U.K. taxes or currency restrictions. As result, they can most advantageously be used by non-residents. Although their base is offshore, they are actually managed by many of the same companies which operate unit trusts and property bonds. They are often based in places like the Channel Islands and the Isle of Man, which are not subject to U.K. tax laws, but many of them are much further afield in places like the Bahamas and the Cayman Islands, where taxes are non-existent or very low.

It is unlikely that the permanent U.K. resident will have much interest in these funds, but the prices of both kinds of funds are quoted daily in the leading national press, the 'offshore' funds under that specific heading. Here are their addresses (telephone numbers in parentheses):

Arbuthnot Securities (Channel Islands) Ltd., P.O. Box 284, St Helier, Jersey (0534 72177)
Australian Selection Fund N.V., Market Opportunities, c/o Irish, Young & Outhwaite, 127 Kent Street, Sydney
Bank of London and South America Ltd., 40-66 Queen Victoria Street, London E.C.4 (01-248 9822)
Banque Bruxelles Lambert, 2 Rue de la Regence, B 1000, Brussels
Barclays Unicorn International (Channel Islands) Ltd., 1 Charing Cross, St Helier, Jersey (0534 2904)
Barclays Unicorn International (Isle of Man) Ltd., 1 Thomas Street, Douglas, Isle of Man (0624 4856)
Bishopsgate Commodity Services Ltd., P.O. Box 42, Douglas, Isle of Man (0624 2391)
Bridge Management Ltd., P.O. Box 508, Grand Cayman, Cayman Islands.
Britannia Trust Management (Channel Islands) Ltd., 30 Bath Street, St Helier, Jersey (0534 73114).
Butterfield Management Co. Ltd., P.O. Box 195, Hamilton, Bermuda
Capital International S.A., 37 rue Notre-Dame, Luxembourg
Charterhouse Japhet, 1 Paternoster Row, London E.C.4 (01-248 3999)
Cornhill Insurance (Guernsey) Ltd., P.O. Box 157, St Peter Port, Guernsey
Delta Group, P.O. Box 3012, Nassau, Bahamas
Dreyfus Intercontinental Investment Fund, P.O. Box N3712, Nassau, Bahamas
Emson & Dudley Trust Management Jersey Ltd., P.O. Box 73, St Helier, Jersey (0534 20591)
F. & C. Management Ltd., Investment Advisers, 1-2 Laurence Pountney, EC4R 0BA.
Fidelity Management and Residence (Bermuda) Ltd., P.O. Box 670, Hamilton, Bermuda
F.I.R.S.T. Managers Ltd., 1 Charing Cross, St Helier, Jersey (0534 29041)
First Viking Commodity Trusts, 8 St George's Street, Douglas, Isle of Man (0624 4682) (London agents: *Dunbar & Co Ltd.,* 36 Pall Mall, London SW1Y 5JH (01-930 7657))
Fleming (Robert) Investment Management Ltd. (Investment Adviser), 8 Crosby Square, London EC3A 6AN
Free World Fund Ltd., Butterfield Building, Hamilton, Bermuda
G. T. Bermuda Ltd., Bank of Bermuda, Front Street, Hamilton, Bermuda
G.T. Management Ltd., London Agents, Park House, 16 Finsbury Circus, London E.C.2 (01-628 8131, TLX. 886100)
G.T. Management (Asia) Ltd., Hutchinson House, Harcourt Road, Hong Kong
G.T. Management (Jersey) Ltd., Royal Trust House, Colomerie Street, St Helier, Jersey
Hambro Pacific Fund Management Ltd., 2110 Connaught Centre, Hong Kong
Hambros (Guernsey) Ltd., P.O. Box 86, St Peter Port, Guernsey (0481 26521)
Haput Management Ltd., 305 Fu House, Ice House Street, Hong Kong (Enquiries 01-283 3531)
Henderson B.S.M Management Ltd., P.O Box N4723, Nassau, Bahamas
Hill Samuel Overseas Fund South Africa, 37 Rue Notre-Dame, Luxembourg
International Pacific Investment Management Ltd., P.O. Box R237, 56 Pitt Street, Sydney, Australia
Jardine Fleming & Co Ltd., 46th Floor, Connaught Centre, Hong Kong
J.E.T. Managers (Jersey) Ltd., P.O. Box 194, Royal Trust House, Jersey (0534 27441)
Kemp-Gee Management Jersey Ltd., 1 Charing Cross, St Helier, Jersey (0534 29041)
Keyselex Management Jersey Ltd., P.O. Box 98, St Helier, Jersey (Enquiries 01-606 7070)

Investing

King & Shaxson Managers (Isle of Man) Ltd., 1 Thomas Street, Douglas, Isle of Man (0624 4856)

King & Shaxson Managers (Jersey) Ltd., 1 Charing Cross, St Helier, Jersey (0534 29041)

Kleinwort Benson Ltd., 20 Fenchurch Street, London E.C.3 (01-623 8000)

Lamont Investment Management Ltd., 8 St George's Street, Douglas, Isle of Man (0624 4682)

Lloyds Bank (Channel Islands) Unit Trust Managers, P.O. Box 195, St Helier, Jersey (0534 27561)

Lloyd's International Management South Africa, 7 Rue du Rhone, P.O. Box 179, 1211 Geneva 11

M. &. G Group, Three Quays, Tower Hill, London EC3R 6BQ (01-626 4588)

Management International Ltd., c/o Bank of Bermuda, Front Street, Hamilton, Bermuda

Montagu, Samuel, London Agents,114 Old Broad Street, London E.C.2 (01-588 6464)

Murray, Johnstone (Investment Adviser), 163 Hope Street, Glasgow C2 (041-221 5521)

Negit Ltd., Bank of Bermuda Buildings, Hamilton, Bermuda

Negit South Africa, 10a Boulevard Royal, Luxembourg

Neptune International Fund Managers, 1 Charing Cross, St Helier, Jersey (0534 29041)

Old Court Commodity Fund Managers Ltd., P.O. Box 58, St Julians Court, Guernsey (0481 26741)

Old Court Fund Managers Ltd., P.O. Box 58, St Julians Court, Guernsey (0481 26331)

Property Growth Overseas Ltd., 28 Irish Town, Gibraltar (Gibraltar 6106)

Royal Trust (Channel Islands) Fund Management Ltd., P.O. Box 194, Royal Trust House, Jersey (0534 27441)

Save and Prosper International, dealings to: 37 Broad Street, St Helier, Jersey (0534 20591)

Schlesinger Fund Managers (Jersey) Ltd., P.O. Box 197, St Helier, Jersey (0534 27311)

Schroder Wagg, J. Henry, & Co. Ltd., 120 Cheapside, London E.C.2 (01-588 4000)

Singer & Friedlander London Agents, 20 Cannon Street, London E.C.4 (01-248 9646)

Surinvest (Jersey) Ltd., P.O. Box 98, St Helier, Jersey (0534 28138)

Surinvest Trust Managers Ltd., 50 Athol Street, Douglas, Isle of Man (0624 23914)

Tokyo Pacific Holdings N.V. Intimis Management Co., N.V. Curacao

Tokyo Pacific Holdings (Seaboard) N.V. Intimis Management Co., N.V., Curacao

T.S.B. Unit Trust Managers (Channel Islands) Ltd., Bagatelle Road, St Saviour, Jersey (0534 73494)

Tyndall Group, Hamilton, Bermuda, and St Helier, Jersey (0534 37331)

United States Trust International Advisers Co., 14 Rue Aldringer, Luxembourg

Warburg, S.G., & Co Ltd., 30 Gresham Street, London E.C.2 (01-600 4555)

Warburg Investment Management Jersey Ltd., 1 Charing Cross, St Helier, Jersey (0534 29041)

World Wide Growth Management, 10a Boulevard Royal, Luxembourg

Chapter 6

INVESTING IN COMMODITIES

THE COMMODITY MARKETS

It is possible to invest money outside the stock market in various other metal and commodity markets. You can, of course, acquire an interest in these markets by investing in the companies who specialize in them, but you can also invest in the actual commodities themselves.

Few small investors go in for this kind of investment. It requires a lot of cash and quite a lot of nerve. It is not advisable to think about these markets unless you have at least £10,000 to invest – and that should not be your entire capital. Despite all the risks, however, the number of investors in these markets has risen over the years; it increased ten times between 1970 and 1975 alone.

The risk is a straightforward one. The prices of commodities vary. They can go up and down with remarkable rapidity. Let's look at some of the reasons for this:

* A commodity may be superseded by another and its price may fall.
* A new source of, for example, a metal may be found, making its production more widespread and bringing down its price.
* Strikes at a major supply point may hold up supplies. The price will then go up.
* A bumper crop may bring prices down.
* A bad harvest may bring prices up.
* Political developments can influence supply in both directions. A war will almost certainly cut off the source for some time and bring prices up. A coup can affect a commodity either way. A country can pursue a policy of not selling to customers abroad and bring prices up that way.
* A recession can cut demand – and prices.

And these are only *some* of the reasons.

At present fourteen different commodities are traded in London, which is one of the world's biggest market places for them. Here is an alphabetical list, including the countries which are the main source of supply. You can assess the risk yourself.

367

1   Barley – British needs are basically supplied from within the U.K.
2   Cocoa – 30 per cent of the world's supply comes from Ghana, the rest from Nigeria, the Ivory Coast, Brazil and the Cameroons.
3   Coffee – from South America, Africa, the East Indies, the West Indies and India.
4   Copper – from the U.S.A., Chile, Canada, Zambia, Zaire and the Sino-Soviet block.
5   Gold – South Africa and the Sino-Soviet block are the main producers, but there are many small ones as well.
6   Lead – from Canada, the U.S.A. and Australia.
7   Platinum – from the U.S.A. and South Africa.
8   Rubber – 90 per cent of natural rubber comes from South-east Asia.
9   Silver – from Canada, the U.S.A. and Australia.
10   Sugar – from Cuba, Brazil, Australia, India, the E.E.C. and the Sino-Soviet block.
11   Tin – from Malaya, Indonesia, Bolivia, Thailand and the Sino-Soviet block.
12   Wheat – the surpluses available come mainly from Canada, the U.S.A., Australia and New Zealand.
13   Wool – from South Africa, Australia, Argentina, New Zealand and the U.S.A.
14   Zinc – from Canada, the U.S.A. and Australia.

No one knows exactly how much of these commodities the Sino-Soviet block could or does produce, but the way these countries deal can be an important influence on commodity prices.

It is important to understand how the commodity markets operate. They are based on what are called 'futures'. First of all, the commodity is offered for sale locally, then the rest is offered in the world market at a price to suit both sides. By the time the commodity reaches its destination the price may have fallen or risen.

This is where the investor comes in. He buys or sells a commodity for delivery in the future. He agrees to buy or sell the commodity in the future in accordance with a standard contract under the guidance of an organized commodity futures market. No one is actually going to come and deliver 50 tons of zinc to you – unless you are a manufacturer and need it for production.

The private investor promises to buy or sell at a certain price on a certain future date. If you think the price of the commodity is going to rise, then you would buy at today's price in order to sell in the future at the new price. If the price moves up meanwhile, the difference between the two prices is your profit.

If, on the other hand, you think prices will fall, you contract to sell at today's price on a specified future date. If the price duly falls you can buy at the lower price and sell at that original price and make a profit.

You can buy and sell these options at any time through a commodity dealer, who like a stockbroker will charge for his services. The commission is usually lower than for buying shares, however, because the amounts involved are much larger; it should average out at about half a per cent.

If you do not have large sums of money available, you may be able to join a 'syndicate', whereby a number of small investors pool their resources and share out the eventual profit or loss according to the proportion invested in the syndicate. The commodity brokers themselves often organize such syndicates, and the agreements are carefully drawn up to protect investors, so that their liability is limited to the amount of their original investment.

There are some snags in this form of investing. The gains are not usually allowed by the Inland Revenue to be capital gains; they are counted as income and taxed accordingly – that is, usually at a much higher rate than capital gains tax.

Commodities offshore

Various unauthorized unit trusts have been set up as offshore funds to deal in commodities. They are scrutinized by the offshore authority where they are based and also by the British government's Department of Industry. Sometimes you can invest as little as £500 to £1,000 in them, but as with any ordinary unit trust the investor has no say in the investment policy of the trust.

Like unit trusts, they lower the risk of commodity investment, and as no dividends are paid it is possible that the investor may only be liable for gains tax and not for income tax when he sells his holding, as he can do at any time.

Investing in commodities can be very profitable, but it is not really for the small investor or anyone who is not fully aware of the risk involved.

Chapter 7

INVESTING IN PROPERTY

RENTING OUT PROPERTY

You may decide that shares are not for you. Having seen the prices of property rise steadily over the years, you perhaps think that would make a more secure investment. In many ways this is true, but the owning and renting of property for income has become much less attractive in recent years. There are several reasons for this:

1 You can no longer get tax relief on a mortgage on a second house. Landlords used to be able to have several mortgages that were all eligible for tax relief, so they made money in two ways, in tax relief and in rents.

2 The mortgage ceiling for tax relief is now £25,000 and there is no guarantee that it will remain this high.

3 When you sell any house or flat which is *not* your principal house, you must pay capital gains tax on any profit you make (see section IV, chapter 1).

4 Rents are taxed very steeply – as unearned income (see section IV, chapter 1).

5 In periods of inflation the costs of upkeep and maintenance have risen sharply, far more sharply than rents as a rule.

6 It is sometimes impossible to get rid of your tenants.

Slowly rising rents and tenants' security of tenure have come about through a series of Rent Acts, starting in 1919. The last one was enacted in 1974. All the Acts have had the same purpose: to give security to tenants and to see that they pay a fair rent. The landlord has come in for little consideration in most of these Acts. For instance, rents stayed frozen from 1939 until almost twenty years later. Landlords were sometimes paying out more on maintenance then they got in rents, unless they were prepared to let their properties fall into a bad state of repair.

Different forms of tenancy

There are various different forms of tenancy:

1   *Fixed term tenancies.* These are for a specific time, whether for as little as a week, or as long as three to five years. Neither landlord nor tenant can terminate them before the end of the period.

2   *Periodic tenancies.* If the tenancy is on a weekly, monthly or quarterly basis, it may be terminated by either side, but note these points about ending a tenancy:

* A minimum of four weeks' notice is absolutely necessary to end any tenancy.
* You may have to give notice for at least the period of the tenancy, unless it is a year.
* You may have to give six months' notice.
* A tenant and landlord may simply agree that the tenancy shall be ended.

3   *Tenancies at will.* These are tenancies where the tenant has agreed in advance to leave when the landlord asks him. This may be difficult to enforce, given the present Rent Acts.

4   *Licences.* These occur when a person is given a right to do specific things on the premises. A lease gives a general right of occupation. The question is whether there is an exclusive right to the premises or not. A lodger, for example, is a licensee; a tenant is not.

Getting possession

If you are a landlord you will find it very difficult to get rid of a tenant who is clean and quiet, pays the rent on time and does not damage your property. These rules apply whether the accommodation is furnished or unfurnished.

If the only way of getting rid of a protected tenant is to offer him money, you are allowed to do this.

You can get possession on several grounds, however:

* If you can prove a tenant has been a bad tenant and caused a nuisance to neighbours, or used the accommodation for immoral purposes.
* If the tenant has damaged the property.
* If the premises have been sub-let without the landlord's permission.
* If the tenant has given notice to quit and withdrawn it after the landlord has re-let or sold the premises.
* If the tenancy is a condition of employment and the tenant leaves the landlord's employ.
* If the landlord needs the house for him or his family to live in. The court will not grant possession if the hardship to the tenant would be greater than that to the landlord.

371

And certain forms of letting do not give the tenant security of tenure:

1   If you let a bedsitter in the house you yourself live in, you can be fairly sure of getting repossession when you want it – as long as you continue to live in the house. Even in these cases, however, the tenant has some rights. He can go to the rent tribunal for a fair rent to be assessed, or he can ask for notice to quit to be extended by up to six months while he looks for somewhere else, and a tribunal will usually grant this, unless the landlord can prove that the tenant is a bad one – not paying rent, damaging the room, etc.

2   If your work takes you abroad for a period and you wish to let your house while you are away, you must tell the tenant in writing that you are the owner-occupier of the house and will be requiring occupancy at the end of the tenancy. Make sure that you get a written acknowledgement that he has received the information.

3   If you have a cottage ready for your retirement and you want to let it meanwhile, you should also give the tenant notice of this before he moves in. Alternatively you can let it to different people for short periods.

4   Holiday lettings are outside the Rent Acts.

5   Some lettings to students are also outside the Rent Acts.

6   Where you provide cleaning, meals or other services.

Fair rents

Getting possession is not the only problem for the landlord. If the accommodation you let has a rateable value of £750 or less outside London, or £1,500 inside it, the rent will be controlled under the Rent Act. This means that only the most expensive houses and flats are outside these controls, and even then the tenant can ask for his lease to be renewed, or his rent reduced, by the rent tribunal.

And then a landlord needs to know how to keep rents rising, so that inflation does not effectively cut his income. This is a very difficult area.

For a start rents are usually constant throughout a lease. When a fixed term ends a landlord may renew it at a higher rent, but if the tenant thinks it is too high he can go to a tribunal and ask to have it lowered. Tribunals fix 'fair' rents. These are not market rents and can be very different from them because no attention is paid to the scarcity of the property in question. *You cannot get rid of or harass in any way a tenant who has had his rent lowered by a tribunal.*

When rent is not paid

If rent is not paid the landlord has the right to take, known as 'distrain', the tenant's goods, and either hold them as security until the rent is paid or sell them to pay it. He cannot, however, take certain personal items such as loose money, clothing, bedding under the value of £50. He must give back to the tenant any proceeds from selling over and above the rent. The consent of a court is required before any goods can be distrained. Eventually, if the rent remains unpaid the landlord can terminate the lease, but this is a fairly long process.

The landlord must write to the tenant, setting out the reason why he has broken the lease. Then either the tenant pays or the landlord can go to court. The court has discretion over whether or not to order that the tenant forfeits the lease. Even if it does, the tenant still has twenty-eight days in which to pay the rent. If he pays he can stay where he is.

The position from the tenant's point of view

If you are a tenant the Rent Acts mostly work in your favour. As long as you are a good tenant – pay your rent, do not damage the premises or upset your neighbours – you can stay for as long as you want provided that:

* The landlord does not live on the premises.
* You get no other services like breakfast or general board or services like cleaning and changing of sheets.
* You do not live in a student's hostel, or holiday accommodation.

You have certain entitlements and obligations under a lease. The landlord cannot, for instance, interfere with your 'quiet enjoyment of the premises'. This has nothing to do with noise, but would apply if your landlord cut your gas or electricity off, or threatened you in any way.

The landlord may or may not be required to do repairs. If you have a full repairing lease you will have to do them all – inside and out. Sometimes the landlord will do outside repairs but not inside ones. Where the rent is under £80 a year in London and £52 elsewhere the landlord is required to do all the repairs, and where the premises are let for less than seven years he usually maintains the outside and essential services. You cannot, of course, expect him to do repairs he does not know about, so it is up to you to tell him.

In return you must pay the rent and treat the premises with reasonable care. Any damage which is done by the tenant or his family must be repaired by them.

Check your lease on all these points. *Repairs can cost a lot of money if you are responsible for them.*

Your lease may allow you to assign it to someone else, or it may not. Generally, even if it does, you will have to have the landlord's agreement that the assigned tenant is acceptable. Leases less than three years long generally do not allow assignment. When you assign you cannot ask for any money for the lease, unless the rateable value of the property is over £750 outside London and £1,500 inside, but you can sell your furniture and fittings. *Take care when you do this not to sell them at an inflated price, because the new tenant can sue and get the excess money back from you.*

Summing up

In view of all these rules and regulations you may well decide that investing in property is not for you. You can always buy property bonds instead (see chapter 5 of this section). That way, you will not have any day-to-day problems.

If, on the other hand, you do decide to go ahead and you want your properties free from time to time, you can gear your letting policy to people who are not likely to stay long.

These include foreign diplomats, executives of overseas companies (make sure the lease goes to the person and not the embassy or the company), and students. None of these is absolutely guaranteed to move, but they are much more likely to than most. Of course, you may have to put up with no tenants from time to time if you cannot find the kind you want immediately.

If you decide to go ahead, take legal advice and read one of the various books which spell out the implications of the Rent Acts in full.

BUYING PROPERTY ABROAD

If you are thinking of buying a second home, you may feel you would like something overseas, to use for holidays now and retirement later.

This can be a good idea, but there are many pitfalls. Property markets abroad are not always so well organized as in the U.K., and do not forget that locals can see a foreigner coming so you may be asked a totally unreasonable price for what you are buying.

If you are thinking of buying abroad, however, the sooner you do it the better. A house is always an asset, wherever it is, and can be sold if you decide later that you do not wish to retire there, or even to use it for holidays. Prices everywhere have been rising in recent years.

The first thing to do is to decide upon the area you are interested in and then take professional advice.

Never buy in a development which is not yet completed, unless you are sure the project is secure, and *never* under any circumstances buy when only the plans are available. Too many people have lost money this way. Don't be caught out. Don't buy anything you haven't seen. If you buy something which needs renovation, check on building costs in the area. Nowhere is cheap anymore.

You can buy property anywhere, and places like Fiji, the Seychelles and the Caribbean are becoming more and more popular. For the moment, however, most British people will buy in Europe, so let's take a look at that.

Buying in Europe

You will find, first of all, that the costs of buying and selling tend to be higher in continental Europe than in the U.K. An estate agent may charge both buyer and seller, the former about 3 per cent and the latter about 5 per cent. On top of that come legal costs and various government charges, which will generally include V.A.T. on the total cost of the property.

The legal process will be conducted through a notary, and transactions are not valid unless carried out in front of one. The purchase is achieved through a formal agreement settled between the parties beforehand, which is then endorsed in front of the notary. Make sure that the seller has full title to the property you are buying, or later on you may find that you have not bought it at all.

You may be able to get a mortgage to help with the payment, but if you do you will find interest rates far higher than in the U.K. Few countries have a mortgage system as good as that of the United Kingdom; it is rare to get an advance abroad for more than 50 per cent of the price of the property. Not only that, you are unlikely to get tax relief on a local mortgage, even if you live there, and you won't, generally, if you are still resident in the U.K.

For this reason, most people who buy property abroad pay cash, unless some kind of group mortgage scheme is available for a large-scale modern development – though it is sometimes possible to get a mortgage in Britain for a purchase overseas and then qualify for tax relief on the interest paid.

There are various schemes. One such has been started by the Save and Prosper Group of unit trusts. S. & P. Villa Developments give ten-year mortgages. The money is paid back through an endowment insurance policy, so both the loan interest and the premium qualify for tax relief. At present this scheme is limited to the Algarve and Minorca, and loans are based on up to half the sterling price or 60 per cent of the S. & P. valuation.

Owners Services runs a scheme with the Scottish Life Assurance Company, under which it is possible to get a first mortgage, a second mortgage, a re-mortgage or a secured bank loan.

Schemes like these seem bound to increase as European countries get more closely interlinked and there is more interchange of personnel between European companies.

The dollar premium

The next step is to get the money out of the U.K. This makes the purchase far more expensive than just the price of the house or flat and the legal costs added together, because all money transferred from the U.K., unless it is to one of the scheduled territories (Isle of Man, Channel Islands, Gibraltar or the Republic of Ireland), must be bought with 'property dollars'. This is a special pool of currency which is usually acquired through a merchant bank from foreign money which has been accumulated from the sale of investments and property abroad.

There is always money available, but the 'premium' – that is, the extra which you have to pay to get hold of the currency – depends upon the level of demand and how much is in the pool at any one time.

In recent years the position has become very complicated. As the pound sterling has 'floated', its value has changed every day, so that the true price of whatever you are buying abroad will depend on the level of the dollar premium and of the pound on the particular day you buy your property dollars.

There is a formula for working out the extra. This is always done in U.S. dollars, and the calculation is based on the last time the pound was fixed – at \$2.60 to £1. Take 100 plus the quoted investment premium on any one day, and multiply it by the current pound-dollar exchange rate. Divide this by 2.60 minus 100. Say the premium is quoted at 75 per cent and sterling at \$1.80, the calculation is:

$$100 + 75 \times 1.80 = 315 \div 2.60 - 100 = 21.2 \text{ per cent}$$

The true premium will be 21.2 per cent not 75 per cent. This means that if the asking price for the property is £10,000 it will actually cost you £12,120. You will have to pay this premium not only on the house but also for any structural alterations which may be needed. This can be important if you are renovating a very old house with few amenities. Furniture purchases must also go through the property dollar market.

Any running costs, however, may be allowed at the ordinary rate of exchange without incurring the premium. These include regular painting, electricity and gas costs, insurance and any local taxes.

Eventually the problem of the dollar premium should disappear, at least as far as E.E.C. countries are concerned, but meanwhile prices might well rise rather more than the premium. In any case, for the time being you will have to reconcile yourself to the fact that as far as buying property abroad is concerned, the British are always at a price disadvantage because of the low value of sterling.

EMIGRATING

If you are emigrating – that is, leaving the country permanently to live somewhere else – the regulations concerning the money you can take with you are quite different. You cannot simply go to the bank, draw out all your money, and take it with you. There are strict rules which you must follow.

All transactions go through the Bank of England. To begin with the Bank has three different sets of rules:

1 *Scheduled territories.* If you are going to a scheduled territory, you are free to take as much as you wish. They are treated for exchange control purposes as part of the United Kingdom. Today they include the Isle of Man, the Channel Isles, Gibraltar and the Republic of Ireland.

2 *Overseas sterling areas.* If you are going to an overseas sterling area, each family unit can take out up to £20,000 for the first four years. A family unit is a husband, wife and any children under eighteen. In addition to the £20,000, they may each take a travel allowance of up to £300 in travellers cheques and £25 in sterling notes, and household goods, personal effects and motor cars, provided these are strictly for the use of the family. Overseas sterling areas include all the old colonial countries – for example, Cyprus and Malta – but not Canada and the territories which were originally under British protection.

3 *Anywhere else.* The rules are the same as for the overseas sterling areas, except that you may only take £5,000.

If at any time in the four years you wish to take out more money you will have to buy the necessary amounts of foreign currency through investment currency market.

After four years, any remaining assets you have here are no longer 'blocked', and you can apply to the Bank of England for their release. These assets can include pensions, annuities, income from investments, or rent from houses and land.

The reason why you have to wait four years is that the Bank of England wants to be certain that you are genuinely emigrating, not just saying that you are in order to get all your money abroad.

There are certain exceptions to these rules: if anyone in the family unit is over retirement age, the £20,000 allowance will be given anywhere. And if you have medical reasons for living abroad and can prove them to the satisfaction of the Bank, they may let you take more than £5,000 to places outside the overseas sterling areas. But they will expect proof, and convincing proof, before agreeing.

Finally, do not attempt to smuggle money abroad. *If you get caught the penalties are severe and all your money may be confiscated.*

LIVING ABROAD

Before you even think of living abroad check on the rules and regulations governing your residence there, and consider the following points:

1 How much time will you want to spent abroad? Any money you get from letting your property while you are not actually living there must be declared as income to the taxman in the U.K.

2 Is your income sufficient? Some countries insist that you have a minimum regular income before allowing you to become resident. Try the embassy of the country for information on this.

3 What is the tax position? Britain has a double tax relief agreement with some countries. This means that overall you may pay less tax. In some places there are no taxes at all. Detailed information is available from Overseas Territories Income Tax Office, 26 Grosvenor Gardens, London S.W.1.

4 What will your personal living costs be in the country of your choice? Will you want many trips back home? Can you grow your own produce? What things can you not do without? Think about this very seriously, because all your plans will come to nothing and you may lose a great deal of money if you find you cannot manage.

5 What about insurance? The cost of medical treatment outside the U.K. can be very high. Do you need insurance to cover it? Remember that the older you get, the more likely you are to need medical treatment. Have you got your house and its fittings properly insured?

6 Will you need a car, or will local transport do? If you have to have a car, check the tax situation if you take a car from the U.K.

7 Do you need a permit if you want to be a permanent resident?

8 Have you insured yourself against a change in the political climate? There can be changes wherever you go to live and foreign residents may not always be welcome. You can insure yourself against this, but it is likely to cost you money, about £1.50 for every £100 worth of assets you insure. It's probably cheaper to cut your losses and run if the worst happens.

The best book of advice on buying property abroad is *Overseas Property Guide* by Arthur Bowers, who is property correspondent of the *Daily Telegraph* and the *Sunday Telegraph*. It will give you a lot of the background, but there is no substitute for your own personal involvement in the buying process.

Chapter 8

OTHER INVESTMENTS

You may decide that you do not want to invest in property or shares or anything else where money is exchanged for a piece of paper which guarantees rights or benefits, or both, to its holders. Yet you may still want to invest in something.

There are many other fields in which sound investments can be made, ranging from stamps to antiques and paintings. Whatever you decide to buy, there will be a number of excellent books to help you. This chapter is intended simply to put forward general advice in just some of the possible areas. No recommendations will be made: for these you must go to an expert in your chosen field.

You can collect almost anything and there is a chance that it will appreciate in value – though of course it may not. If this happens with, say, your antiques, you will just have to use them as furniture in your home. If you are a beginner with not much money try to spot the next vogue. Always buy things you think are attractive. Beautifully made objects in almost any field can go out of fashion, but they always return after a few years. Meanwhile you can buy at low prices. The year 1977, for example, saw a vast number of jugs, plates, ornaments and general bric-à-brac to mark the Queen's Silver Jubilee. If past experience of such occasions is any guide, in a few years these ornaments will be selling at high premiums on their purchase prices.

Royal occasions of all kinds have been celebrated in this way in the past, and almost all the souvenirs produced have turned out to be good investments – if fairly modest ones. This is because they are usually produced in limited editions – that is, a fixed number only. Inevitably many get lost and broken; then the souvenirs become rare, and their prices rise.

Limited editions of all kinds are produced for these occasions – books, medallions, pots, plaques, lithographs, almost anything in the ornamental line. Not all of them become worth a great deal of money, but some do. They are rarely a profitable short-term investment. If you buy something new today, think in terms of your grandchildren benefiting.

But there are all kinds of frauds. A limited edition might not be as limited as is claimed. Beware of the claims made by glossy advertisements. Check before buying if you possibly can.

THE BEST INVESTMENTS

What are the best investments then? The most reliable guide is to see what auctioneers think. Here is how Phillips of London view what will be sound hedges against inflation, bought at present prices:

Items under £500

* Books – Victorian cookery books.
* Carpets and rugs – Caucasian rugs, smaller rugs and saddlebags.
* Ceramics and glass – English blue and white, eighteenth-century continental figures, good early eighteenth-century baluster glasses, miniatures.
* Clocks and art objects – English and French nineteenth-century.
* Jewellery and watches – gold bracelets, Victorian and Edwardian small diamond brooches, good Victorian level watches.
* Oriental art – ivories
* Paintings, watercolours, prints – old master drawings and prints. And good modern British painting is underpriced.
* Pewter.
* Silver, gold and plate – small, good pieces of Georgian silver, including boxes, spoons and plate.
* Textiles, art nouveau and deco – Gallé glass, metal toys.

Items from £500 to £2,000

* Books – good travel and exploration books.
* Carpets and rugs – Persian.
* Ceramics and glass – good quality Worcester, Minton and Coalport vases by reputable artists, finely engraved commemorative glass.
* Clocks and art objects – bracketed and long case clocks, good bronzes.
* Jewellery and watches – good diamond rings, Fabergé.
* Oriental art – oriental swords and sword fittings.
* Paintings, watercolours, prints – old master paintings and drawings, fine engravings.
* Silver, gold and plate – eighteenth century continental silver, including flatware and candlesticks.
* Textiles art nouveau and deco – art deco bronze and ivory figures, art nouveau jewellery.
* Wood carvings.

BUYING ANTIQUES

There is such a wide choice when it comes to buying antiques that it is difficult to know where to start. If you are serious about collecting, it is best to stick to one particular kind of piece, or period. That way you will build up your knowledge and have a better chance of picking up something really good than if you dabble about here and there. Here are some useful tips for you to follow:

1   Start off by trying to *find a kind of antique that appeals to you personally*. One of the nice things about antiques, as opposed to bank notes or share certificates, is that they can be put on show in your home while they make money for you. It seems a pity to collect Spode china, for example, if you don't like it yourself.

2   In choosing an area, you should also try to *find one that has not been over-exploited before*. For example, 1890s posters, blue and white printed earthenware, and English literary autographs are still in some expert's opinions undervalued. You then have the chance of pioneering a collection with a relatively low outlay.

3   If possible, approach your collecting in an orderly and professional way. *Keep a book as a 'catalogue'*, entering for each item everything you can find out about it – where bought, for how much, previous owners, previous appearances in sales, etc. This catalogue will be invaluable when you come to sell the collection. It can be handed over to the auctioneer and will help him in making *his* catalogue.

You should also have each major piece photographed. These photos can then be used in the eventual sale catalogue; they will also, like the catalogue, be of immense use if by an unhappy chance your collection is stolen. In that case the catalogue and pictures can be given to the police immediately.

4   *Never buy damaged pieces*. If you do, you will soon find that what to the seller is an 'honourable scar' or 'hairline crack' becomes magnified into a 'bloody great piece broken off', or simply 'A.F.' ('all faults'), in the auctioneer's catalogue.

5   If you are not used to buying antiques, and have no great knowledge of them, it will save you money in the long run to *operate through a reliable dealer*, accepting his advice on which pieces to buy and letting him bid for you in the auction rooms.

Whatever the dealers' associations say, the 'ring' still operates in many sales, and, while in no way wanting to encourage this nefarious practice, you will come to grief if you run counter to it and antagonize the dealers. Let the wily professional take the strain. The commission you pay him will be justified.

6   Nevertheless, the best way of collecting antiques is to *make yourself an expert in what you are collecting*. Do your homework: read books on the subject, visit museums and attend sales. It could become a delightful hobby which will not only make you money but also stop you dying of boredom after you retire.

Buying and selling at auctions

You can buy your pieces from a shop or a dealer, but you may like to try your hand at buying in an auction. Anything can be auctioned, even property; some auctioneers specialize in one particular range of goods.

If you do want to try buying at an auction first go to several simply to study the techniques. Buying at auctions involves skill, if you are not going to lose what you want or find yourself paying a ridiculous price for it.

When you are beginning you can always ask a dealer to buy for you. Put a price limit on what you want to buy and watch how he goes about it.

When you buy at an auction you compete with other prospective buyers and the object goes to the person who names the highest price. You do not usually have to pay anything to buy, but recently some auctioneers have split the commission they expect for auctioning an item – usually 10 per cent – between the buyer and the seller. Previously only the seller paid.

One problem with buying at an auction is that the quality of the goods purchased is not guaranteed under the Supply of Goods (Implied Terms) Act, 1973. But you might be able to claim under the Misrepresentation Act of 1967, if you feel you were told a deliberate lie about the item you have bought. Supposing a chair is described as a genuine Chippendale and when you get it home it is clearly a fake. In that case, you may be able to claim your money back. (For more about auction law, turn to section VI, chapter 3).

If you are selling you must get the item to the auctioneers in time for it to go into the catalogue. If you wish you can set a reserve price below which you do not wish to sell. If the item does not reach the reserve it is withdrawn from the sale and either sent back to you or put in another time – when you can change the reserve if you wish.

COLLECTING SILVER

One of the most pleasant aspects of collecting silver is that you can use and enjoy your investment at the same time as it is growing in value for you. Some pieces of antique silver, especially when they are of particular historical interest, fetch very high prices and are just for the wealthy collector, but silver is also good for the beginner because there is a wide range of items to be had at prices from a few pounds up.

Silver is not as valuable as gold, but it has proved a good investment for many people. What makes it especially attractive is that with British silver at any rate, you know what you are buying because of the hallmark. Gold, of course, is also hallmarked.

Rule number one, then, is know what you are buying. Is it silver, and if so, what kind? If it is British silver (or gold) it will carry a hallmark. This is a measure of the standard of the precious metal and was introduced in London in 1238 (in 1975 hallmarking was extended to include platinum). Silver which passed the Goldsmiths' Guild test was marked with a leopard's head. The marks developed, and today there are four Assay Offices in the United Kingdom – in London, Birmingham, Sheffield and Edinburgh – (there is one in Dublin too) which authenticate silver, gold and platinum. Formerly there were a number of other Assay Offices.

The hallmark is a row of small letters and pictures stamped into the metal. Together these tell you how old the silver is and who made it. It also includes the Assay Office mark which identifies the particular office at which the article was tested and marked, and the standard mark which denotes that the precious metal content is not less than the standard indicated. A 'lion passant', for instance, appears on every piece of sterling silver. It faces left holding a paw in the air (when it faces right is means it came from Newcastle and was made in the years from 1721 to 1727 only). Sterling silver is 92.5 per cent pure silver; the rest is metal alloy. There are also marks which commemorate special events. The illustration below is an example of a complete hallmark, including the 1977—Silver Jubilee comemorative mark. It shows the sponsor's mark, followed by the mark for sterling silver, the London Assay Office mark, the date letter for 1977, and the 1977 Silver Jubilee mark.

The illustrations on p. 384, reproduced by courtesy of the Assay Offices of Great Britain, give the pre- and post-1975 standard marks and Assay Office marks for silver, gold and platinum.

Continental silver is less easy to identify. It often has a lower silver content than sterling silver, perhaps as little as 80 per cent. This cannot legally be sold as silver in Britain, but it may be worth buying as an antique or collector's piece. Any silver which came into the country after 1842 had to be assayed and hallmarked so that people knew what they were buying. The best bargains in continental silver are from Spain or Portugal, though Dutch is popular with buyers.

There are many books on silver and its hallmarks. If you use one, you can easily tell whether the piece you are thinking of buying is one of those prized by collectors.

Get your silver valued for insurance purposes. There is no laid down

Standard Mark

British Articles

Prior to 1975	Standard	From 1975
	22 carat gold Marked in England Marked in Scotland	916
	18 carat gold Marked in England Marked in Scotland	750
	14 carat gold	585
	9 carat gold	375
	Sterling silver Marked in England Marked in Scotland	
	Britannia silver	
—	Platinum	

Imported Articles

Prior to 1975		From 1975
916	22 carat gold	916
750	18 carat gold	750
585	14 carat gold	585
375	9 carat gold	375
925	Sterling silver	925
958	Britannia silver	958
—	Platinum	950

Assay Office Mark

British Articles

Prior to 1975	Assay Office	From 197
gold & Sterling silver — Britannia silver	London	gold, silver & platinum
gold — silver	Birmingham	gold & platinum — silver
gold — silver	Sheffield	gold, silver platinum
gold & silver	Edinburgh	gold & silver

Notes – (i) Some variations in the surrounding shields are found before 1975. (ii) All Assay Offices mark Britannia silver but only London (prior to 1975) had a special Assay Office mark for this standard.

Imported Articles

Prior to 1975		Assay Office	From 19	
gold	silver		gold & silver	plat
		London	unchanged	
		Birmingham	unchanged	
		Sheffield	unchanged	
		Edinburgh	unchanged	

fee for valuation, but as a general guide you will pay something like £2 basic fee, plus 1 per cent of the valuation up to £20,000, plus 20p an article after the first item.

Don't go wandering into a shop asking a dealer to make you an offer to get an idea of the value. He will give you a price which will allow for a profit for him on resale, so you may be very disappointed at how low he rates your treasure, which may well have a higher insurance value.

Silver plate

Silver isn't always what it seems to be. Very often it is silver plate. This consists of a coating of silver on copper, and the process has been used for over 200 years. Even though its worth in silver is small, pieces of silver plate *can* be valuable as collector's items. Like silver, it is hallmarked, often including the letters E.P.N.S., which simply means electroplated nickel silver.

COLLECTING BANK NOTES

Your money may well be worth more than its face value, and collecting bank notes can prove quite a profitable hobby. Pre-decimilization notes, for instance, which are in 'very fine' condition – that is, showing no signs of wear – can be sold at a premium of about 10 per cent. This means that the old 10s note may sell for 55p, and the old £1 note for £1.10.

Obviously this sort of profit is only worthwhile if you deal in large amounts. There are some quite recent notes, however, which fetch much better prices, particularly where there are oddities in the water-marking or the serial numbers or where only a small number of those particular notes were issued. Some £1 notes issued in 1967, for instance, are fetching up to £8.

Any Bank of England notes issued before 1900 are valuable. They are fairly rare and may be worth more than £100 each. When you get this far back the actual denomination of the note ceases to have any impact on the price; it is the rarity value which is important. If you go back as far as the eighteenth century, prices run between £100 and £2,000.

Some of the Treasury notes issued in the 1914-18 War and known as 'Bradburys' sell at between fifty and a hundred times their face value. Other Treasury notes, which were withdrawn in 1928 when the Bank of England took over the issue of notes, command good prices. Specimens signed by C.P. Mahone or B.G. Catterns are worth buying. The £5 notes are worth more than £20 today.

COLLECTING STAMPS

Unlike collecting gems, antiques or silver, which can be very expensive, we can all have a go at stamp collecting. There can be few people who did not try this hobby as a child, but for adult collectors it is a very serious business. Like collecting gems and antiques, stamp collecting has been more rewarding for the investor in recent years than either the stock market or bank deposits.

But, as with all collecting, you have to know what you are doing. Stanley Gibbons – the best known British dealers, who produce annual catalogues – say that nothing after 1930 is worth the serious collector's attention, apart from a few exceptions which for one reason or another have become scarce. *Rarity is all in stamp collecting.* Here are a few examples of pieces at 1976 levels:

* 1922 2½d British Empire Exhibition, worth £100.
* 1957 1d or 9½d Scout Jamboree, worth £10 each.
* 1958 2s British Empire Games, worth £16.
* 1963 1d or 5½d Freedom from Hunger, worth £20 each.
* 1974 28p Churchill Centenary, worth £2.

If you find you have some of these stamps tucked away and want to sell, you must knock at least 25 per cent off these prices. Remember that catalogue prices are dealers' *selling* prices not buying prices. If you have a few hundred pounds to spend Stanley Gibbons runs a general investment advisory service. Experience shows, however, that major discoveries by amateurs have always been rare and are virtually non-existent today.

First day covers have been popular with serious stamp collectors for years. Until recently these were simply stamps with a postmark showing the date they were issued. They were often good investments.

Today they have become an industry, and the post office sells the stamps on fancy envelopes with a special postmark. As more and more people have begun buying first day covers, they have become devalued, and it is more difficult to make a profit on them. First day covers can be provided by the post office for a few pence above the face value of the stamps, but some dealers have recently started offering a more fancy service for providing covers for clients which can cost a considerable amount of money and – more important – may be a doubtful invest-ment. If you buy first day covers:

* Either use the post office or buy and post the stamps yourself, or use a recognized stamp dealer.
* Buy a complete set.
* Make sure you are not paying for an envelope rather than the stamps themselves.

Generally, if you choose correctly, you ought to make money on stamps. Prices have risen steadily. A random selection of twenty-four rare stamps showed an annual increase in catalogue value of 20.5 per cent in the decade 1966-76. In 1975-76 – a difficult year – the catalogue value increased by 29.5 per cent.

INVESTING IN GEMS

Many people have been badly caught investing in gems. For example, people who bought those little packages of diamonds which the buyer is not supposed to open for a period after purchase, otherwise he cannot get his money back later on sale, even if the price of diamonds has gone up in the meantime. If you see one of these schemes – now fortunately rare – ignore it.

You really need a great deal of money to invest in gems. The small stones in most rings are not worth a great deal. These should be bought just for pleasure.

Diamonds consistently do well, but the coloured gems have done even better in recent years. The prices of fine sapphires have gone up almost ten time over the last five years, emeralds six times and rubies three times. If you have a few thousand pounds needed for a really good one-carat gem (a carat weighs 0.2 grams) you can expect to make a profit of around 50 per cent a year, because good quality gems are in short supply and more people are keeping their best stones rather than selling them for currency, which is falling in value.

Take expert advice before you buy. A bad stone may be worth only about a tenth as much as a good one. Colour, clarity and cut are the keys, and only the very skilled can judge.

Size, which is what matters if you are investing, is of no significance until you reach half a carat for diamonds, two carats for rubies, four for sapphires and one for emeralds.

In Britain most dealing is done through London's Hatton Garden, where about fifty merchants operate. If you are sensible you will buy through them and not through advertisements from private people.

This is a very conservative trade, but new dealers have been emerging recently who will buy for you at trade price plus commission. Look out for them.

The London Diamond Bourse and the London Diamond Club are two places where you will find reputable gem 'brokers'. They do not normally deal with the general public, but individual brokers will sometimes advise.

There is little possibility of a properly supervised and managed diamond 'fund' for smaller investors because of the problems of grading diamonds. There are a number of different assessment scales in the world, and much depends on the experts' view. If such a fund could be set up it would also assist in selling and would cut down the excessive profit margins to which small investors are subjected.

INVESTING IN WINE

There can be few wine drinkers who do not think at some time of 'laying down' some bottles of wine as an investment.

First, you must think about where to store it. In some cases the merchant or shipper will be prepared to do that for you, and that has the advantage that you will then have no temptation to nip down and deplete your investment by drinking the occasional bottle.

You may prefer to keep it at home, however, if you have suitable space available. Wines like to be kept in dark, cool places, but modern houses are rarely built with the cellars which suit wines so well. In fact the actual temperature is not that important, as long as it does not go over 70°F or below 40°F. What is important is that the temperature should not vary much. All wine will go off if the temperature keeps changing sharply. Lie the bottles on their sides. This prevents the cork from shrinking and letting in air.

If you do start a cellar, whether in your own home or at the shippers, always keep a book of your purchases. This should record the name of the wine, the name of the shipper, the year, the price, the quantity bought, any comments on it, and the earliest and latest maturity dates. You do not have to keep your wine till maturity, however. It is saleable at any stage along the way.

Wine buying can be fun. It is not too expensive, if you buy the wine young and then leave it to mature. But it does have its risks, and these should not be under-rated.

The logic behind investing in wine seems sound. Some wines are ready for drinking very soon after they are made. Others go on improving if they are kept – sometimes for up to fifty years. And as they improve they rise in price. In theory then you only have to pick the right wine and your profit will follow automatically.

In practice it does not always work out like that. Wine prices do not always rise as expected. Perhaps there turns out to be too much of a particular kind at a particular time, or, as it matures, its taste does not fulfil its early promise. So wine buying is as much a risk as any other kind of investment – though if the worst comes to the worst you can always drink it.

Only the best wines are worth laying down. On the whole these are French wines, with a few from Germany and a very few from Austria and Italy.

Vintages vary from year to year from superb to bad, and any graduation in between. You will need a wine shipper's advice as to what is worth buying in any particular year.

Champagne also comes in vintages. In some years when quality is poor no vintage is declared, but there are also non-vintage champagnes produced every year. Even good non-vintage champagne will improve for some time after it has been shipped. Vintage champagnes are not sold until they are five years old.

Port also comes in vintage and non-vintage years, each individual shipper deciding for himself whether a particular year will be a vintage one for him. The quality varies enormously from year to year, and the length of time it takes to reach maturity also varies. The 1963 vintage, for instance, which was regarded as very good, will not really be ready for drinking until 1980. Anyone who bought in the early years can expect a good profit.

Most people are mainly interested in quite straightforward wines, however. Here, by area rather than by year, are some examples of the average length of time it takes wines to mature. All cheaper wines may improve with time, but most can be drunk at once.

France
* Alsace: the better reserves and 'grand vins' will improve for up to about six years.
* Loire: there is a great variety and no 'average' maturing period. Some sweeter wines will last fifty years, and others deteriorate quite quickly.
* Red Bordeaux: five years is a minimum, but some wines last for fifty years or more. Middle quality wines improve for about twenty years.
* White Bordeaux: ten to fifteen years.
* Red Burgundy: there is a great variety here, some wines are for early drinking, some later. Take the advice of a wine merchant or shipper.
* White burgundy: well-balanced vintages improve for up to ten years. Most vintages also have light wines which are ready for drinking almost immediately.
* Red Rhone: vintages from the north keep longer than those from the south. Best ones keep for twenty years or more.

Germany
* Mosel: these wines are often drunk young, but improve if kept for a year. Some will keep up to fifteen years.
* Rhine: almost all of these wines are good to drink after two or three years. Some improve for ten years, but bottles more than seven years old are unusual.

You can see from this brief list that there are many varieties within each region. Add to that the differing qualities and quantities each year, and it is easy to see that buying as an investment is not always as easy as it might appear. *You must get expert advice.*

Chapter 9

PROVIDING FOR YOUR RETIREMENT

It is never too soon to think about providing for your old age. Start in your early twenties if possible; the longer you leave it, the more it will cost. If you think that twenty is too soon, think of how we pay our national insurance contributions from the moment we go out to work, and that is for the barest minimum pension at retirement age.

If you are going to augment the state pension with schemes of your own, the longer the period you do it over, the greater your chances of achieving a pension somewhere near your old salary levels.

Suppose you are a married man and you want to retire on an income of about two thirds of your pre-retirement salary; you want that income to be inflation-proof, and you want your wife to have a continuing income should you die before her. To achieve this you will have to have to hand at the end of your working life between seven and ten years' pay. Yet it is impossible to say what that sum will actually be, because no one knows what the rate of inflation will be. All we know is that between 10 and 20 plus per cent has been normal in the past few years.

In this chapter we are going to see how these very reasonable aims can be achieved. Let's start with the state pension, which we all get if we have been working.

THE STATE PENSION SCHEME

A new state pension scheme starts in April 1978. It is commonly called the Castle scheme, because it was introduced by Mrs Barbara Castle when she was Minister of Social Security; it was part of the Social Security Pensions Act of 1975.

This scheme provides a new formula for state pensions (though a similar one proposed by Sir Keith Joseph when the Conservatives were in power (1971-74) died when Labour was returned to office). What is new about the scheme is that it provides not only a basic pension for everyone who has contributed but on top of that a further, varying, slice of pension. This slice depends on extra contributions, which are related to the size of your income, and is known as 'the flexible tier'. This relates only to contributions made after April 1978.

Today there are very few people, except women who have never worked or married women who have chosen to be 'contracted out', who do not qualify for a state pension. The basic pension has gone to the employed, the self-employed and even the unemployed, if the necessary national insurance contributions have been paid. Payment has been compulsory since 1948, so there are very few people still working who have not paid enough.

The state scheme divides the state pension into four parts:

1   *The flat-rate state pension.* At present this goes up a little most years. From November 1977 it will be £17.50 for a single person and £28 for a married couple. This adds up to £910 and £1,456 a year, clearly a rock-bottom income. Unless you have no fixed outgoings except food and fuel, you are likely to be poor, if this is absolutely all you have.

To qualify for the flat-rate pension you must have paid contributions from the age of eighteen to retiring age. Students are exempt, and anyone who was over eighteen when the national insurance scheme started in 1948 is exempt as far as the period before 1948 is concerned, provided they kept up their payments until they retired. There is a three-year qualifying period, but there can be few people alive who retired before 1951. If you have been sick or registered unemployed you will have been credited at the time with your national insurance contributions. If you have failed to pay for any part of the time, your pension will be scaled down accordingly. If you are going abroad for any considerable time, you should take steps to see that you are covered, if you want the full pension when you retire.

2   *The flexible tier*, or Castle scheme, which will only apply to people who retire after April 1978. And is only for those employed by other people; if you are self-employed you will have to make other arrangements, or you will find yourself with only the basic pension when you retire.

Employers have the option of contracting out of this scheme, if they already have a suitable company pension scheme. But even where there is a company scheme, some employers have decided to contract in so as to give their employees the benefit of both schemes. In this case the employer may scale down the employee's contributions to the company scheme, and also his benefits.

The flexible tier formula is complicated, and it is difficult to tell how much you will get when you retire. Here is an example. To make it clear it has been necessary to keep it very simple, so it is probably an over-simplification in comparison with most real life cases.

The man who is twenty-five in 1978 pays into the Castle scheme for forty years, until he is sixty-five. At the end of this period he will be entitled to a pension of 25 per cent of that part of his earnings between one and seven times the single person's flat-rate state pension. This means that he gets 1/160th of that part of his income for each year he contributes. However, a man of forty-five or over with twenty years or less to work to retirement would get 1/80th for each year he contributes.

This is because the scheme is related to a quarter of 'average' weekly earnings. At the start of the scheme maturity is put at twenty years; after that, it will be the average of the best twenty years.

This kind of scheme differs from a normal company's final salary pension scheme (see later in the chapter) because the Castle scheme is not based on final salary. A company scheme might give you 40/60ths or 66.7 per cent of *final* pay for forty years of service, whereas the Castle scheme will only produce 40/160ths or 25 per cent of revalued earnings between one and seven times the flat-rate state pension.

Assume the 25-year-old man earning £60 a week joins the scheme in 1978, and that the flat-rate state pension for a single person is then £20 a week. The pension earned during the year 1978-79 (assuming regular weekly earnings throughout) is 1/160th x £40, which is 25p. This 25p will be revalued each year in line with an earnings factor which will be announced by the minister each year and which is supposed to enable the 25p to keep pace with inflation.

If the man had no further pay increases and there was no inflation over the next forty years – both highly unlikely – the employee would get 40 x 25p, or £10 a week, when he was sixty-five.

But although the annual revaluation provides protection against inflation, it makes no allowance for a higher salary through promotion. In contrast, as I have already said, most company schemes are now based on *final* salary. An employee might start with half the national average earnings but finish up with earnings of four times the national average. The 1/160th or 1/80th which he earned in his first year of service still provides 1/20th of his pension when he retires at the end of his career.

Unlike the majority of private schemes, no money is invested to underwrite future demands under the Castle scheme. The scheme is financed on a pay-as-you-go basis from the flexible national insurance contribution, which means that your future pension rights are vulnerable to changes in the ratio between the numbers of people who have retired to the numbers still at work. Future Castle pensions are also vulnerable to changes in government pension policy, as are all state pensions.

An employee who is contracted out of the Castle flexible tier must get better benefits (the contracting out rules stipulate this). Further, employees' contributions to a company scheme will normally qualify for expenses relief, whereas no such tax relief is available on contributions to Castle. It is therefore likely that most employees will prefer to be contracted out of Castle. However, the contracting out terms are complicated. There is a system of rebates for employers and employees, and this rebate system may make it financially advantageous for young employees to contract out and for older employees to contract in.

Some employers have decided that the whole contracting out exercise is not worth the time and trouble and run their own pension schemes entirely on top of Castle. Others have decided to cut back their own company schemes to compensate for benefits being provided under Castle and also to compensate to some extent for the increased contributions which Castle would require both from employers and employees. Care should be taken to make sure that employees are not totally overburdened by pension contributions.

3 *The state graduated scheme.* This applies to relatively few people. It was introduced in 1961 and discontinued in 1975. When you retire you will be entitled to any pension which you earned during this period. Not everyone was involved in the scheme. Some companies, for example, only contracted women employees in, as they were often not eligible for the company pension. (This no longer applies; company pension schemes must now be open to women on equal terms.)

The amount you will eventually get – or are getting, if you have already retired – depends on your weekly or monthly earnings during the period and whether you were 'contracted out' of the scheme for any part of the period. In any case you are unlikely to get much from the scheme. The Department of Health and Social Security issued certificates telling you how many 'units' you had standing to your credit. Each unit was worth 2½p a week, £1.30 a year. No one is going to get rich on amounts like that.

4 *Supplementary benefits.* These only go to the very poor and are designed to bring the money they have available to spend above the poverty level. Basically, it has been recognized that the flat-rate pension is not enough to live on, and those who do not have money from any other source are entitled to a supplementary benefit level of £17.90 for a single person and £28.35 for a married couple, plus an allowance for rent and rates.

A married couple with only the normal flat-rate pension of £28.00 and paying £10 in rent and rates would be entitled to supplementary benefits to bring the basic pension up to £38.35 – that is 35p (to reach the £28.35 minimum) plus £10 for rent and rates.

Every case is dealt with on its merits. Your assets will be assessed – how much you have in the bank, whether you own your house, whether you have any investments. Do not think, though, that you can rely on supplementary benefits to see you through, rather than making some arrangements of your own. You will still be badly off, even at the maximum benefit levels.

Until 1975 pensions were paid for partly out of the flat-rate national insurance stamp and partly by graduated contributions. From April 1975 national insurance stamps were done away with, except for the self-employed. Social security contributions are now expressed as a percentage of earnings – again with the exception of the self-employed, who still have to stamp cards.

Investing

The rates of state social security contributions can be increased virtually any time, but the following rates are a useful indicator. The percentages are percentages of the employee's earnings.

date	employee contribution	employer contribution	total percentage of earnings
August 1975	5.50%	8.50%	14%
April 1976	5.75%	8.75%	14.5%
April 1977	5.75%	10.75%	17.5%
April 1978	6.75%	12.25%	19%*

*The 1978 contributions are for employees participating in the Castle scheme.

It is not compulsory in law to retire at sixty or sixty-five, but your company may insist that you do and it is at these ages that you become eligible for a state pension. If you are able to defer your retirement, and you want and are capable of going on earning, you will get a bigger pension when you eventually do retire.

You can draw your pension if you wish, however, even though you are still working – though if you are a woman aged between sixty and sixty-five or a man between sixty-five and seventy your pension will be reduced if you are earning more than £40 a week. If this is the case it is probably best to defer taking up the pension until you actually retire.

How to claim your pension

As you near sixty (woman) or sixty-five (man), you should take steps to register your claim to a pension, so that it begins to be paid the moment you retire. As a rule the Department of Health and Social Security writes to everyone entitled to a pension, enclosing a claim form. *If you have not received this three months before you retire, make enquiries at your local social security office.*

If you are a married woman and are entitled to a pension in your own right, you must make a separate application. If, on the other hand, you are claiming a pension on your husband's contributions you must still make a separate claim and give notice of your retirement, even if you do not work outside the home. You cannot claim on your husband's contributions before he is sixty-five and retired. Fill in the form immediately and send it back. If you do not claim your pension, or notify the Ministry of your retirement, your pension will be delayed and you may lose benefit.

The form will ask you to state the date of your retirement. It will be either the day you stop working, if you are over sixty or sixty-five, or your actual birthday if you are retiring on that date. Give the day on which you wish to be treated as if you had retired, assuming that you will be taking up the pension, even though you are still working when you fill in the form.

Your pension will normally be paid in advance weekly at any post office. If this is inconvenient, however, you can arrange for it to be paid in arrears four-weekly or quarterly, by a crossed order which you must pay into a bank account. If you prefer this way, ask the local social security office for form NI. 105, which gives all the details.

The Ministry of Health and Social Security has issued a leaflet, NI. 15, which explains all your pension rights in detail. It is free from any local social security office and can be found in many post offices as well.

A final point: do claim your pension. You may feel you do not need it and that you do not want to live on the charity of the state. This is foolish: *you are entitled to your pension and you have been paying for it – or your husband has – over many years.*

Is the Castle scheme with us forever?

There have been many different schemes since state pensions were first introduced by Lloyd George in 1908. Then the rate for men was 25p a week, and 50p for a married couple. This was the first time the state had recognized the need for some government assistance to the aged.

There was no change in principle until 1948. Then the Beveridge pension scheme arrived, along with a package of other benefits which were the foundation of the welfare state as we know it today. These included unemployment and sickness benefits, death grants and widows' and maternity allowances. All were incorporated in the National Insurance Act of 1946. In 1948 the pension was £1.30 for a single person and £2.10 for a married couple. Ten years later these had increased to £2.50 and £4.00 respectively.

The next big change came in 1959, when the Conservative government set up the graduated scheme, which came into effect in 1961. This was ended in 1975. Then in the late sixties came the Crossman scheme – the first earnings-related plan. This never came into operation and died with the Labour government in 1970.

Then it was Sir Keith Joseph's turn. In 1973 he introduced a State Reserve Scheme in the Social Security Act of that year. It was similar to the later Castle scheme, with the very important difference that the money raised in contributions would be 'funded', that is put into investments to pay for future pensions.

That scheme was dismantled by the next Labour government, and the Castle scheme, which relies on current contributions to pay for pensions, was introduced. This means that each working generation must pay for the pensions of the retired generation. As the birth rate falls and the proportion of old people becomes greater, the burden on those still at work could become quite heavy.

This brief history of pensions raises the question of how long the Castle scheme will last. In principle, in terms of benefits, it seems likely to stay for some time at least – though a Conservative government might well return to 'funding'. Pensions have been bedevilled by politics since they were first brought in and a period of tranquillity for pension holders seems desirable. At the moment some retired people have a flat-rate pension, a graduated pension and an occupational scheme. Soon the flexible tier will be added to this lot, making looking after one's pension quite a complicated business.

PRIVATE PENSION SCHEMES

Contracting out of the Castle scheme

If an employer wishes to contract out of the earnings-related part of the Castle Scheme he must have a pension scheme of his own which fulfils the following conditions. They are not onerous:

1   He must provide minimum pensions of 1/80th of employees' earnings for each year they are contracted out of the state flexible tier scheme. The actual amount may be geared to final earnings, or to contributions paid year by year.
2   The amount of the pension must be at least equal to the state earnings-related pension.
3   There must be a widow's benefit in the scheme for death in service, which gives at least five-eighths of the employees pensionable earnings. Widows' post-retirement benefits must be at least half the guaranteed minimum pension of the employee.
4   Employees must be able to claim their pension at the state retirement ages of sixty and sixty-five. If they go on working to sixty-five and seventy for women and men respectively, the pension must be increased by a minimum of 8½ per cent a year. After sixty-five and seventy no further increases are permitted.
5   Some guaranteed pension must be assured if the employee leaves before the retirement age. This pension must be revalued in line with the national increase in pensions as time goes on.
6   Men and women must be treated alike in terms of eligibility for schemes. Higher entry age and less good benefits for women have had to go under the Sex Discrimination Act – though this has not changed the retirement ages. If these ever do change, there is likely to be a downward movement for men rather than a rising of the age for women.

If your pension scheme fulfils all these conditions, your company can be contracted out of the flexible tier scheme – though you still have to go on paying for the flat-rate pension.

In deciding to start a scheme the employer will have the following points in mind:

* The preservation of a good employer – employee relationship.
* The total cost of the scheme, and how much he can afford to pay in contributions to balance those of the employee.
* How difficult it would be to run. Most large employers have had to set up special departments to operate their schemes. This could be prohibitive for a small employer.

If an employer does decide to contract out of the earnings-related scheme there is some financial saving for both employee and employer. The total cut in social security contributions is 7 per cent of the employee's earnings, of which 4½ per cent goes to the employer and 2½ per cent to the employee.

Eligibility for company schemes

Just because you work for a company does not mean you can automatically join their pension scheme. Most schemes insist that you have a minimum of one year's service, or they do not allow you to join until you are twenty-one, twenty-five or even thirty. This is to weed out those who do not stay for a reasonable length of time with a company. Some schemes used to be for men only, but that is now illegal; other companies have different schemes for executives and factory workers.

If you are a partner in the firm or run your own business, you are not allowed to participate yourself in any scheme you may set up for your employees – unless you become a limited company, in which case you can be treated as an employee with all the national insurance benefits and company pensions. This applies even if you are a director and own almost all the shares.

Should you join a company scheme?

The first step when considering joining the pension fund is to read the rules and ask questions on any aspect that bothers you. These are some of the questions you could consider:

* How will the pension be calculated? Will it be inflation-proof both before and after retirement?
* Is the scheme approved by the Inland Revenue? This has tax implications (see later in chapter).

* What are the widows' and orphans' benefits?
* How is the period of employment calculated? Is there any lump sum of money if death occurs before retirement? Are there any provisions for early or late retirement? What happens if you leave before retiring?
* How much do you pay and how much does the employer pay? How are these contributions invested?

Most people pay between 3 and 6 per cent of their income in private pension contributions, but about a third are in pension funds where they pay nothing and only the employer contributes.

How much should you pay? It is difficult to say, because it is important to be in a good scheme and pay, rather than in a bad scheme and not pay. If you pay 4 per cent and your employer 8 per cent, you will get a better pension in the end than in any scheme where only your employer pays and he pays less than 12 per cent. Five per cent is the more usual employee contribution.

If you do not have to pay, you must make as many enquiries about the scheme as if you were paying. You may find that you will have to supplement your company pension with some other form of regular saving.

Very few schemes are identical. All will have some element which refers only to the particular needs of the employees in a particular company. Remember that if you are an employee it is only by joining a pension scheme that you have any hope of raising the seven to ten years' salary that you will require on your retirement to maintain a reasonable standard of living.

The Castle scheme may be good for those with low earnings, but anyone earning more than the maximum of £105 a week to which the scheme applies will lose out with every extra £1 he earns. Remember, too, that for every pound you put into a company scheme your employer (on average) will put in twice as much, and you will get the benefit from the total contributions. So if you are paying 7½ per cent of your salary into the pension fund and your employer pays 15 per cent (though this would be very high), you are getting the equivalent of an extra £12 a week, if you earn £80 a week.

There are some tax advantages too. Anything you pay into a pension fund is sliced off your income completely. And of course you pay no tax on the contributions your employer puts in. Allowing for tax at a standard rate of 35 per cent, the £6 a week you put in and the £12 from your employer (in the example above) are worth £24.30 a week in salary terms. Put another way, if you had to pay tax on the £18, it would be worth only £11.70 to you.

A further advantage is that the money you pay and the money your employer pays on your behalf is invested. The money which is invested

398

may – it depends on the skill of the fund's investment managers – grow in capital value and will certainly earn dividends, which are *free of tax*. Some of this money may be paid out in bonuses to pensioners or be used to raise the level of pensions.

Things to watch

How much of your salary is your pension based on? It may be all your pay or only a part of it. Schemes may include or exclude overtime, bonuses and any other extras in calculating your pensionable pay. As a rule the Inland Revenue will insist that fluctuating items in your pay are averaged out over the last three years and included in a pensionable pay. If the 'floating' items in your salary are substantial they can affect your pension.

For a pension contribution to be eligible for tax relief the scheme must be approved by the Inland Revenue. If it is not, the amount you pay in contributions will not be taken off your taxable income and you will also have to pay tax on your employer's contributions.

The maximum pension that the Inland Revenue allows anyone in a private scheme is two-thirds of final pay. This means that the company may have to limit your eligibility to forty years (that is 40/60ths, or two-thirds). When this is the case there is no point in men joining a scheme until they are twenty-five and women twenty.

When you retire your pension is treated as earned income and taxed under normal P.A.Y.E. You will also be taxed on your state pension, even though there is no tax relief attached to your national insurance contributions while you are working.

How will your pension be calculated?

The pension you are entitled to can be calculated in a variety of ways:

1 The most common way is to pay 1/60th or 1/80th or some other fraction of your final pay for each year you contribute to the scheme. This type of scheme favours men, when their pensions finally arrive, because they will have five extra years in which to contribute. The total benefit over the entire pension period is about the same for men and women, however, because women tend to die later than men. It just means living longer on less.

2 Instead of being based on final pay, the pension may be the same fraction of your average pay for each year of service. If this is the method chosen, salaries are usually treated in bands and the company should have a table showing you the pension at various salary levels.

3 Where companies are small, the employer and the employee may pay in a fixed amount of contributions, which are invested and then used at the time of retirement for whatever pension the

399

money will buy. These are known as 'money purchase schemes' and are not very common, because the employee is at the mercy of the financial situation when he retires.

4 You may get a fixed amount of pension whatever you earn. This is usually at a very low level and is of little use to the higher paid. It may also be at such a low level that the employer cannot contract out of the earnings-related scheme. In these cases the earnings-related element may bring the total pension up to a reasonable amount.

5 You may be offered what is called an 'integrated' scheme. This will give you a pension which is a certain proportion of your final earnings, often two-thirds, less any state pension you may get. Say you are earning £72 when you retire; two-thirds of that would be £48, but you must take off the married man's state pension of £24.50, leaving you with a private pension worth £23.50, not £48. These schemes have become complicated with the advent of earnings-related pensions. They are not attractive, but you will be stuck with it if that is the method chosen by your employer. It is scarcely worth changing jobs just to get into a good pension scheme – though for a man in his fifties it could be. A job giving maximum pension rights for the rest of his life could be worth more than a big increase in salary for the few years left to retirement.

Of all these alternatives the one based on final salary is most preferable.

A capital sum

Some schemes allow you to receive a capital sum when you retire, deducting an appropriate amount from your monthly pension. The standard formula approved by the Inland Revenue is 3/80ths of final pay for each year of service.

Some schemes offer the pension of 1/80th plus 3/80ths of final pay as a capital sum. Put together this is considered to be about the same as a pension only, with no capital sum of 1/60th.

A lump sum can be useful, because you may then be able to finish paying off your mortgage if it is not cleared and so not have to worry about that when you retire. Or you can buy an annuity (see section I, chapter 13), which will boost your post-retirement income and bring tax advantages as well. By doing both you can sometimes increase your net income after tax by 30 per cent.

WILL YOUR PENSION BE ENOUGH?

In a period of inflation you may well think that your pension will not be enough for you to live on when it arrives. You can increase the amount you have by taking specialist advice, or you could consider some of the saving and assurance schemes discussed in chapters 3 and 13 of section I or regular saving in unit trusts, discussed in chapter 5 of this section.

If you fall into certain categories you may have particular reason to worry, however.

If you change your job

Very few of us stay with the same employer for forty years, so when you join a scheme you must find out what happens if you leave.

The 1973 Social Security Act which came into operation in April 1975 requires all company schemes to preserve pension rights for employees who leave if they are aged twenty-six or over and have completed five years' service; some schemes give you the option of taking your money out when you leave. Some pension schemes provide for preservation as from year one. Others provide for transfer payments. Yet others inflation-proof preserved pensions.

For example, if you joined the Civil Service scheme at twenty-five and left at thirty-five and were entitled to £1,000 a year preserved pension at the date of leaving, this £1,000 would increase each year in line with the Retail Price Index until you reach the age of sixty (the Civil Service retiring age), when it would become payable. After this the pension would be increased each year in order to maintain its real value.

If you are contracted out of the Castle scheme your 'preserved pension' will be 'dynamized' in a similar way. This is again a difficult technical area. It will pay you to examine the provisions of your own pension scheme carefully before making any final decision to change jobs.

If you have the option of taking your money out when you leave and you decide to do so, remember that you will lose all the benefits deriving from the employer's part of the total contribution. This is an Inland Revenue rule.

A tidier alternative is to transfer your pension rights. Transferability can operate in two ways:

1 A lump sum can be sent to the pension scheme of your new employer.
2 A pension can be paid based on your final salary and the number of years you had worked for the company at the time you left. This is kept by your new employer and paid to you on your retirement. Not all schemes permit transferability, so you could well end up with several small pensions from a variety of companies when you retire. But this is preferable to taking a refund at any time.

401

If you are self-employed

The self-employed always come off worst when it comes to any benefits, and pensions are no exception. Under the new Castle scheme, for example, they will only get the flat-rate pension and are not eligible for the earnings-related part. Yet they are the section of the population most exposed to risk. They may have no capital when they retire and a very limited pension. This means that they have to look after their pensions themselves.

At present the flat-rate contribution for self-employed men is £2.66, and £2.55 for women (reflecting women's lower average earnings). The gap between men's and women's rates has been closing in recent years, and eventually they will both pay the same.

The insurance companies have developed all sorts of schemes to help the self-employed, but they must follow certain government rules about the amount of money they are permitted to put away each year towards their pensions. At present it is 15 per cent of their earnings in any one year.

Those who earn more than £10,000 a year are allowed to invest 15 per cent of their incomes to a ceiling of £20,000. This means that the maximum each year that they can put away is £3,000. At £10,000 it will be £1,500; at £11,000, £1,650, and so on. There is also a 5 per cent of earnings limit on life assurance contracts up to a ceiling of £20,000, so that the maximum amount allowed here is £1,000 for anyone earning £20,000 or more.

These contributions are eligible for tax relief, and the more you earn the more this is worth. It is easy to see, however, that at the higher salary ranges particularly, the employed may come off much better than the self-employed as there is no limit on their contributions.

To make sure you get the best scheme possible, seek the advice of a pensions expert. There are many possible combinations and you will be able to choose whatever suits you best. This is a very complicated area and you are unlikely to make the best decision without some assistance.

If you wish to retire early

You cannot get a state pension until you reach the state retirement age, unless you get a disability allowance. But some people who are quite fit would like to retire early. If you only contribute to the state scheme the only way you can do this is to have some form of capital to live on until you reach retirement age. But remember, if you do not continue to pay full national insurance contributions, that pension will be scaled down.

Those in private company schemes usually do better, but not always. Some private schemes allow for pensions on early retirement on certain terms; others will not pay out until retirement age. In the former case, if the terms are not punitive, you could do better drawing your pension early, because the extra years' benefit from, say, retiring five years earlier, will more than make up for the cut in the rate of pension.

Some schemes might allow you to retire early but take, say 5 per cent off your pension for every year early that you retired. So if you retired five years early your pension would be cut by a quarter. You might get more total benefit over the total period you are pensioned for, but you would be a lot poorer while it lasted.

Some schemes offer the best of both worlds and let your maximum pension under your particular scheme run from sixty (in these cases women may or may not be able to go at fifty-five).

For most people, however, early retirement will probably have to remain a dream, for this is how the average private pension works.

Let's take a man of fifty-five who would like to retire. We'll assume he is earning £100 a week, which if he stayed at work until sixty-five would rise to £150. His pension is worked out at 1/60th for every year of service, and he has been with the company for thirty years. If he wants to take an early pension, this is likely to be no more than half the amount he would get retiring at sixty-five. Even this may not be allowed, and he may have to wait until he is sixty-five before getting the money. There are two sums he must work out.

1   If he continued working until he was sixty-five, his weekly pension would be based on forty years with the firm and a final salary of £150 a week. He would then get 40/60ths of £150, or £100 a week. Add on the state pension and his total pension would be over 80 per cent of his final salary.
2   If he retires at fifty-five and his pension is calculated on the same formula, he may only get 30/60ths (for thirty years' service) of his final salary of £100 a week, reduced by an early-retirement factor of 50%, giving him £25 a week. Even is his salary remained unchanged for the period to retirement, the difference in working to sixty-five rather than fifty-five could be as much as £42 a week – £67 instead of £25 a week.

You can of course make up these differences by regular saving, but it will mean that throughout your working life you will have to put away much more of your capital towards your retirement than would otherwise be the case.

Remember, retiring early might be fun and give you a better life, but you must consider all the aspects before deciding to do it.

If you wish to retire abroad

There can be problems if you wish to retire abroad as far as your pension is concerned. Retiring abroad is far more common than you would think, and is not simply confined to the very rich. More than 150,000 people are drawing British state benefits abroad. Almost 100,000 of these live in America or the Commonwealth countries of Canada, Australia and New Zealand, many having gone out on retirement to join their children who have emigrated.

There is no problem in taking your pension abroad when you retire, but what happens to that pension afterwards can be . Often no increases in pensions are payable abroad. This means that despite inflation – and inflation happens everywhere – those who retire in, say, 1965 on a basic pension of £4, or £6.50 for a married couple, will still be getting that amount rather than the £17.50 or the £28.00 which is paid to anyone who has stayed in the U.K.

This does not apply everywhere; there are, for example, reasonable social security agreements between Britain and the other E.E.C. countries. And some countries – Australia is one – will pay retired people a pension even if they have not paid the relevant contributions there. This is done in an attempt to keep families together in the new country, for there is a tendency for emigrants to return home when their parents get old.

The situation is different for every country, and you should study all the methods of adjusting pensions before you retire. You should write to the Department of Health and Social Security (Overseas Group), Newcastle-upon-Tyne NE98 1YX, and ask them what your position will be in the country to which you plan to emigrate.

If you are a woman

Although you will get the same flat-rate pension, you are likely to get less than a man on the earnings-related part of the state scheme, because despite the Equal Pay Act the gap between women's and men's wages is still very wide.

This has implications, too, if you are in a private scheme. Women are allowed to retire at sixty. This means they get less pension each week whatever kind of scheme they have been in – though by the time they die they will probably have had as much in total as most men, if not more. For the moment, at least, the government has turned its back on any proposals for equal retirement age.

There have been a number of improvements in recent years as far as women's pension rights are concerned. They now have to have equal access to private pension schemes, on the same terms as men. But many women, particularly the older ones, may have been excluded from pension schemes in the past and only recently have been able to join. Inevitably this also means that they will end up with a lower pension than a man.

All this may not matter so much for the married woman, who gets a pension on her husband's contribution, but it means that the single woman can often find her income sharply reduced after retirement.

It is just as important for a woman to be in a pension scheme as a man, whether married or not. Married people who have been used to living on two salaries will find it difficult living on one pension.

A single woman pays national insurance contributions at a slightly lower rate than a man – though this gap is narrowing.

Some married women who opted out of the N.I. scheme before 11 May 1977 are covered by their husbands' contributions. If they did not opt out, or have started working since that date, they must pay full contributions.

In other cases it is rarely sensible for a woman to pay full contributions, because she will not get a full single person's pension to supplement the £28.00 she and her husband will get from his contribution anyway. The maximum she is allowed is the difference between that and two single persons' pensions of £17.50 each together. This means that from all her years of contributions she will get only £7.00 a week. The money could be far better utilized in another form of saving.

Women have advantages in comparison with men in their rights as widows. Any widow over fifty inherits the whole of her husband's pension rights under the Castle scheme. This privilege is not similarly extended to men.

Because women live longer and are generally younger than their husbands – only 35 per cent of women are older than their husbands – the widow's element can be a very valuable addition to pension rights.

Widows' pension rights in private schemes vary enormously, but today they must meet government requirements if the company concerned is contracted out of the earnings-related part of the state scheme.

Some older schemes have no widows' rights (these cannot be contracted out of the Castle scheme), but in most schemes the employer will give a 50 per cent pension to a wife in return for the employee taking a slightly lower pension while he is alive.

In some schemes the employer gives a guarantee of a minimum pension for a number of years. If the husband then dies suddenly soon after retirement his family will continue to receive this pension until the time is up. Five years is normal, but it is sometimes ten.

If a woman is in a private pension scheme in her own right and has dependents she may find that she is not so well treated as a man and may have no benefits for them written into the scheme. But more and more funds are allowing dependents' pensions to women on the same terms as men.

If you are in a private pension scheme yourself and have dependents fight for the right. If you cannot get these benefits consult an insurance broker, or get your firm to do it for you. You can get single premium insurance policies which in the event of your death will give your children a guaranteed income until they are able to earn their own living. In similar circumstances a man should of course take out a policy of this kind. They are not expensive.

Chapter 10

Gambling

The government makes money out of gambling, so do the bookmakers; the punters – the people who actually do the gambling – do not. Of course a few people win large sums of money on the football pools or the horses, or on some other kind of bet, but on the whole the odds are weighted very much in favour of the people who organize the business, and the government, which collects tax on the various forms of betting.

If you look at the table opposite, you will see that the government is now collecting almost £300 million from the country's gamblers. The figure has more than quadrupled in the last ten years, as new taxes have been introduced to replace the old ones, which did not bring in such large sums of money.

The football pool betting duty makes up a third of the total, and the general betting duty, which covers all other betting primarily collected from the bookmakers, more than half. The biggest item in the gaming duties, which covers gaming clubs and machines, is bingo, which brings in half the total.

As you can see, gambling is big business for the government and a valuable source of revenue. Because it is impossible for gamblers to win overall, gambling cannot really be considered part of an investment policy. But many people spend money on it, partly for pleasure and partly as a serious business.

You can bet on anything – the weight of your baby when it is born, the colour of its eyes, its sex, which party will win the next general election, or how many runs a particular batsman will score in a game of cricket.

Some bets are particular favourites with people. I asked Ladbrokes, one of the big bookmakers, for some they had had recently. They had just taken money on the haggis-eating contest, and a £2,000 bet at odds of 33-1 on whether more than a quarter of an inch of rain would fall in La

BETTING AND GAMING DUTIES: RECEIPTS

	Betting duties					Gaming duties				Total betting and gaming duties
	Pool betting duty	Bookmakers' licence duty (a)	General betting duty (b)	Betting premises licence duty (c)	Total betting duties	Gaming licence (premises) duty (d)	Gaming machine licence duty (d)	Bingo duty (e)	Total gaming duties	
1966-67 …	34,148	436	10,831	—	45,415	1,987	2,689	4,676	50,091	
1967-68 …	32,896	—	30,237	—	63,132	1,907	2,861	—	4,768	67,900
1968-69 …	39,493	—	54,435	—	93,928	2,802	2,935	—	5,737	99,665
1969-70 …	46,207(f)	—	58,989	3,380	108,577(f)	1,394	7,705	1,351	10,450	119,027(f)
1970-71 …	45,341(g)	—	71,149	400	116,890(g)	1,717	7,910	3,918	13,545	130,435(g)
1971-72 …	62,061	—	79,591	3	141,655	2,668	7,787	4,237	14,692	156,347
1972-73 …	69,187	—	86,786	—2	155,971	3,005	7,576	4,855	15,436	171,407
1973-74 …	72,073	—	97,248	—5	169,316	2,540	8,266	5,338	16,144	185,460(h)
1974-75 …	87,925	—	131,375	—	219,300	3,850	9,235	6,160	19,245	238,545(i)
1975-76 …	95,192	—	146,292	—	241,484	5,301	8,222	9,965	23,488	264,972(j)
1976-77 … (estimate)	100,000	—	165,00	—	265,000	6,000	9,000	15,000	30,000	295,000

(a) To 23 October 1966.
(b) From 24 October 1966.
(c) From 1 October 1969 to 27 April 1970.
(d) From 1 October 1966.
(e) From 1 October 1969.

(f) Includes £8.7 million due in respect of earlier years.
(g) Includes £2.4 million due in respect of earlier years.
(h) Includes £521,009 Northern Ireland revenue from 1 January.
(i) Includes £2.9 million Northern Ireland revenue.
(j) Includes £3.6 million Northern Ireland revenue.

Source: The Annual Report of The Customs and Excise. This table is updated once a year and published in December.

Paz, Bolivia, between 4 and 27 April. They told me that the existence of the Loch Ness monster is a favourite bet, as the monster seeking season comes round. Again, many Americans who bet in Britain – there are fewer legal chances for them to do so in the U.S.A. – are regular gamblers on whether aliens, alive or dead, will land on earth from outer space.

This may give you some idea of the variety of events you can bet on – though the average person is more likely to stick to the football pools and the occasional bet on a horse in one of the big races like the Derby or the Grand National.

THE FOOTBALL POOLS

Football pool forms are as familiar in many families as the daily newspaper; as many as 5 million individual gamblers stake a total of well over £200 million in a season. The average amount staked is around 40p for individuals, though syndicates bet much more. They may have many members who contribute an equal amount each week and share any proceeds.

Really big wins on the pools are few and far between, but there are many smaller prizes to temp the punter and keep him hoping for the big one. The pools companies reckon that the chance of winning a prize of £100,000 or more is about the same as the chance of being murdered.

The big prizes go on the Treble Chance pool, where the punter selects eight draws each week from the list on his form, and 90 per cent of the stake money goes on this.

Only between thirty and forty people win prizes of more than £100,000 in a season. The publicity which results from a big win of £500,000 or so is extremely important for the pools companies, as it brings an upsurge of business each time. The pools companies offer the big winners an investment advisory service. It may seem impossible if you have not had a big win, but some past winners have managed to get through hundreds of thousands of pounds and end up as poor as they were before they won.

The pools company has to pay tax on all the money they receive, but any win is tax-free to the punter. When all the administration is done and taxes are paid the promoter only makes about 1½ per cent profit. Tax and prizes together take up almost 70 per cent of their total income, and the distribution and running of the pools is costly administratively. About 28 per cent of the money which comes in on the pools goes out in prizes. This means that punters *overall* must lose over 70 per cent of their money.

This is how the wins are paid out. The promoters call them 'dividends'.

1 *The Treble Chance pool.* The first prize takes 60 per cent of the prize money, with a limit of £500,000, the second prize 10 per cent, and

the third 9 per cent. The fourth to sixth prizes are 8, 7, and 6 per cent respectively. Any surplus money is equally divided among the lower dividends in the same pool. To win the Treble Chance you have to select eight draws on any one Saturday. The more draws there are, the more people get high points, and the smaller the individual dividends.

Some people study form each week in selecting their draws; others put them anywhere, perhaps in the same positions each week, as the order of the teams varies. Most people do several lines. This is known as a 'permutation'. You can if you wish pay all your money at the start of the season and give the company your regular permutation; they will then check it every week.

2   *Ten homes, four aways and four draws pools.* These are less popular, but they are the ones where punters believe that skills come in. It is easier to win on one's home ground, but some clubs have a good away record.

If you invest enough in these on a system it is alleged that you can get through the season in balance, or losing very little. But your wins are unlikely to be great either. Anyone who gets a one-column forecast correct gets all the money available for prizes. If no one gets it right, then the money is divided or given to the person nearest an all-correct forecast.

3   *Easier six.* In this the results of all six matches selected must be forecast, and the marks are 1 for a home win, 2 for an away win and 3 for a draw. The punter who forecasts most accurately wins the whole of the prize money.

There are of course a few rules. They vary a little but not much between promoters:

1   There is a minimum stake and a maximum stake. On Littlewoods' Treble Chance the minimum is ½p per column and the maximum 3p. On its other pools the minimum is 3p and the maximum £2.
2   Your coupon must be sent off with a postmark showing that it was posted *before the match took place*. Moreover, it will not be accepted by the promoter if it arrives after 3 p.m. on the day the matches are taking place.

If you think you have won the Treble Chance you must claim as soon as possible after the matches end, and certainly not later than the Monday following. You claim via registered letter, enclosing a complete copy of the winning entry and stating:

The name and address on the coupon.
The number of points claimed.
The reference number.
How the coupon was submitted (whether the promoter had a collector who took the coupon from you at home, for example).

If you win on other pools you should automatically get the money by the following Saturday. If you do not, you then claim.

Your claim will not be allowed if:

* You have not sent any money with the coupon.
* You have not signed it, or it comes from the address of a school or college, or is sent in on behalf of an employee or spouse rather than yourself.
* If you are under eighteen.
* If it is illegible in any way and not absolutely clear.
* If it gets lost in the post, or does not reach the promoter for any reason, or is damaged. For this reason you may be safer with a collection if there is one near you.

There are further rules for abandoned or unplayed matches, and more 'small print' in the rules which the company will send you. Study them carefully.

I have no advice on how to win. If I had, I would have taken it myself. Some people swear by skill and study, but it is interesting to see how many winners pick randomly or win after the first few tries. You will have to have your own philosophy.

THE HORSES

Most people, unless they are firmly against gambling on moral grounds, have a flutter at least once in their lives, even if it is only on a horse whose name they fancy or a jockey who has a long list of wins.

Though this type of gambling is not nearly so widespread as doing the football pools, the stakes (the money you put up) are much higher. The amount of money the industry is taking in is thought now to be reaching £1,500 million a year – seven and a half times as much as the pools companies.

Most of this money goes on the big races, but there are professional gamblers whose lives are spent at the racecourses. As long as you are eighteen years old you will have plenty of opportunities for betting.

All bets are made on 'odds' – that is, you win a stated amount for every pound you stake. The less chance a horse has of winning the 'longer' the odds, the more chance the 'shorter' they are. A horse with a string of failures may be quoted at long odds of 100-1. This means that if it wins you will get £100 for every £1 you have staked. The favourite could be at 2-1 only, or 'evens' – when you only win £1 for every £1 bet.

If you bet 'each way', this means your stake is split between a win and a place – if the horse comes in the first three or four for classic races where the field is over a certain number. Say you put down £2 at 5-1 and the horse wins. You will then collect £5 on your first £1; you lose your second £1. If it comes second or third you collect on the other £1, but only at about a quarter of the odds. Place bets are not allowed when there are five horses or less, and the third is not permitted when there are only between five and seven horses in the race.

There are a variety of very complicated bets whereby you can increase your winnings. I will describe these later on. First, the places where you can bet:

1 *Bookmakers.* They can take bets on the course or off the course in a betting shop. There are some differences depending on which you choose. Let's say you bet £1 at 10-1 to win on course and the horse wins. Theoretically you should get back your £1 and your £10 win, but bookmakers today expect the punter to help towards the tax they have to pay, so they deduct 4 per cent from the £11 total due to you. That means your net winnings are £10.56; the tax amounts to 44p.

If you bet off-track in a bookmakers office, you do a little worse. On the same bet, 8.5 per cent is taken off for tax, betting levy and bookmaker charges. This means that your net win would be £11 minus 93½p or £10.06½.

You can also place a bet with a bookmaker by phone. To do this you will have to have a certain amount of credit permitted by the bookmaker; he will check on this before allowing the bet. The same win again gives you £10.06½ net, the charges being the same.

In one way or another over 90 per cent of British punters bet via bookmakers.

2 *The totalizator.* This was set up by the government in 1929, when off-course cash betting was still illegal. Its aim was to provide another form of betting and raise money for the improvement of racing. You can bet in either cash or credit on the course or in one of the totalizator betting shops. The money you get is worked out by dividing the total money placed on the race by the number of winning tickets. There is no fixed deduction, but it usually averages about 18 per cent. This would then bring your net winnings down to £9.02.

Form is far more carefully studied in horse racing than in the football pools, and there is no doubt that favourites are favourites because they are outstanding horses with a good record. But all kinds of things can go wrong, and favourites don't always win. If they did, racing would be far duller. Some jockeys have a good record, too – though it is doubtful whether you would win much overall by following one particular horse or jockey through the season.

If you want to study form there are always the newspapers. All the dailies except the *Financial Times,* which specializes in speculation of another sort, give daily racing cards, and most of them have a number of staff tipsters. Tipsters' records vary and are by no means consistent, so do not follow them if you fancy another horse. There are also two racing

411

dailies, the *Sporting Life* and the *Sporting Chronicle*. They give an enormous amount of detail about each race. It will take you some time to work your way round the terminology. For the truly professional there are weekly publications from a London shop called Turf Newspapers, which produces *Timeform* in two editions, one for the eight months of flat racing and the other for the ten months of National Hunt steeple-chasing for £60 per season (1977 price).

If you have a win you may still not be satisifed with it. There are various ways of increasing your winnings, if you happen to be lucky a second time or more:

A double: links two horses in one bet. The horses are in two different races, and if the first one wins the whole of the stake money and the winnings are automatically transferred to the second horse.

A treble is similar, but there are three horses. The chances of making a treble are obviously less than on a double.

The accumulator works on the same principle, but with four horses or more. There have been cases of people winning on seven or more horses, but you need pretty strong nerves for this and a relaxed attitude if you lose in the end.

Forecasting usually entails betting on the first and second in a race and, depending on the size of the field, can sometimes be linked to take in the two horses who will come first and second in any order for one stake.

These are the most common sorts of bets but there are others. They come with such names as *Any-to-come* (A.T.C.), where winnings from one race are reinvested as the punter thinks fit in other races, and *Up and down,* where two horses are backed singly, each with an A.T.C. bet on the other. A *Rounder* is when three horses are backed singly, and if one wins the other two are backed on a double. And a *Roundabout* is a Rounder with double stakes.

Then come the really complicated bets. A *Round Robin* involves ten bets – three horses are linked up and down on each pair, plus three doubles and a treble. A *Patent* is three horses backed in three single bets, three doubles and a treble. The gamble involving the most separate bets is a *Heinz,* so-called because it involves fifty-seven bets on six different horses. In between it and the Round Robin come a *Canadian* (twenty-six bets and five horses), a *Flag* (twenty-three bets and four horses) and a *Yankee* (eleven bets and four horses).

Owning a horse

Perhaps you would like to be on the other side of the racing business and own a horse yourself. Anyone can be lucky and buy a good horse, which turn out to win large prizes and can later be sold for stud, but the chance are that these horses will go to the big names in racing. The fact that the

412

average horse wins around £750 a year and can cost more than £2,500 in training and other expenses is a sobering thought. Most owners run at a loss and hope to make it up eventually with big prizes or wins on other horses. Some people go into a syndicate with a horse, and you can then get your original investment in it returned with a profit when it is sold for stud. Race horse owning is still very much the preserve of the rich, however. For the ordinary person it is simply out of range.

You may be interested to know where the prize money comes from: there are four sources: owners' entry fees, the racecourses, the levy board (the body that levies money from British bookmakers) and sponsors who put up money in exchange for an advertisement on the course.

In 1977 the basic prizes for some of the big flat races were:

The Derby – £80,000
The King George and Queen Elizabeth Stakes – £110,000
The Eclipse Stakes – £40,000

British owners and punters also go for the French races, where the prizes are even higher – though more goes to a French horse if it wins. The best prize of all is the Prix de L'Arc de Triomphe at £150,000, followed by the French Derby at £107,397 and the Grand Prix de St Cloud at £72,636.

GREYHOUND RACING

Betting on greyhounds has been a popular British pastime for over fifty years. Despite a decline in attendances in recent years, more than 6 million people still go to one of the forty-nine racecourses around the country which operate under the rules of the National Greyhound Racing Club. Since 1960 off-course betting has been allowed, and this has reduced both the numbers actually watching the races and the money which goes on on-course betting.

GAMING

It is well known that casinos and gaming clubs make vast profits, though no one is certain of the actual figures. They are kept a well-guarded secret. One thing seems certain: if gamblers knew what the levels of these profits were many of them would be deterred from gambling with the odds so stacked against them. On averge there is a 6 per cent bias in favour of the 'house', the gaming club. This is called the percentage.

You must remember, if you gamble, that in most cases it is luck and not skill when you win. Most gamblers work on systems and will swear that their particular one works. This is simply not true; no technique or system can be guaranteed to beat the draw. Never lose sight of this fact, and if you can only afford to lose very little limit your stake firmly. Above all, once you have reached your limit never try to recoup your losses by staking further money.

Games vary enormously, however, and some do involve a considerable degree of skill. Poker is the obvious example. Bridge also requires skill, but it is not counted by habitués of gaming clubs and casinos as gambling in the same sense as the others. Others involve not so much skill as prodigous memory, to remember exactly what cards have already been drawn. Blackjack is the leader among these. And some games are all risk; roulette is an outstanding example of this.

Gambling games can be divided then into *games of chance* – games in which there is no element of skill, called by gamblers 'mechanical games', such as lotteries, raffles, bingo, 'one-armed bandits', most dice games, and some card games like faro, baccarat, and roulette – and *games of skill and chance*, which give the skilled operator a better chance. There is still an element of luck, but the player can bend it to his advantage to some extent. These include most card games – poker, gin rummy, bridge, blackjack and pinochle – and also backgammon.

If you wish to join a gaming club, the entry fees are expensive; such clubs are only for the relatively rich. Entry to casinos is often free, and there are few limits on what you can win – or more frequently lose.

There are several excellent books which you can study if you are interested. Cuthbertson's *Card Games* is a complete encyclopedia. Unfortunately it is out of print, but you may be able to get a copy second-hand. *Challenge to Chance* by E. Lennox Figgis, also out of print, discusses gambling systems most entertainingly. But remember, no system can win.

BINGO

Bingo, which is simply a form of the children's game Housey-Housey, has become a very popular part-time betting activity with housewives. A much smaller proportion of the takings goes in tax than on the football pools; it is only 5 per cent. Even so the £299 million which is now staked every year on Bingo brings the government nearly £15 million in revenue each year.

Each player sits at a board marked with squares with numbers in them. Numbers are called out at random, and if the player has that number on her board she – it is usually a she – covers that number with a piece of plastic. When all the squares are covered it's Bingo! and the first player to do this is the winner.

To play bingo you will have to become a member of a club. This takes twenty-four hours and costs around 50p. Then there is an admission charge, which in the bigger clubs will be between 15p and 25p. About twenty games are played each session, and there will be a charge for each

414

'chance' (stake). This cannot be more than 10p, and the total taken on each chance must not add up to more than £5. Most people who are regular bingo players spend about £5 a week on it, but there are some who bet up to £50. Prize money varies, but in the bigger clubs it may be as much as £160 a game, and sometimes linked games offer even higher prizes.

A FINAL WORD

Many people condemn gambling, but I believe this can be a mistake. For most people it is a source of relaxation and pleasure and costs them very little. A bet of 40p a week on the football pools is not going to break anyone's budget; nor is an occasional flutter on the St Leger. All forms of recreation and entertainment cost money, and if you are sensible you will regard betting in that light. For most of us gambling is just building castles in the air, and there is no harm in that.

Some people, however, find gambling compulsive, and whether it is bingo, the pools, or the horses you start becoming addicted to, you should stop if this happens to you. Once it gets out of hand gambling is just as family- and soul-destroying as too much alcohol or drugs. Those who find their gambling has got out of control can go to Gamblers Anonymous, 19 Abbey House, Victoria Street, London S.W.1. (01-222 4252) which will try to help cure them of their addiction – because that is what it is.

Your Money and the Law

Chapter 1

GOING TO LAW

Litigation can be very expensive. You will have to pay a solicitor and possibly a barrister to represent you. Getting any legal advice is also expensive. But if you do not have any spare money over and above your daily necessities, do not despair: this does not mean that you cannot get legal advice or take action in court. In this chapter I will look at three ways of taking legal action which need not result in any cost to yourself.

LEGAL ADVICE

This is a relatively new service, introduced in 1973. The procedure is far more informal than that for legal aid. You simply go to a solicitor who is party to the scheme (not all of them are, and some will not consider legal aid cases either) and give him details of your financial situation. He will say whether you are eligible or not. Your local Law Society branch or Citizens' Advice Bureau will give you a list of solicitors who are in the scheme.

Whether you are eligible or not depends on your disposable capital and your disposable income.

The former is any money which you actually have available, leaving aside personal and household effects. It would, for instance, include any savings or investments you have and any income from them. The latter is your total income from all sources, taking off any liability for tax and national insurance contributions and anything you may need for your dependents.

The levels of disposable income and capital change all the time. Only a solicitor can tell you if you are eligible at any one time.

If you are eligible there are a variety of things the solicitor can do for you. They include:

1 Giving general advice, and writing letters and conducting negotiations on behalf of clients.
2 Drawing up legal documents such as wills.
3 Sometimes – but not usually – conveyancing.
4 Advising on what action should be taken in court – though the solicitor cannot take this action himself. Suppose you have to appear before an industrial tribunal over a redundancy payment. The solicitor can prepare the papers for you, but the scheme does not cover his appearance before the tribunal on your behalf.

This legal advice service is known as the 'green form scheme'. Applicants may be referred to the local supplementary benefits office for a financial assessment rather than the solicitor taking it upon himself. Sometimes the service may be totally free; at other times the applicant may have to make a contribution.

Legal advice and assistance can be transformed into full legal aid, if that becomes necessary.

LEGAL AID

The legal aid system began in 1949 under the first Legal Aid and Advice Act. Before that, going to law really was the prerogative of the rich, unless a barrister felt charitable towards a particular case. Legal aid is designed to give everyone equal rights before the law, and you should not hesitate to seek it should the occasion arise. The financial qualifications are the same as for legal advice and assistance. You are expected to pay only what you can afford, and there is no stigma involved. It is the right of every citizen to be adequately represented in court, whether he or she has the means to pay or not. The richer you are, therefore, the more likely it is you will be turned down. Check to see if aid is available for what you want. It does not extend to many tribunals. Legal aid is divided into two parts:

Aid in civil cases

If you do not have a solicitor, get a form from your local Citizens' Advice Bureau, the court office, or the committee of the local branch of the Law Society which runs the scheme in your area. Ask them to issue a certificate. If this is refused and you think you have got a good case, you have the right of appeal to the area committee of the Law Society, but you can take it that you will be granted a certificate if you have any case at all.

The chances are that you will be applying for aid in a divorce case; nearly half the total applications are for divorces. But the law is being tightened up, and certificates will not be granted so freely in divorce cases in the future as in the past, for it is felt that the system has been abused. Your certificate may apply to action in any court from the House of Lords down, but not for an action before a tribunal.

Aid in criminal cases

Getting legal aid for criminal cases is generally much faster than for civil cases. If you are accused of a criminal offence you simply fill in an application form after you are charged. The request is considered by the clerk to the justices, who may grant it unconditionally or may ask for a down payment to be made to the court. If he does the latter, or turns down the request altogether, then the application form is put before the magistrate.

The same attention is not paid to the accused's assets in a criminal case as in civil matters. The magistrate only considers whether the accused has the money *readily available* to pay. Only after the case is finished is consideration given to the applicant's ability to pay the whole or part of his costs, in instalments if necessary.

Legal aid must be granted regardless of assets in murder cases. It is generally expected that it will also be granted in trials by a judge and jury and in certain other circumstances: when a case raises a difficult point of law; when the accused is in danger of suffering damage to his reputation or livelihood or of losing his liberty; or when the accused is unable to follow the proceedings or defend himself because of a lack of understanding of English or mental incapacity.

Well over 99 per cent of applications for legal aid in criminal cases are granted.

SMALL CLAIMS

It may well be that you do not want to pay for advice from a solicitor, and would not be granted legal aid on such a trivial matter, yet you do wish to make a claim upon someone. This is where the Small Claims Court comes in. It deals with claims for which you do not use a solicitor. And, as its name implies, it is there to deal with small claims, mostly under £100, though arbitration is available through the County Court for claims less than £200. The Small Claims Court, which is not a court but a voluntary arbitration scheme, might well deal with matters such as:

* Failure to pay for work done, goods delivered, or money lent.
* Failure to supply goods ordered, or delivering the wrong or defective ones.
* Damages caused by negligence. This could arise following a road accident if you feel the accident was the other driver's fault, and you do not want to risk losing your no-claims bonus.
* Salary in lieu of notice, or any salary owed.
* Rent arrears, possession of property.

If the amount you are claiming is £100 or less, it is advisable to use the Small Claims Court, because costs in ordinary courts are not allowed for claims under £100, even if you win your case. For claims over that, go to a solicitor for advice.

This book is not the place to go into the details of how to make a claim (there are many helpful books on the subject), but broadly you can take steps to recover the money once you have made a formal complaint or demand in writing and have followed it up with a reminder, which states that you will be applying to the court for restitution.

Next you must supply the court with details of what you are claiming. These 'particulars of claim' can be quite short, but should be enough to let the defendent know why you are making the claim and how much you think is owed.

To start the action you must fill in a form called a 'request'. When this is filed at the court a fee (not more than £5) for the issue of summons must be paid. The court bailiff will then serve the summons and this involves an additional small fee. You can serve the summons yourself, but this may not be a good idea – though you can always try to find the defendant if the court fails to do so.

If the defendant then decides it is not worth the bother of arguing in court he may well pay up, or he may decide to ignore the summons. If he does not turn up to defend the claim, the plaintiff (the person making the claim) will get judgement. If he does turn up the court will decide whether he is liable and to what extent.

If the claim is accepted by the court, the plaintiff can ask for any expenses he has incurred to be paid by the defendant. These may include court fees and witness fees. If your claim is not allowed in full, you may be able to recover only a certain proportion of your costs.

If the judgement does not go the way you want, you can appeal, but think carefully before you do this. It will cost money, and if you have lost the first round, the chances are, unless you have new evidence, that you may end up losing more than your original claim.

The Lord Chancellor's Office has produced an excellent booklet to help both plaintiffs and defendants called *Small Claims in the County Court*. It is by Michael Birks and is available from all branches of H.M.S.O.

Chapter 2

CONSUMER PROTECTION

Standards of consumer protection are high in Britain and many official bodies exist to help consumers. The government Department of Prices and Consumer Protection watches over the whole retail area on behalf of the shopper.

As a result, most shopkeepers and providers of services today recognize their responsibilities to their customers. But not all do. There are still some, for instance, who are well aware of their customers' rights but nevertheless try to avoid their own responsibilities. A few even go so far as to try to persuade the customer that he has no legal rights at all against the shop.

Two instances of flouting the law are particularly common. The first is refusing to give cash refunds and trying to persuade customers to take a credit note instead. The second is trying to persuade customers that they should return defective items to the manufacturer rather than, as one is entitled in law, returning them to the shop where they were bought, and leaving the shopkeeper to deal with the manufacturer. *Watch out for these dodges and do not stand any nonsense.*

It is important for you as a consumer to know your rights, at least in outline, because if you wish to complain about something you have bought or some service you have used, you must be sure that you actually have the right in law to complain.

YOUR RIGHTS AS A CONSUMER

Britain has a long history of consumer protection. The first-ever government Act to help the consumer was introduced as long ago as 1893. It was the Sale of Goods Act, and it is still the basic law in the area, though it was amended in 1973 to close a variety of loopholes which some manufacturers had managed to find in the original law. A common example was putting special clauses into order forms and guarantees which limited the buyer's rights. In the case of cars, for instance, you used to find that you could not buy a car at all unless you signed such an agreement.

In 1967 the Misrepresentation Act was passed. Under this the customer can claim compensation if he has been deceived by the seller.

420

This Act applies not only to everyday goods which are bought in the shops, but also to houses and anything bought at auctions.

Next came the Trade Descriptions Act of 1968, which punishes traders who make false or misleading statements about the goods or services they offer. If the description turns out to be false, a customer is entitled to return the goods and get the correct ones or his money back.

Customers may have to rely on descriptions of goods on the outsides of packets and tins which they cannot open until they get home. If something turns out not to be what is described on the packet, take it back. The law will support you, and anyone who deliberately misdescribes anything which is on sale is liable to a fine. Remember, though, that genuine mistakes can happen, so do not be over-hasty in demanding your rights. Listen to what the shopkeeper has to say first of all. In some cases, if it regards the case as a serious one the court may order financial compensation to the complainant.

When you buy something, it does not matter whether you pay in cash or in instalments. You have the same legal rights. If you buy on credit, of course, you can always take matters into your own hands and refuse to make further payments until an article is replaced or repaired. But take care if you do this. You may not be able to prove your case and could end up with a court ordering you to pay.

The Fair Trading Act, 1973, provided for the appointment of the Director General of Fair Trading and a Consumer Protection Advisory Committee. This checks on all consumer matters and sees that the law is obeyed. It deals with consumer credit, monopolies and mergers, and restrictive practices, and any trade practices which it thinks might be harmful to the consumer.

As well as amending the 1893 Act, the Supply of Goods (Implied Terms) Act of 1973 also laid down that:

1 Goods are of *merchantable quality*.
2 They may be *fit for the purpose* for which they were bought.

Merchantable Quality

This requirement basically means that a customer must know the true condition of any product when he buys it. It does not mean, therefore, that whatever you buy must be perfect, only that you must know when it is not. Goods clearly marked 'seconds' or 'imperfect' cannot be returned on the grounds that you did know of this when you bought them.

Nevertheless, even something imperfect can be expected to function. If bits are broken and parts are missing (and this is not stated on the goods when you buy them) you will be entitled to your money back. If you buy a fridge for instance, which is badly scratched on the outside, and you can see this before you buy, you will be unable to get your money

421

back after delivery, but if it does not function when you get it home you can send it back and get a replacement or your money back.

Remember 'merchantable' does not automatically mean 'perfect'. It simply means 'fair' or 'reasonable'.

This is what the Act says: 'An article must be fit for the purpose for which articles of that kind are commonly bought, as is reasonable to expect, having regard to the description applied to it, and the price paid (if this is relevant) and any other factors.'

Fit for the purpose

For a product to be fit for the purpose for which it was bought, it must function satisfactorily and be properly designed. If an electric kettle gives you a shock every time you switch it on, it is obviously not fit for its purpose, which is boiling water safely. Any one who had known of its condition at the time of purchase would not have bought it.

But you could not, for instance, automatically get your money back if you bought a face cream which brought you out in spots. It would have to bring everyone out in spots before that was the case. Manufacturers and shopkeepers cannot be expected to know of and cater for any particular allergy you might have.

You may buy something with a particular use in mind. If you make that use clear when you buy, and if when you get it home the article, though merchantable in some other circumstances, is unsuitable for the purposes you have described, then you are entitled to take the article back and reclaim your money. But you must have a cast-iron case. If you are at all doubtful about the article try to get down in writing the purpose for which it is being bought. Otherwise you may have difficulty in proving your case.

Buying from samples

The law here is very clear. If you make an order after studying samples, the good ordered must be identical in colour, shape, quality and any other characteristic with the sample from which they were chosen.

Buying by mail order

Many people buy through mail order after seeing an advertisement in a catalogue or a newspaper. In such cases you cannot examine the goods before taking them away, so you are forced to rely on the supplier's description. If there is any difference at all between the description of the goods and those which you receive you are entitled to your money back. But you cannot return something just because you do not like it when you see it. It is simply a matter of whether the description tallies with the actual article.

Newspapers, which rely for the bulk of their revenue on advertising, are very anxious to maintain high standards in advertising, particularly in the mail order sphere. If you have any complaints, do not complain only to the advertiser, but also to the editor and advertising manager of the newspaper. They can put pressure on any recalcitrant advertiser who does not immediately offer a replacement for the faulty item or give you your money back. *Do not think that you are being a nuisance by complaining. It is a neighbourly act.*

Guarantees

Should you or should you not sign a guarantee when you purchase goods? You will very probably have heard people say that a guarantee is not worth the paper it is written on, that you sign away some of your consumer rights or that the articles must be covered by the 'merchantable quality' and 'fit for the purpose' rulings anyway, so why bother with a guarantee at all?

Some of these comments used to be true in certain cases. If you did not sign a guarantee, you did not place yourself within the limits of the conditions in the guarantee. But all that has now changed.

Shopkeepers and dealers are no longer allowed to put limiting clauses in any guarantee they may offer. If they do, these clauses can be disregarded. *It is now in your interest to sign guarantees. Unless you do so, you may find that you have rights only against the person who sold you the goods and not against the manufacturer.*

Services

The consumer is not nearly so well protected in the area of services. If you use the services of, say, a shoe repairer or a laundry, no sale of goods is involved. Such shops are still allowed to have printed conditions which limit their liabilities in the event of poor or bad service or even damage to the article they are holding. This can mean that the customer is treated unfairly. A bill to bring services into line with sales is now being considered by Parliament. Some traders in service industries put disclaimer notices in their windows or give customers disclaimer notes which deny responsibility for almost anything. Ignore these and check your rights with your local Citizens' Advice Bureau or Consumer Advice Centre.

When you lose your rights

In certain circumstances you may lose your rights under the law. We have already seen, for example, that when a defect is pointed out before you buy, you cannot get your money back.

The same applies when you are known to have examined something carefully yourself before buying and the flaw is such that your examination would have revealed it. You would have better protection in law if you had made only a very superficial examination.

If you are buying a car, for instance, it might be better to rely on the sellers' word that it works properly rather than test it yourself. If you have tested it, you will have no case against the dealer. So, if you know nothing about cars, either get in an experienced person to test it, or take the dealer's word for it. If you have a car tested by the A.A. or R.A.C., they will accept responsibility for any faults they do not discover.

This is particularly important with cars, but the same principle applies to everything you buy, even though the purchase may not be particularly important in your overall budget.

Finally, if you buy privately from someone who is not in the business of selling that particular item it is assumed that you have examined whatever you are buying and are satisfied with its condition. You will have no redress under the law.

HOW THE LAW IS ENFORCED

Below the Office of Fair Trading, which supervises all consumer law, are the trading standards officers (who used to be the weights and measures inspectors). They are employed by local authorities and are responsible for seeing that the various laws protecting the consumer are not flouted. If you have a problem and cannot get satisfaction from the retailer, go first to them. They do not deal with all aspects of consumer law, themselves, however.

Local authorities employ environmental health officers (previously public health inspectors and before that sanitary inspectors), who are responsible for the cleanliness of restaurants and foods shops and for the quality of food. And many councils now have Consumer Advice Centres, which offer a wide variety of advice. Check in your area. These centres exist not only to help you if something goes wrong, but also to help you make the right choice in the first place.

There is also a second tier of government-sponsored organizations. The best known of these are the National Consumer Council, the Scottish, Welsh and Northern Ireland Consumer Councils and the councils for the various nationalized industries. These organizations are not responsible for enforcing the law, but advise the government on general policy matters. They do not normally deal with individual cases.

Next come a wide variety of voluntary organizations. These do not have anything to do with law enforcement either, but they have plenty to say for themselves and put a lot of pressure on official bodies for action.

The Consumers' Association is the best known of these. It publishes the various *Which* magazines, which are almost essential reading for sensible consumers. Among these publications is *Money Which*. This can help you with your money problems, but even more useful is the general monthly publication *Which,* which sets out the pros and cons of a wide variety of products. *Which* will always suggest a 'best buy', but you can easily work out your own individual choice from the range of information offered.

Chapter 3

BUYING SECOND-HAND GOODS

BUYING FROM A SHOP OR DEALER

We saw in the last chapter how the customer is protected by the law when he buys anything, and how the law also protects you when you buy imperfect goods – or 'seconds'.

These laws for the protection of shoppers also protect people buying second-hand, as long as they buy from a shop or a dealer, rather than from a private seller or at an auction (see below). Anything you buy from a shop or dealer must be of 'merchantable quality', as I set out in the last chapter, even if it is second-hand.

The problem is whether the goods are 'saleable', and this will depend to a large extent on the price being asked. Almost everything which is sold is worth *something,* so it is a matter of getting the price right for the condition of the article in question. The wise buyer will look particularly carefully at anything second-hand before buying – though he will actually be in a less strong position legally than the person who makes no such examination, as the latter cannot be presumed to have known what the defects were at the time of buying, whereas the careful buyer can.

Cars are a notorious example of this. If you are sensible you will get a qualified engineer to examine a car before you buy it. But if a fault then develops, the dealer can argue that you ought to have known about it, as the engineer should have discovered any fault that was there at the time. *If the A.A. or R.A.C. check a car for you before buying, they now accept responsibility for any defects they overlooked.*

Even if you do not have a proper inspection of a car – or indeed any other purchase – before buying, anyone who deals fraudently with you can be prosecuted under the Trade Descriptions Act. A dealer who puts a car mileometer back to persuade the buyer that the car has been less used than it has been, can be fined and the customer compensated. If you complain to them, the local trading standards officers will carry out an inspection for you.

Under the Supply of Goods (Implied Terms) Act of 1973 a garage cannot put anything in the 'small print' of a sale contract which takes away the buyer's right to a car which is serviceable, even though it is second-hand.

BUYING AT AUCTIONS

If you become a collector of any of the things discussed in section V chapter 8, you will probably at some time try your hand at buying at an auction. Remember that special rules apply when you buy at auctions.

Most important of all, you will have no protection as far as 'merchantable quality' goes – though you can sometimes claim under the Misrepresentation Act of 1967 if what you buy turns out to be a fake (if it was claimed to be genuine) or is not what the catalogue said it was.

There are certain regulations regarding the proper conduct of auctions, however:

* The highest bidder always gets the goods, unless there is a 'reserve' price which the bidding does not reach. If you have made a bid and want to change your mind, you must do it before the auctioneer's hammer falls. After that you are the owner whether you want to be or not.
* The auctioneer is usually the agent of the seller, but he can sign the purchase agreement on behalf of the buyer once it has actually been bought.
* An auctioneer is not allowed to buy articles from a seller without the latter's permission. If he does buy with permission, he cannot deduct any commission from the selling price. Anyone can claim against an auctioneer, if he thinks the auctioneer has cheated by buying himself. Such a claim can be made even quite a long time after the event, and it is then up to the auctioneer to prove that he had the consent of the seller to buy.
* If you set a reserve price, the auctioneer must know what it is, but bidders are not told. If the highest bid is below the reserve, then the person who made it cannot insist on buying whatever is under offer.

    In a house auction the printed conditions must state whether the seller has the right to bid and if there is a reserve below which the seller will not sell.

426

* It is illegal for two or more professionals to get together and agree not to bid against one another – which means that one of them can get something at a lower price than if the bidding was open. This activity is known as 'the ring'. The penalty can be from six months' to two years' imprisonment.

    If you think this is happening, you may have trouble proving it. But if you can do so, you are entitled to get the object back from the dealer, and, if he has already sold it, you are entitled to damages from all the dealers who were involved in the ring.

* No seller can take part in the bidding himself in an attempt to push up prices, or employ what is called a 'puffer' to bid for him. Any seller who wants to take part in the bidding will have to give this information in the catalogue, or it will be announced by the auctioneer when the 'lot' – as each item or set of items is called – is called by the auctioneer.

    If a buyer is tricked by this ploy, he can make the seller take the object back or claim damages from him. If two people engage in fake bidding, they can be sued for criminal conspiracy.

* Auctioneers must not pretend to accept bids which have not been made. This is known as 'taking bids out of the air' and can result in a prosecution for deception.

UNSOLICITED GOODS

In the past many people used to receive an enormous variety of goods through the post accompanied by an invoice, so that if the recipient liked them he could simply send back a payment. This is called 'inertia selling', and can be very annoying. Some companies even went so far as to threaten people who ignored their offers, and did not return them, with court action. All this has now been outlawed under the Unsolicited Goods and Services Act of 1971. Should you receive anything through the post in this way you can just ignore it, and you need not spend any money on postage to send it back to the company involved. You can become the legal owner of anything which comes to you in this way by:

1 Doing nothing. If the firm does not come to collect the item within six months, it belongs to the person to whom it was sent. Take care, however, not to stop anyone collecting it.
2 Writing to the company concerned and telling them to come and collect the goods, giving a name and address for collection. On receipt of such a letter, they must act within thirty days or the goods belong to the person to whom they were sent.

Chapter 4

THE LAW ON CREDIT PURCHASES

It's all very well to appreciate why borrowing to buy the things you need is a sensible thing to do in a period of inflation when the value of money is falling, but it is also very necessary to understand the law as it relates to the various methods of financing any purchases whereby you defer payment over a period. The aim of the law here is to protect both the purchaser of the goods and the seller, or lender of the money.

To begin with, all agreements which provide credit up to £5,000 are covered by the Consumer Credit Act, apart from house mortgages. The figure of £5,000 excludes any interest you will pay during the period of the contract and any deposit you may put down at the beginning. So if you buy a boat for £5,500 and put down a deposit of £1,000 you are borrowing £4,500 and so are subject to the Act. *Remember, it is the amount you actually borrow which determines whether you are covered by the Act.*

The regulations under the Consumer Credit Act, 1974, are being phased in gradually. Since May 1977 those who operate in the business of giving credit must have a licence to do so, if they make credit agreements of more than £30 and from November 1977, credit reference agencies who amend their files on a consumer's credit worthiness will be required by law to send the revised information to any traders to whom they had supplied earlier information on a particular customer. Potential customers who are refused credit must now be told the reason why.

First of all you must understand the difference between the two forms of credit purchase – *hire purchase* and *credit sale*. In general a hire purchase agreement is complicated and a credit sale simple. This is because with hire purchase you do not own whatever you may think you have 'bought' until you have made the last payment under the agreement. You literally 'hire' it until that point.

What happens is that the finance company buys the goods from the retailer and then hires them out to the buyer, signing them over when the last payment has been made. There are about 1,000 companies in this business, but a few big ones dominate. If you arrange for a credit sale, on the other hand, you own the article from the moment you take delivery.

428

This basic difference of ownership at the point of the agreement means that there are important differences in the two contracts – differences which can have important legal implications. Let's look at some of them:

Defaulting on payments. With hire purchase the lender has the right to take the goods back if the 'hirer' defaults on the payments. With a credit sale he cannot. This further means that you cannot sell something that you are buying on hire purchase, because you are not the legal owner. There is no such prohibition with a credit sale – though if you do sell you may find that you are liable to make the whole remaining payment immediately. So check the contract.

The hirer – for that is what you are until you finish paying – is protected by the law in some ways. If less than one third of what is owed has been paid and payments stop, the finance company has the legal right to send someone round to take the goods back. If more than a third has been paid, however, the company must get a court order before it can retrieve its property. If you have defaulted because you are in financial difficulties a court may allow you to keep the goods. In that case it will fix a new scale of payments. In contrast, if you miss one payment under a credit sale deal, you become liable to pay the rest immediately.

The golden rule is, *if you get into difficulties over keeping up your payments, tell the company*. It will not want to go to court any more than you do and will often modify the agreement so that you can pay off over a longer period.

Returning the goods. Under a hire purchase deal you can insist at any time that the company takes the goods back. When this happens you will not have to pay more than half the total hire purchase price, if the article has been kept in good condition. The court may rule that the payment is even less. If you have bought under a credit sale, you cannot cancel the agreement and send the stuff back, unless it is defective.

When there is a court order against you. If the bailiffs come to take away your furniture and other effects, they cannot take anything which is currently being bought on hire purchase, because it does not, legally speaking, belong to you until you have paid off the loan. The bailiffs can take anything away that you may be buying on a credit sale, because in that case you are the rightful owner.

Maintenance of the goods bought. Hire purchase agreements are complicated and often very long with a great deal of small print. Very few people bother to read the small print, but whether you read it or not you are bound by all the conditions of the contract. These will vary, but you will usually find that you are required to keep the goods in a sound condition and insure them against all risks until you are the real owner. If you buy something on credit sale, you can knock it about as much as you wish.

Under the Act you can claim that you were misled when signing any credit agreement, but you will be lucky to get away with it. But when you buy on hire purchase or by means of a credit sale you are sometimes allowed a cooling-off period. If you sign an H.P. agreement in your home, or a credit sale over £30 away from trade premises, the dealer must send you a second copy within seven days. You then have five days to reconsider and you can cancel any agreement without giving a reason. This is extremely useful for people who feel that they have been pressurized into an agreement which on more sober reflection they know they cannot afford.

If you sign the agreement on any trade premises – say a shop – you do not get the same cooling off period. The reasoning behind this is that in the former case you may have been lured into a purchase you were not actually thinking of. In other words, you were a passive buyer. When you buy in a shop the position is reversed; you are actively in pursuit of goods and it's the seller who is the passive one.

Buying a car. It does sometimes happen that someone buys a car in good faith, only to find out that it still belongs to a finance company because the previous owner has not finished his payments. When this happens the individual cannot have the car taken away from him, but a dealer who buys in similar circumstances does not have the same protection.

Chapter 5

DEBTS AND BANKRUPTCY

NON-PAYMENT OF DEBTS

If you are in debt and do not pay, there is a legal limit to the amount of pressure which the person or organization to whom you owe the money can put upon you, no matter how large the debt.

You are of course obliged in law to pay your debts, but a creditor must pursue his claim against you in an orderly way. He must send you a bill, followed by further requests for payment, and eventually take court action. What he may not do is pursue a debt in such a way that he causes alarm, distress or humiliation to the debtor – or indeed his family. The legal term for this is 'harassment'. It can be said to occur because of the frequency of the demands, the way they are made or the place where they are made.

It is illegal to pressurize a debtor in any of the•following ways:

* By sending letters threatening to take court action which look legal because they are printed on special forms. These are called 'blue frighteners', and if someone sends you one you can send it to the police.
* By going to someone's home and threatening them or demanding the money.
* By threatening that you will send round a debt collecting agency. In fact debt collecting agencies themselves have to take care. They are not allowed to threaten to inform a debtor's employers of the situation by pretending that they need information. If this happens they can be prosecuted.
* By blackmail. If anyone tries to blackmail you over a debt, go to the police immediately. This is a criminal offence and is severely punishable.

GOING BANKRUPT

Sometimes it happens that our debts get too much for us and we can see no way of settling them. If this happens you can go 'bankrupt'. It is far more common with companies than with individual people.

When it does happen with individuals it is often because they are unable to meet tax demands. For one reason or another they have been paid gross and not net of tax, and they have not put money by to settle the tax bill when it comes in. Eventually the Inland Revenue will want the money. It will give time to pay, but if the money is not forthcoming it will eventually ask for the person to be declared bankrupt.

Of course it is not only the Inland Revenue which asks for people to be declared bankrupt. All kinds of creditors may come forward for their money, and any one of them, or the person himself, can ask for the state of bankruptcy to be declared. It could be because of something as simple as taking on too many hire purchase commitments.

The 'act of bankruptcy'

Bankruptcy proceedings cannot begin until the debtor has committed what is called 'an act of bankruptcy' – which generally means that he has failed to comply with a bankruptcy notice. To get this notice served the creditor must first go to court to get an order that the debt must be paid. If it is not paid, then he can serve a bankruptcy notice on the person owing the money. If the debt still remains unpaid within seven days, this amounts to 'an act of bankruptcy'.

But this is not the only way it can happen. The debtor may simply say he is not paying his debts; he may have disappeared in an attempt to avoid his creditors; he may dispose of his property in a way which stops creditors from getting their hands on it and so having their debts paid that way.

A petition for bankruptcy may be filed with the court either by the debtor himself, or by his creditors. If it is a creditor's petition, a copy of the petition then goes to the debtor, who must later present himself before the court.

A preliminary hearing follows, then the court registrar may issue a receiving order, or he may decide, for a variety of reasons, that there is no point in going ahead with the case. As a rule, however, the receiving order will go out.

The Official Receiver

When the receiving order goes out, this means that all the debtor's assets are put under the control of the Official Receiver, so that the debtor can no longer deal with his own property. After this, the debtor must make a statement of all his assets and liabilities, and it is at this time, too, that he should put forward any scheme that he has for paying off his creditors.

Sometimes agreement can be reached at this stage, but if not there is a public examination of the debtor in court, during which every detail of his financial affairs – including how he reached the present situation – will be discussed.

It is at this point that a person may be actually declared bankrupt, either on his own request or on that of his creditors. All his property is then transferred to the person who has been designated his 'trustee in bankruptcy'.

The person who is declared bankrupt is only allowed to keep clothes, bedding and any 'tools of his trade'. He is not allowed to have a bank account nor to seek any form of credit. This means that he will have to surrender all his credit cards etc. If he is working, he is allowed to keep only as much of his earnings as is 'reasonably' needed for his keep and that of his family. The rest must go to the trustee. This includes any profits from a personal business, again apart from what he needs for his keep.

Even so, the state of bankruptcy can come as a great relief to many people. They no longer have any control over their assets, someone else has taken over the responsibility for their debts, and for the time being at least it is necessary only for the bankrupt and his family to survive.

Paying off the debts

The next step is for the trustee to try to pay off the debts. Naturally he will try to pay them all in full, but some creditors' demands come before those of others.

Preferred creditors are entitled to have their debts paid in full before the others. They include, in order of priority, the Inland Revenue, a local authority levying general rates, and any employees of the bankrupt.

Once they are paid up it is the turn of the *ordinary* creditors, followed finally by the *deferred* creditors. These include the husband or wife of the bankrupt, and possibly any partners he or she may have had in business. They also include banks and suppliers of any goods and services.

In his efforts to pay everyone off, the trustee will want to value all the assets of the bankrupt. Many people who see themselves running into trouble will try to beat bankruptcy by signing over some of their assets to a husband, wife or children. Or they may decide on their own 'preferred' creditors and pay them off rather than anyone else. The trustee, however, may, for example:

* Reclaim money which has been paid to any creditor in the past six months, if he can prove that the now-bankrupt was insolvent at the time. If the bankrupt can prove he was pressurized into making the payment, his action will not be regarded as fraudulent and therefore illegal.
* Reclaim any property which the bankrupt has given away within two years of his bankruptcy. This may be to his family, but can be to anyone at all. The trustee has the gift set aside and uses it to pay off the creditors.
* Reclaim any property given away within ten years of bankruptcy, unless the bankrupt can prove he was solvent at the time.
* Reclaim any property, apart from these time limits, if it can be proved that there was an attempt to avoid creditors. The crucial question is the intention in the mind of the now-bankrupt when he made the transfer.

Discharging a bankrupt

The court can discharge a bankrupt at any time. The person involved may ask for the discharge, or the trustees may do it if they have settled all the debts. If the bankruptcy was caused by circumstances outside the control of the bankrupt, he may get a 'certificate of misfortune' and be granted an absolute discharge.

If, however, he is held to have behaved recklessly, or even to have attempted to be fraudulent, the court may suspend the discharge for a few years, depending on how seriously the court regards his misconduct.

If all the debts have not been paid, it may grant a 'conditional discharge'. This means that at any time in the future, until the debts are

433

paid in full, the bankrupt can be made to put any assets he acquires towards finalizing the payment of his debts.

Whatever happens, people who extend credit are likely to look on a former bankrupt with suspicion for a long time. This is unfortunate, but bankruptcy is far better than ruination of one's family, or running away, or plunging even deeper into debt once the writing is on the wall.

Take legal and financial advice immediately you feel you may be reaching the point of no return financially. Even if the situation seems desperate, ways of paying off creditors may still be found.

Chapter 6

FINDING A SOLICITOR

Most of us use a solicitor at some time in our lives, even if it is only when buying a house or making a will. As in any profession some solicitors are better than others. How can you make sure that you choose correctly?

First of all, solicitors do not advertise – they are not allowed to – so the chances are that if you are, say, buying a house you will use a local solicitor, chosen either simply because he happens to have a convenient office or because a friend has recommended him. If you cannot find one in this way, you can ask at your local Citizens' Advice Bureau, or write to the Law Society. They will supply you with a list of solicitors in your area, but will not recommend a particular one. Their address is 113 Chancery Lane, London W.C.2.

For the money you pay you are entitled to good service and proper advice from your solicitor. He must, among other things

* Keep everything you tell him secret. If he breaches your trust, you are entitled to damages.
* Keep proper accounts of any money you send him. These accounts must be regularly audited.

He is liable if you suffer loss through his negligence. This does not mean, however, that you can sue automatically if a solicitor's advice turns out to be wrong. He may honestly and painstakingly advise you in a doubtful case and his advice may later turn out to be wrong. If he is

434

negligent, however, you should be able to get full satisfaction, because all solicitors are heavily insured against claims of this kind.

The Law Society may recompense you, if you lose money through a solicitor's dishonesty.

If you are dissatisfied with your solicitor for any reason at all – including feeling that you have been overcharged – you can report the matter to the Law Society. They may be able to help you, but they do not have the power to order a solicitor to pay compensation. Most reliable solicitors, however, take note of what the Law Society says.

Index

Index